THE RIGHT TO BE ONESELF

What does the right to be oneself entail? And how is it manifest in our understanding of the law?

The leading commentator on this subject explores these questions, taking an ambitious and multi-faceted approach. To answer them, he draws on private law, jurisprudence, constitutional law, as well as history, art and literature. This treatise, translated from the Italian original and expanded to give a more international perspective, is the seminal work on the development of identity-protection through law.

The Future of Private Law

Series Editors

Marija Bartl, Anna Beckers, Simon Deakin, Daniel Markovits, and Hans-W Micklitz

A new wave of scholarship is remaking and invigorating private law. Legal regimes that were long understood as invisible systems of technical rules governing purely private relations are being reconsidered in their social, economic, and political context. This scholarly trend interacts with three major developments in 20th century private law. First, private law itself has undergone a series of fundamental transformation. Openly public and political values were inserted into private law regimes both before and immediately after 1945, only to be rejected in favour of a purported re-privatisation of law and society alike in the heyday of neoliberalism. Neoliberalism itself is now subject to increasingly intense critique, under the mounting pressure of multiple social and environmental crises. Second, private law has had to respond to fundamental transformations in the global economy, which have simultaneously placed inherited legal orders under economic and political pressure, and denaturalized previously unquestioned doctrinal arrangements. And, third, private law has been challenged by the call for and recognition of legal pluralism as a constitutive feature of legal systems.

Legislatures and courts, responding to these forces, have relied on private law to achieve openly moral ends, such as social justice, gender and ethnic equality, and more recently, sustainability, climate change and intergenerational justice, as well as adaptation to a digitalized economy and society. Scholars have similarly begun to observe the regulatory character of private law, its connection to public values, and even its 'constitutionalisation'. These developments blur the boundaries between what has been perceived as the 'classical' private law of the nineteenth century and the new regulatory private law of the twentieth. Along the way, they are redefining the relation between private law, societal values, and political objectives. Even 'classical', formal, or, as it is sometimes labelled, 'neutral' private law, is becoming inflected with political objectives. The possibility that the basic concepts that traditional private law scholarship deploys could themselves be related to hegemonies based on race, gender, or class, or the outcome of colonial imaginaries and interests, only reinforces the importance of unmasking the supposedly neutral or technical quality of private law. All these developments suggest that private law will in the future become even more clearly interwoven with normative objectives and societal claims. The question of which values will infuse private law therefore becomes unavoidable.

Changes in the economic regime that private law governs – both domestically and at a global scale – are reinforcing the need for new approaches. Within countries, private actors (including civil society organisations, trade and industry groups, and even individual firms) have gained the power to influence law-making and legal enforcement, and to create their own regulatory orders. Private forms of rule-making and administration have therefore become a part of private law, both by constraining the state from making effective law, and by empowering non-state actors to use law as a tool for promoting private interests. Moreover, across countries, a liberal commercial order that once purported to separate international economic law from domestic private law has been displaced by a transnational commercial regime that openly confers on private law a central role in global economic arrangements. Digital technologies, and the new forms of regulation that they enable – including in particular data- and code-driven regimes that fuse legal regulation with technical infrastructure and interfaces – further reinforce these trends. These new forms of digital governance threaten the state's traditional monopoly over legal regulation, while breaking down the legal categories through which private law has traditionally constrained state over-reach. In short: non-state actors have increasingly used private law for their own increasingly political ends, and states have sought to shape nominally private economic arrangements in order to promote national economic and geopolitical interests. Critical legal scholarship is beginning to expose the ways in which these developments within private law are not simply failing to address inequalities of resources and power, but actively perpetuating them.

Such developments are not entirely new, but they were previously confined to the borders of private law. Now, under new conditions, they appear in a vivid and insistent light. Together, these developments demand a new orientation from private law and place private law scholarship at the centre of the broader development of legal thought. The objective of this series is to publish books that answer this call.

This objective requires the series to embrace a broad understanding of private law, which combines the traditional core of private law with regulatory private law and its interaction with international economic law and legal pluralism. Substantively, the series stresses the need to think through the future of private law and to understand anew its pillars, modules, and institutions, including its most fundamental conceptions of the person, contract, tort, and property. The series will also pay close regard to legal process, by attending to interactions among the several national private law orders and between domestic and transnational law. To this end it will aim to analyse the relationships among different levels of legislation and between law, private regulation and technology. It will also pay close attention to the way private law is made to work in practice through a variety of public and private enforcement mechanisms, on the part not just of the executive and judiciary, but via non-state actors.

Methodologically, the series is committed to exploring the breadth and depth of the challenges private law is facing from the perspective of multiple disciplines. We expect the series to reflect the growing debate about exactly what doctrinal method consists of, as part of which a comparison of legal methods with those of other disciplines is becoming increasingly necessary. Thus not just the paradigms of other disciplines in the human and social sciences, but the methods they typically employ, ranging from statistical and other quantitative approaches to the ethnographies used in fieldwork and the hermeneutic techniques employed in the analysis of texts, will be of interest. Contributions from scholars engaged in critical analysis of inequalities and power relations, associated with race, gender and class among other categories, are among those we particularly welcome, as are contributions from legal researchers engaging with the data sciences across a broad range of applications, including but not limited to those associated with artificial intelligence. Our hope for the series is that it will expand the boundaries of private law scholarship as conventionally understood, while retaining the coherence necessary for private law as both discipline and practice.

The Right to be Oneself

Guido Alpa

•HART•
OXFORD • LONDON • NEW YORK • NEW DELHI • SYDNEY

HART PUBLISHING
Bloomsbury Publishing Plc
Kemp House, Chawley Park, Cumnor Hill, Oxford, OX2 9PH, UK
1385 Broadway, New York, NY 10018, USA
29 Earlsfort Terrace, Dublin 2, Ireland

HART PUBLISHING, the Hart/Stag logo, BLOOMSBURY and the Diana logo are trademarks of Bloomsbury Publishing Plc

First published in Great Britain 2024

A catalogue record for this book is available from the British Library.

Library of Congress Cataloging-in-Publication data

Names: Alpa, Guido, author.

Title: The right to be oneself | Guido Alpa.

Description: Oxford, UK ; New York, NY : Hart Publishing, 2024. | Series: The future of private law | Includes bibliographical references and index. | Summary: "What does the right to be oneself entail? And how is it manifest in our understanding of the law? The leading commentator on this subject explores these questions, taking an ambitious and multi-faceted approach. To answer them, he draws on private law, jurisprudence, constitutional law, as well as history, art and literature. This treatise, translated from the Italian original and expanded to give a more international perspective, is the seminal work on the development of identity-protection through law"—Provided by publisher.

Identifiers: LCCN 2024004874 (print) | LCCN 2024004875 (ebook) | ISBN 9781509972449 (hardback) | ISBN 9781509972487 (paperback) | ISBN 9781509972456 (Epub) | ISBN 9781509972463 (ebook)

Subjects: LCSH: Persons (Law) | Personality (Law)

Classification: LCC K625 .A94 2024 (print) | LCC K625 (ebook) | DDC 342.08/5—dc23/eng/20240205

LC record available at https://lccn.loc.gov/2024004874

LC ebook record available at https://lccn.loc.gov/2024004875

ISBN: HB: 978-1-50997-244-9
ePDF: 978-1-50997-246-3
ePub: 978-1-50997-245-6

Typeset by Compuscript Ltd, Shannon

The Right to be Oneself

The whole world is a stage,
women and men are only actors
entering and leaving the scene.
Everyone plays many roles in their lives
and the acts are the seven ages of life
Shakespeare, *As You Like It*

The less we are free to decide
who we are or to live
as we wish
the more we strive to present a façade,
of hiding the facts and playing a part
Hanna Arendt, *Judaism and Modernity*

To live, one needs an identity, i.e. dignity.
Without dignity, identity is poor, it becomes ambiguous,
can be manipulated
Rodotà, *Living Democracy*

Contents

A Premise

SOME DECADES AGO, Hans Mayer published a book entitled *Aussenseiter*: the outsider, the outcast, the loser, the social pariah or, metaphorically, the loner as isolated, non-integrated. The book was translated into Italian two years later under the title *I diversi*.[1] The translation of the book is faithful, but the title appears somewhat reductive: 'different' in the singular has a meaning – and not only a quantitative one – different from 'different' in the plural: *different* is a noun adjective that indicates a single individual; *different*, in the plural, indicates a group that differs from the majority because it is perceived and qualified as a minority. The different can be reproached, mocked, persecuted even in its individuality, not only for belonging to a minority. The different person Mayer proposes is considered different within his own group; he is a different among the different. The women, the Jews, the homosexuals that his text gives us, as if they were the protagonists of a novel, are extracts from the Bible, from Marlowe's and Shakespeare's tragedies, from painting, from poetry, from philosophy; they are individuals who have been able to make of their diversity an instrument of affirmation, of catharsis, of redemption.

Mayer concluded his work with a wonderful quote from Goethe: 'it is not good to linger long in the world of abstractions. Esoteric doctrine only does harm when it becomes exoteric. To teach how to live, there is nothing better than life itself'.

Jurists should ponder this maxim seriously: they are accustomed to dealing with reality and fictions, and they know that in law fictions play an important role, so important that they equate fiction with reality. If we remove the mask from law, we do not deprive it of its essential characteristics, but highlight its strength; it is an ambivalent strength, because it can be used against the different, or in its favour. But it is also an ambiguous force, because when it stands guard over what is different and protects it, it demands its unveiling. Hence the paradox of law: to protect what is different, law must 'recognise' it, that is, it requires it to remove its mask.

In the imagination, in social reality, in the categories of law, one encounters so many different people in addition to those identified by Mayer: foreigners, immigrants, heretics, the poor, the disabled, the infirm, the native-born and so on. Every society has had, and still has, its different ones, ie its outcasts. Signs, classifications and rules vary, and for them the 'right to have rights' is a goal, but a difficult goal to achieve.

[1] H Mayer, *I diversi* (Milan, Garzanti, 1992).

It seems easy to recognise the different. But this illusion is twofold: the different changes, just as people considered *normal* change. Each person wears his or her own mask; his or her image resembles that rendered by a shattered mirror. Beneath the mask there is no individual always equal to himself or herself, reducible to an unrepeatable *unicum*. And yet law needs certainties; it tends to simplify a reality that is multiform and in perpetual evolution. Signs evaporate, classifications multiply, rules do not keep pace with the transformations of technology. There is a need for identity, but what identity?

Unlike in the past, 'personal identity' has become a polysemous expression with many margins of ambiguity.

1

'Identity': A Multifaceted Self

I. PATHS OF IDENTITY AND PATHS OF LAW

THE COMMON LANGUAGE knows different types of identity: individual identity is flanked by group identity and, gradually widening the circle, collective identity, social identity, national identity. Each is defined in its role and has its own history. The law does not normally give a literal definition; it uses synonyms, it refers to identity factors, and it is concerned – today – with defending each one from harmful treatment related to those identity components. On the one hand, it defends those factors, as if they were offshoots of the person, from appropriation or alteration, elevating them to inviolable subjective rights, such as the right to one's name, the right to physical integrity, the right to one's image, the right to the proper processing of personal data; on the other hand, it defends the person from discrimination based on those identity factors, such as gender, sexual orientation, ethnicity, social origin, and so on.

In the course of time, certain aspects that were at first ignored have become relevant to law; others, at first meticulously regulated, have lost their legal relevance; law has become the medium of power dynamics, of social and economic instances, from time to time modelling the legal form in which to incorporate the person. And it has done so by delimiting the person's freedom of action, delineating their social position, establishing power relations with other citizens. In most cases, law has compressed the development of the person; only recently has it taken as its primary purpose the protection of the person in all its dimensions.

When one specifies that identity is to be considered in a (at least) threefold dimension, considering what a person believes he or she is (who am I?) and how he or she wants to be represented (how am I?) and how others represent him or her (how do they see me?), one grasps a psychological dimension of identity, which is accompanied by a social dimension, an anthropological dimension, a political dimension, and a cultural dimension. And this considers the person both as *self* and in relation to the *other*.

These aspects constitute the foundation on which the law builds its identity dimension.

As can be seen, identity means, on the one hand, the uniqueness of a human being who, from the outside, is an unrepeatable being and different from others and, on the other hand, *hypseity*, ie the way the person perceives himself or herself and wants to appear. Identity also means identity of treatment, insofar as it wants to preach *equality* between human beings.

Law codifies the criteria for identifying individuals. These criteria have been formed over time, with historical fluctuations in order, importance, and consistency; and the law deals with the characteristics that the person wants to exhibit, choosing at different times between unmasking and concealing.

In everyday language, identity refers objectively to living beings, to human beings, to men and women, to individuals, to *persons*. In legal language, the human being is translated into concepts that by their nature are abstract.

When Roman jurists developed terminology and concepts, they distinguished human beings according to their role in the world of law, and used the term *person* to indicate the *role* each person played in that world.[1]

Between then and now there have been many changes.

By today's linguistic convention, the terms 'person' and 'man' or 'woman', 'human being', 'individual', allude to the same meaning, ie to a living being who is endowed with certain identifying characteristics, and who therefore *cannot but be a* person, even under the law.[2]

But in Roman law, *personae* were related to their role: the father of the family, the married woman, the unmarried woman, the adult child, the minor child, the slave, the freedman (ie freed slave), the citizen, the foreigner, and so on. And it was debated whether slaves were in the proper sense *personae* rather than things.

If only those who had power, a 'status', could consider themselves well-rounded people, what were all the others? They were anonymous individuals.

In the Middle Ages and until the end of the *Ancien Régime*, the Latin term *personae* continued to be used in legal texts according to the meaning of Roman law. In other contexts, *homines* was used to refer to common beings.

In the mediaeval period, social roles multiplied. 'Serf' became a newly recognised identity while, in the nobility hierarchy, the different ranks and titles of nobility, reflecting the ecclesiastical hierarchy, were also established. Stratifications became fixed and immutable, dividing individuals into *states*, which remained unchanged until the French Revolution.[3]

[1] M Brutti, *Il diritto privato nell'antica Roma*, 3rd edn (Turin, Giappichelli, 2015) 97ff.; U Vincenti, *Categorie del diritto romano. L'ordine quadrato* (Naples, Jovene, 2019) 4 (and formerly U Boniolo, G De Anna and U Vincenti, *Individuo e persona. Tre saggi su chi siamo* (Milan, Bompiani, 2007); A Schiavone, *Eguaglianza. Una nuova visione sul filo della storia* (Turin, Einaudi, 2019) 53ff (and already Ius, *L'invenzione del diritto in Occidente* (Turin, Einaudi, 2005) 155ff; taking up these legal profiles, in a philosophical perspective, R Esposito, *Due. La macchina della teologia politica e il posto del pensiero* (Turin, Einaudi, 2013) 91ff.

[2] More extensively, G Alpa and G Resta, *Le persone fisiche e i diritti della* personalità, 2nd edn, *Trattato di diritto civile* directed by R Sacco (Turin, UTET, 2019).

[3] F Calasso, *Medioevo del diritto.I.Le fonti* (Milan, Giuffrè, 1954) 154ff.; Ascheri, *I diritti del Medioevo italiano. Secoli XI–XV*, 2nd edn (Rome, Carocci, 2003) 185ff. Di Renzo Villata, voce *Persone e famiglia nel diritto medievale e moderno*, in *Digesto italiano delle Discipline Privatistiche-Sezione civile*, XIII (Turin, UTET, 1995) 457–527.

Nobles, clergymen, and soldiers had their own individuality, and thus their own identity – political and social – for which the law provided terminology, categories and rules. They were therefore distinguished from others by their office.[4]

Other individuals, who were not identifiable through their *dignitas*, belonged to categories that at one time would qualify as artisan, mercantile, intellectual, technical or manual, and at another would belong generically to the vulgar, to the serfs: they were peasants, labourers, soldiers, and remained such throughout their lives. No one remembered them except family and friends; their short life stories were shrouded in anonymity.

Those to whom a higher lineage was reserved by birth also had a name, which went with a title. To these titles, moreover, were attached immunities and privileges, offices, emoluments, pensions, as well as the guarantees offered by law, such as the right to be judged by one's peers, the right to royal protection, the right to wear arms, and to bear distinguishing marks. The Magna Carta represented this complex state of affairs icastically.

For everyone else, identity was marked by geographical origin, the places where they were born and lived their lives; their language, religion, social status.

Until the eighteenth-century revolutions, these privileges, codified by law in the statuses of the *Ancien Régime*, prevailed. After the revolutions, privileges diminished, but did not disappear. Each person – that is, each individual – was granted certain basic rights, called 'human rights', because they are inherent in the essence of living beings.

Relations between individuals were governed by civil law, and the rights granted to them referred to as 'civil rights': rights granted to all, except for those who had been sanctioned, for which their 'civil death' had been decreed. The individual's relations with the state, with authority, were governed by public law: but social rights and political rights did not align with civil rights. Later they would be properly established for all, but at different ages.

In the civil law of the last few centuries, the individual was configured with an even more abstract notion: he or she was defined as a *subject of rights*, because he or she was recognised in the abstract as the owner of rights; and when in the sphere of civil law one spoke of rights, from the end of the eighteenth century to the first half of the twentieth century, one spoke of the right to *property*: in the abstract, it was recognised as available to all, but in concrete terms it was reserved for the few. The individual was relevant to law insofar as he or she was the *owner*: the owner of real estate, of movable property, including precious metals, and, if the individual owned nothing, he or she was the owner of his or her labour power.

[4] Further insights can be found in G Alpa, *Status and Capacity. La costruzione giuridica delle differenze individuali* (Roma-Bari, Laterza, 1993).

Civil law throughout the nineteenth century centred on the right to property. This 'terrible right'[5] also underpinned public law governing the relationship between citizen and state. In fact, the right to property differentiated individuals such that it became one of the requirements for exercising the right to vote.[6]

Civil law and public law enabled, with skillful manipulation, the deprivation of individuals of all rights. The degradation of the individual, reduced from human being to *Untermensch*, to slave, to what was reached under Nazism: in the concentration and extermination camps human beings were reduced to a number, a labour force harassed and then annihilated. The individual – qualified as a Jew, and with this ethnicity also the Roma and homosexuals – no longer had any legal subjectivity. Auschwitz did not only signify the abyss of immorality and abuse; it showed the extent to which law could be instrumentalised.[7]

After Auschwitz, the reactions to the horror lead to a re-evaluation of natural law and the correction of the extreme interpretations of positivism: the individual could no longer be considered a creature that must be respected and protected at all costs and in all situations. This led to a new qualification: the individual who is a *person as such*, the holder of inviolable rights such as the right to life, the right to physical integrity, the right to health. Torture, experimental compulsory health treatments, subjection to the servile state, discrimination were prohibited.

In this context, 'person' does not have the meaning used by the Roman; it acquires a more pregnant meaning. This is why it is usually said that with the post-World War II constitutions, *the individual becomes a person*, no longer an abstract concept, but a flesh-and-blood man or woman,[8] with his or her needs, aspirations, dignity and precisely *inviolable* rights.[9]

This era has been defined by Norberto Bobbio as the *age of rights*.[10]

The past has left its marks in language, behaviour, relationships and, of course, in regulatory texts.

Every age has obeyed the classificatory categories of jurists: the archaeology of knowledge applied to law shows us that each individual is qualified by criteria that carve out his or her identity.

[5] S Rodotà, *Il terribile diritto. Studies on private property and the commons* (Bologna, Il Mulino, 2013).

[6] Alpa (n 4).

[7] M Barberis, *Introduzione allo studio del diritto* (Turin, Giappichelli, 2014); on the annihilation of the person in the horror of the extermination camps, H Arendt, *La banalità del male. Eichmann in Jerusalem* (Milan, Feltrinelli, 1964) and TW Adorno, 'Criticism of Culture and Society' (1949) in *Prisms. Essays in cultural criticism and society* (trans Carlo Mainoldi) (Turin, Einaudi, 1972) 22; and now Chapoutot, *La rivoluzione culturale nazista* (Roma-Bari, Laterza, 2019) 204ff.

[8] P Grossi, *Society, law, state: a recovery for the law* (Milan, Giuffré, 2006) 231.

[9] S Rodotà, *Dal soggetto alla persona* (Naples, Edizioni Scientifiche, 2007); and in the extensive philosophical literature, V Possenti, *Il nuovo principio persona* (Rome, Armando Editore, 2013).

[10] *L'età dei diritti* (Turin, Einaudi, 2014); a topical reflection on this issue is now proposed by G Zagrebelsky, *Diritti per forza* (Turin, Einaudi, 2017).

It is not so long ago that the role of law changed, no longer being to consolidate differences to protect the privileged, but rather to guarantee inviolable (human and fundamental) rights to all, and to recognise their identity. In this sense, identity is no longer constructed in each person's past, but looks to the present and the future, and becomes a *choice* and an *opportunity*.

Personal identity can then be metaphorically described as a cornucopia in which dignity, religious beliefs, political and trade union allegiances, ethnicity, gender and sexual orientation, language, disability, genetic origins are protected. The original social condition is no longer the sole determinant of the individual's place in society; on the contrary, freedom and equality are preached, and the prevalence of merit and the recognition of abilities allow each person to develop his or her personality.[11]

Personal identity is associated with the recognition, guarantee and exercise of human and fundamental rights. Identity cannot be discriminatory, but presupposes the *fight against discrimination*.

The ultimate aspiration becomes, as Stefano Rodotà theorised, to ensure that everyone has the 'right to have rights'.[12]

'Identity' is therefore a word with many meanings and by its very nature mysterious and ambiguous: it traverses the centuries, carrying with it the onerous baggage of the past; it is reflected in the present and projected into the future.

II. THE VOCABULARY OF LAW

The use of terms in the world of law has been mentioned.

Jurists have been concerned with persons ever since the idea and representation of law was formed. The tripartition of civil law into *personae*, *res*, *actiones* in the *Institutions* of Gaius, a famous jurist of the second century AD, was taken up again in Justinian's *Institutions* in 533 AD and has been used with that meaning ever since, even influencing the layout of the books of which the civil codes of the nineteenth century are composed.

The Civil Code currently in force in Italy also follows this order, starting from the discipline of persons and the family (Book I) to regulate the rights of *natural persons*. In the enunciations that follow one another, the person is frequently mentioned, in relation to simultaneous death (Article 4), the right to a name (Article 6), protection of a name (Article 7), protection of a pseudonym (Article 9), abuse of the image (Article 10), domicile and residence (Article 43), absence (Article 48), presumed death (Article 58) and kinship (Article 74), precisely to configure a set of rules that establish how the person in his or her identity, composed of name-image-pseudonym-physical integrity,

[11] Alpa (n 4) ch 1.
[12] Rodotà, *Il diritto di avere diritti* (Roma-Bari, Laterza, 2013) 18ff, 41ff.

and as the holder of the corresponding rights and remedies, is to be treated in civil law.

The right of persons is thus summarised in certain rights established by the Civil Code, among the many that this and other laws recognise.

This is still a neutral expression, because it is true that 'person' in the context of the code is something more than 'individual'. That is to say, it indicates the individual holder of rights (which, subject to birth, are recognised only for those who are conceived (Article 1c.2 of the Civil Code), but it is also true that these rights could be modified by the law, even to the point of suppressing them, as happened with the approval of the racial laws, and as Article 1c.3 of the Civil Code provided when Book I (*Delle persone e della famiglia*) was enacted by Royal Decree No 1852 of 12 December 1938, which came into force on 1 July 1939.

The *law of persons* is an area in which the *rights of the person* are protected. The rights of the person is therefore an area left to the will of the legislature.

In each case, reference is made to the person, not to man. The expression 'human rights' took on its own very precise meaning from the late seventeenth century, as a result of natural law: at that time people spoke of man's 'natural rights', but by the end of the eighteenth century the Declarations of Rights referred to the rights of man and of the citizen; the catalogue of these rights primarily concerned the relationship between the individual and the community, the state, the authority, and thus involved public law.

Until the 1948 Constitution, the two levels were separate; afterwards, by way of interpretation, they came closer together, and an osmosis was created, whereby the rights governed by the Civil Code are irradiated by the Constitution, and constitutional norms have made it possible to create new rights that are defended with the remedies of the Civil Code.[13]

The person is therefore still the 'legal guise' of man, but its meaning has been enriched with constitutional coverage.

Jurists are not satisfied with these definitions. Legal logic demands that the right has an object – one takes as a paradigm the right to *things*, such as property, and its conventional limitations, such as easements, use, usufruct, habitation – one wonders what the object of a person's rights is, with regard to his or her connotations, ie name, image, pseudonym. As mentioned above, however, the Code does not refer to the right *to* name, image, etc, but rather *to* these connotations.

What is the relationship between the person and his name, image, etc? Should one reason in terms of ownership?

[13] For initial references see R Bifulco, M Cartabia, A Celotto, *L'Europa dei diritti* (Bologna, Il Mulino, 2001) 28ff; P Manzini and A Lollini, *Diritti fondamentali in Europa* (Bologna, Il Mulino, 2015) 7ff.; P Gianniti (ed), *I diritti fondamentali nell'Unione europea* (Bologna, Zanichelli, 2013) 483ff; L Trucco, *Introduzione allo studio dell'identità individuale nell'ordinamento costituzionale italiano* (Turin, Giappichelli, 2004).

Even more intriguing is the law's approach to the *body*.[14] Here too, law has had a hesitant, ambiguous attitude towards the body, usually never mentioning that Article 5 of the Civil Code, on acts of disposition of the body, is an exception in the history of Italian civil codes, and in the history of the civil codes of continental European states. For the body, too, the same question arises: is it an object of property? The law has therefore not stated that man could be an object (and not a subject) of law; and where man has been degraded to an object, it was under the presumption that he was no longer person but a thing. After several millennia, the problem remained open; it was solved, as we shall see, by changing the terms used. And what about the result of all these components, identity? Is each individual the master of his or her own identity?

III. IMPOSED IDENTITIES AND CONSTRUCTED IDENTITIES

Represented graphically, the individual is a multicoloured, iridescent entity, presenting some characteristics that remain constant, and others that change over time. These can be real, virtual, or coercively 'imposed'. Real, because the image of the individual physically retains something of itself even with the passage of time: a notation immediately proven by comparing photographs that accompany a person from birth to death. If they are compared, there is a feature that tends to remain constant: physically it is the eyes, the gaze, the concept of self that is projected externally; psychologically too, the character presents certain constants. Other features are destined to be sculpted, modelled, modified by the events of life; even the ideal image is engraved by intellectual adventures, by familiarity with certain people, by the environment, by personal history within community, nation of state history. These are virtual characteristics, because the image of the person, beyond its internal construction, is constructed externally by the evolution of the social, medical and biological sciences, which the law translates into binding rules.

If one looks at the person from the point of view of IT practices, websites, social networks, one recognises their *digital identity*.

The law builds around the person an compulsory cage, regulating in an almost obsessive manner what the person is called, what sex he or she is, what community he or she belongs to, his or her state of freedom or servitude, whether he or she is to be classified as poor, illiterate, citizen or foreigner. Again. It seems incredible to think that only 80 years ago, law could determine whether an individual's blood should be considered 'pure or impure', whether a person should be considered 'normal' or 'abnormal', and so on.

Law has constructed the individual's social status, his or her way of positioning themself in society, his or her way of constructing personality and

[14] S Rodotà, *La vita e le regole. Tra diritto e non diritto*, 3rd edn (Milan, Feltrinelli, 2018) 73ff; S Rodotà (n 12) 160ff, 250ff.

culture, his or her way of dressing, eating, observing the rules of ceremonial, etiquette and manners. Law regulates his or her affections, aspirations, intimate relationships.

Here, unlike the other sciences, which construct identity on the basis of their constantly evolving categories, which are verifiable and susceptible to rectification, modification and alteration,[15] and with margins of approximation, law constructs identity with *binding* categories: the individual cannot escape them except with the authorization, or at any rate the intervention, of authority. Law *prescribes* a person's way of being and living.

This consideration familiar to jurists, and to scientists concerned with legal anthropology, eludes sociologists who study the ways in which people construct themselves, as if the individual will alone could exhaust the factors that sculpt identity.

Every individual has a 'future behind him',[16] to use Hanna Arendt's expression, because his or her past that sculpts his or her present has been constructed by the ordering categories of law.

Identity then turns from *fact to precept*, from a real world as interpreted by the social sciences into an imaginary world constructed by norms. In this world too – according to different conceptions of law – one encounters the person in many dimensions: from the statement that must be interpreted according to canons established by law to the human being in his corporeity, from the abstract concept to concrete life. Life and rules – to use an expression dear to Stefano Rodotà – are marked by law.

The relationships an individual has with others are also governed and shaped by law: family, association, community and authority law relationships. Not only the person as 'self', but also the self and the other, the self and others, are governed by law.

And the '*others*' also suffer the same fate, ie the same legal construction: the others can be minority or majority, white or black, faithful or heretical, western or eastern, and so on, in an iridescent collective qualification.[17]

Underlying the original legal construction of identity is this conception: since nature is governed by God-given laws, law must adapt human laws to the laws of nature. *Natural* identity has thus come to haunt the individual for centuries; only contemporary law has managed to definitively dissociate law from nature. 'Definitively' is a big word: law is made up of advances and regressions and each position cannot be said to have been definitively conquered.

[15] Identity as recorded in social relations, constructed on the one hand and ascribed on the other, stands out in Georg Simmel's studies (see in particular *La differenziazione sociale* (It trans) (Rome-Bari, Laterza, 1982 1st edn Leipzig, 1890); *Individuo e gruppo* (Roma, 2006, Armando Editore, 1st edn, 1908); in this perspective see F Crespi, *Identità e riconoscimento nella sociologia contemporanea* (Roma-Bari, Laterza, 2004) and now A Honneth, *Riconoscimento. Storia di un'idea europea* (Milan, Feltrinelli, 2019).

[16] *The future behind us* (Bologna, Il Mulino, 2011).

[17] For all see A Pizzorusso, *Minorities and Majorities* (Turin, Einaudi, 1993).

Laws show a world that must be discovered: like the identity of the person, they must be placed in their historical framework, in their temporality, in their flow. Max Weber would say: conditioned by the laws of nature, society, politics and economics.

Dike and Nomos[18] have much to say about identity, and it is precisely by taking both law and justice into account that those who wish to decipher this legal concept must embark on a journey that does not delve into the unfathomable abyss of the unconscious, but must take it into account;[19] does not exhaust itself in the bureaucratic cataloguing of distinctive signs, but is aware of it; does not limit itself to the description of norms, even if it draws nourishment from them, but through the description of the ways in which personal identity is configured by legislators, judges, academics, breaks it down and reconstructs it. The journey, however, is not out of time, but within time: and from when it begins to when it ends, the identity that it first examined has already changed. Identity therefore becomes an elusive concept, even for the jurist. That is why the jurist attempts to fix it once and for all through its crystallisation in norms, which at the moment they are set give the illusion of having grasped it forever.

Identity is a multifaceted self, which presents itself as one and threefold: the self as such, that is, the individual as he or she perceives himself or herself and how the individual positions himself or herself in being himself or herself; the self as he or she projects himself or herself externally and how he or she constructs himself or herself for others; the self as perceived externally, by others, who construct his or her identity on the basis of their culture and social rules.

Identity is singular and plural. When it is plural, it becomes group identity, and if it embraces all those who live in a given historical moment in a given aera, it becomes a collective identity that can be coloured, according to national culture, language, religion, traditions.

In these pages, the gaze is turned towards the individual and the group, since the individual exists because he or she is compared with the *other*, and may be part of a group or be an outsider to it. The individual therefore experiences a problem of *recognition*, which implies the drafting of canons of expression, of behaviour, of appearance that are stratified, giving rise to a model with which to compare oneself, a mirror in which to be reflected.

The individual is full of synonyms, but they are not mere linguistic variations; each of them has a meaningful meaning, whether we are talking about living beings, human beings, men and women, or more sophisticated categories created by law such as citizens, foreigners, stateless persons, immigrants.

[18] According to the meaning proposed by M Cacciari and N Irti, *In Praise of Law* (Milan, La Nave di Teseo, 2019) with an essay by W Jaeger.

[19] In the very extensive literature see M Mead, *Mind Self and Society from the Standpoint of a Social Behaviorist* (ed CW Morris) (Chicago, 1934); E Goffman, *La vita quotidiana come rappresentazione* (It trans) (Bologna, Il Mulino, 1969; 1st edn New York, 1959).

Law has created imaginative categories, such as the *Untermenschen*, which legitimised the Nazis' persecution of the Jews; it created discrimination based on 'race' by borrowing this pseudo-scientific invention from the biological and anthropological sciences of the late nineteenth century.

The progressive abstraction from reality ends up constructing a law consigned to law and technology: the masks of law hide the faces of life, as Paolo Zatti has icastically written.[20]

The evolution of the construction of rights traces the way in which law has considered the individual from time to time.[21] The person, today, with the universal declarations of rights and the guarantees provided by the constitutions, is no longer a mask, no longer an abstract concept, but is also considered in law to be a human being in the flesh, a value in itself, to which the legal system provides every form of protection. This network extends to defend the individual's character, and to protect him or her from discrimination.

Article 21 of the Charter of Fundamental Rights of the European Union prohibits discrimination based, in particular, 'on sex, race, colour, ethnic or racial origin, genetic features, language, religion or belief, political or any other opinion, membership of a national minority, property, birth, disability, age or sexual orientation'. Furthermore, the Union respects cultural, religious, linguistic diversity (Article 22); ensures equality between men and women (Article 23); and protects children (Article 24) and the elderly (Article 25).

Article 21 outlines some of the distinguishing characteristics of persons: the term 'person' is repeated almost obsessively in the Charter. In order to fully understand the meaning and normative scope of these provisions, one cannot ignore how distinctions and discrimination arose, and why there was an urgent need to place them at the heart of the Bill of Rights as of many modern constitutions.

The identification of the person proceeds hand in hand with *its differentiation and thus with its distinction*. This process directly affects the social sciences, especially sociology and anthropology, as well as psychology and medicine, but also economics and politics. What role has law played in this process? In order to understand it, one has to break down the provisions, deconstruct the legal form to highlight its components, go to the root of the terms and rules.

[20] P Zatti, *Maschere del diritto volti della vita* (Milan, Giuffré, 2009).
[21] Rodotà (n 9).

2

The Representation of Identity

I. A UNIVERSE OF SIGNS AND SYMBOLS

INDIVIDUALS AND THEIR groups have been identified throughout history using signs, symbols, tattoos, coats of arms, documents, numbers, codes, arithmetic formulas and algorithms, as well as robes, uniforms, headgear, footwear, belts and jewellery, ranks and weapons, flags and banners. Some of these artefacts may have acquired a sacred significance, to distinguish those who displayed or wore them, or were forced to display and wear them.

Symbols and distinctive signs correspond to privileges or positions of subjugation and marginality.

The factors of discrimination have come down to us via very different routes: the discrimination of women goes back to primordial times; the discrimination of the Jews from the destruction of the Temple of Jerusalem and the diaspora; the discrimination on the grounds of sexual orientation acquired different names and meanings in the Middle Ages and later centuries; discrimination on the grounds of social conditions continued until the twentieth century; and so on.

But these boundaries are blurred; signs often disappear and then re-emerge.

Historical analysis warns us that certain distinctive criteria deemed to have disappeared reappear in different guises:[1] think of the new slavery, which in fact reproposes the establishment of a right of man over man; think of the condition of immigrants and stateless persons; think of the mentally ill. All human conditions to which contemporary philosophy – the works of Michel Foucault immediately come to mind – has devoted extensive studies to investigate the evolution of social classes, forms of power, and the metamorphosis of the ego.

The law has played its part in this – hence the need to distinguish rights and criteria of recognition and discrimination, going back to the origins of distinction and classification, and to the world of legal forms. It is an investigation that must necessarily be carried out *diachronically for each* criterion of discrimination, for each right linked to it, for each area in which it operates.

[1] For all see V Groebner, *Storia dell'identità personale e della sua certificazione. Scheda segnaletica, documento di identità e controllo nell' Europa moderna* (It trans) (Bellinzona, 2008; Muenchen, 2004).

Distinctive signs are at the same time outward signs, because they are used to 'recognise', to 'be recognised' and to 'recognise oneself' – as if they were a mirror in which the individual's outward appearance is reflected, but also his status and rank – and the role that that individual plays in society. The distinctive signs that construct the individual are not random, nor are they free, but are ordered by law because they precisely place the individual in the *social order*.

There are constants that run through the different historical phases, and enable large geographical areas to be standardised according to ordering factors, rights and duties, identification criteria and distinctive signs.

But, as stated above, the identification criteria, the distinguishing marks, do not change *en bloc*; they take root in the constituent fluctuations of the individual's 'mask'; they perpetuate; they take root, perhaps they evolve while keeping their roots intact, crossing the centuries.

In contrast to the external image of the individual, there is also the image that the individual sees from within and decides to expose – if he is able to do so – in a free and conscious manner. Political history, literary and theatrical history tell us of the self, of its double,[2] of falsified identities, of constructed identities, of exchanged identities: all hypotheses opposed by law, which aims to make the real identity coincide with the imposed identity.

When does this correspondence erode? When does erosion become fracture?

The erosion begins with the spread of the mass media: the history of the right to privacy is the most overt example of this. The fracture begins with the affirmation of information technology, in which more than one identity manifests itself: real identity, understood as the personal identity, is flanked by digital identity, which splits into identity constructed by data collectors and manipulators, and identity constructed by the person concerned who disseminates data on himself or herself through the network and 'social'.

Another identification process linked to biological technology is also consolidating this: the comparison between registry and biological identity, which do not always correspond. The law tends to privilege the anagraphic identity, but cracks have appeared in this approach, because the individual may want to know his biological origins. In this case, the evolution of law has meant that a link can be made between biological identity and the claim to know one's origins.

As can be seen, law sometimes plays a conservative and constricting role, sometimes a liberating and guaranteeing role. Usually the first is played in ancient times, the second in modern.

[2] With the Menecmi Plautus inaugurated the theatre of misunderstandings, later taken up by Shakespeare, Molière and Goldoni: G Ferroni, *Il testo e la scena. Saggi sul teatro del Cinquecento* (Rome, Bulzoni, 1980). And see O Rank, *Il Doppio. Il significato del sosia nella letteratura e nel folklore* (Milan, SE, 1972). Luigi Pirandello, on the other hand, will make an introspective reading of it, the misunderstandings being introduced in each person, in the awareness that we were given 'a reality that does not exist' once and for all, but is 'continuously infinitely mutable' (*Uno,nessuno, centomila* (Turin, Einaudi, 2014; 1st edn 1926).

II. COMBINATIONS AND INTERSECTIONS OF IDENTIFICATION AND DISCRIMINATION CRITERIA

Within a society, forms of discrimination affect both the individual as an individual and as a member of a community; but individual discrimination can also affect the individual within his own community.

Combinations are almost compulsory, as it is difficult for a discrete criterion to be isolated and not combined with others. As an individual's way of being, sex is always combined with another criterion: with 'race', skin colour, ethnic or social origin, genetic characteristics, and so on. Being a white or black woman in a class society changes her legal situation a great deal; so does being a rich or poor woman, or a woman belonging to a high or low social status: history teaches us that queens and mistresses of kings were placed in a situation not of minority but quite equal to that of men; indeed, it was the men who, if lovers of the queen, or of the king, placed themselves in a situation of power and wealth that was only temporary and mocked by the other courtiers. The history of the kings, queens and mistresses of France and England tells of innumerable such situations. Each can be catalogued on the basis of its characteristics in the light of the conventions and beliefs of the time in question. However, according to the rules of nobility, the noble woman who married a commoner lost her noble title, but if the man was a servant she became free, whereas the noble man who married a commoner made her noble: '*la verge anoblist, le ventre afranchist*', according to the French and English Dictionary.[3]

On the contrary, being female can become a further form of discrimination if this attribute is coupled with another discretional criterion: from a religious point of view, women can be treated less favourably than men, as happens in the religions of the Book, in which women assume an ancillary position.

And so it is with regard to individual discrimination versus collective discrimination, as is the case for minorities within a community, within a state, or of a state within an empire, confederation or federation.

Individual forms of discrimination must therefore be viewed in terms of each type of discrimination and how these connect with each other.

The deciphering – with terminology and categories constructed by law – of signs, symbols, distinctive traits, and their conversion into rights or into factors of discrimination is part of every culture, and is so ingrained in the way we think and act that we often do not even realise that behind a painting or a literary passage there is a legal construction that conditions the way we appear and are represented.

[3] Which in the title states: 'composed by Mr. Randle Cotgrave, with another, in *English and French*' (London, 1673). The expression is found in RJ Pothier, *Traité des personnes et des choses* (1st edn, 1778; Paris, Hachette, 2017) 966.

3

The Secrets of Painting and Literature

I. THE PORTRAIT

THE DISTINCTIVE TRAITS of individuals are so ingrained in the habits of life that they seem natural to us, such that they become accepted as unreflected data. They are at the same time a broadly cultural product to the manufacture of which law has made its contribution.

Law is a product of culture. Through the lens of law we can fully read artistic representations of identity.

The portrait of a person rendered by a painting, or a page of a literary work, effectively and immediately reveals a world of references and connections concerning identity that tend to be overlooked or ignored by an ordinary observer or reader.

There are many examples; Van Dyck's portrait of Elena Grimaldi is emblematic. The painting comes from the brush of the Flemish painter, a pupil of Rubens, who worked in Genoa in the years of his youth, between 1621 and 1623. At that time Genoa was queen of the seas, its economy based on trade and finance, and the noble families – who had been granted the privilege of engaging in trade without losing their titles – seized the opportunity to commission the painter with an important task: to immortalise themselves, their wealth, their power. For the Marquises Cattaneo, Van Dyck painted several portraits, including one of Elena Grimaldi, who had married Giacomo Cattaneo. 'The portraits of the Cattaneo family,' emphasises Federico Zeri,[1] 'are among the supreme examples of the painter's portraiture, marked by unsurpassed aristocratic dignity and acute characterisation, which combines social determination with an inner investigation of the subjects'.

The painting depicts a lady standing in front of her palace, dressed in a long black dress adorned with a row of golden buttons and a rich *gorget*, on a terrace showing columns and brocades behind her, while gentle tree-lined hills loom in the background. But what strikes the observer most is the red

[1] F Zeri, *Van Dyck. Marchesa Elena Grimaldi Cattaneo with negro servant* (Milan, Rizzoli, 1999), a book resulting from a conversation with Marco Dolcetta.

stain of the parasol, which shelters the lady from the rain heralded by the dark clouds that occupy the entire left-hand corner of the painting, and the attentive solicitude of the 'negretto' – the black slave holding the parasol. The gazes are eloquent: the lady gazes determinedly at her observer; the servant reveals sadness and self-denial, albeit dressed in luxurious clothes.

What does the jurist glimpse in this work? First of all a subject, a woman, who, because of the robe she wears and the outline, has her own strong individuality, an identity marked by eloquent symbols: the dress is decorated with many buttons, which are a sign of nobility because at that time buttons could only be used by nobles and clergymen; she is a woman who comes from a rich and powerful family, the owner of sumptuous palaces, a sign of proprietary identity that in Genoa is passed down from generation to generation, and is associated with noble titles and public offices; the marriage unites two aristocratic families that have accumulated their wealth through trade and money-lending. Historians tell us of Genoa's economic fortunes in the Mediterranean and of the role of noble bankers to the rulers: Andrea Doria, admiral of Charles V, was given the title of Prince of Melfi and Duke of Tursi in exchange for military aid with the galleys he owned and the numerous loans he gave to the Emperor without repayment.[2]

In the painting, all these data reconstruct an identity: first of all the identity of a subject, who stands out from the anonymous crowd, who has her own personality, her own history, her own 'dignity' understood as rank in the society in which she lives and in the era in which she lives; that subject has a name and a surname, she has his own way of dressing, she is provided with goods, and she has a servant who, being black-skinned, is probably a slave. The lady is free because she enjoys the *status civitatis* (she belongs to the Republic of Genoa) and the *status libertatis* (being a married woman she is subject only to her husband's power) and is noble. On the other hand, the boy holding the parasol is one of many, who arrived at the palace as a result of a sale contract or perhaps was born in the palace of a slave, since those born of slaves acquired the status of slaves.

The painting sums up a tangle of legal rules of great depth, concerning status, property and the family, social stratification and the division of power, commerce and finance, together these regulate everyone's life down to the tiniest detail, to govern the way they dress, the way they stay in society, the way they organise their homes, the countryside, their holidays in the fiefdom.

[2] Andrea Doria succeeded in freeing the city of Genoa from the French, reconstituting the nobility by grouping the families into 'hotels' and giving a new constitution to the aristocratic republic. The most important Genoese families, experts in commerce, were granted many privileges by the Emperor of the Two Worlds: in particular, that of preserving their noble titles and enriching them, in exchange for the right to trade, which outside the Republic was considered incompatible with noble dignity, and that of governing the city and its territory, on both sides of the Giogo, with the elective offices limited to the families grouped in the Alberghi.

Even the palaces, the splendid palaces of Strada Nuova, which had caught Rubens' imagination, bear these signs: on the ground floor are the warehouses for storing goods, on the first floor the flats where the owners live, complete with terraces and hanging gardens, and on the top floor the servants' quarters.

The depiction of human subjects is present in all painting, from classical paintings depicting gods and stories described in classical works, allegories and fantastic worlds, to paintings with a religious content, depicting characters and stories from the Bible, dedications of churches as well as miracles or sacrifices of saints. Paintings concerning individual subjects or families are reserved for monarchs. Michel Foucault elects the scene of Velasquez portraying *Las Meninas* with Philip IV, Marianne of Austria and their children as an emblematic example of the structure of that society's way of thinking.[3]

The philosophy of the image reveals many things.

Burckhardt teaches that the depiction of the individual in isolation was born in the Renaissance period in Italian painting.[4]

Only recently has Peter Burke tried to correct this approach. But his thesis stands the test of time. And, indeed, the individual who has no dignity of his own is indistinct, part of a crowd. If he does not have a dignity, he acquires it because he is the subject of a portrait, as is the case with the *Girl with the Pearl Earring*, Vermeer's jockey, or the Fornarina, Raphael's mistress.[5]

Tzvetan Todorov places the origins of pictorial individualism in Flanders, dating back to the fifteenth century: the realism of the Flemish painters is expressed in the reality of human faces, and is a reflection of the philosophy of William of Ockham, who, precisely by distinguishing the laws of men from the laws of God, legitimises the representation of real life; human figures are no longer linked in painting to the representation of edifying episodes of religious life or the imaginative version of pages from the ancient classics, but can relate to scenes from everyday life.[6]

Thus Erwin Panofsky, in his book on early Flemish painting, expounds the thesis of the *ars nova*, invented by Flemish painters at the beginning of the fifteenth century, consisting of 'veiling symbols under the appearance of real objects'. This direction finds its earliest traces in Giotto and Duccio, but is more pervasively and clearly developed in later centuries. The individualist portrait par excellence is the mirror tondo of the Pandolfini couple by Jan van Eyck of 1434. Note that these are images of a bourgeois couple, the rising social class in that part of Europe at the time.

[3] *Le parole e le cose* (It trans) (Milan, Rizzoli, 1967).

[4] *La civiltà del Rinascimento in Italia* (It trans) (Milan, Newton Compton Editori, 2020). The work, originally written in 1860, was supplemented with chapters and essays up to the German edition of 1928; note that the author used the expression *Kultur*. A wide-ranging debate was opened on his thought: see R Fubini, 'Considerazioni su Burkhardt, Il libro sul Rinascimento in Italia, De Sanctis e Burkhardt' (2000) 158 *Archivio Storico Italiano* 85.

[5] *The Renaissance* (Bologna, Il Mulino, 2001).

[6] 'In Praise of the Individual. An Essay on Flemish Painting in the Renaissance' (Sant'Oreste, Rome, 2001).

In any case, whether one is to believe Burckhart or Panofsky, in painting the individual as such, with his somatic characteristics, his personality, his unrepeatability, was born in the fifteenth century. Peter Burke persuasively establishes the relationship between individualism, the Renaissance and portraiture: in portraiture, 'self-awareness, self-confidence, resoluteness, singularity' emerge. Fame and social competition are the springs of this *nouvelle vague*, which is affirmed by the rise of the productive bourgeoisie. And indeed the crowds receive legitimacy in painting when they have obtained it in social and political life. There are two images that remain firmly in the memory: the Marianne leading the people to the storming of the Bastille – we are now at the end of the eighteenth century – and the Fourth Estate marching animated by social redemption and the aspiration to political participation, to arrive at the beginning of the twentieth century.

In Eugène Delacroix's painting, Marianne becomes the symbol of the secular and democratic French Republic;[7] Marianne wears the Phrygian cap and leads the people against the armigers; the people are dressed in shabby clothes; the revolutionaries are carrying randomly collected weapons; they advance victoriously, crushing the militia, recognisable by their uniforms and equipment; Marianne's chest is bare, but hers is a chaste nudity: she is a woman who fights unclothed and sings the praises of redemption, holding the Tricolor like a sabre; in the background are the towers of Notre Dame and the piles of smoke and dust raised by the clash. Marianne is a woman without a name, who acquires one, invented, for the heroism she shows.[8]

Pelizza da Volpedo's *Quarto Stato* of 1901 also depicts the anonymous crowd. In the centre of the painting are three figures: two men of mature age, wearing simple clothes as was the custom among the common people of the time, with a woman, fully dressed, but barefoot; she carries a half-naked child around her neck, covered in a vest. The men's gaze is not threatening but determined, that of the woman expresses the desolation of the last; behind them a crowd that speaks with their hands and faces: the hands are turned upwards, representing poverty waiting to be rescued, the faces expressing questions but also strength – the strength of despair.

II. THE STORY

In literature, too, we can read through the eyes of the jurist many pages by authors that illustrate the reality of the person, and of his social relations, that is, his individual identity and his social (or collective) identity; identities

[7] M Agulhon, *Marianne au combat: L'imagerie et la symbolique républicaines de 1789 à 1880* (Paris, Flammarion, 1979).

[8] It is debated whether this depiction is a reminder of 14 July 1789 or rather represents the 28 July 1830 uprising against the libertarian laws of the reactionary government appointed by Charles X, King of France.

sculpted by law that does not transpire from the page, but are almost naturally imprinted on it. A scene from Daniel Defoe's *Robinson Crusoe* is emblematic.

It is a *count philosophique* in which the good savage, nicknamed Friday, becomes a servant, one might say 'naturally'.

The contrast between the encounter with the naked and savage Friday and that with the other prisoner and predestined victim of the cannibals, who use the island where Robinson survives, for their ferocious banquets, is stark: the first word the prisoner freed by Robinson utters is a qualifying term. Not knowing the nationality of his saviour, the prisoner expresses in Latin the differentiating term of belonging: 'Christianus sum', which sums up in itself, almost as if it were the essence, the distinctive coordinates of the individual: he is civilised, he is baptised, he is therefore a person; he has his own dignity conferred on him by his knowledge of Latin, his own status, deriving from belonging to a religion and a community (Christianity), that is, he is not a savage, nor an infidel. And a 'brother'. The specification of belonging to Christendom precedes that of nationality.

Robinson asks him what country he is from, and the other replies: 'Spanish'. At this point Robinson, in the heat of the moment (he is freeing the unfortunate man and has to hold off some 20 cannibals) incites him to fight. He does not ask his name ('We will talk later; now we must fight'), but turns to him with the qualifying expression corresponding to his rank: 'Sir …'.

The relationship between Robinson and the Spaniard is therefore one of respect: although the Spaniard will be subservient to him because he is indebted for the life Robinson saved him, he will not be treated as the wild Friday, 'naturally' a servant.

In the past, these pages were considered the product of an elite culture aimed at a small circle of users. In this respect, too, there is contiguity between literary wisdom and legal wisdom. The production of law is also the work of an elite that governs a silent (and subordinate) majority. Singular, in this sense, is the lesson that can be drawn from the Renaissance behaviourists. 'Without ever precluding the reasons of nature and reality' they tend to intensify the naturalistic origins of men. Not only do they make a case for statuses, but they point to the way in which each person must behave in order to live up to his status. There is thus a tension between reality and ideality: between nature and the way to conform to it.

III. MORAL WORKS AND THE 'CIVILISED' MAN

The plastic image of identity in all its classificatory components that emerges from portraits and literary passages is revealed with equal intensity in moral works, in treatises on the etiquette of court societies, in manuals on the education of civilised men.

In order to decrypt the text, it is worth considering that its author assumes the social structure as an inescapable given; he does not normally question the equity of roles; rather, he tends to emphasise distinctions. Each of the behaviourists works by enriching his contribution with references to classical culture, to evangelical values, to models of tradition; the texts therefore vary in literary value, in the pleasantness of expressive modes, in depth of content.

Some, like Giovanni Della Casa, remain at the threshold of inwardness; they are all overthrown on the outside, on appearances, on etiquette; others, like Baldassar Castiglione, are more solid, more cultured, more acute. Castiglione and Della Casa belong to the petty nobility, but live pleasantly in the world of the powerful and build a comfortable life for themselves. The former (1478–1529) was the son of a man-at-arms and a Gonzaga; he lived in the courts and became an ambassador; the latter (1503–1550) came from a noble and well-to-do Florentine family, lived under the aegis of the Farnese family, embarked on an ecclesiastical career, became an archbishop, ambassador and secretary of state. Michel de Montaigne (1533–1592) belonged to a noble family from Périgord, but soon made the great rejection, distancing himself from the court, and preferring to spend much of his existence in simplicity and meditation. He did not appreciate the courtier's model of life; all his work was dedicated to the inner grammar, even if his asceticism was not mystical; the content of his message was interwoven with classicism, common sense, reasonableness; he succeeded in demonstrating that *mediocritas* can, in addition to being golden, be a pleasant viaticum for an honest and tranquil life. Baltasar Gracidn (1601–1658), the son of a doctor of fair social standing, built his career in the Society of Jesus. But due to his independence, his biting spirit and his intellectual freedom, he did not rise to the top of the order. Throughout his life, he taught in colleges and associated with a few wealthy gentlemen with whom he shared his passion for erudition. In his works, the court is no longer the scene of life; nor the Renaissance man its protagonist; but the whole world, with its flatteries, illusions, disillusions and perfidies, is the terrain in which the individual, ie the Hero, the Wise, the Prudent, must compete. These are the models that Graci6n paints; his is an inner discipline, sometimes seasoned with attention to externals; but above all a path towards the unfolding of intelligence seasoned with prudence and cunning, with dissimulation and constructed appearances. There are not just two dimensions – reality and appearance, political life and moral life – but a multiplicity of planes, in which one must know how to move wisely. The position established by nature – the social condition – is at the same time the incentive, the *réservoir of* energies, the starting point for being able to make full use of the rational and intellectual faculties with which each person, as a man, is naturally more or less endowed.

In the old order, where everyone is placed by fortune/nature in their 'right' place, there is continuity in the values that permeate the common mentality, and the jurists champion them up to the Enlightenment and the Revolution.

Even in the second half of the eighteenth century, the privilege of nobility made the Marquis de Sade immune from many crimes. The story of de Sade is emblematic in this regard. If sanction intervenes, it is not because he violated human life, sexual freedom, or the personal freedom of his victims (behaviour typical of all libertines of the time, tolerated if not protected by authority), but for other reasons. Because the ideas professed by de Sade upset the established order and were considered irreverent and subversive. The use of religious symbols in the (imaginary or real?) exploitation of bodies is a symptom of subversion and therefore must be severely repressed.

But let us take a closer look at the texts and return to Castiglione.

It is worth quoting a page from the beginning of Book I of the work. It is both the 'manifesto' and the table of values, the guide to reading and the purpose of the writing: it is a page that betrays the way of understanding social differences and the distinctive symbols of men. From here, the teaching to become a perfect courtier departs.

Castiglione does not exclude that one who is not born noble (ie is 'ignoble') cannot perform meritorious deeds; but by descent, and the education received, he believes that the noble is 'naturally' led to virtue (I, xiv), whereas for the ignoble the path to virtue is artificial and more difficult.

On closer inspection, Castiglione's description of the courtier corresponds to the characteristics of the nobles of high lineage and good reputation that he frequented. He also attributes to the courtier the duties that nobles take on. The courtier must devote himself to arms (I, xvii), hunting, ball games, vaulting on horseback (I, xxii), dancing (II, xi), conversation (II, xvii); he must dress elegantly but without excess (II, xxvii); he can make puns (II, Lxiv) and also witticisms (Il, Lxv); he must know Plato and Aristotle (II, xLviI), painting and sculpture (II, LII).

But, given his natural superiority and virtues, how should he treat individuals who are not his equals?

Castiglione does not like promiscuity, uniformity, or worse, homologation: the courtier must distinguish himself from all others. His cultured and accurate manual is also aimed at this: at distinction, that is, at the exaltation of the noble traits that a person (already noble) must strive to highlight externally with apparent signs, and in his cultural formation, with choices of certain value. And again in the opening paragraph (I, xiv) he clarifies his message:

> Nobility is almost like a bright light that shows and makes us see good and bad deeds, and enkindles and spurs us to virtue with the fear of infamy, as well as with the hope of praise; and since this splendour of nobility is not revealed in the works of the ignoble, they lack the stimulus and fear of that infamy, nor do they seem to be obliged to go further than their ancestors did; and the noble are not obliged to reach at least the goal they were shown by the first. However, it is almost always the case that in arms and other virtuous deeds the noblest men are the most distinguished, because a certain strength and propriety of their beginning is linked to everything

> that derives from it and makes it similar to itself; as we see not only in the breeds of quarrymen and other animals, but also in trees, the scions of which almost always resemble the trunk; and if they degenerate, it is due to the bad farmer.

And so it is with little men, who, if they are cultivated with good charity, are almost always similar to those from whom they proceed and often improve; but if there is no one to look after them well, they become like savages, and never mature. It is true that, either by the favour of the stars, they seem not to have been born, or that some god with his own hands has formed them and adorned them with all the goods of mind and body; just as many are seen to be so inept and rude, that one cannot believe that nature, out of spite or mockery, has brought them into the world.

This is because nature expresses *subtle distinctions* in terms of appearance, health, attractiveness. It is therefore the courtier's task to correct the gaps that nature has shown, and to bring the gifts of nature and the gifts of lineage back into conjunction. Castiglione does not hide – he makes Gaspare Pallavicino say so – that many, born of the noblest blood, are full of vices; and other ignoble ones have illustrated their posterity with their virtue (I, xv). He also admits that fortune may be the cause of differences. But this is the answer he entrusts to Count Ludovico da Canossa: even if virtue can reign in 'lowly men', the courtier must be of noble birth because of the universal opinion that accompanies nobility (I, xvi).

The idea of nobility expressed in these passages is symptomatic of the Renaissance and sixteenth-century mentality.[9]

Precisely because he endeavours to be different, the courtier must not mingle with the 'inferiors': it is not appropriate for him to honour a country party with his own person (II, ix), nor to measure himself in feats of strength with the peasants, by whom he might be beaten (II, x); he must be discreet, and thus not dance with the inferiors (II, xi), and let himself be seen rarely (II, xii). If, however, he wants to approach the ignoble, this must result in his greater greatness and distinction: he must show that the nobleman's worth 'is not increased by being a prince' (II, xi).

We have recognised in this rule the dictates of behaviour scrupulously observed by Manzoni's characters. At the end of the novel Count Attilio celebrates Renzo, Lucia and Agnese, but does not forget his own lineage. He does not admit them to his table, but serves them, as if to emphasise sympathy that does not, however, exceed natural limits.

Much milder, and aimed at exteriority, is Monsignor Della Casa. Here the social condition dictates the law in a precise manner as to the style of dress (vii),

[9] C Donati, *L'idea di nobiltà in Italia. Secoli XIV–XVIII* (Roma-Bari, Laterza, 1988) 38ff. The vast literature on the subject is fragmented into the history of the nobility of individual regions and families and stocks, monarchies, titles and coats of arms: O Brunner, *Vita nobiliare e cultura europea* (It trans) (Bologna, Il Mulino, 1972).

to be in company (x), to participate in ceremonies (xiv); he recommends discretion in the use of titles, now given to all (xxv), and caution in the use of mottos (xx). He is not so much concerned with solid culture, or the cultivation of virtues: the young man he wishes to teach is invited simply not to tell lies (xiv).

The *Galateo* is, in short, a manual of social propriety, with which one learns to be pleasant. There are no ideals; aspiring cardinals, diplomats, gentlemen of the chamber, personal secretaries of the powerful find their gospel in these clear pages, from which an entirely formal mediocrity emanates.

Its beneficiaries are those who belong from birth to the world of the powerful, and those who have the means to enter it. All the others, the 'non-honest' bourgeois, those who exercise professions, trades, commerce, not to mention those who are peasants or serfs, are not even in the background. They are simply ignored, as they belong to a world of their own, not communicating with the former. It is not possible to establish an equal relationship with those from a lower status: Della Casa is so convinced of this that it is the subject of a small treatise, *De officis interpotentiores et tenuiores amicos*, precisely the manual of behaviour between friends of different social rank. The basic idea that emerges is that there can be no true friendship between persons of different social rank: the feelings of those of weaker status will be marked by calculation, flattery, falsehood, envy; and those of those higher up the social ladder will be marked by deference, benevolence, and instrumentalisation.

Appearances, titles, dress code and ceremony are the hallmarks of a society of good manners; a new civilisation is emerging. According to Norbert Elias, good manners are a means of identification of a person's social status.[10]

Sometimes symbols, rituals, differentiations are the object of an almost obsessive cult, as happens in the Baroque era, marked by the Spanish manner. Emblematic is that passage Manzoni's *The Betrothed* where the altercation between the haughty nobleman and the future Friar Christopher is described. The passage is too well known to dwell on it even briefly. It is worth remembering, however, that the altercation, which later led to a duel, arose precisely from the violation of a rule of etiquette: the nobleman was denied the right hand ('with your equals the right is mine') and drew his sword: he was not to blame, but his honour was saved.

Among the philosophers of the sixteenth and seventeenth centuries, who constitute the other *side of* behaviourism, Michel de Montaigne stands out, as mentioned above.

A genuine exception to a host of thinkers who accept the conditions of individuals as reflecting an order of nature that is immutable and therefore natural, unchangeable and therefore *just*, Montaigne dedicates some acute reflections to

[10] N Elias, *La civiltà delle buone maniere* (Bologna, Il Mulino, 2009).

the social order. And he also manifests in these his modernity, his probity, his intellectual courage.

So far, it has been found that most behaviourists – as well as the jurists who act as notaries of history – consider it a serious misfortune to be born a serf, in the lowest classes, and only value those born into the free and wealthy, possibly noble social categories. Only those who come into the world with such connections or qualities have the opportunity to enjoy all rights and thus automatically gain an advantage over most.

However, Montaigne reverses the pyramid.[11] He does not cite the parable of the talents, nor the passages of scripture in which the humble are exalted and the grave responsibilities of the powerful are highlighted. He simply stops to consider the misfortune of greatness; he does not even choose the opposite, the way of the humble; he keeps to the middle path. He is a son of his time, and therefore does not intend to oppose the natural order of things. He only remarks, indicating his own aspirations ('limited and fearful elevation … in firmness, in prudence in health, in beauty and even in wealth') that he would rather be third in Paris than first in Périgueux.

He does not like to 'argue with a miserable stranger' but neither, in passing, does he like to 'cleave the crowds in worship'.[12] He claims to have behaved in such a way in his life as to exceed the degree of fortune in which God places 'his birth'. And *en passant he* notes: 'every natural constitution is similarly just and tranquil'. He then explains how difficult it is to be a king, to whom all bow, whom all flatter, whom all fear. The life that opens up to him is smooth, but lacking in courage, and false (VII, l.III).

In the second essay[13] dedicated to honours, Montaigne does not discuss the vanity of human things, but asks what their purpose is. And here is the answer: it was a fine invention, accepted in most governments of the world, to institute certain vain and worthless signs to honour and reward valour. The distinguishing marks of individuals, such as the style of dress, privileges, titles, orders of knighthood, emblems, are useful (not vain) means to honour and reward their valour. Hence his dismay that distinctive signs have lost their original essence, as they have been disseminated, multiplied, offered to such a large number of people who did not deserve them, as to empty of meaning the honour they were meant to represent.

So far, one might say, we find some novelty; but Montaigne continues to be a child of his time. He accepts the given order, and suggests how – by pursuing the middle path, not that of heroism or holiness – it is possible to elevate oneself morally.

[11] M de Montaigne, *Saggi* (Milan, Bompiani, 1986).
[12] ibid 147.
[13] ibid 290.

In the essay entitled 'The inequality that exists among us' he goes further.[14] Here he clearly distinguishes between social position and moral position, between appearance and essence, between mask and reality: even the powerful fall ill, suffer, go into rages, that is, they are human, even though their appearances, their way of dressing, of living, the court with which they surround themselves give them a semi-divine position. In other words, 'the goods of fortune, although they are such, one must also have sensibility to manage them'. In short, 'the advantages of princes are imaginary advantages'. The conclusion is the precept taken from Cornelius Nepot's *Vitadi Atticus*: 'mores cuique sui fingunt fortunam'. And virtue that gives the sign of fortune, of nobility.

The equality that Montaigne celebrates is therefore that of the virtues: the pursuit of the virtues the path in which all men find themselves in an identical position; not therefore the equality of departure – which Montaigne neither discusses nor proposes to subvert – but equality in the pursuit of what is good.

It is a dimension that grows, and distances itself from those of the Renaissance behaviourists, because it doubles reality: that of appearances, ordered according to nature, wealth, honours, and the inner one, ordered according to the search for values.

Less explicit, more profound, and richer in suggestion and references to classical culture is the text by Baltasar Gracián, which in some ways can be compared to Castiglione. Gracián mentions Castiglione more than once in his wide-ranging work: in a letter to his protector, Don Vincenzo Giovanni de Lastanosa, in which he describes 'the man for all hours', endowed with a universal will and capable intelligence, with infinite ambitions,[15] and in the same proem of the *Hero*[16] where Castiglione, then already so famous as to be called 'the count' par excellence, is compared to the great masters of the past: Seneca, Aesop, Homer, Aristotle and Tacitus.

The man who emerges from advice, from suggestions, from events, that is, the hero, the wise, the prudent, the intelligent, is a well-rounded man, who uses his experience of the world to conquer it. Gracián's reading is not edifying, but it is striking for the acuity with which he scrutinises the human soul, exploits circumstances; he grasps the spirit of situations. Not professing discredited inclinations, knowing the fortunate to make friends, and the unfortunate to escape them, enjoying a reputation for complacency, finding each person's weak point (the art of bending the will of others to one's own talent), keeping friends who are helpful, doing and showing off what one does are just some of the titles of his thoughts. They are precisely the teachings to take the right path to

[14] ibid 283.
[15] B Gracián, 'El Discreto' in B Gracián, *Obras completas* (Madrid, Ediciones Catedra, 1969) 95.
[16] B Gracián, *Obras completas* (ibid) 5.

success, to 'get to be somebody'. When one has reached the position, seasoned with good virtues, one must not lower oneself: 'he who lowers himself, immediately loses the superiority that his greatness of spirit gave him, and moreover loses esteem'.

This prepared the new idea of nobility proper to the seventeenth century; nobility does not necessarily imply a gentle spirit, defence of traditional values, and so on; nobility means belonging to the class of the privileged by rescript of the monarch (acquired, or accidental nobility) or by historical ancestry (natural nobility).

4

The Distinctions of Individuals in the World of Law

I. THE TERMINOLOGY OF JURISTS AND THE MASK OF BOETHIUS

In this complex and varied context, it may seem curious to think that the law has not been able to convey an unambiguous meaning of the term 'person' over time.

As mentioned in the opening of the discourse, in the world of law, 'person', 'man', 'individual', 'subject of law' do not have the same meaning.[1] Eineccio says: 'Man and person in law are two very different objects. Man is an entity that has a reasonable soul in its body. The person is a man considered in a certain state.'

Thus, the person is an individual with attributes established by law. Distinctive signs are attributes of the person. But what is the relationship between the person and those attributes?

Behind this question lies a centuries-old dispute: since man cannot be the object of rights, how can one justify the exercise of rights over the body, over the name, over the image? And, again, when we speak of the rights of the person, are we talking about a multiplicity of distinct rights or a single right with many representations?

As will be seen, the German science of the second half of the nineteenth century is responsible for answering this question. How it got there is the result of a long journey of terminology that jurists cultivated with a care that was as skilful as it was maniacal.

In a recent, penetrating essay, Bartolomé Clavero[2] takes his starting point from a passage by Boethius, later taken up by the most authoritative vocabularies of the seventeenth century, according to which the person is 'naturae rationalis individua substantia'. Law appropriates this definition so as to specify that the person is a human being endowed with reason and an

[1] *Elements of Roman Civil Law in the Order of Justinian's Institutions* (It trans) (Naples, 1831) § 75, 55.

[2] B Clavero, *La Máscara de Boecio: Antropologías del Sujeto entre Persona e Individuo, Teología y Derecho* in the review *Quaderni Fiorentini*, XXXIX (2010) 7ff.

individuality, and differs from man in that he is the hypostasis of his place in a society: in other words, he is an individual who enjoys status. The person is an abstract, 'disembodied' creation, which differs from the individual, from man, who, in his carnality, if he does not possess a status can be the *subject of* rights; the person-abstract concept, on the other hand, can only be the *subject* of rights. In short, person is confused with dignity, so that there are men who have no person, because they have no dignity: 'it is always a matter of having a capacity, a dignity, in accordance with the prevailing order of political and social hierarchies'.[3] Person therefore means *having*, not *being*. Being a 'person' as we think of it today alludes to another problematic, exquisitely theological, which concerns the person of God and the mystery of the Trinity.

When the term is referred to human affairs, Clavero points out how this appropriative conception of the person, which sculpts the figure of the individual endowed with dignity, spread not only in law and theology, but also in seventeenth-century political philosophy. And he takes as an example the pages of Hobbes in which the term 'person' is appropriated and explained in this way: the person is the transfiguration of man endowed with freedom, but only insofar as he participates in the state, a freedom that comes from the state, and which finds its legitimisation in the state.[4] The man of law is the person as an abstraction, a fictitious representation of reality, which Hobbes describes first in *De corpore*, then in *De homine*, then in *De cive*: there is a logical sequence in the passage from the physicality of the body to man and finally to the citizen, who is endowed with freedom insofar as he is legitimised by the State.[5]

But there is a decisive phase that radically changes the conception of the individual, the phase of the emergence of natural rights, whereby man is the recipient – by his very nature – of rights and thus of freedom.

We must not, however, fall into the error of considering man and his rights as a whole, a conception that affects every being as such. Differences are always in the background and re-emerge when they need to be asserted. To speak of human rights without removing the mask, without understanding what lies beneath their veil, runs the risk of imagining a situation of freedom when in dramatic reality one is in the presence of individuals and groups living in the suffering brought about by discrimination.

Law has hidden carnality under that veil, the individual composed of mind and body, flesh and bone, with its feelings and emotions, the individual living in palpitating reality, transfiguring it into a pale image, into a simulacrum, an idea, a legal concept.

[3] ibid 14.

[4] A Amendola, *Il Sovrano e la maschera – Saggio sul concetto della persona in Hobbes* (Naples, Edizioni Scientifiche, 1998); L Negri, *Persona e stato nel pensiero di Hobbes* (Milan, Jaka Book, 1987); N Bobbio, *Thomas Hobbes* (Turin, Einaudi, 2004).

[5] Negri (ibid) 33ff.

If we look at the individual underlying the abstract configuration, we realise that man exists, ie comes into consideration, only if distinguished from other men; and that distinctions between individuals are related to two fundamental factors: the natural factor and the social factor. The former is based on the conception of nature translated into the world of law; the latter depends on the birth that is constructed on man in consideration of his natural condition.

From nature we derive the distinction on the basis of sex, which leads to the discrimination of women; the distinction on the basis of sexual orientation, which leads to the discrimination of homosexuals; the distinction on the basis of 'blood' (and birth) and thus 'race', which leads to the discrimination of Jews; the distinction on the basis of skin colour (sometimes combined with blood), which leads to the discrimination of Blacks; the distinction on the basis of birth, which leads to the discrimination of serfs; the distinction on the basis of economic and social conditions, which leads to the discrimination of the poor, beggars, the homeless and the 'landless', who are immigrants.

This is therefore the path to understanding the different meanings of 'person', the way in which law constructs the image and role of the person, the way in which law can discriminate against or protect the person.

II. DELVING AMONG ANCIENT JURISTS

We can add some further notation to the way in which difference in the sixteenth and seventeenth centuries was constructed in the legal sense, by examining the non-systematic, but compilative works of the authors of vocabularies and lexicons. Here are a few examples.

In the index of titles and subjects covered by Conrad Lago's most famous work,[6] one finds the indexes of the classifications of 'subjects': reference is made to lawyers, slanderers, office takers (*munera*) and other categories such as enchanters, forgers, plagiarists, etc, Christians (with reference to the lawfulness of binding themselves by means of civil contracts), curators, masters (and their *potestas* over servants).

We therefore do not find a true classification by *gender* or status categories; we find an objective classification by *powers*, from which the existence of the categories and classifications is induced. And this in two parts that constitute as many aspects of subject law: the right and *quality* of persons,[7] their differentiation according to *dignity* and *vileness*.

The principles that can be deduced from the introduction of the law of persons are essentially two: one derives from the crossover between (Roman)

[6] C Lago (Haas), *Methodica juris utriusque traditio* (Lyon, 1546).
[7] ibid 68.

civil law and Christian doctrine; the other is the rationalisation of the categories, and derives from the formal description of the then existing social conditions. The equality of nature makes it right that there should be no preference between men, because all enjoy and obey the same law ('nam cum natura pariter nos eadem lege in hanc vitam producat, aequum esse videtur ut nemo alteri preferatur, sed omnes eadem lege utantur').[8]

Hence there is the possibility for a Christian to enslave another man to himself, and the death penalty for heretics and Jews who have a Christian in their power.

Again, no power is legitimate unless it is conjoined to a benefit ('nulla potest dici legitima potestas personae quae non est coniuncta beneficio').[9]

Power over the person is conferred in the interest of the person who is *sub potestate*. But the fine jurist, who must justify the differences, observes that the teaching must be taken as a rule of *faith*, not as a *political* rule. It is true that according to Paul's teaching, those baptised in Christ are neither free nor servants ('inter Christianos non habeat aliqua esse in personas potestas');[10] just as there is no difference between men and women, if baptised in Christ. However, this – according to Lago – does not mean (as some believe) that there can be no differences in *potestas*. In that Pauline passage, 'one does not speak of political freedom, but of faith and spirit'.[11]

Lago also clarifies why he proceeds by inferring concepts and not categories of subjects. At a certain point in his discourse, where he asks how differentiations arise, he laments the lacunae of Roman sources; and indeed, according to tradition, those born of legitimate marriages and of free parents are free. Reference is also made to the naive and libertines, but it is not made clear how one becomes such and why.

Private authorities concern the administration of property and ownership. The former concerns the relations between fathers and sons, masters and freedmen, guardians and pupils, and curators. Property does not extend to the person, at least not over children; and as for servants, it is lawful to sell them and use them as one might use an ox; but without abuse. Public authorities are for political and ecclesiastical purposes.

It is not relevant here to follow the author in describing private powers, where a traditional construction is found.

At the very least, it can be emphasised that the causes for the extinction of parental authority also include civil death resulting from sentencing to severe punishment, such as deportation or forced labour. It is also unclear why the author insists on the relationship between master and freedmen: how many slaves were freed out of gratitude at the time?

[8] ibid 113.
[9] ibid 70.
[10] ibid 71.
[11] Lago (n 6).

On the condition of the servants Lago insists. After all, he is keen to highlight the maximum limit to which the master's authority can be extended. He emphasises how the containment of this power is necessary because 'the lust for domination is so insolent in man that, if you are a little indulgent, it immediately becomes oblivious of all humanity'.[12]

In any case, although the condition of the servant has improved, the author emphasises that it remains, in his time, the worst condition in which an individual can find himself. Under civil law, servants are treated in the same way as dead or non-existent persons: while they cannot own anything in common, nor can they hold civil offices, make wills or be witnesses, act as arbitrators, judges or litigants, they can instead be defendants and resist their master's claims; while they cannot take on obligations, perform public occupations, they are, however, authorised by their master to own a peculio. Servile status is acquired by capture or birth, especially from a servant mother. It is the law of nations that disposes of it. But the *rationale of* human consortium finds remedies for those who find themselves in this status (ransom, liberation due to serious illness, proof of their ingenuity).

The distinguishing features of the dignity (and cowardice) of people are:

(a) sex ('it is not our fault if we are born male or female'; weakness – *imbecillitas* – resulting from sex cannot be corrected by law)[13]
(b) nobility of birth (acquired by virtue, by act of the emperor, by enfeoffment, by custom). However, Lago quotes Juvenal in the eighth satire: 'Nobilitas sola est, quae moribus ornat'.[14]

The other dignities mentioned are the military, those of jurists, lawyers and judges, and clerics; followed by: tabellarians, philosophers, those who practise the mechanical arts; and merchants, whose dignities or virtues are debated, given the dubious honesty with which they are deemed to operate.[15]

An equally interesting document from the same era is Antonio de Nebrija's *Vocabulary*.[16] Here, status is defined as 'conditio hominis in qua ut plurimum potest'.

The etymology of servant – 'servus non a serviendo sed a servando' – indicates that the person, even though subject to this deterrent condition, retains his existence (one insists on the benevolent treatment owed by masters to servants).[17] Dignity is a power or a condition or a prerogative.[18] Power concerns women and sometimes men.[19]

[12] ibid.
[13] ibid.
[14] ibid.
[15] ibid 119.
[16] A de Nebrija, *Vocabolarium utriusque iuris* (Venice, 1596).
[17] ibid 310.
[18] ibid 115.
[19] ibid 272.

But let us come to one of the greatest jurists of the first half of the seventeenth century, Hugh Grotius.

Grotius distinguishes between civil liberty and personal liberty. While civil liberty, which concerns an entire people, can be circumscribed, alienated, subjected to an authority (eg the monarch), personal liberty cannot be conculcated: 'liberi homines in commercio non sint'.[20] This is because, he further explains,[21] no man can be a slave. When it is said that men or peoples are 'naturally free', this must be understood as happening 'by natural right that precedes every human act'.[22] In other words, and continuing, Grotius admits the compatibility of servitude and humanity; no man has the right never to become a slave.

In support of his assumptions, he recalls Seneca's authority, according to which man is neither free nor servant, but *fortune* subsequently imposes one or the other of these poles on each; and he refers to Aristotle's authority. According to the Stagirite, being a servant or free is a consequence of the law. Those who have fallen into servitude for a legitimate cause must therefore be content with their state, according to St Paul's maxim *(I Corinthians*, VII, 21): 'do not be sorry for your lot'.

However, Grotius deduces from this that there are no *naturally* enslaved peoples; anyone with the use of *reason* must be able to freely choose what is to their advantage or disadvantage (minors and the mentally handicapped are therefore excluded). Slaves are the prisoners of war to whom everything can be made to suffer with impunity.[23] Grotius, too, takes the etymology of *servus* from Pomponius,[24] who sees the purpose expressed by the name as resale (and thus preservation in life); but he also specifies that it is the law of nations that regulates these relations, according to the principle of 'utility'.

But Grotius goes further: he specifies that, according to the law of each people, a relationship of servitude cannot normally be established between citizens: Socrates had already suggested this to the Greeks,[25] but the Christians did the same and so did the Turks. He adds, however, that the Christians have maintained the custom of sparing prisoners until ransom has been paid; and as a rule each retains what he receives unless they are persons of considerable rank *(eximiae dignitatis)* over whom only the state or its own head can claim rights, according to the customs of most nations. The characters of prisoner and dignitary are thus elided, and the latter prevails over the former. Social rank prevails over bad luck in battle. Dignity prevails over general categories; fate is not always malignant with the loser, if his status is superior. Prisoners of war

[20] U Grotius, *De iure belli ac pacis* (Amsterdam, 1646) l, I, ch III, § XII.
[21] ibid l, II, ch. VII, § I.
[22] ibid l, II, ch. CXXII, § XI.
[23] ibid 1, III, ch. VII, § II.
[24] Pomponius, *Dig* l, I, tit XVI, *De verb. Signif.* leg CCXXXIX, § I.
[25] Plato, *The Republic* I, IV (quoted in the margin by Grotius (n 20) 1, III, ch VII, § IX).

must be treated with clemency[26] and the right of life and death exercised over them must be applied with equity.

In this kind of domestic jurisdiction, one only strikes if there is a crime. The authors referred to for their *auctoritas are* various: Seneca, Pliny the Younger, Plutarch, Job. And also Moses, who speaks of Israelite slaves; but for Grotius the term must be understood as concerning every man, just as 'neighbour' is used generically.

The authority most emphasised in this passage by Grotius, however, is Philo the Jew, who recalls the equal nature of masters and servants, in which the better or worse condition depends only on fate.

And,' adds Grotius, quoting Philo, 'according to God's law, the rule of righteousness is not that which derives from Fortune, but that which indulges nature'.[27] Hence also, according to Grotius, the rule of the Sabbath, the day on which even slaves are given to rest.

These constructions, represented here in a non-systematic, but episodic and emblematic manner, are protracted over time; the legal formulas seem neutral, aseptic, indifferent to political, social and economic upheavals; they bounce from century to century, without changing terminology but modifying their content.

The Jews are mentioned in the *Institutiones juris Regni Neapolitani* by Oronzo Figheri[28] in the part dedicated to criminal law, under the title of the offence of *lesa majesty divina.*[29] Alongside heretics, simoniacs, schismatics, infidels, apostates, sacrileges, perjurers, blasphemers, magicians, and violators of asylums and sepulchres, infidels are counted, among whom are the Jews. They, says the jurist, are punished with fire if they attempt to detach co-religionists who have converted from the Christian faith; they are punished with exile and confiscation of property if they circumcise a believer; if they have two wives, they will be condemned for bigamy, unless they resort to repudiation, which is permitted by Mosaic usage. If they have a Christian servant *(mancipium) they will be* punished with exile and the servant will be set free. They may be servants of the clergy.

Towards the end of the eighteenth century, however, the fundamental distinction of men between free and servants (slaves) was set aside. In the *Institutions* of Oronzo Figherio it only appears in a note on the law of persons. It is interesting to note that the first *division of* men is not between free and servants but between clerics and laymen.[30] The author recalls that only two constitutions

[26] Grotius (n 20) l, III, ch XIV, § III.
[27] Lago (n 6) 381.
[28] O Figherio, *Institutiones juris Regni Neapolitani;* 4th enlarged edition (Naples, Tipografia di Michele Moreffi, 1782).
[29] ibid 189ff.
[30] ibid 94.

are in force in this regard: one on the flight of servants and handmaids; and the other on the flight of the *mancipio*. The first, issued by William I, forbade the capture of runaway servants, and ordered their return to their master, under penalty of confiscation of their property; the second, issued by Frederick II, established that runaway *mancipes* were to be handed over to the royal bailiffs (*baiulos*) who enslaved them for a year, in order to return them to their owner. If they were not claimed within the year on the basis of well-founded evidence, they were attributed to the tax authorities.

In any case, the author notes, the custom among Christians is that slavery rights are not exercised except against enemies of the Christian religion; Roman rules apply to them.

A distinction based on religious belief thus emerges. Indeed, active contrariety (enemies of the Christian religion) leads – as if it were a penalty – to servitude. It is the same distinguishing criterion – religious belief and role within society with reference to religious belief – that Figherio applies to describe the status of the person. Clerics, according to the traditional partition, are distinguished into regular and secular; in any case they are 'alien' from civil law because their life is governed by their own laws: this entails the recognition of privileges such as the ecclesiastical forum, exemption from public burdens both personal and real; they are immune from the[31] franchise and can receive six bushels of flour without paying tax (*vectigal*).

The second division stems from the feudal system still entrenched at the time and family ties. People are distinguished into *homines sui juris* and *homines alterius juris subiecti*. The former are barons insofar as they have received a barony by royal title; those who have a fief without the title of baron are vassals, or are called *milites* or feudatories (Figherio specifies that counts who administer justice, marquises who have fiefs on the border of the kingdom and princes also have the title of barony). All others are *subiecti* subject to the jurisdiction of the barons. Vassals owe personal and patrimonial benefits (*angariae*).

As far as family ties are concerned, children are subject to parental authority until the death of the father unless they are emancipated, or paternal forbearance is established with regard to their independently managed economic activities, or they are daughters, to whom the Neapolitan custom applies. Marriage, for Neapolitan women, is a kind of emancipation; they need not be brought into the groom's house because consent is sufficient to achieve the effects of marriage.[32]

Pupils and minors constitute the third category of *homines alterius juris*.

In the early eighteenth century, and again in the second half, a few years after the French Revolution, civilists continued to repeat Romanist classifications.

[31] ibid 103.
[32] ibid 140.

Let us first consider the outlines, the orders other than French, and the authors translated into Italian. These are the addresses closest to the Roman tradition. Here too we can proceed by symptomatic examples, by *excursus*, by hints.

Heinecke's work, in the Latin version and in the Italian translations, enjoys immense popularity. The *Elementa juris civilis*, according to the order of the institutions, is a model for the legal treatment of civil law. In particular, for the law of persons, the Neapolitan edition of 1728, the Venetian edition of 1737 and again the Neapolitan edition translated into Italian in 1830 are admirable for their simplicity, clarity and systematic intent, but also interesting for their attempts to adapt to the reality of the time.

While Grotius looks at the question of the position of the individual in society from the point of view of public law, Heinecke examines it from the point of view of civil law: and here he makes use of the terminology used by Grotius himself to distinguish man as an element of nature (*homo*) from man as a member of a society endowed with autonomy and a social role (*persona*). The natural man living in a social aggregate is therefore always accompanied by status. Status decrees his membership of 'persons' or 'things'. Heinecke specifies: '*status* … is that quality proper to man in society that accords him different rights according to the difference in this quality'.[33]

Status differs according to quality: status is the quality proper to a man in society to which different rights are attached (thus the servant, the foreigner, the citizen). Natural status has regard to the *natural condition of* the individual (sex, strength, etc); civil status has regard to his *social* condition.

Heinecke grasps the contradiction in these statements. But having to justify servitude, while adhering to the thesis of historians who consider servitude repugnant because it is against nature, he recognises that servitude is an unnatural institution but not rejected by the law of nature and the law of reason. And contrary to the nature of things; Scripture, however, approves of it. The author quotes St Paul's letter to the Corinthians here, taking it from Grotius.

The law of nature is also invoked to justify the condition of the son according to the principle 'foetus tamquam accessio ventris, ad dominum ventris pertinet'; and again to apply the principle that the son follows the condition of the mother. From the marriage of a prince with a subject, no prince is born unless the mother is elevated to princely dignity by the emperor:[34] 'ratione ventris, sive matris, cuius conditio in liberali causa inspicitur, non vero patris'.

Heinecke questions whether the distinction still applies in his time. He denies it, even though he admits the existence of serfs. It is due to: birth from a handmaiden; residence in a place where the law provides for servile status; deprivation of citizenship, if the foreigner is without a certain domicile ('d'aria fa i servi', is

[33] JG Heinecke, *Elementa juris civilis* (Naples, 1778) 54.
[34] ibid 56.

the principle applied by the Palatine Elector to allocate himself cheap labour). Wandering travellers, gypsies, stragglers, outcasts thus had no escape.

This is followed by the traditional categories: the naive, the freedmen and those who have rights and are not subject to anyone (*sui juris*). This succession of categories tends to appear in Italian authors slowly over time, coinciding with the absorption of the canon law table of values into civil law. Gravina in *Istituzioni*[35] devotes only one mention to the Roman distinctions, while insisting on the statuses connected with the individual's position in the family.

This is easily explained by the fact that serfdom (and slavery) had all but disappeared in Christian European countries; it survived in the colonies. Ambiguous was the attitude towards infidels, especially Turks. Slavery proper was dying out, at least in France and the Italian states. It survived instead in Germany, as Alexis de Tocqueville[36] and the admirable studies of Marc Bloch[37] pointed out in the last century.

[35] GV Gravina, *Institutiones juris civilis receptioris libri quatuor* (Venice, 1746).
[36] A de Tocqueville, *L'antico regime e la rivoluzione* (Milan, Rizzoli, 1981; 1st edn 1856).
[37] M Bloch, *Servitude in Medieval Society* (Florence, La Nuova Italia, 1975; 1st edn 1939).

5

Discrimination and Human Rights

I. HUMAN RIGHTS AND PROPERTY

Innate rights to be granted to an individual as such are discussed in ancient philosophy.

In 1965, Leo Strauss published an essay on the history of the philosophy of natural law and the separation from this conception of individual 'natural rights' related to man. The natural law of the ancients has little in common with the reason-based natural law of the Enlightenment, nor with the neo-naturalism of the early twentieth century, based on the opposition to positive law, nor with contemporary natural law, based on substantive justice as opposed to formal justice.[1] Natural law can only be understood if it is historicised. The natural law of the moderns moves from an ordinistic conception of nature, but it is a secular conception, which does not exchange nature for divinity. Man, as such, has natural rights – to life, liberty, property – but history takes it upon itself to limit them, sometimes to suppress them.

In the extraordinarily acute pages of Hanna Arendt one finds the fiercest critique of the traditional conception of human rights: 'the conception of human rights,' she writes in *The Origins of Totalitarianism*,[2]

> foundered the moment individuals appeared who had lost all other specific qualities and relations except their human quality. … If an individual loses his political status, he should find himself, according to the implications of innate and inalienable human rights, in the situation contemplated by the declarations proclaiming them. Exactly the opposite happens: a man who is no more than a man seems to have lost the qualities that prompted others to treat him as their fellow man.

And again:

> [F]or the confirmation of my identity I depend entirely on others; and it is the great grace of companionship that makes the loner a 'whole again', rescuing him from the dialogue of reflection in which one always remains equivocal, and giving him back the identity that allows him to speak with the single voice of a non-exchangeable person.

For Arendt, these assertions are fully justified and are consistent with the consideration of those who – as Jews – were deprived of the very essence of humanity,

[1] L Strauss, *Natural Law and History* (Chicago, University of Chicago.Press, 1953).
[2] H Arendt, *The Origins of Totalitarianism* (New York, Harcourt Brace Jovanovich, 1973).

being considered *Untermensch*, being assimilated to things, the object of property and therefore of appropriation and exploitation. The Jewish identity becomes a burden that shifts the past into the future (*a future behind it*) and condemns those who bear it to suffer harassment, persecution, torture and murder. The proclamation of human rights has not prevented genocide, the Shoah, anguish of all kinds perpetrated against individuals or entire communities.

Human rights have been the subject of extensive scrutiny[3] but also of much criticism, which means that their vitality, on the one hand, has been strengthened by their normative elaboration, ie their transformation from principles of philosophical and political significance to precepts that impose their observance; on the other hand, they retain their fragility and abstraction charge, because proclaiming them does not mean respecting them, and their generality does not automatically mean respect for diversity.

Studies of international law document their history and their force, at the conventional level. Constitutional law studies indicate their limits, within the framework of national legal systems. Studies of domestic law explain how they can be applied, by way of interpretation, and whether they can be filtered through the 'counter-limits' that the legal system can put in place in order not to comply with them if they ever conflict with constitutional law or public order.

The fact that their substance almost coincides with that of the fundamental rights of the European Union and national constitutional principles makes this eventuality entirely marginal, if not impossible in practice.

But the proclamation of human rights, in itself, is no guarantee of their implementation.

It is on their origin and their connection with the right to property and with the entrenchment of the idea of race (well before it was reduced to a biological belonging) that the criticism is levelled at human rights in the present hour, a historical phase in which they are redeemed from their origin and positivised so that they can be recognised and guaranteed as fundamental rights.

Their enucleation from the *ius gentium* referred to by Ulpianus allows Vitoria to isolate the freedom to move from one land to another (*ius peregrinandi*), the freedom to trade, the right to acquire property (including the appropriation of *res nullius*), the freedom of establishment and to become citizens of other provinces than the one of origin. It is therefore the legitimation of *dominium that is* their primary function, *dominium* that is also exercised over one's own person.

The *regime of differences* therefore becomes the foundation of society, of the order within the categories of individuals, of the hierarchy existing between them. If men organise themselves into a rationally upright society, they can also exercise *dominium*. And so we distinguish the barbarians, capable of reasoning, from the aborigines, the natives, the 'savages', who have a weak capacity

[3] The literature is boundless: see however V Ferrone, *Storia dei diritti dell'uomo: L'Illuminismo e la costruzione del linguaggio politico dei moderni* (Roma-Bari, Laterza, 2014).

for reasoning, and therefore must be guided, and are unable to take full advantage of property. They are included in the human category, they are not *others*, but they cannot claim the same rights as the conquerors because they are placed at the bottom of the hierarchy that governs the *societas christiana*.[4] Locke perfects the shift from human rights to property rights, and sees in the lands used by the Indios an infinite expanse of *res nullius*. In other words, everyone is equal, but the subject is a historical, social and cultural construction, so that at its birth the subject already finds its place within the hierarchy. Next to the hierarchy therefore stands race, to which gender – with the discrimination of women – and age are then associated. Property, gender, race and age radicalise this hierarchy, which overlaps with the equality of human rights.

The parable of human rights runs through the nineteenth century, and develops together with the cult of the right to property, legitimising colonialism, which resorts, in a certain direction,[5] to the same arguments of Spanish jurists and theologians to legitimise the conquest of the Indies, so that the critique of human rights ends up being confused with the critique of the right to property.[6]

II. PUFENDORF, DOMAT, POTHIER

With Pufendorf, one discovers the essence of the person in his or her 'human dignity', which must be recognised in every individual, whatever his or her social role. Unlike Hobbes and Grotius, Pufendorf condemns slavery. His ideas walk through and pervade French legal culture, which becomes an authentic driving force for the re-foundation of civil law.

At the same time as Pufendorf wrote his fundamental work on the law of nature and of peoples (published in 1672), Domat wrote the *Loix civiles*, which saw the light of day in 1689.

Due to its influence on Pothier's works and Napoleon's codification, Domat's thought is very relevant in the history of civil law and thus in the construction of the notion of 'person'.

Domat can be taken as the prototype of the model of legal reasoning with regard to the conception of the person (Lib Prel, tit II, sect II). Indeed, he distinguishes the status of persons – ie the set of 'qualities' of a human being – into natural and civil. The 'natural' state relates to a person's sex, birth and age; the

[4] P Costa, 'Dai diritti naturali ai diritti umani:episodi di retorica universalistica' in M Meccarelli, P Palchetti and C (eds), *Il lato oscuro dei diritti umani.Esigenze emancipatorie e logiche di dominio nella tutela giuridica dell'individuo* (Madrid, Editorial Dykinson, 2014) 27ff, 33–35.

[5] An address that goes along with, rather than against, the justification given by the need to acquire uncultivated or under-cultivated land to feed overpopulated nations: see 'L'Europa e gli "Altri". Il diritto coloniale fra Otto e Novecento' 2004/2005) XXXIII/XXXIV *Quaderni Fiorentini*.

[6] As Marx lucidly argued, *On the Jewish Question* (1843) (Italian trans) (Bompiani, Milano, 2007).

'civil' state, on the other hand, is determined by the 'arbitrary laws' of men, depending on the Roman tradition (liberty, citizenship, family) or local laws; considering the situation in France at his time, he records the distinction of persons into noble and ignoble, ecclesiastics, citizens and plebeians, of free or servile condition, the latter not being a personal condition but linked to domicile or the nature of the goods possessed.

While acknowledging that there are no slaves in France, Domat describes their condition according to Roman laws. Again in the Italian language edition of the *Loix civiles* published in Naples in 1796, he comments specifying that there are no slaves in the Kingdom other than the Turks, 'taken in the act they do as privateers'; they may be sold but their legal movement is freely permitted only within the borders of the Kingdom; they may be freed, but even if free, they may not leave the borders without royal authorisation, under penalty of being returned to slavery.[7]

Although remarkable, Domat's conception – in the eyes of today's jurists – is not without flaws.

There are several cracks in his conception of natural law the first concerns the mixing of natural and civil laws; the second concerns the separation of natural and civil law; the third concerns the hypostatisation of *statuses*.

More precisely, one cannot consider birth out of wedlock and hence the acquisition of the *status of* 'bastard' (with limitations in the law of succession) a condition that comes from nature; it is clear that the natural fact of birth does not make any distinction with regard to the rights inherent in the person, other than that of equality. In this perspective, the legal construction of the person appears to be the crystallisation of categories, prejudices, social conditioning, which codify objective inequalities; there is thus an interpretation of external data according to pre-constituted models that does not distinguish what is called natural from what is superimposed on nature; rather, a selective interpretation is assigned to what is said to be 'natural' according to canons drawn from pre-constituted social convictions.

It is then unclear how the distinction between the laws of nature and civil laws can work: Domat first illustrates what he calls natural laws and juxtaposes them with civil laws, which are 'arbitrary', but does not say that the former are better than the latter, that they constitute the ideal model or that they should be their corrective.

Finally, the notion of *status* taken from Roman law – in which Domat laments a lacuna due to the absence of a definition – is not clarified in its origins and causes; *status* is not regarded by him as a juridical instrument, a social selector, a pillar of social aggregation, but rather as an element of nature, and thus coming from the Creator who imprinted that order on the world.

[7] J Domat, *Le leggi civili nel loro ordine naturale*, 3rd edn (It trans) (Naples, 1796; 1st edn 1723) 188.

In short, the cornerstones for the constitution of the notion of the 'person' in the past – Roman law, medieval law, natural law, pre-Napoleonic civil law – seem to waver because they are the result of hypostasis or anti-historical operations, veritable anachronisms to which the jurist refers to give a founding reason for privileges. Tradition is a tool to justify the present and to argue for its continuity with the past; in other words, to make ideologically oriented but not explicit operations.

Much flatter is the discourse of Pothier, whose *treatise* on the universe of law also includes persons. His is a very simple and aseptic description of the status of persons, their distinction by nature, 'race' (ie family), the social role they play, with rights and duties. The basis is always Roman law, but medieval law is recalled wherever royal provisions (the references are all to the French legal system) introduced innovations. Ecclesiastics, nobles, the third state and serfs (the latter in all the varieties of condition peculiar to the different regions) are the backbone of society To the third state, which, along with the serfs, was the most populous category, he dedicates only a few lines: after all, for the eighteenth-century French jurist, the law of persons is a law of privileges. Those who have none are of no interest to the law. In addition to social status, the *civitas* and the position of the foreigner is taken into consideration. A diminished position, both with regard to political rights and with regard to civil rights (in particular inheritance, since the property of foreigners was acquired to the royal estate by virtue of *albinaggio*). More attention is given to civil death, as a sanction alongside criminal death, limiting or excluding the civil rights of convicted and imprisoned persons, to infamy, which is an intermediate sanction, and then to distinctions due to age, gender and illness. Power, guardianship and curatorship, all conditions in which the person's rights are restricted, close the discussion.

III. NATURE AND HUMAN DIVERSITY. THE PHILOSOPHERS

The necessity of distinction, the natural superiority of certain individuals over others, the immutability of the social order, even though discrimination is lessened and access to power is widened, are the humus on which the works of certain Enlightenmentists, who have gone down in history for the contribution they made to the building of the new order, are nourished.

In the Esprit des lois, for example, Montesquieu never forgets his own aristocratic background, nor does he scruple to reserve for the *noblesse* its fundamental role in the apparatus of the state. On the contrary, he deprecates the alliance between the monarch and the bourgeoisie, which threatens the privileges of the nobles, historically long-standing and legitimate in their legal foundation. The judgement given about him by Helvétius – 'he has retained his prejudices as a nobleman of toga and gentleman' – could not have been more appropriate.

Precisely in limine to his celebrated work, Montesquieu seems to reply to Helvétius: 'I have elaborated my principles not from my prejudices, but from the *nature of thing*'.[8] And indeed, among the principles, ie 'what makes a government act', Montesquieu posits: *virtue* for democracy and *moderation*, ie 'equality among the nobles' (certainly not equality between the nobles and those belonging to inferior states); *honour*, for monarchy, *fear* for despotism.

Among the characteristics of the laws in the monarchic regime, he emphasises how honour is the foundation and result of nobility (*l'enfant et le père*); and emphasises how nobility must be hereditary, not to stand between the power of the prince and the weakness of the people, but as a link between these two; the *maggiorascato* is the right to alienate property, the *retratto* is the possibility of recovering property otherwise sold to the family estate, privileges are granted to lands where the dignity of the fief reflects the nobility of the person who owns it.[9]

The basis of the distinction of statuses depends, according to Montesquieu, on nature;[10] on climate, as men are different in different climates,[11] and it is to climate that he traces the birth of slavery: hence to a natural cause, precisely for this reason unchangeable; a cause found in the world order, pre-constituted and not elaborated by man. Hence the criticism of Roman law, which allowed slavery for debt and the sale of oneself and one's children (voluntary operations and therefore 'against nature'); the other two causes of slavery besides the act of will (promise), namely capture in war and birth, are also criticised by Montesquieu. He does not approve of slavery at home, where it would be a sign of despotism; but he only admits it in hot countries, where slavery is a necessary consequence of the climate. As for the social order, in the last part of his work Montesquieu asserts the rights of the nobles against the monarch's prevarication.

Rousseau deals more extensively with the equality of men – and thus with differences – in his *Discourse on the Origin and Foundations of Inequality among Men*, which dates back to 1755.[12] It is here that we find the well-known argument of the wild man, of the myth of uncorrupted nature modelling the pure and whole primal man. And it is here that Rousseau polemises with Hobbes and his idea of the natural man as a beast bent on evil. However, Rousseau agrees with the English philosopher in his criticism of the definitions of natural law.[13]

And this is how differences arise. First, as a result of the climate, the seasons, and the environment, which force men to adapt, out of an instinct for

[8] CL de Secondat Baron de Montesquieu, *De l'esprit des lois* (1st edn 1748; Paris, Hachette, 2017).

[9] ibid 93.

[10] Montesquieu, therefore, also seems determinist.

[11] Montesquieu (n 8) XVI, vol II, 47.

[12] J-J Rousseau, *Discours sur l'origine et les fondements de l'inégalité parmi les hommes* (1st edn 1755; Paris, Folio, 1985).

[13] ibid 83.

preservation;[14] group life, however, gives rise to the first differences: some sing better, some are more beautiful, some are stronger; in short, the first differences lead to vice because they give rise to vanity, hatred, pride, and envy. Then one begins to cultivate the art of metals and agriculture.[15] And it is from agriculture that the second difference starts, that is, being an owner (to each his own). In this way, following Grotius's intuition, Rousseau emphasises that a right other than the law of nature is born.[16] In this way, the other inequalities, by wealth, by fortune, by the employment of talent, are also gradually born. Hence also arise the forms of government, which are due neither to nature nor to parental authority, but to the will, to the contract.[17] Rousseau, however, criticises Pufendorf, according to whom the will can also enslave man, because man can by contract transfer property and thus everything he possesses, but cannot be the subject of a contract.

'Essential gifts of nature', such as life and freedom, are not susceptible to change; man has no right to dispossess them.[18] He is against slavery; man does violence to nature when, by admitting slavery, he allows a human being not to be born a man. And it is in this way that the rights of nature are violated and the distinctions between rulers and ruled are introduced into the political aggregations. Under the tyrant, the despot, all men become equal again because they are all exposed to his will; they are no longer nothing, and the circle closes at the point from which we started.

The difference between Rousseau and Voltaire in terms of status is extraordinary. Rousseau began work on the *Social Contract* in 1760 and printed it in 1762; Voltaire in the same years worked on the *Encyclopaedia*, published the *Treatise on Tolerance* and then the *Philosophical Dictionary.*

Voltaire takes a similar attitude to Montesquieu, ie he considers men to be equal by nature (but, since they have to satisfy needs, they are diverse) and ends up describing equality as chimerical; Rousseau is much more modern, and, if one may say so, revolutionary and idealistic for his time.

He opens the *Social Contract* with the icastic expression: 'Man is born free, and everywhere he is in chains'. And he specifies that the social order does not come from nature, but is founded on conventions, When he describes the forms of government, he shows appreciation for the aristocracy, understood, however, as the government of the wisest, and therefore not connected to honour, tradition, origins. In any case, the government is conventional and representative.

Voltaire lashes out against privileges ('magistrates, peasants, priests equally pay the taxes of the state') and against masters; Rousseau ruminates on the

[14] ibid 95.
[15] ibid 103.
[16] ibid 104.
[17] ibid 113.
[18] ibid 114.

freedom to disobey, to 're-enter natural liberty by right' when the government usurps sovereignty, ie violates the social pact.

Different again is the proposal of Gaetano Filangieri, a Neapolitan nobleman, who, inspired by the *Esprit des lois*, published *Science of Legislation* in 1780. In his world, which one wants to see as ideal, but which takes concrete nourishment from the reality of things, an attempt is made to remedy the ills of the society he describes by identifying possible legislative measures. First of all, he seeks to remedy the differences between individuals, which arise due to the unequal distribution of property: 'Property is what generates the citizen, and soil is what unites him to his country'.[19] He is well aware that he is writing in antagonism to the interests of the class to which he belongs ('the class, against which I write, if it is the most powerful in the state, I hope it will also be the most docile and the most reasonable'[20]). And he admits that distinctions are necessary: 'in democracies themselves, where political equality is of the nature of the constitution, there is always a nobility of opinion'; just as he admits that in a monarchy the 'distinction must be more sensitive, because the constitution of the government does not require political equality, and it is right, according to the spirit of the government, that the nobility should be adorned with certain honourable prerogatives'.[21] But he states that between the monarch, the nobles and other men, space must be made for a non-hereditary body without innate powers, which he identifies in the magistracy.

In this, Filangieri comes close to Montesquieu's design; but quite different is the sub-attitude towards feudalism. With investiture, the sovereign

> donates or sells to a private citizen and his descendants, a large portion of his authority over another portion of citizens, who, without their consent, are degraded from their political condition, condemned to new servitudes, obliged to new duties, deprived of a part of their dearest prerogatives

and subjects to the will of a man who was their equal.[22] What is more, the abolition of feudalism would empower the noble class.

Feudal lands, inalienable by nature – he emphasises – 'put back into the circulation of contracts', would acquire a new value: this operation, restoring freedom to people and things, 'would in time form industry, agriculture and population'; in other words, beyond the economic benefits, Filangieri sees feudalism as an instrument of oppression and an obstacle to the free circulation of wealth; its abolition would restore 'to a large part of the citizens their natural rights'.[23] Statuses are detrimental to the freedom of the market, as well as the freedom of individuals.

[19] G Filangieri, *Scienza della legislazione* (Milan, 1817) 1, I, voi I, 356.
[20] ibid 54.
[21] ibid 55.
[22] ibid 61.
[23] ibid 72.

Nature comes to be, once again, the mirror of society; but the natural order is assumed by Filangieri in the opposite way to that of conservative politicians. Since by nature all men are equal, the 'ranks', which the Enlightenment respected, without going so far as to suppress every prerogative, every distinction, every property, are admitted and justified as long as the fundamental rights due to each as a man are respected.

This is why Condillac, in his instructions to the prince of Parma, outlines a state in which the ranks are maintained: 'It is not possible today, because of our vices and prejudices, to do what legislators might once have been able to do', ie to redistribute property equally.[24] What can be done is to aspire that in society 'there is no birthright, title or privilege that absolves the individual from performing his duties as a citizen'; at the same time 'the quality of a citizen must be respected even in the last man in the state'.[25]

The distinction is admitted 'because we are not capable of being brothers and conforming to the intentions of nature'; there must be 'classes of citizens more honoured than others' but no one must be humiliated, the law must make sacred and inviolable the rights of each.

> The third state will respect the big ones without being demeaned, and the big ones in turn are obliged to respect in the person of the bourgeois and peasants the rights of humanity, and the *quality of* a free citizen who contributes to making the law he must obey.[26]

These are ideas circulating in Enlightenment Europe. On the other hand, in the works of Jeremy Bentham, well known in France, we read the condemnation of slavery, without, however, disturbing the social order. 'The owners should not be alarmed at this change' (ie, the abolition of slavery). 'Those who own the land have a natural power over those who can only live by working'.[27]

We have thus arrived at the threshold of the Revolution. The bourgeois found their tribune in Abbot Emmanuel-Joseph Sieyès, who claimed power against the nobles and clergy in the name of the principles of majority and equality in the third state. But in this state there is no place for Blacks from the colonies, who can be kept in their slavery, women and the ignorant, and above all the poor, the *populace*, the *canaille*. For them, for these categories distinguished on the basis of race, sex, culture and census, the principle of equality does not triumph; the equality of the three states, the equality of the citizens, experiences its highest contradiction: while it claims rights and proclaims the abolition of privileges, it reaffirms discrimination and positions of subjection for other categories. The democratic process has stalled halfway up the social ladder.

[24] EB de Condillac, *Cours d'étude pour l'instruction des jeunes gens. De l'étude de l'histoire*, t VIII (Paris, 1798) year VI, 227.

[25] ibid 229.

[26] ibid 230.

[27] J Bentham, *Traités de législation civile et pénale* (ed E Dumont) (Paris, 1802; Brussels 1840); the quotation is from the 1840 edition, t II, *Principes de Code civil* 17.

Sieyès is the brilliant champion of the new order: but more than in the work that made him famous,[28] his genius for demolishing distinctions – although not *all* distinctions – emerges *from the Essai sur les privilèges*, written the previous year.

Sieyès, too, does not intend to abolish the proprietary classes and other differences between individuals. However, like Condillac, he wants to recognise an essential nucleus of rights for everyone, consisting of *civil* and *political rights*. 'The attributes by which citizens differ from one another are beyond the quality of citizenship,' he says; 'the inequalities of property and profession are like differences of age, of sex, of stature. They do not distort equality in the quality of citizenship'.[29] Hence the need to abolish privilege; this 'miserable invention' that constitutes 'a dispensation for those who benefit from it and a source of discouragement for all others'.[30] In a footnote to the second edition of the *Essay*, in 1789, Sieyès adds: 'It is natural that all individuals, all living beings should be different from one another' (in other words, difference is the very reason for non-identity, that is, for the multitude); but 'in nature, superiority or inferiority does not exist by right, but by fact: he who knows how to impose himself on others becomes superior'.

What he fights is the shift from fact to law, founded not on the principle of equality, but on privilege: privilege acquired by the lucky few through the fact of birth;[31] whereas citizens must be equal, so that each can offer his commodity, his labour, in a 'continuous exchange'.

Differences are founded on a false hierarchy; the real hierarchy, the power legitimately exercised, is founded on equality.

IV. HUMAN RIGHTS IN NORMATIVE TEXTS

The rights associated with man, which, as we have seen, have a varied denomination – human rights, innate rights, essential rights – are the result of very complex machinations in the world of law. And we can say, without fear of hazard, that it is precisely on this terrain that the closest confluence of philosophical–political and legal thought takes place.

They have been elaborated doctrinally, eminently by scholars of moral philosophy and philosophy of politics, and have gradually multiplied, moving from the first elementary formulations in which, according to Grotius, there were four essential rights (the right to life, the right to personal liberty, the right to resist unjust law, the right to property) – to longer lists of rights in which moral imperatives and the conditions for living in a civil society are coagulated, as conditioned by culture and the economic and social situation.

[28] E-J Sieyès, *Qu'est ce-que le tiers état?* 1st edn 1789 (Paris, Folio, 1989).
[29] E-J Sieyès, *Che cos'è il terzo stato?* (trans U Cerroni) (Rome, Editori Riuniti, 1992) 85.
[30] E-J Sieyès, 'Essay on Privileges' in Sieyès (n 29) 95.
[31] ibid 113.

From the works of philosophers to texts prepared by jurists, accepted by legislators, applied by judges, the step was not a short one, as we learn from their history.

There has been much discussion about the circular 'itinerary' of the rights contained in the Bill of Rights and the first Declarations of the late eighteenth century, and whether human rights could be recognised as having effects in the context of relations between private individuals, overcoming the private law/public law dichotomy.

Qualifying the individual as a *man was* not only intended to emphasise his difference from animals, as a being endowed with reason, but to define his political nature in a pedagogical sense, as a being who had his own awareness, his own capacity to interpret his role in society, his own culture, and his own participation in active life, ie in the distribution of power in society. The conscious and therefore cultured man is capable of being *civis*.[32] But to give complete order to this intellectual and political revolution, thought is not enough: it is necessary to consolidate, in a certain sense 'consecrate', its contents in legally binding rules. A bond that is established between all individuals in a covenantal manner, because these rules do not descend from above but emerge from below. Hence the division of powers and the creation of law, which focuses us on the legislator – the will of individuals transfused into law – the result of the 'social contract'.

With the codification of these rights, ie with their transposition from a doctrinal text to a normative text, the work of the doctrine, from a source of inspiration and elaboration, turned into a predominantly exegetical work of normative texts, but some legislators – using different formulas and alluding to different techniques – left the field open to the novelties created by the interpreter.

An examination of the legal texts reveals their philosophical and political ancestry. They set out the rights recognised as belonging to man both in his relations with authority (rights that belong to public law) and in relations between men (rights that belong to private law).

In the two traditions – the French and the American – there is a succession of declarative texts and texts organising society, with 'constitutional' value.

The revolutionary scope of these texts is given first and foremost by the proclamation of rights: to declare is to make explicit publicly an act of commitment, to *declare* is therefore linked to *doing*. And doing means refounding the idea of man that is linked to his natural origin, which makes him equal to other men, who are precisely his *fellow* men. This implies that a society founded on such a declaration cannot allow a differentiation of human beings determined by their origins (as was the case with the distribution of individuals in statuses).

[32] R Koselleck, *Critica illuminista e crisi della socità borghese* (Bologna, Il Mulino, 1994) 17–68.

At the same time, the break with the past implies the impossibility of going back to the old order of society, and assigns these declarations a pedagogical role.[33] The naturalist influence can thus be seen in the declarations of rights and constitutions adopted in the late eighteenth century and throughout the nineteenth century.[34]

In addition, these declarations, being inherent to the social model transposed into a legal framework, become the yardstick of a nation's cultural identity, a heritage of values with which their history is imbued, and, by extension, a connotation of each individual who is part of that nation.[35] The search for what is good and right is placed at the foundation of the social covenant.

The study of these experiences is vital for understanding how human rights, destined to become 'fundamental' in contemporary constitutions, are born and how they evolve. And, of course, the vicissitudes of the principle of equality are its backbone.[36]

Protected rights are not always placed in an exhaustive list. Legislators follow different models: they name certain rights, refer to categories of rights, replace and supplement them.

The starting point is the 1776 Declaration of Independence of the United States of America, the intellectual origins of which are nourished by Locke's philosophy, which we can describe as proto-Enlightenment.[37] And it is here that we find the Russovian formula proclaiming the equality of men:

> [A]ll men are created equal; … they are by the Creator endowed with certain inalienable rights, … among these rights are Life, Liberty, and the pursuit of Happiness; … to secure these rights governments are instituted among men, deriving their just powers from the consent of the governed; … whenever any form of government tends to deny these ends, the people have a right to alter or abolish it, and to institute a new government founded on such principles, and to organise its powers in such form as seems to the people best fitted to procure their Safety and Happiness.

Property and economic interests are protected as an expression of freedom, and with them trade.

Historians debate the basis of these claims.

The soul of the American Declaration seems to consist primarily of economic interests, which are protected to the extent that good governance is established.

[33] C Fauré, *Ce que déclarer veu dire:histoires* (Paris, Les Belles Lettres, 1997) 236.

[34] For the first bibliographical references see G Alpa, *Status e capacità. La costruzione delle differenze individuali* (Roma-Bari, Laterza, 1993); memorable are the pages by N Bobbio, *L'età dei diritti*, now in *Etica e politica* (Milan, Mondadori, 2009) 1168ff; and by S Rodotà, *Dal soggetto alla persona* (Naples, Edizioni Scientifiche, 2009).

[35] Fauré (n 34) 236.

[36] See for all, A Schiavone, *Eguaglianza.Una nuova vision sul filo della storia* (Bologna, Il Mulino, 2019).

[37] For an extensive account of the intellectual origins of the American Revolution, see J Israel, *The Great Fire. How the American Revolution Conquered the World, 1775–1848* (Turin, Einaudi, 2018).

The connection between innate rights and economic prosperity is provided by an appropriate division of powers based on the consent of the governed.[38] It is debated whether the disappearance of the term property among the fundamental rights signifies, in the American experience, a criticism of the property tradition, but the prevailing opinion is quite the opposite: property was so inherent to liberty that there was no need to mention it explicitly, since the legitimacy and relevance of this right could not be questioned.[39] It is debated, however, whether the document was based on a Protestant idea of the 'common good' or whether the Declaration is the prototype of individualist proclamations.

In the American experience, the enumeration of rights, their transformation, and their integration takes place verbatim in the Constitution of 1787, which deals with the role of the States within the Confederation, and in Article IV(2) states that 'The citizens of each state shall be entitled in all other states to all the privileges and immunities of citizens'.

The 9th Amendment of the US Constitution makes it clear that the rights protected in the text do not preclude other rights from being protected even if not explicitly mentioned.

The amendment, proposed by James Madison in 1791, reads: 'The enumeration in the Constitution, of certain rights, shall not be construed to deny or disparage others retained by the people'. The amendment was introduced by the Anti-Federalists, who wanted to limit federal power, which was seen as a threat to individual liberties. In truth, the text is somewhat obscure, because while the first part is reasonable by suggesting that the rights enumerated in the text do not constitute a closed list, the second part is much less so: what are the 'other rights' held by the people? Does the people mean every individual? And who assigns the rights not mentioned? Is this a blank bill of exchange?

In fact, the 9th Amendment was not applied for more than a century and a half. But, in connection with other Amendments, it was mentioned in the first US Constitutional Court ruling that created the right to privacy, with the 1965 case *Griswold v Connecticut*. The issue was whether a Connecticut law prohibiting the sale of contraceptives was in conformity with the Constitution. In that case Justice Douglas pointed out that 'the specific guarantees of the Bill of Rights have a penumbra, formed by the radiations of those guarantees that support the protected rights by giving them life and substance'.[40] The Court held that the law violated a constitutionally guaranteed right: the right to privacy. The Court had thus created a right that doctrine had long elaborated: witness the essay

[38] L Hartz, *The Liberal Tradition in America* (Milan, Feltrinelli, 1960); a classic is Beard's work, *An Economic Interpretation of the United States* (1st edn 1913; New York, Dover Publications, 2004); quoting Locke can be found in *Two Treatises on Government* (1689) (London, Hackett, 1980).

[39] L Strauss, *Naturreht und Geschichte*, 1st edn 1949 (It trans) (Venice, Neri Pozza, 1957) 240ff.

[40] 381 US at 484. The opinion was concurred in by Chief Justice Warren and Justices Clark, Goldberg and Brennan.

by Senator Warren and Justice Brandeis published in 1890 in the *Harvard Law Review*, the first and most important American legal journal.[41]

The 9th Amendment, along with other provisions of the Constitution, was also referred to by the constitutional judges when they drafted the right to abortion. Further, in a landmark judgment, *Roe v Wade*,[42] the judges held that state legislation could not intrude into the secret sphere of the individual and therefore that it was legitimate not only to provide medical interventions to bring a pregnancy to term but also to terminate it.

Today, the Ninth Amendment is contested by jurists attached to tradition, qualified as 'conservatives', who, with the expedient of the original meaning of the constitutional text (the so-called originalist interpretation) would like to circumscribe the scope of constitutionally guaranteed rights. But this is an entirely marginal direction.

Certainly indebted to the thinking of Enlightenment philosophers is the Declaration of Rights of 1789, which marks the beginning of the French Revolution.[43] It is the most significant European document of the eighteenth century. Approved by the French National Constituent Assembly on 26 August 1789, its full title is the *Declaration of the Rights of Man and of the Citizen*. It is the first normative sign of the Revolution that consecrates the end of the Ancién Régime, founded on a rigid division of society into social categories called *statuses*, and even expressed in the political body in the form of the States General (of the nobility, the clergy and the bourgeoisie).

The 1789 Declaration is the landmark text of the declarations of rights in all the countries of Europe in which the reaction to absolute government and the proclamation of freedoms to all citizens on the basis of the principle of formal equality is recorded. It has become a historical monument, so to speak, and a reference model, even though it was only in force for four years.

The Declaration bears traces of Jean-Jaques Rousseau's thought. Its title can be misleading: it is true that the expression 'man' is used in a neutral sense, ie it includes women and minors as well as men, but each of these categories then had a particular status in civil law (and a few years later in the *Code civil*), so that the representation of the individual as 'man' gives rise to an abstract conception.

The principle of equality is assured to all men who are 'born and remain free and equal in rights'.

The opening is solemn:

> The representatives of the French people constituted in the National Assembly, considering that ignorance, oblivion or contempt for the rights of man are the

[41] S Warren and L Brandeis, 'The Right to Privacy' (1890) 4 *Harvard Law Review* 193.

[42] *Roe v Wade*, 410 US 113 (1973).

[43] D Mornet, *Le origini intellettuali della Rivoluzione francese* (1715–1787) (It trans) (Milano, Jaka Book, 1983); J Israel, *La Rivoluzione francese. Una storia intellettuale dai Diritti dell'Uomo a Robespierre* (It trans) (Torino, Einaudi, 2015).

> sole causes of public disasters and the corruption of governments, have resolved to set forth, in a solemn declaration, the natural, inalienable and sacred rights of man, so that this declaration constantly present to all members of the social body, may incessantly remind them of their rights and duties; that the acts of the legislative and executive powers may be treated with greater respect by being compared at all times with the purpose of every political institution; that the claims of the citizens, founded henceforth on simple and incontestable principles, may always result in the maintenance of the Constitution and the happiness of all. Accordingly, the National Assembly recognises and declares, in the presence and under the auspices of the Supreme Being, the following rights of man and citizen.

Basic rights are thus set out in a linear manner:

> Article I – Men are born and remain free and equal in rights. Social distinctions can only be based on common utility.
>
> Article II – The aim of every political association is the preservation of natural and imprescriptible human rights. These rights are freedom, property, security and resistance to oppression.
>
> Article III – The principle of all sovereignty resides essentially in the nation. No body or individual may exercise an authority that does not expressly emanate from it.
>
> Article IV – Freedom consists in being able to do everything that does not harm others: thus, the exercise of each man's natural rights has as its limits only those that ensure the enjoyment of these same rights by other members of society. Such limits can be determined only by law.

The organisation of the structural apparatus of society, the form of government, is described in an embryonic way. But even here, the recognition of rights is closely linked to the way society is organised. Human rights and good governance are an inseparable pair.

In 1793, it was replaced by the Declaration inspired by Robespierre's ideas: it is a republican declaration in which the duty of social solidarity (Article VIII), and security, as well as property are emphasised above all; the purpose of society is still common happiness (Article I), and the evangelical–Kantian imperative is at the basis of social relations: do not do unto others as you would not have them do unto you (Article V). The difference between the two texts is remarkable: the first is an expression of divinity, understood, secularly, as Goddess Reason, the second incorporates divinity into law, which becomes the common divinity; the first is a table of values, which anticipates the reformulation of the powers that govern the nation in the form of a written constitution (which will be approved in 1791), the second is identified with the Constitution, it is in fact the amended text of the Declaration of 1789 that becomes the Constitution of 24 June 1793, in which power is entrusted entirely to the people, having been guillotined shortly before Louis XVI (on 21 January 1793).

However, *social distinctions are* admitted, which can only be based on common utility (Article I). Alongside personal freedoms, the guarantee of property, defined as an inviolable and sacred right, is affirmed (Article XVII).

Relevant for our purposes is Article VI, according to which all *citizens* (not therefore all men) are 'equally eligible for all dignities, posts and public employment according to their capacity and without any distinction other than that of their virtues and talents'.

Since social organisation was based on property, the basic distinction was between *owners and non-owners.*

A few years later, the Jacobin Constitution (24 June 1793) was approved. It bears the same name, but differs from its predecessor in that the natural law influence is more pronounced. It codifies the purpose of society as 'common happiness', guarantees the enjoyment of man's natural rights (Article 1), guarantees the principle of equality to all men who 'are equal by nature and before the law' (Article 3) and specifies that these natural rights are equality, liberty, security and property (Article 2).

The Declaration-Constitution of 1793 is also an icon, to which the French people and the intellectual elite remain attached.

On 22 August 1795, the period of the Terror over, the French gave themselves a new constitution. This too enunciates human rights (liberty, equality, security, property (Article 1)) and protects property as 'the right to enjoy and dispose of one's property and rents, the fruit of one's labour and activity' (Article 5).

But the great novelty of this Constitution is that alongside rights it also enumerates *duties*, the first of which is respect for the law (Articles 1 and 3 of the 'duties' section). It adds:

> All the duties of man and citizen derive from these two principles, imprinted by nature in all hearts: 'Do not do unto others what you would not have them do unto you. Do constantly to others the good that you would like to receive'.

It is still a declaration that returns under the aegis of the Supreme Being, a 'bourgeois', censorious constitution that prepares the rise of Napoleon and the Civil Code of 1804.

A different model can be found in the Austrian legal system, where even human rights are codified in the civil code, which could then be considered as the constitution of private individuals.

The Austrian Civil Code of 1811 (ABGB), which came into force in the Italian-speaking provinces of the Empire in 1816, contains a provision denouncing its natural law origin. It states in §16: 'Everyone has rights that are evidently the result of reason alone and must therefore be considered as a person. Slavery and personal servitude, and the exercise of relative power, are not permitted in these states'.

Of note, for our purposes, is the distinction between *Mensch* and *Person*: man as such is a *person, ie a holder of rights.*

From the *personality* recognised by law, which corresponds in this context to the essence of humanity, derive rights that only *civil society* recognises and guarantees.

When the Civil Code first appeared, the Austrian commentators did not doubt that these rules referred to natural rights, ie rights created by the philosophical natural law approach. And it could be argued whether in this way the Austrian commentators wished to take up the teaching of Eineccius and the other Roman law scholars (thus going back to Gaius) or, as I believe, wished to assign the term *person* a deeper meaning.

Speaking of *a right* consisting of the 'right to take all those actions (but only those) that can be taken with a social status of being independent', the meaning of the terms used and the opening provision of the civil code seem to lean towards the second option.

Reading the first commentaries on the Austrian Civil Code, one discovers that the rights that derive from this conception of 'person' are either natural or acquired. As for the former, they derive 'from the character of personality'. Slavery occurs when a man is the object of another man's ownership; servitude when a man is considered to be the appurtenance of a property.[44] It is therefore a state of freedom: the person is by nature free. And it was precisely this freedom that the Austrian Empire guaranteed to its rulers.

This provision has again provided work material for contemporary jurists in the construction of the category of personality rights. Austrian doctrine disputed whether innate rights included other rights in addition to those ordinarily included in the category of natural rights, and concluded that although the list was originally reduced to the essentials (life, personal liberty, resistance, honour, property), the evolutionary interpretation allowed the protection of life, liberty, health, privacy and dignity to be based on this provision.[45]

Common law, for its part, does not present an organic framework for regulating the person, in itself considered, but expounds jagged aspects of it. No manuals, treatises, or sections of works devoted to 'person law' are to be found in legal literature, except in texts dealing with Roman law. There is certainly talk of the person (*natural person*) in the manuals that illustrate individual sectors, mirrors of private law, but it is only an incidental description. One thinks, in contract law, of the rules on natural capacity and the contracts of the minor; in family law, of the relations between parents and children or between spouses; in law concerning forensic medicine and bioethics, one thinks of the rules concerning birth and death, the embryo and the foetus; in the discipline of *torts* we find the protection of certain rights that in the continental cultural horizon are part

[44] *Commentario sul Codice civile universale per tutti gli Stati ereditari tedeschi della Monarchia austriaca* (ed Francesco de Zeiller) (Milan, 1815) t.I, 108ff.

[45] K Oliphant, Z Pinghua, C Lei (eds), *The Legal Protection of Privacy Rights: Chinese and European Perspectives* (Leiden, Brill/Nijhoff, 2018) 32ff.

of the discipline of the person because they concern his attributes, ie 'personality rights' such as honour and reputation (*label and slander*, *defamation*), confidentiality (*privacy*) and personal integrity (*personal injury*).

This sphere of rights borrows its rules from both customary civil law and customary constitutional law. And it is interesting to note that these rights received new impetus in England from the debate on citizenship and minority rights. This debate expanded when the Human Rights Act came into force in 1998.

Thus, it is not the roots of private law but those of public law that form the basis of the 'law of the person'. In his philosophical work entitled *The Province of Jurisprudence Determined* (1832),[46] John Austin treats the natural person (*single or individual person*) only as a member of an aggregate (*body*) and therefore the person is seen as an individual who, together with the other members of the group to which he belongs or to which he is ascribed, contributes to forming the will of the group, be it a society or even Parliament itself.

According to Stein, one can nevertheless identify common features of *common law* and *civil law* in the law of persons due to the spread of canon law in England; but beyond these pale assonances, it is the last two centuries that have brought the European systems[47] closer together with the advent of modern law shaped by the demands of the industrial economy.

More realistic is the approach of Buckland and McNair,[48] who confirm the impression of the *civil*, opening the chapter on the subject – not by chance exposed under the angle of territoriality and the personality of law – with an unequivocal observation: 'the rubric "persons" is of comparatively small importance in our law, since the law is territorial and every subject of the State is a citizen of it'.[49]

V. HUMAN RIGHTS AND THE CONSTITUTIONS OF THE NINETEENTH CENTURY

The Italian revolutionary constitutions, which follow in the wake of the French Revolution, are similar in concept and text to the last French Constitution of 1795: see eg the Constitution of the Roman Republic and the Constitution of the Cisalpine Republic of 1799. But there are exceptions.

[46] (Cambridge, CUP,1995) 126ff.

[47] ibid 135–36.

[48] *Roman law and Common law* (Cambridge, CUP, 1936) 20ff.

[49] Even more widespread is Lee's commentary on Justinian's Institutions. And here, in addition to the classical arguments, one finds open the question of whether the slave was a 'thing' or a 'person'. And the answer is: 'both qualifications', because he was considered as an object of rights, but as a 'person', in late Byzantine law influenced by theology, he was a 'being capable of rights and duties' (Nicholas).

Of a more libertarian and guarantorist tone is the Constitution of the Neapolitan Republic, also of 1799, which distinguishes *rights*, according to the usage of the time, ie rights and duties: the rights of man, the rights of the citizen, the rights of the people and, correspondingly, similar duties in the same sequence.

All men are equal and therefore also equal in rights; the only distinctions allowed are those arising from moral qualities (Article 1).

The rights of man involve the free exercise of his physical and moral faculties, and to 'use the action of the body according to his needs'; the rights of liberty, of opinion and volition, of manifestation of opinions and volitions, of property and of *resistance* to those who impede the exercise of the rights thus recognised are recognised (Articles 2–9).

The rights of the citizen are protected by public force: these are '*natural and civil rights*' (Article 10). Civil rights are not defined, but in the cultural context of the time they concerned property and family relations. Citizens' rights also include equality in punishment and the right to vote and stand for election to public office.

The rights of the 'people' – which is not defined, but concerns the totality of citizens – relate to the establishment of a free constitution (Article 13), the form of government (Article 14), making war (Article 15) and the imposition of contributions (Article 16).

Duties concern man (respecting the rights of others, aiding other men, feeding the needy, enlightening and instructing others). The duties of the citizen derive from the general will that reflects individual wills; alongside them are enumerated the duties of public officials.

The principle of equality is reaffirmed at the end of the text – composed of 421 articles (this is probably the longest constitution in the world) – as it is emphasised that there is 'no superiority' between citizens, except that of public officials, but only in relation to their functions (Article 396). Evident throughout the text is the oppression of the Bourbon regime, the yearning for freedom, the repudiation of all absolute power, and the suppression of abuses, particularly those of the public administration and the police.

The Restoration gave rise to the restoration of the laws that predated the French Revolution and the Napoleonic Empire. But the revolutions of 1848, which upset the order of the restored European monarchies, gave rise to constitutions that were less generous and less noble than those of the eighteenth century.

The Statuto Albertino, ie the Statute of the Kingdom of Sardinia, of 4 March 1848, is an emblematic example of this; despite the jubilation of sacrifices that it cost the Italian patriots, united in the secular and libertarian faith, despite Charles Albert's hesitations, the text that was approved is notable for the narrow space reserved for the rights of the *citizen*. Human rights are ignored. There is no proclamation of human rights, only the declination of the rights and duties of the citizen.

Man is seen as a *ruler*, ie a subject of His Majesty. The term *person* is only used when referring to the King: 'the person of the King is sacred and inviolable'; it is the King who appoints to all State offices (Article 4).

Equality applies to citizens, who are equal not among themselves but *before the law*: it is the law that therefore conforms their *status*, which may vary by *title and rank* (Article 24). Everyone enjoys civil and political rights, subject to exceptions determined by law (Article 24).

Home (Article 27) and property (Article 29) are inviolable, but not the human person, with the exception, as mentioned above, of the person of the King.

Quite different is the tenor of the Constitution of the French Republic of the same year, which appears modern and guarantorist, despite being coeval with the Statute of Albertine. But it is a republican constitution, approved in a state that, while respecting religion, appears secular as a whole.

In the preamble it 'recognises rights and duties that are *prior and superior to positive laws*' (Article III). That is, it codifies in law the superiority of rights and duties to the law: it does not say to whom these rights and duties pertain, whether to all individuals or only to citizens, but it is understood to allude to citizens (see Article VIff). The Republic protects the citizen in the *person* (and again in the family, religion, property and work: Article VIII). There are similarities with the Constitution of 1795, but here the tenor is more general: a programme of a social nature is also accepted, which hinges on fraternal assistance (Article VIII). It is proclaimed that slavery cannot exist on any French land (Article 6). Terms and concepts are employed that will be used by twentieth century constitutions; Article 4 reads: 'No one shall be deprived of his natural judges'. Noble titles and distinctions of *birth, class or caste* are abolished 'forever' (Article 10). Class is a socio-political concept, caste is a term not previously used and more fluid: the former evidently reflects the socialist values that were beginning to emerge at the time (the Marxian Manifesto dates back to 1848); the latter is an expression of privileges and a separate elitist social body.

A similar expression – without the reference to social classes, however – can be found in the text of the Constitution of the Roman Republic, by Mazzini, of 2 July 1849: 'The democratic regime has equality, liberty and fraternity as its rule. It does not recognise suits of nobility, nor privileges of birth or caste' (Article II). Following the French example, this Constitution promotes 'the improvement of the moral and material conditions of all citizens' and regards all peoples as *brothers* (Article IV). It ensures that the exercise of civil and political rights 'does not depend on religious belief' (Article VII). It includes among the guaranteed rights the right to citizenship, detailing its modalities. And it states that '*persons* and property are inviolable'.

This is a very relevant statement, because if one re-reads the texts examined so far, one can see that this is the first time the term '*person*' has appeared in a constitutional text: one has spoken of 'man', 'citizen', 'ruler', 'people', 'needy', but the term 'person' has not been used except for the King. If everyone has equal dignity, every individual is a person on a par with the King.

VI. THE RIGHTS OF THE INDIVIDUAL IN NINETEENTH-CENTURY CIVIL CODES

The Napoleonic Code (the French Civil Code) came into force in France in 1804 and in the Kingdom of Italy in 1806.

The Napoleonic Code deals with the rights of the individual in his relations with other individuals: these are rights of a patrimonial nature, centred on property, the institution on which the new order founded by the 'Hero of France' is based. Exported from the provinces conquered by Napoleon, the French civil code is the model for nineteenth-century codifications.[50] But each code has its own characteristics.

Annibale Giordano, a civil court judge, printed a commentary on the civil laws of the Kingdom of the Two Sicilies in 1743; those statutes were replaced in 1819 by a new code promulgated by the King Ferdinand I., many changes.

Although it was modelled on the Napoleonic Code, the differences between the two are dazzling. The first distinction, codified in the preliminary provisions, is between *nationals* of the Kingdom of the Two Sicilies and *foreigners.*

Both categories are subject to the Sicilian laws if they are residents in the territory of the Kingdom (Article 5); but the laws oblige nationals, even if they are non-residents (Article 6). Giordano, in his extensive commentary, points out that a distinction must be made: the personal statute (personal laws), the royal statute (royal laws), and the police and security laws.[51]

Personal laws indicate the status and capacity of persons.[52] National status is the result of nature (when one is such by 'birth or origin') or of law, when one becomes such according to the conditions prescribed by law 'in order to purge the defects of birth or origin'.

The *longa manus of* the law is justified by the progress of commerce and civilisation; as commerce and communication thicken, each person brings his status with him: personal laws 'are inherent to the person'; this implies, for example, that the Sicilian cannot contract marriage abroad without parental consent, if under 25 years of age; or that he can be legitimised by subsequent marriage (Giordano points out the opposite treatment of the English). Jurisprudence, applying special laws, makes exceptions: for instance, ambassadors, ministers, envoys, enjoy the privilege of the proper forum 'according to the law of nations'. Alongside these hypotheses, the author includes others taken from French jurisprudence, such as practical law and Roman sources.

By contrast, the real laws relating to property distinguish between movable property that follows the domicile of the owner and immovable property that follows the law of the place where it is located even if it belongs to foreigners.

[50] On this point see G Alpa, *Diritto civile.Due secoli di storia* (Bologna, Il Mulino, 2018).

[51] A Giordano, *Commentary on the Civil Laws of the Kingdom of the Two Sicilies* (Palermo, 1843).

[52] ibid 29.

Police laws affect everyone. Foreigners are granted only civil rights (and not political rights) under the constraint of reciprocity.

As for the expression 'civil rights', it includes the right to contract and negotiate securities, to make a will, to sue in court, and to own property. Giordano is a firm believer in this in the light of natural law principles. For foreigners, the author is especially concerned to emphasise the abolition of the right of *albinaggio*, by virtue of which the state confiscated the assets lying within the borders and property of the foreigner who died without being naturalised.

Giordano recalls cases that document the application of this legislation. One of these had divided the two branches of the Imperiale, a noble family, in court; the Genoese branch (foreign) and the Neapolitan branch (national). Although the descendants belonged to the same family, the interweaving of kinship had failed to overcome the distinction between nationals and foreigners, so that the Genoese family could not claim any rights to the assets of a Neapolitan relative who had died intestate. The assets had been forfeited by the treasury. Giordano refers to the Digest, Book L, tit 15, which states that 'one is born not only to the giver of life but also to the State'.

The registration of civil deeds is the same for all; 'dissimilarities arise from property law, institutions and social conventions'.[53]

They, even if they do not belong to natural law, 'are no less respectable and less necessary'. The jurist thus justifies differences in status and census on the basis of paranatural law.

The analysis of the models of the civil codes can stop here. What is relevant is to emphasise how they, throughout the century, recant, on the one hand, the rules on property relations, and on the other, govern a field of relations in which the state, and thus public law, does not interfere. Civil society and state are separate: civil law pertains to the former, public law to the latter.

This distinction is not only technical, but eminently political. Throughout the nineteenth century, the individual, for civil law, is legally relevant insofar as he is an owner and, for public law, insofar as he is literate and has a census; with the industrial revolution and the new economic organisation based on capital and no longer only on land ownership, the owner–rentier is joined by the entrepreneur–master.

VII. HUMAN RIGHTS AND DISCRIMINATION

A whole century separates the eighteenth- and nineteenth-century declarations and constitutions from contemporary declarations and constitutions. If one looks at the technique with which the texts are drafted – without considering, of course, the exceptional historical events that took place during that period,

[53] ibid 124.

ie the Second Industrial Revolution, the First World War, the Russian Revolution, the Great Depression, the Second World War, the Shoah – one can see certain assonances, which sound like a defeat, because the need to reaffirm human rights means that they, though proclaimed, had not been definitively conquered. And one also notes the need to emphasise *the legal irrelevance of distinctions*.

Distinctions cannot be translated into reasons of inequality, or persecution: *discrimination* is not allowed.

The civil codes marked another history: there is a singular continuity between the nineteenth- and twentieth-century codes. Indeed. In certain experiences, the continuity is given by the application of the same text, as in France and Austria, and its adaptation to the new requirements is entrusted to special legislation and doctrinal and jurisprudential interpretation.

Public law supersedes civil law with the Weimar Constitution of 1919 and the post-war constitutions in other countries.

The Universal Declaration of Human Rights was approved by the United Nations in 1948; two years later the European Convention on Human Rights was approved. These declarations that have different force (the countries that have signed it across the entire globe the first, the countries adhering to the Council of Europe the second), a different wording, an apparatus of remedies and two different courts. Remedies and courts are very relevant, because the Declaration has only a persuasive effect, inviting states to act in such a way as to protect rather than violate human rights. The Convention is enforced by the Strasbourg Court, which has the power to impose a compensatory sanction on a state that has violated the human rights of one of its citizens, who turns to the Court to obtain justice, having been unable to obtain it in his own state despite having gone through three levels of judicial process.

A comparison of the texts reveals how the sensibilities of the drafters, who also came from different cultures – those who converged on the universal text were more varied, those who converged on the European text were more cohesive – found themselves on the same positions.

The general opening clause and the distinguishing criteria are almost the same.

Universal Declaration:

> Article 1 All human beings are born free and equal in dignity and rights. They are endowed with reason and conscience and must act towards one another in a spirit of brotherhood.
>
> Article 2 Everyone is entitled to all the rights and freedoms set forth in this Declaration, without distinction of any kind, such as race, colour, sex, language, religion, political or other opinion, national or social origin, property, birth or other status. Furthermore, no distinction shall be made on the basis of the political, legal or international status of the country or territory to which a person belongs, whether independent, under trusteeship or otherwise, or subject to any limitation of sovereignty.

European Convention:

> Article 1 Obligation to respect human rights The High Contracting Parties recognise the rights and freedoms set forth in Title I of this Convention to every person under their jurisdiction.
>
> Article 14 Prohibition of discrimination The enjoyment of the rights and freedoms set forth in this Convention shall be secured without discrimination on any ground such as sex, race, colour, language, religion, political or other opinion, national or social origin, membership of a national minority, property, birth or other status.

What is striking is the way the text is written.

The Universal Declaration recalls the Russovian definition of human rights, and uses the expression 'dignity', on which we shall dwell at the end of this discourse, specifying in any case that the textual absence of this word in the European Declaration does not imply its absence among the value parameters that the Strasbourg Court uses to scrutinise the conduct of states. 'Brotherhood' recalls the opening words of the American Constitution and the French Declaration of Rights.

The enumerations of the distinguishing criteria are equivalent, and both have a closing clause that allows them to be extended.

On the closure clauses, the debate that continues to fuel the American literature on the subject has not taken place. This is because the two politically conflicting conceptions of the constitution between 'evolutionists' and 'originalists' did not clash. In fact, in the United States the closing formula legitimised the jurisprudential creation of new rights, not contemplated in the original text, such as the right to privacy with its subsequent elaborations concerning the right to use contraceptives, the right to abortion, the right to have sexual relations between consenting adults of the same sex, and gay marriage.

The distinguishing criteria listed in the two texts correspond to each other, and also correspond to the lists in the post-World War II constitutions, as well as the list included in the European Charter of Fundamental Rights half a century later. And this is a sign of the persistence of distinctions and discrimination. It is a sign that certain traits – psychological, somatic, apparent or hidden but 'revealed' – are part of archetypes that are transmitted over time and become such deep-rooted prejudices that they are considered 'natural'.

Nature therefore plays an essential role in legal thought and its translation into normative texts.[54]

[54] See N Irti, *L'uso giuridico della natura* (Roma-Bari, Laterza, 2013).

6

'Nature' and Sex Discrimination

I. THE IDEOLOGICAL USE OF NATURE AND RELIGION

THE EXPRESSION 'NATURE' referring to man can be read in different ways: as a force that distinguishes man from animals and things, through rationality, conscience, the expression of feelings, or on the contrary as an instrument of oppression. Sex, sexual orientation, blood, skin colour are data connected to the individual and derive from the co-essentiality of human being and nature; in fact, they portray man's 'natural' way of being. Alongside individual data, collective data are constructed: women constitute a category 'handicapped' by '*imbecillitas sexus*', Jews and homosexuals constitute a minority to be marginalised, black-skinned men a race to be subjugated or colonised. Then there are the socially constructed minorities, such as heretics, subversives, the poor.

There is, however, a difference between the first and second groups of distinctive traits, because the first group is the result of an old classification based on persistent data that originates from birth and marks the individual for ever, as if it were an indelible mark against which one cannot fight, indeed one *should* not fight because it is nature that demands it. The second are the result first of Christianisation and then of secularisation; they are therefore more recent and mainly concern the individual immersed in his environment, in the social formations in which he develops his personality.

II. NATURE

The idea of *nature* that penetrates legal culture is the result of the thinking of Western history. The semantic and historical analysis of the Latin word, which corresponds exactly, in its phoneme, to the Italian one, is a path that winds its way from the Greek *fusis*, indicating human nature, the nature of things, poetic nature, to the Latin *natura*, which in Lucretius indicates not only things, animals and man, but also physical force, cosmic force, the life-giving power, as the generator of life itself in its various phases, from conception to birth.

Scholars decline different meanings of it, linked to the 'laws' that govern the universe, and then descend through the branches to medieval theology and philosophy, in which nature is related directly to God (natura *naturans*) who created the world (*natura naturata*), to the science of the Renaissance and the seventeenth century; according to the Spinozian conception, it is confused with God, up to the so-to-speak ideological and secular revisitation carried out by the Enlightenment[1] and then by the powerful analyses of its transfigurations by Hegel and Marx.

André Pellicer demonstrated the unification of *fusis* and *nature* in the first century BC and the consolidation of its semantic value: nature as a mode of being, encompassing man's innate character, his physical and psychic aspects, and thus spontaneity, naturalness, but also necessity; nature as property, quality, and thus power; nature as universality and as cause.[2]

Behind this evocative and complex term lie the orders of society: its physicality, but above all its moral order, laws and law. Nature is already placed by the Latin rhetoricians and philosophers at the basis of the family; it is considered as the foundation of friendship and of society itself, which is 'good' if it conforms to nature: Socrates and Plato unite nature with justice; the Romans named the law of nature as the law of all men, *ius gentium*, and civil law as the law of *cives*: thus Gaius in the opening of his Institutions, in that 'what is *according to nature is the rule of law*' (Leg I, 44).

In legal thought, the 'nature of things' becomes a real source of law.

III. NATURE AND RELIGIONS OF THE BOOK

Consider the idea of nature that emerges from the religions of the Book.[3]

In the conception, nature is the fruit of God's creation; it is identified with the world, and the world is God's creation *ex nihilo*: before creation there was nothing; after creation God placed himself at the helm of the world: 'In Judaism, the material nature of the world has never been inferior or subordinate to the spiritual: all reality is the fruit of divine creation and, by virtue of this, its goodness and positivity must be preached and appreciated.'[4] There are many passages in the Bible that ground this tradition in which soul and body support each other, in a synergy that leads to the realisation of the person, and the man–woman relationship is not only aimed at procreation, but also at

[1] Ehrard, L'idée de nature en France dans la moitié du XVIIIe siècle (Paris, 1963; 1994).

[2] *Natura. Etude sémantique et historique du mot latin* (Paris, 1966): *fusis* is a mode of being, which appears at birth, and, in a translated sense, is innate; while natura, according to Ciceronian usage, is the proper and external character of things and persons. This is a semantic analysis, while for the philosophical analysis see Naddaf, *The Greek Concept of Nature* (New York, 2005).

[3] The Jewish position is treated in 'The Concept of Nature in Greek Thought and the Bible' (1974) *The Monthly Review of Israel* 252; D Hillel, *The Natural History of the Bible* (Cambridge (Mass), CUP, 2005). And see E Levinas, *Totalità e infinito* (Milan, Jaca Book, 1990).

[4] G Laras, *Natura e pensiero ebraico* (Milan, Jaca Book, 2015) 27.

exalting the importance of eros and physical pleasure.[5] And again the passages in which man – Abraham representing him universally – comes to know God through nature. That is, he comes to God through the observation of nature and its laws. Behind this representation lies the idea of 'a design and order of reality as creation'.[6]

It is natural, therefore, that women are submissive to men and that their relationship cannot be approached as one between persons of the same sex. And yet figures of extraordinary women emerge from the Bible, such as Ruth, Deborah, Judith, Esther.

The interpretation of God's word is reserved for men. In the synagogue, women are separated and placed in the women's gallery. And woman is created from Adam's rib, so she is the result of a derivation rather than an independent creation.

And yet man is born of woman, which proves that the two sexes are inseparable.

In the Gospel, the woman has a greater prominence, potentially equal to that of the man: Jesus entertains women, imparts teachings to them, not caring about the rabbinical prescriptions that forbade it (Luke 10:39).

He recognises the equal dignity of man and woman (*cf* Luke 13:16) and it is to a woman, and a foreign one at that, that he addresses the highest praise for faith (Matthew 15:28). Man and woman are complementary: the two shall be one flesh (Mark 10:6; Gen 18–20).

But the Christian tradition accepts the subalternity of women. It is Paul who writes in the *First Letter to the Corinthians* (1 Cor 14:34–35):

> [L]et the women in the meetings be silent, for it has not been entrusted to them to speak, but let them be submissive, as the law says. If they wish to be instructed in anything, let them question their husbands at home, for it is unseemly for a woman to speak in an assembly.

And in the *First Epistle to Timothy* (1 Tim 2:9–15):

> I also want women to be dressed with decorum, adorned with modesty and truthfulness, not with braids of gold, pearls, and luxurious garments, but with good works, as befits women who make profession of piety.

The Koran is no exception. In Sura II, the heifer, verse 228 reads:

> Let the divorced women observe a three-cycle retreat, and they are not allowed to hide what Allah has created in their wombs, if they believe in Allah and the Last Day. And their spouses will have priority if, wishing to reconcile, they take them back during this period. They have rights equivalent to their duties, according to good custom, but men are superior. Allah is Mighty, He is Wise.

[5] ibid 28.
[6] ibid 37.

The interpretation of the Koran also leads to the subordination of women to men. In Sura IV, on women, verse 34 states:

> Men are preeminent over women because of the preference Allah grants to one over the other and because they spend [on them] their wealth. Virtuous [women] are the pious ones, who protect in secret that which Allah has preserved. Admonish those whose insubordination ye fear, leave them alone in their beds, beat them. If they then obey you, do nothing more against them. Allah is Most High, Most Great.[7]

And with regard to same-sex relationships – ordinarily between men, those between women being ignored – Genesis 19 and Leviticus 18 and 20 condemn this practice, punishing it with the death penalty. In the Gospels, there is no mention of the matter, while Paul interprets the episode of the destruction of Sodom and Gomorrah not as the effect of the violation of the principle of hospitality,[8] but as the condemnation of an abominable practice (Romans I, 24–27; Corinthians I, 6, 9; I Timothy I, 1,10).

In Greek history, which begins with the myth of Padora, woman is the cause of all evil.[9] She is an ambiguous character, reflected in all-female versions of divinity, from Juno, mother of the gods, to Venus, repository of pleasure, to Athena, symbol of intelligence. All virtues, moreover, are feminine. In classical works, woman reflects all these aspects, positive and negative, from the capricious Helen to the hard-working and patient Penelope. And in the Roman world, woman is seen as a necessary complement to man, always in an ancillary position.[10]

IV. THE IDEOLOGICAL USE OF NATURE AND SEX DISCRIMINATION

In short, the man–woman contraposition is a constant in human history, at any latitude and at any time in history. From the point of view of identity, it is found in the conception of nature, in the narrative of each person's life, and in the organisation of the family, which has its own history, and again in the organisation of society with its distribution of power. The position of women until the middle of the twentieth century, and beyond, is considered inferior and complementary to that of men: beyond the pages of Scripture, the natural physical weakness of women compared to the strength of men (*imbecillitas sexus*) has repercussions on the allocation of work within and outside the family, and their marginal role even within the social aggregate. Law reflects this condition, not

[7] J Baldock, *Le donne nella Bibbia* (Milan, Rizzoli, 2019); E Bosetti, *Women of the Bible* (Assisi, Cittadella Editrice, 2010).

[8] T Roemer and L Bonjour, *L'homosexuaité dans les Proche-Orient et dans la Bible* (Paris, Labor et Fides, 2005) 65ff, 120ff.

[9] E Cantarella, *Gli inganni di Pandora* (Milan, Feltrinelli, 2019).

[10] E Cantarella, *L'ambiguo malanno.condizione e immagine della donna nell'antichità greca e romana* (Milan, Feltrinelli, 2010).

only because legal rules are written by men, but because law in this is precisely the mirror of society, of social conventions, of the common mentality. But Pothier in the *Treatise on Persons* points out that, in addition to the weakness of sex, the role of women in the family must also be taken into account: women are expected to behave discreetly, away from the public eye, and for this reason they cannot be assigned public offices, which would require them to expose themselves to the outside world, removing themselves from the protection of domestic walls.

Already at the moment of her birth, her destiny is sealed: sublime is the novel within the novel, the story of the Nun of Monza with which Alessandro Manzoni depicts the legal status of Gertrude, who was brought up in such a way that entry into the convent and the monastic choice were expressions of free will, while on the contrary they were an expedient to avoid the dispersion of the ancestral heritage. The rules of status persecute women for centuries upon centuries, the male culture gradually constructs them as the object of feelings, desire, faithful cooperation and the pious conduct of a life dedicated to hearth and family.

Hence redemption, emancipation, freedom, the fight against discrimination, the demand for equal opportunities, the more-than-justified antagonism destined to support individual acculturation and careers, family formation, child-rearing, the sharing of work and power. It will take a long time to realise that *imbecillitas sexus* is a mystification, that law supports discrimination, oppression, marginalisation as an instrument of preservation; its change will be achieved at the price of grave sacrifices and difficult struggles.

The complex history that the law of the past gives us is a valuable document for understanding this path, which is both a path of civilisation and morality. And it should be noted that even today there is a tendency to see a woman's legal status more in the environment in which she lives – the family, associations, the world of work and the professions – than in terms of the individual path she takes.

V. THE BEGINNING OF WOMEN'S EMANCIPATION

It is precisely the law that helps us understand the line of the journey, its stages, its cadences, as if it were a sort of crusade in which little by little the citadels of preservation are conquered. A simple historical account, of events, would not be as effective or as clear-cut in its demarcation, because, of course, there were women who became true myths for their great wisdom and loveliness (the Queen of Sheba), for their courage (the women of the Bible), for their cunning (Cleopatra), for their high intellectual capacities (Hypatia), or artistic skills (Artemisia Gentileschi), for their mystical virtues (martyrs and saints), for their political and power management skills (Mary Stuart, Elizabeth I, Christina of Sweden, Catherine de' Medici, Catherine of Russia, Maria Theresa of Austria) and literary women (Vittoria Colonna, Jane Austen, the Brontë Sisters, Virginia Woolf) – from the eighteenth century onwards, in particular, in all countries that were opening up to progress and novelty – but they were appreciated more for their exceptionality and for their ability to place themselves on the same level as men, and perhaps even above them, than for their individuality. Comparison, not individual value, tended to contain their merit, not exalt it.

By way of summary, and merely by way of example, in a literature that is at times overflowing in tone and content with the intention of striking at the female sex, and at times suasive and mellifluous in order to record its 'natural' ancillary role, I would like to recall the work of a now little-known eighteenth-century author – but appreciated by Benedetto Croce – Vincenzo Martinelli, who published first in London, in 1752, and then in Italy, his manual on the *Istoria critica della vita civile*, a sort of etiquette, a summa of wisdom and advice for the deportment of cultured people, an essay on morals, politics, economics.

Martinelli explains that:

> [T]he principal object of their destiny in the world is evidently the propagation of the species, as is shown by the structure of their bodies; and in Sacred Scripture, and in the Greeks and Latins, they are found to be praised only for their fecundity, their subordination to their husbands, and their love for their children; Nor is it seen that their care is only for the internal conduct of the family, and this only as far as education is concerned; the husbands always appear as absolute directors, and with a kind of sovereignty over the wives themselves. Martinelli justifies the choice that women can be given a lesser education because the legislator has excluded them from all offices and social roles, from theology as well as law because 'Judging and Advocacy are from God (8–9).

Once again, the Enlightenment is the starting point of the women's revolution.[11]

Louise-Feliticé de Kéralio, writer, publicist, editor, admitted to the Academy of Arras thanks to Robespierre, publishes from 1796 to 1789 the most important works of French literature by women, and after the advent of the Revolution founds the *Journal d'État et du Citoyen* in Paris, becoming the first female editor-in-chief of a newspaper in history. She was a member of the Club des Cordilleres, which was also open to women at the initiative of her husband, and was responsible for the *Société fraternelle de l'un et l'autre sexe*. It is to her that we owe the most heartfelt demand for women's rights, the *Cahier de doléances des femmes* that opens up the debate on the position of women in society and politics. She managed to overcome the Terror, the fall of Napoleon and the return of Louis VIII, but, having been compromised by her support for the King's death sentence, she was forced to take refuge in Belgium. Soon afterwards, Olympia de Gouges wrote *The Declaration of the Rights of Women and the Citizen* (1791). She will not make it through the days of the Terror, and will be guillotined.

[11] G Duby and M Perrot, *History of Women in the West*, vols 1–5 (Roma-Bari, Laterza, 1995).

In the Preamble, aimed at the feminine, Olimpia faithfully reproduces the text of the 1789 Declaration by paying tribute to 'the sex superior in both beauty and courage, in the sufferings of motherhood'. Hers is not a claim for greater rights, but merely an affirmation of the equality of women with men in work, in participation in public life, in taxation, in the exercise of freedoms.

From Condorcet to the humanist philosophers of the nineteenth century, to the socialists, there were thinkers who carved the furrow to achieve the longed-for equality.

Cristina di Belgiojoso and Anna Maria Mozzoni are other apostles of women's freedom. Their sarcastic accents, their heartfelt claims, are also argued in legal terms. Belgiojoso was not a jurist, but she could justifiably be given the title of lawyer: *Della presente condizione delle donne e del loro avvenire* is a memoir published in the 'Nuova Antologia di scienze, lettere ed arti' (I, 1) in Florence in January 1866. Modern society must reflect new principles, not be a vehicle for old prejudices:

> Removed, by man's will, from all study that does not relate exclusively and directly to the imagination, such as the so-called fine arts, i.e. music, painting, embroidery, adornment of the person, etc., etc., and from all participation in the affairs of society, women remained confined within the walls of their homes, where most of them were able to find a pasture for their industriousness, making the master of the house welcome with their work, and from all participation in the affairs of society, women remained confined within the walls of their homes, where the greater number of them were able to find pasture for their own industriousness, making it pleasing to the master of the house to live there, and relieving him entirely of those cares that he judged petty, boring and too inferior to his greatness. (9)

And again:

> Educated to please the man and to be passionately loved by him, she is mostly not consulted on the choice of a companion and lord, to whom, her love will be exclusively due for the entire life of both of them: fortune is valued, the name, the rank, the social status of he who asks her to marry him, and nothing more, under the puerile pretext that after a few months or a few years of marriage the attractions of the person are no longer observed, and that the only lasting elements of happiness are riches and the satisfactions of pride (14).

His thoughts are on a woman's education, her admission to the professions, her serene life in a free family. And it is a thought for the legislator who is about to dictate the law for the new nation.

More argued, and more subtly technical, is the speech by Anna Maria Mozzoni, who, being a jurist, prides herself on reading the draft laws and then the Civil Code of 1865 from the point of view of women's rights, trampled upon by a traditional and narrow mentality, which was unable to innovate even when dictating the rules of the new codification, which, as such, is valid for today but above all for the future.

His criticism focuses on family relations, the subordination of wives to their husbands, the legal incapacity of women to administer their own property, working conditions, and all the other rules that juristic men have written for their own benefit. Hence his very articulate programme in favour of the equality of the sexes, and thus in favour of the elevation of women to the level of men, written in his book on *The Liberation of Women*:

> 'I. That she be given a national education with broad programmes. II. That she be equal to other citizens in majority. III. That she be granted the right of election, and be at least a voter, if not eligible. IV. That the balance be restored between spouses. V. That the separation of marital property be common law. VI. That adultery and concubinage are subject to the same legal tests and consequences. VII. That the husband may not represent his wife in any legal act, without her express mandate. VIII. That the relationships of obedience and protection be abolished, the one being unjust and the other illusory. IX. That in case the wife does not wish to follow her husband, she may submit her reasons to a family council composed of both sexes. X. That the husband may not alienate his property, either for a consideration or free of charge, or obligate it in any way, without the wife's consent, and reciprocally. – Since the squandering spouse must be maintained by the other, it is only right that the control should be mutual. XI. That the mother be a contuctressor, according to natural law. XII. That the father, in dying, should himself elect a contumitor, and that the mother in her turn should elect a contumitor to her children. XIII. That the search for paternity be admitted, and subject to the legal proofs, to which adultery is subject. XIV. Let the law on seduction be made more severe, and protect women until the age of twenty-five. XV. That the woman be admitted to guardianship and family council. XVI. Let the guardian have the same rights as the guardian; and where there is a dispute, let the family council judge in the first instance, and then the pupil court. XVII. That all professions and employments shall be open to women. XVIII. That women may acquire rights of citizenship otherwise than by marriage'. (38)

In order to claim her rights, women must transform themselves into jurists and fight the law to obtain from the law the recognition of their prerogatives, ie nothing other than the application of the principle of equality.[12]

VI. WOMEN IN CIVIL CODES: THE FAMILY

In a society such as the one which, having emerged from the Revolution, was preparing to enter the new century, the family model to be favoured corresponded to the type of social model that had been chosen: the expression of an authoritarian regime, the *Code civil* also imprinted the regulation of the family on the principle of authority. The debates before the legislative body are very

[12] Mary Wollstonecraft's book, *Vindication of the Rights of Woman* (1792) (London, Penguin, 2004) is situated, albeit in a polemical form, within democratic thought.

eloquent in this respect; as is the constant, untiring attention that Napoleon gave to the very part of the Code that concerned family relations. And certain phrases, which have become famous (*'le mari se doit de pouvoir dire à sa femme: madame, vous m'appartenez corps et fune; … madame, vous ne sortirez pas; madame, vous n'irez pas à la Comédie; madame, vous ne verrez pas la telle ou telle personne*') by the First Consul denounce, without a shadow of a doubt, the sentiment that inspired the legislator in the construction of the rules of family government. In other words; the direction of the family lay with the husband; the wife fulfilled a necessarily vicarious role (Article 213: 'The husband owes protection to his wife; the wife obedience to her husband'; Article 214: 'the wife is obliged to live with her husband, or to follow him wherever he sees fit to establish his residence; the husband is obliged to keep her with him, and to provide her with everything necessary for the necessities of life, in proportion to his substance and condition'); children were completely subservient, until the age of majority (21); paternal consent to marriage was required up to the age of 21 for women, up to 25 for men; the husband-father summed up all powers, the puissance *paternelle* and the *puissance maritale*, so that the wife was subject to him without being able to dispose either of the property acquired after the marriage or that brought as a dowry (Article 217: 'the wife, even in a regime of separation of property, may not make donations, alienate, mortgage, or make gratuitous or onerous purchases without the husband's participation in the deed or without his consent in writing'; Article 1421: 'the husband alone administers the community property; he may sell, alienate, mortgage it without the wife's consent'; Article 1428: 'the husband has the administration of all his wife's personal property; he may independently exercise all the real-estate and possessory actions that his wife holds'). And the image of woman that emerges from this – 'robustness and boldness are man's', Locré observed in a commentary a few decades after the Code, 'woman's shyness and modesty; they cannot be part of the same work and the same labours, nor give themselves to the same occupations; and not the law, but nature has distributed its share to each of the sexes; woman needs protection because she is weaker, man is freer because he is stronger' – is precisely that of woman as a 'vicarious' subject, excluded from political life as well as from most professions. An image, moreover, so ingrained in nineteenth-century French (and European) society that it was revived in the same terms at the end of the century in the pages of Maupassant's *Une vie*. In an incisive manner, Arnaud portrays the female figure that emerges from the Code Napoleon: 'is there any need to insist on the fact that the 'Code of Liberty' was not about the emancipation of women? How many expressions remain in today's language that derive from the more or less conscious consideration of the role reserved for women by the Code Napoleon?' 'Weak sex, woman of the hearth': woman does not have the right to sit at the table of the social game; marginalised in the shadow of her 'lord and master', 'she attracts the thunderbolts of the members of the group if she tries to get out of that condition'. And in the family sphere, no better condition is reserved for the children (who, in the case of serious 'disobedience' can be imprisoned by their father), especially those who are not recognisable, such as adulterers and incestuous persons, treated as 'bastards' (to use Napoleon's merciless terminology).

The secular, bourgeois model of the family, built according to 'a distinctly individualistic legal framework' thus corresponded to a 'strong command structure' functional to the nineteenth-century capitalist society that intended to guarantee a 'strong family in a strong state'.

Taken as an inspirational model, the Code Napoléon leaves deep traces in the Italian Unitary Code of 1865. There are, however, some innovations in family law, even if, in substance, the 'authoritarian' line does not change. On the one hand, implementing Cavour's principle of 'free Church in a free State', the institution of civil marriage is introduced (but the institution of divorce is excluded, following a long debate in Parliament); the separation of the spouses is maintained, if cohabitation has become impossible; but a privileged position is ensured to the husband (Article 150 c 2: 'an action for separation is not admissible for adultery on the part of the husband, except when he keeps the concubine at home or, notoriously, in another place, or when there are circumstances such that the fact constitutes a serious insult to the wife'); the husband is still considered the 'head of the family' and the wife 'follows his civil status, takes his surname and is obliged to accompany him wherever he sees fit to establish his residence' (Article 131); the husband retains the management of the family (Article 152: 'it is the husband's duty to protect his wife, to keep her close to him and to provide her with everything necessary for her needs in proportion to his wealth'), even if the wife is required to contribute to her husband's maintenance 'if he does not have sufficient means' (Article 132(2)), and (albeit attenuated) marital power, which is expressed in the 'authorisation' to which the wife's activities of alienation and purchases are subject (Article 134: 'the wife may not donate, dispose of real estate, mortgage it, contract loans, assign or collect capital, set up a security, or settle or take legal action in relation to such acts, without the husband's authorisation'; authorisation is not required if the husband is a minor, absent, interdicted, sentenced while serving his sentence; separated through his own fault; when the wife is a merchant); in the most serious cases the father can have the child placed in an education and correction home, but certainly not in prison.

However, the road to the emancipation of women, and of the 'family' as a whole, is a rough one. Many years had to pass after the introduction of the 1865 Code before new legislation changed the situation of women in the family and society;[13]

In Italy, feminist movements (such as the English Women Suffrage Committee) that engage in political struggle to promote better conditions for women do

[13] See in particular M Fioravanti, *Il lato oscuro del moderno. Diritti dell'uomo, schiavitù ed emancipazione tra storia e storiografia* in the review Quaderni Fiorentini, 2013, 9ff.

not have much luck. The words of John Stuart Mill, but also those of Marx and Millet, remain unheard for a long time. And if many agree in admitting that 'man is no longer born in the place he will occupy in life' and that 'the subordination of women arises as an isolated fact in the midst of the modern institutions of society … and is the only vestige left of an old intellectual and moral world destroyed everywhere', the social conscience, even before the political order, seems to legitimise what Mill called the worst servitude of women, who 'are in a very different position from that of any other species of servants, since the gentlemen husbands more than the servitude and obedience of their wives demand the domination of their feelings'. And female 'liberation' proceeds slowly.

In 1877 there was a law admitting women to testify in public acts; in 1893 (and 1907) there were measures that mitigated marital authority, excluding authorisation for the benefit of separated women and working women; and in 1919 there was a law abolishing marital authorisation and admitting women to participate in family councils, to exercise all professions and to hold all public offices, except those of a jurisdictional, military and political nature. These measures were certainly of great importance, but unable to completely change the vicarious position of women in the family and society. Some attempts at more substantial revaluation were unsuccessful. The parliamentary commission set up by the Guardasigilli Niccolò Gallo in 1908 to revise the first book of the Civil Code failed to complete its work, even though it was aware of the serious condition reserved for women in civil legislation: 'in family law,' the Guardasigilli observed, 'it will be necessary to see what different appreciation can be given to the condition of women in the institutes that concern them; it is appropriate to examine whether any element of subjective incapacity of women should not disappear'.

The arduous and humiliating path of emancipation does not only concern the family, but also women in society. Emblematic is the fate of women in the legal professions, to which they will only be admitted after the First World War. The arguments used by jurists – men, of course – seem laughable to us today, yet they reflected the mentality of the time; the exceptions that could be counted were very rare.

VII. WOMEN IN THE LEGAL PROFESSIONS

Tu gisti colà, Vergin preclara ove di molle pié l'orma è più rara.[14] With these words, taken from the ode *La laurea* (1777), Giuseppe Parini crowned

[14] G Parini, *The Degree* (1777) in *Il Giorno. Le Odii* (Milan, Rizzoli, 2011).

Maria Pellegrina Amoretti with his poetic wreath, who had earned the laurel for her degree in *utroque iure* obtained at the University of Pavia on 25 January 1777 on the subject of dowry. A double merit, not only because she was one of the first women graduates, but above all because the degree in which Amoretti had graduated was quite singular: the study and practice of law was in fact reserved for men, for reasons that tradition, social organisation and the government of politics had entrenched to such an extent that this sort of exclusivity was considered an entirely natural, indisputable, and indefectible fact.

Yet in many ways woman was no stranger to the world of law. On the contrary, she was an integral part of it, so much so that she was even its symbol: Themis, the wife of Zeus, symbolised order and law; her daughter Dike, the Roman *Iustitia*, symbolised justice, the fundamental principle underpinning civil society and the driving force behind its development.

At the origins of Western culture, in Greek tragedy but also in Greek poetry and philosophy, the theme of justice is the unbroken thread that gathers around it all the problems of humanity, from the relationship with the Absolute to the relationship between people, from the distribution of power and goods to the future of humanity. Justice is prosperity, hence fecundity: only the image of woman, her body, combined with the natural procreative gift, stands out in the representations of justice. The icons collected on justice by Cesare Ripa are very beautiful, but the painting that struck me most is the one that stands in a room of the Ducal Palace in Genoa, once a palace of justice and detention. Here, Giovanni Andrea De Ferrari depicts justice in the guise of a florid youth, with sword and scales, but without a blindfold, and with a cornucopia carried in her arms, signifying that justice, though severe, is the harbinger of prosperity. Was it mere mythology, mere oleographic depiction, or did the presence of women in the creation of the idea of justice go beyond myth and aesthetics? It is no coincidence that one of the most complex and courageous characters in Greek tragedy is a woman, Antigone. Antigone defies the law, the law of the state, by virtue of an ethical law, pity for her father and peace for the dead; she expresses the drama of the conflict between official law and justice as an innate value, and she can only do so as a woman, because women in those days did not belong to the legislative body, which was reserved for men. Men could criticise the text of the law when it was to be passed, but once it was passed they had to observe it. *Dura lex sed lex*.

Woman is therefore entrusted with the highest and most difficult task: that of identifying the boundary between law and justice, and thus of delineating the boundaries of just law. In Greek thought, however, alongside Antigone we find Diotima, a seer and priestess, Socrates' tutor in erotic matters, and the protagonist of Plato's Symposium. These two components – it is not daring to emphasise this – accompany the entry of women into the world of law and the legal professions. And it is no coincidence that in the same ode by Parini, so much emphasis is placed on the gracefulness of the woman with a law degree. Take note too of the difficulties of the male world of the jurists to accept such an unusual presence: 'Oh lovable sex, which reigns over the soul/with such mighty enchantment/what generous soul is it that scorns/the novelty of your boast?'

Male generosity on the entry of women into the world of law has always been very rare: women became *sui iuris* only with the abolition of marital guardianship, in Italy in 1919, and with a very limited application of the new rules. This is the *discrimen* between the legal status of a woman as a person, as a member of the family, as a member of society, and of a woman as a legal practitioner. For the other professions, the notary and the judiciary, as well as for political representation, it would take decades more, not only because entry into the world of law was still surrounded by hostility, opposition, cultural delays and petty limitations, but also because exercising the functions of a notary or the judiciary meant carrying out a public role; and offices that implied a public function or the exercise of a public service were only suitable for men.

Discrimination against women transcends the great events of history, goes beyond the Enlightenment period, the French Revolution and the Declaration of the Rights of Man and of the Citizen, is consolidated in the Napoleonic Civil Code and is not even undermined by the Italian Civil Code of 1865, even though Anna Maria Mozzoni, one of the great icons of the battle for equal rights, had a way of writing, in a persuasive and elegant style, an essay with the eloquent title, *La liberazione della donna* (*The Liberation of Women*). This 1864 essay contains valuable observations on the draft civil code then being drafted. It is worth dwelling on these pages because they clearly show that the professional status of women had to overcome not one but two obstacles: equal treatment in the area of individual and family rights, and equal treatment in the world of work. The two dimensions are inextricably intertwined, so that without one the other could not proceed or even dissociate. And so it was: the turning point of 1919 implied an irreversible change – even if, as historians have documented, achieved with so much effort and observed with so much caution – both in the legal position of women as such and in the legal position of women as exercisers of a profession that did not involve the assumption of a public function.

In this long journey, professional historians assist jurists: just think of the history of historiography,[15] the political and social history of the West,[16] the history of the professions.[17] But jurists add a *quid pluris* to these narratives: on the one hand, their contribution to the creation of the legal rule and its

[15] M Palazzi, 'Storia delle donne e storia di genere in Italia' in S Bellassai, M Malatesta (eds), *Genere e mascolinità. Uno sguardo storico* (Rome, Carocci, 2000).

[16] G Duby and M Perrot, *Storia delle donne in Occidente* (Roma-Bari, Laterza, 2003).

[17] M Malatesta (ed), *Atlante storico delle professioni* (Bologna, Il Mulino, 2009).

interpretation, so as to make discrimination a cogent fact,[18] on the other hand, their subtle intelligence aimed at arguing the reasons justifying discrimination. Yes, the history of women's entry into the legal profession is not only a political and social history; it is a history that insinuates itself, 'creeps' so to speak, into the mentality and culture of jurists, into tradition, it is chased in legal texts, in judgments, in manuals, in specialist literature.

It is to this perspective that I would like to give more attention, since there is no need to repeat, summarising and thus debasing, the beautiful pages of Francesca Tacchi.[19] On the threshold of the new civil code Mozzoni attempts, with an accurate analysis of the position of women in public opinion, religion, the family, society and science, to build the basis for a reform of the rules of private law that would improve their position and guarantee their emancipation:

> G.G. Rousseau considered woman in nature; Balzac spoke of her from the point of view of masculine interests; La Bruyère subjected her to a fine analysis without any reform in or around her; Madame Neker only saw her from the point of view of local institutions, which often clashed with the true nature of beings and things. No one, among many, purposely studied the influence of institutions on her character and condition.
>
> Since woman, like man, has special aptitudes, she also, like man, has the right to develop them. She has the right because, since she has the right to work, the choice of her work lies in her alone; she has the right because she actually and practically works and produces; and in industry and commerce, and in the arts and teaching, she is already on a large scale, and at this time she has aptitudes that one would perhaps have had the itch to deny her. Finally, she has the right, because society has the right, that the function be exercised by those who can do it better; and if, among several competitors, a woman shows greater aptitude, she has the right.
>
> The woman was and always is considered to be outside the law, with the help of her weakness, which one has every study and ingenuity to exaggerate to the point of ridicule, and with the opportune *enactment of* her pretended incapacity, to disprove which splendid facts arise everywhere in vain.

Mozzoni's discourse unfolds in two stages. Firstly, she examines women 'in the face of law', and, starting from the principle that the purpose of law can only be to guarantee each individual the development and exercise of his faculties and not to impose on him or her any other limitation than that of the rights of others, she declines all the classifications and prejudices that have prevented this principle of natural law from being fully shared and applied.

[18] I highlighted this in *Status e capacità. La costruzione giuridica delle differenze individuali* (Roma-Bari, Laterza, 1994).

[19] F Tacchi, *Eva togata. Donne e professioni giuridiche in Italia dall'Unità ad oggi* (Turin, UTET, 2009).

It is a discourse that goes far beyond the equality of the sexes and the vindication of women's rights: the questions that Mozzoni asks herself and addresses to the reader – they could also be addressed to the contemporary reader – are extremely subtle. She writes:

> '[I]n our times (I speak of civilised and progressive countries) what, in the face of the philosophical principle of law, does the ostracism of Jews mean? What, the barriers raised to free association by diversity of belief? The disinheritance of the son who has left his father's religion? The phrase common to many codes, tolerance of cults? The enslavement of coloured races? The suppression of female intelligence and activity?'

Hence the prejudices that lurk about paternity, and thus about parenthood, which excludes the mother's rights over her offspring, which lists the wife's duties and the husband's rights, which drowns the wife in her husband's shadow, which penalises the wife in crimes where the husband is treated more lightly, which reduces the wife to the mercy of her husband's power.

In the pages then addressed to the Minister Guardasigilli who had, if it were possible, worsened the position of women in the family and society, Mozzoni explains how it is necessary to overcome the obstacle of public office by not only allowing women more prominence in family relationships, but also by opening the doors to work, private and public employment, the professions and teaching. More. The law, informed by the 'old caryatid of Roman law, which by now the centuries should have gnawed away', is incompatible with the new Italy and the new generations. The legal argument goes hand-in-hand with the political one, and a crucial question arises: if the Civil Code is to reflect the needs of society, why introduce rules that are no longer in step with the times and indeed are overtaken by the same beliefs that are now widespread in society? Why are legislators more retrograde and jurists more conservative than models that have been overtaken by the times and by social evolution itself?

Animated by the principles advocated by mid-nineteenth-century socialism, Mozzoni with subtle acumen, paints, in a few lines, the legal condition of women articulated in the different situations on the social scale, and discovers that – curiously enough – the condition of women of humble extraction is more egalitarian than that of women of noble or bourgeois extraction: the former condemned to boredom, the latter condemned to live in the professional light of their husbands.

The criticism of 'Mr Gabba' is fierce: the balance between the sexes advocated by the jurist 'is a real imbalance for anyone who has a florid sense of justice and understands how facts strangle selfish theorems everywhere, as soon as they are born'. Gabba himself, a professor at the University of Pisa, had written on the legal condition of women, justifying their *deminutio*, and insisted on the theme in his work against the introduction of divorce, in his work on *Le donne non avvocate* (*Women not lawyers*) and then in the report he gave at the third National Juridical Congress, held in Florence.

With many aspirations, peppered with expectations, the phase of legitimised discrimination ended with the First World War, and that of the rise to formal equality opened. It was necessary to overcome the dictate of the Civil Code, arrive at universal suffrage, overcome discrimination with a clear constitutional dictate. Above all, a civil conscience and a widespread mentality had to be formed that would break through the wall of prohibitions. It would take half a century and a Second World War to change this mentality and to form a new civil conscience and to approve a new Constitution, it would take almost a century to reform the discipline of the family and to recognise women as having equal dignity with men.

7

'Nature' and Discrimination Based on Sexual Orientation

I. ANACHRONISMS AND HISTORICISATIONS

NATURE AND ACTS 'against nature' dominate the moral, religious and legal conceptions by which those who are attracted to persons of the same sex are evaluated.

Dealing with forms of discrimination due to sexual orientation is very complex. Unlike other figures of diversity, dating back in time, this has only recently been defined in terms of 'homosexuality'. We must therefore beware of anachronistic projections, because the very identification of diversity in the affective and sexual sphere is inextricably linked to culture, social practices and, in this case, the state of science. And it must be borne in mind that for many centuries it was the individual acts, rather than the affections, that were taken into consideration, however they were performed, even if they occurred between persons of different sexes and even between spouses. Legally relevant was the act, qualified as 'against nature', therefore morally reprehensible and criminally relevant; the act was punished with corporal punishment, sometimes with imprisonment and burning. The behaviour was not taken into account, nor was it thought that the subject had been induced to perform the act because of a mental illness.

It is rare to find in classical sources characters – historical or fictional – who present a constant propensity for their own sex. Usually reference is made to single acts, or single relationships; the propensity for one's own sex coexists with bisexuality and is not a definitive election.

In Greece, however, this practice was not matched by a moral judgement. The fact that on Olympus there were frequent love affairs or encounters of this kind, that Jupiter, the father of the gods, had abducted and loved Ganymede, that in *The Iliad* Achilles placed Patroclus at the top of the pyramid of his affections, that in the Athenian chronicles it was claimed that Alcibiades nurtured a particular affection for Socrates, that in the historical sources it was reported that Alexander the Great had loved Hephaistion, indicates that in the collective imagination, in the figurative arts, in lyric poetry, in comedy, same-sex love was not an object of scandal. One of the best-known and most studied of the Platonic dialogues is the *Symposium*, which tradition has handed down to us as the text in which *platonic love is* codified.[1]

In Rome, mentality and customs were different, the propensity for the same sex barely tolerated, more often blamed. Valour, prestige and *auctoritas* were nevertheless a safe screen for any criticism or aggression. Thus Caesar was jokingly mocked by his soldiers, but appreciated as a valiant commander, Nero feared and hated for his blood-thirsty despotism, not because he had contracted three marriages with men with impunity, Hadrian respected for his wit, not despised for the love that had bound him to Antinous.

Pagan culture was indifferent or at most tolerant. Rather, the moral evaluation of same-sex love is linked to more solid and authoritative religious traditions.

Precisely for this reason, one cannot read ancient history with the eyes of the present: the most appropriate terminology and table of values must be found for each era.

From the biblical episode of the destruction of Sodom and Gomorrah we derive the reasons for condemning sodomy, a behaviour that is morally reprehensible as a *sin*.[2]

The religions of the Book are opposed to any behaviour that is not functional to the preservation and development of society and the protection of the family (ie that can disrupt the social order); the non-procreative sexual act is contrary to the divine will, is immoral and therefore illegal.

There are passages in Leviticus that, at least on literal interpretation, sound like curses:

> 22 You shall not lie down with a man as you do with a woman: it is an abominable thing.
>
> 24 Do not make yourself unclean with any of these practices, for with all these things the nations I am about to drive out before you have made themselves unclean.
>
> 29 Every one who practices any of these abominations, every one who commits them, shall be cut off from his people.
>
> (Leviticus 18:22; 24; 29)

[1] KJ Dover, *Homosexualité grecque* (Grenoble, La pensée souvage, 1980); M Foucault, *La volonté de savoir* (Paris, Gallimard, 1976), and *L'usage des plaisirs* (Paris, Gallimard, 1984); Halperin, *Cent ans d'homosexualité et autres essais sur l'amour grec* (Paris, Epel, 2000); JJ Winkler, *The constraints of desire: the Anthropology of Sex and Gender in Ancient Greece* (New York, Routledge, 1989).

[2] D Sherwin Bailey, *Homosexuality and the Western Christian Tradition* (London, Longmans, Green, 1955) 73–74; M Brinkschröde, 'Christian Homophobia: Four Central Discourses' in M Groneberg (ed), *Combatting Homophobia* (Muenster, LIT, 2011) 166; T Römer and L Bonjour, *Homosexuality in the Bible and the Ancient Near East* (Turin, Claudiana, 2007).

No explicit condemnations of same-sex sexual practices are found in the Gospels, whereas they are found in the letters of Paul of Tarsus:

> We also know that the law is made not for the righteous but for the unrighteous and rebellious, for the wicked and sinners, for the sacrilegious and the irreligious, for those who kill father and mother, for murderers, for fornicators, for sodomites, for slave traders, for liars, for perjurers, and for anything else contrary to sound doctrine.
>
> (1 Timothy 1:10)

Christian thought is fuelled by sentiments and words of condemnation because acts with persons of the same sex imply social 'disorder', conflict with the sanctity of the family, and violate the rules of creation.

Augustine writes: 'Crimes that go against nature, such as those committed by sodomites, must be condemned and punished everywhere and always' (Confessions, c III, 8). John Chrysostom reiterates: 'Not only are the passions of homosexuals satanic, but their lives are diabolic' (*Homilia IV in Epistola Pauli ad Romanos*). Thomas Aquinas states: 'In sins against nature in which the natural order is violated, God himself is offended as the orderer of Nature' (*Summa Theologica*, II-II, q 154, a 12).[3]

However, attitudes towards same-sex sexual acts have had a sinusoidal pattern over time, showing long periods of persecution alongside short periods of tolerance.

Social status, however, was an excuse, as was the case in the England of Edward II in the early fifteenth century, or in the France of Henry III in the second half of the sixteenth century, in Venice in the eighteenth century, and in Prussia with Frederick II, in Bavaria in the reign of Ludwig II, in Berlin in the 1920s and 1930s. Even Popes such as Sixtus IV della Rovere and Julius II della Rovere together with extraordinary masters of the arts, such as Michelangelo, Leonardo, Cellini, Caravaggio, Canova, Winckelmann for so many intuitable reasons were not the object of aversion or retaliation.

In the second half of the nineteenth century, medicine was the laboratory in which an attempt was made to settle this phenomenon scientifically, starting with the coining of a new term: *homosexuality*.[4]

But placing the phenomenon within a scientific framework did not exclude it from continuing to be discriminated against and persecuted.

[3] J Boswell, *Alla scoperta dell'amore.Critianesimo e omosessualità* (Rome, Castelvecchi Editore, 2015). Only recently has there been more openness since the Dutch Catechism, although the official position is in the sense of defending the individual from aggression but deploring the practice as immoral because it is an expression of disorder: Various authors, *Il nuovo catechismo olandese* (Alba, Editrice Elledieci, 1969); see also the English version, *Catholic Faith For Adults A New Catechism* (London, Herder Pablications Ltd, 1967) (authorised edition of the Dutch Catechism).

[4] M Foucault, *History of Sexuality.II. The Will to Know* (Milan, Feltrinelli, 1978).

II. THE QUALIFICATION OF THE 'DIFFERENT'. MEDICINE AND PSYCHOLOGY

It was not until 1990 that the World Health Organization (WHO) de-listed homosexuality from mental diseases.

However, psychologists are divided.

Some see homosexuality as a *natural* tendency, ie a condition dictated by the psyche, or biological inheritance; it cannot be escaped from; others see it as the result of social conditioning, family life and social life. For a long time it was believed that homosexuality could be corrected through therapeutic or psychiatric treatment.

What is striking about this human condition is that over two millennia and possibly more it has been the subject of repressive measures.

> Throughout history, homosexuals have encountered very different modes of tolerance or intolerance, but the great novelty at the end of the last century was their becoming a public feature and acquiring a dimension of claiming rights and equality in difference. This led to the homosexual person becoming a citizen or citizen, thanks to the laws enacted to make possible the recognition of the affective bond between persons of the same sex and the possibility of creating a family.[5]

III. THE PATH OF LEGITIMISING DIVERSITY

The path to decriminalising homosexuality has been long and tortuous. Italy was among the first states to decriminalise homosexuality, with the Zanardelli code of 1889; the United Kingdom did so only in 1967, Germany in 1969, Spain in 1979, France in 1982, Ireland in 1993.

Particularly heated was the press campaign organised by the jurist Ulrichs in the years preceding the founding of the Prussian Empire, for the recognition of the rights of homosexuals (of whom psychologists and anthropologists had claimed to identify specific distinctive traits of psychophysical origin) and following the founding, by other scholars for the repeal of § 175 of the penal code then in force, which criminalised fornication and lust between men or of persons with animals.[6] At the same time, a well-known physician, Hirschfeld, had theorised the naturalness of love for persons of the same sex (believing, moreover, that an intermediate sex, the third sex, could be identified between men and women), created a vast cultural movement in favour of homosexuality and activated the first civil rights movements.[7] The collapse of the Empire

[5] V Lingiardi, *Homosexuality and Homophobia* (Milan, Il Saggiatore, 2013).

[6] In the literature on the subject see IV Hull, *Sexuality, State and Civil Society in Germany* (Ithaca, New York, Cornell University Press, 1997); H Puff, *Sodomy in Reformation Germany and Switzerland* (Chicago, University of Chicago Press, 2003).

[7] The Zanardelli code of 1889 had ignored homosexuality: see G Dall' Orto, *La 'tolleranza repressiva' dell'omosessualità. Quando un atteggiamento legale diviene tradizione* (Bologna, Il Mulino, 1988) 37ff.

and the Weimar Republic introduced forms of extended freedom that favoured the spread of a tolerant attitude towards homosexuals, which was to be seen especially in Berlin in the 1920s.

For a long time the law affected the practice of diversity, not the condition of, or way of being, homosexual. Only with the advent of Nazism did the homosexual condition become a crime in and of itself, and, in addition to the extensive application of § 175 of the penal code, special minute legislation was introduced providing for systems of 'prevention' and medical treatment of homosexuality, and for punishment, this being considered a crime against the purity of the race. From here it was a short step to internment and annihilation in extermination camps.

The history of these events has been investigated by an extensive literature, especially abroad.

With the approval of the new constitutions, the action of the civil rights and diversity movements and the initiatives of LGBT associations, the hostile attitude towards homosexuality has gradually eased.

It was not until 2000, with the Nice Charter, that discrimination on the grounds of sexual orientation was explicitly stigmatised (Article 21), even though at the level of interpretation the principle of formal equality and the prohibition of discrimination on the grounds of sex have founded tolerant orientations in almost all systems of Western countries.

The paradox of protection is that it presupposes 'disclosure': a person is protected if he denounces his diversity. But how is diversity defined? By his acts, his behaviour, his feelings, his 'nature'?

Michel Foucault begins *The Will to Know*,[8] his history of sexuality, as follows:

> Sodomy – that of ancient civil and canon law – was a particular type of prohibited act; its perpetrator was merely its legal subject. The 19th century homosexual, on the other hand, has become a character: a past, a history, and a childhood, a character, a form of life; a morphology too, with an indiscreet anatomy and perhaps a mysterious physiology. Nothing of what he altogether is escapes his sexuality.

One could discuss this conviction at length: reading this passage, it seems that homosexuality was only relevant because it legally configured a case under canon law or criminal law. In reality, if one studies the phenomenon, one is convinced of the opposite: law has never formulated definitions and solutions *autonomous* from the religious moral or political and social conceptions that existed at the time when it intervened to repress homosexuality. On the contrary, it has made itself the bearer of legal forms to prevent, prohibit, punish acts and behaviour 'against nature'.

Foucault also argues that it was only at the end of the eighteenth century that sexual relations 'against nature' were legally sanctioned because, like incest, rape and adultery, homosexuality was considered one of the crimes that

[8] Vol I (Milan, Feltrinelli, 1988).

disrupted the family. The prohibition of incest is based on biological, religious and moral arguments; the prohibition of rape is placed to safeguard the consent of the betrothed, and seals, where appropriate, class endogamy; the repression of adultery reinforces the husband's power over his wife and prevents uncertainties over the paternity of children; homosexuality is opposed to procreation and constitutes a brake on the propagation of the species.

Family historians accredit this perspective and place the repression of sodomy in the context of the cultural and religious climate of the Reformation and Counter-Reformation.

In other words, sodomy presupposes that marriage (understood as the legal institutionalisation of sexual union) must be directed towards procreation; sodomy does not entail procreation and is therefore a threat to the survival of society.

However, this historical progression must be corrected.

As mentioned above, the notion of homosexuality constructed at the end of the nineteenth century marks a break with the past and favours the transition from the atomistic conception founded on single acts to a syncretic conception founded on quality, that is, on *identity*, which is a permanent way of being of the individual. From the physical dimension, the focus shifts to the psyche, which becomes the working ground for understanding the individual's identity and correcting its nature – but also to mock it.[9]

The social reaction is expressed in a stigma that persecutes the individual throughout his life.[10] Even the lexicon with all its variants, including dialect and slang, becomes an instrument of discrimination: the homosexual becomes the *different person* par excellence.[11]

IV. THE IDENTITY OF THE DIFFERENT

On the website of the WHO, studies, statistics and recommendations are collected on the health situation of minorities in different areas of the world. The results of these reports indicate, in a 2019 publication, that homosexual behaviour is one of the causes of the spread of HIV, which is found above all in the poorer classes, since the poorest are unable or hindered by their economic conditions to provide themselves with preventive tools, are poorly informed, and are often unaware of the risks to which they expose themselves.[12] Children are the most affected.[13]

[9] M Barbagli, *Modern Homosexuals. Gays and lesbians in Italy* (Bologna, Il Mulino, 2007).

[10] E Goffman, *Stigma.Notes on the management of degraded identity* (Verona, Ombre Corte, 2018).

[11] G Stella, *Negroes and Faggots, Guides & Co. The eternal struggle against the other* (Milan, Mondadori, 2018).

[12] 'Breaking Barriers Towards more gender-responsive and equitable health systems' (New York, WHO, 2019).

[13] ibid 11. 'Countries must consider the inequities and disparities within and across groups and geographic areas in accessing health care, learn how gender norms and unequal power relations impede access and identify the key barriers to access for women, men, and lesbian, gay, bisexual, transgender and intersex populations.'

The WHO thus attests to a link between *gender-related* sexual behaviour and the spread of socially dangerous diseases[14] and emphasises the need to make each individual responsible so that the misuse of gender can result in harm to society.

Obviously, these considerations must be measured, because they tend, if taken to extremes, to criminalise those who appeal to gender in order to affirm their identity. They also provoke reactions against anything that brings uncertainty about sexual identification or sexual orientation.

A vicious circle then arises: those who are different are criminalised, so they are forced to act covertly; this prompts them not to avail themselves of medical aid to treat themselves if they are infected, with the consequence that those who come into contact with them risk putting their health at risk. Identity is correlated with social exclusion, poverty, social conditions and health. WHO studies highlight the correlation between the status of the different and social marginalisation. Sex is seen only in its physical and biological aspect, gender in its cultural and social aspect. Gender identity also implies role awareness and is the result of inner experience with respect to the sex assigned by the community.[15] The conclusion of these studies is that gender should not be used to discriminate against individuals even in the field of health.[16] The WHO recently denounced the situation of the different in the world. Violence and discrimination are common in countries in Africa and Asia.[17]

[14] ibid 25.

[15] 'Sex refers to the biological and physiological characteristics, such as chromosomes, hormones and anatomy, that distinguish males and females. While sex is often referred to as a binary category – male or female – there are other categories that do not fall under either of these categories, such as intersex. Gender encompasses socially constructed norms, roles, behaviours, activities and attributes that a given society considers appropriate for individuals based on the sex assigned to them at birth. Individuals are socialised into a gender and are taught behaviours considered appropriate for women and men, including how to interact with others of the same or opposite sex. Gender roles are also affected by age, class, race, ethnicity and religion, as well as by geographic, economic, and political environments. Gender identity is a person's deeply felt internal and individual experience of gender (as male, female, a blend of both or neither), which may or may not correspond with the sex assigned at birth or the gender attributed to them by society. Gender identity includes the personal sense of the body (which may involve, if freely chosen, modification of appearance or function by medical, surgical or other means) and expressions of gender, including dress, speech and mannerisms. Gender equality means equal opportunities for women and men to access and control social, economic and political resources, including equal and fair protection under the law. It means that the different behaviours, aspirations and needs of women and men are considered, valued and favoured equally and that there is no discrimination on the grounds of gender in the allocation of resources or benefits.'

[16] B Ki-Moon, 'Message to Human Rights Council meeting on Violence and Discrimination based on Sexual Orientation or Gender Identity' (New York, ONU, 2012) 30, available at www.un.org/sg/en/content/sg/speeches/2012-03-07/message-human-rights-council-meeting-violence-and-discrimination. United Nations. 'Ending violence and discrimination against lesbian, gay, bisexual, transgender and intersex people' (2015), available at www.ohchr.org/Documents/Issues/Discrimination/Joint_LGBTI_Statement_ENG.PDF.

[17] 'Report of the Independent Expert on protection against violence and discrimination based on sexual orientation and gender identity' Council of Europe human rights session (June 2017).

8

Nature and Discrimination Based on 'Race', Skin Colour, Physiognomy

I. THE INDIOS

IT IS ALWAYS something adherent to nature considered in its physical consistency and appearance that racists believe (or pretend) to find in individuals qualified as different. Sex and fluidity in the woman and the homosexual respectively, the semblance of humanity in the Indian, purity of lineage in the Jew and the Roma, dark skin in the native and the slave.

The first different ones are, historically speaking, the American Indians, inhabitants of a continent whose existence was unknown, and who, not belonging to the European or East Indian populations, were doubted to have common roots with the known ones, and to be descended from the same creation.

The most compelling description of the mentality still prevailing today with regard to the 'different', the 'other' is found in the analytical examination of the reports on the conquest of the Indies conducted by a scientist with a structuralist orientation, Tzvetan Todorov. Todorov uses the discovery of the Indios as an emblematic historical example of the operation of commonly practised discriminatory categories.[1]

Through the descriptions of the first discoverer, the conquerors, the evangelisers, the problem of how to consider *the other* emerges forcefully. Is the Indio a human being or a beast? Can he be an object of property? Is he to be considered an intermediate being between man and the other natural kinds? Or is he a dimidiate man?

This is a unique experiment, because it is the first contact with the New World, and thus the reactions that modern Western culture expresses for the first time in history towards populations of unsuspected existence. Hence the need for a choice: whether to treat, culturally before socially and juridically, the Indian as the black, the slave, as the enslaved Moor – all legally inscribable in the categories of the Roman law tradition *(capite deminuti*, *serfs*, etc); or whether to establish a category, at the same time cultural, social and juridical of a new type.

[1] T Todorov, The Conquest of America. The Problem of the Other (Turin, Einaudi, 1992).

The problem is complicated by the fact that the conquerors, the preachers, the educators, who are all bearers of a caste culture in a more or less arrogant way, are uncomfortable facing the savage, who is not without a social dimension: on the contrary, the society the conquerors come across is organised, complex, caste-like. Todorov notes[2] how Moctezuma I, when he decided to codify the laws of his people in the mid-fifteenth century, formulated 14 prescriptions. Of these, only two were comparable to European ones (the punishment of adultery and theft); the others were aimed at regulating precedence, ie etiquette and rituality: in a word, diversity.

The situation also mirrors that from which the conquerors viewed the society of the natives. The inability to recognise others as equal and different at the same time is not only peculiar to the conquerors; it is also peculiar to the natives.

However, not all human categories considered inferior by Europeans are on an equal footing. European culture, not without disagreements and contrasts, isolates a diversity within diversity: the other, the Indio, is considered different from the Black African; and not being equated with the latter, he may receive better legal treatment. However, even when the humanitarian orientation prevails, based on the consideration that the Indios are human beings, this does not mean that all differences are overcome; the Indio is pagan, and therefore must be coercively evangelised.

The problem of the legal status of the Indios is felt so acutely and seriously that the Catholic kings set up a junta of theologians and jurists as early as 1500; and in 1503 the first rules are issued. Freedom is confirmed to the Indios, with only three exceptions: Indios *caribes* (*anthropophagi*), Indios who rebel; Indios already held as slaves by other Indios. Slaves are branded with iron, like Blacks. But a few decades later, exceptions and branding are suppressed.

Given the regime of freedom, however, the question of capacity in the strict sense opens up: what legal treatment should be given to the Indios?

Noting that they do not know how to live like the conquerors, being bearers of a different culture (we would say today) or not being civilised (we would say then), the Indios are considered *incapable*. Theologically, it is debated whether, in addition to baptism and marriage, it is appropriate or even licit to administer the other sacraments to them. The question arises as to whether, used as a labour force, they should be treated with respect or privilege over slaves. The theological dispute is finally resolved with Pope Paul III's bull *Sublimis Deus*, in 1537, which not only admits the possibility of administering all the sacraments to the Indians, but by virtue of this excludes the possibility of enslaving them and depriving them of their property. Evangelisation thus becomes an instrument of liberation.

[2] ibid 83.

Improvements in the juridical treatment of the Indios are due to two great Dominicans: Las Casas and de Vitoria.

Bartolomé de Las Casas (1474–1566) was the most radical critic of the conquest and thus of the behaviour of the conquerors. Relying on natural law of divine origin, he believed that titles to acquire lands in the New World were not legitimate, as they were based on common law of human origin.

His Dominican confrere Francisco de Vitoria (1486–1546), a lecturer in Salamanca, took a less rigid stance: he retained the titles on the level of natural law, but admitted their legitimacy in the case of the voluntary subjugation of the Indios; the path to this assessment was traced by Vitoria through the law of nations, which he included in natural law. In January 1539, Francisco de Vitoria was asked to summarise in a lecture (*relecci6n*) his thought as he had developed it in the university courses of the first chair of Theology he held in Salamanca. His choice fell on the Indios (*De Indis*). His curiosity for the New World was combined with the theological problems opened up by the conquest, with his expertise in international law and with the idea of a universal state, composed of an international community of states replacing the Christian community of European states, making Vitoria one of the founders of international law.[3]

The summarising lecture is divided into three sections: the first is dedicated to discussing the issue of the ownership of the barbarians (Indios); and he resolves the issue in a positive sense, because the then newly discovered lands are not under the dominion of either Catholic kings or the Pope; to the barbarians, even if they are heretics, he recognises the right of ownership. In the second section, Vitoria discusses the titles with which the Spaniards seized the possessions of the Indios; and he points out that, even if they rejected the Good News brought to them by the foreigners, thus falling into mortal sin, they should not consider themselves unworthy of the dominion of their possessions. In the third, Vitoria explains the legitimate titles on which the Spanish imposed their rule over the Indios. He recognises the *jus peregrinandi* to the Spaniards, in order to trade by bartering for products the Indios lack, receiving in return gold, silver and other goods they have in abundance. Finally, he allows the subjugation of barbarians only if they are dangerous, hostile or hinder the preaching of the Gospel.

The Indios are therefore not only free, but are put on an equal footing with the vassals of Castile; this is by implication recognised by Columbus, and officially in 1501; however, there is an insistence on the introduction of laws so that they are assured humane treatment and are not overworked. The limitation of their legal capacity is modelled on that of minors and the poor (*miserables*).[4]

[3] J Malagòn Barcelò (ed), *Las relacciones de Indis y De jure belli de Fray Francisco de Vitoria, O. P. fundador del Derecho Internacional* (Washington DC, Union Panamericana, 1963). In today's text the lecture is collected together with the one on the law of war (*De jure belli*), and printed in Cologne and Frankfurt in 1696.

[4] A Garcìa-Gallo, *Manual de história del derecho español* (Madrid, Autopublication, 1959) 682.

Obviously, this minority discipline comes in the form of 'special protection of their interests'. They are allowed to live according to their own customs, provided they respect religion and royal laws; malice is not presumed in their acts; their statements cannot be used against them; they are judged in summary proceedings by indigenous judges. Intensive labour legislation is also initiated in their favour, even more favourable than that reserved for the Spanish,[5] with regard to the working day, rest, etc. This legislation developed to such an extent that it had to be collected in codes.[6] One speaks, in short, of authentic privileges.

Work is in any case compulsory; the Indios are divided into departments, ruled by a Spaniard; work is paid but not at market prices, but according to the rates set by the governor. Thus, agricultural or mining companies (*encomiendas*) are established, not without contrasts, which serve to reward the conquerors, pioneers, the 'populators' of the new lands. Their juridical nature is much debated, not least because the new lands belonged to the kings of Castile, who, having offered them to the Pope, had them returned to him as a donation. In any case, the *encomiendas* are given in concession to the *encomendero*, who pays a tribute for this. Between the de facto and juridical treatment of the Indios, historians place a large hiatus.[7]

II. THE JEWS

In the case of the Jews, discrimination is based on artfully constructed prejudices consolidated over time: a religious prejudice, which takes its cue from the Gospels on the trial and death sentence of Jesus in order to blame contemporary Jews and all their descendants; a moral prejudice, based on the practice of lending money, from which indifference and ruthlessness towards the needy would derive; an economic prejudice, stemming from envy of their wealth, accumulated by exploiting the resentment of debtors, by resorting to usury; an ethnic prejudice, based on the 'purity of blood' that was not to be contaminated by the descendants of the persecutors of Jesus; a cultural prejudice, stemming from envy of their millenary, august tradition. Prejudices were accompanied by the invention of imaginary crimes, such as the kidnapping of Christian children to be destined for deity sacrifice, the celebration of satanic and bloodthirsty rituals, the creation of spy and subversive networks, in a crescendo of hateful accusations that fomented intolerance and sedimented hostile feelings.

[5] ibid.

[6] A first attempt is made by Gáspar de Escalva y Aguero, in 1636; and then by Alonso Peña Montenegro, in his *Itinerario per istruzione degli Indios* (1668).

[7] The legal capacity of the Indios reveals a design that appears, at that time, much more advanced than that reserved for the Eritreans and Libyans in the colonial phase. The treatment reserved for the Jews in the racial legislation is, if possible, even more execrated.

In other words, the legal status of the Jews is not a constant in public organisation, changing from era to era, people to people, sovereign to sovereign, historical phase to historical phase.[8]

Medieval and modern law record these variations of an ordinarily persecutory regulatory treatment, punctuated only by occasional privileges. In reality it depended on the arbitrariness of the lord

> who could revoke at whim the privileges already granted. And thus legitimised the thousand anguish used to their detriment. When they had become well impoverished and almost all the citizens had become their debtors, the convenient theory of *servitus quasi publica* legitimised their confiscation or expulsion.[9]

On the other hand, the privileges were very little: preservation of the faith (when they were not obliged to abjure, thus becoming Marranos[10]), worshipping in synagogues (when these were not burnt or looted), access to their own courts (but only for marriages and successions). Tax treatment was mostly vexatious, even to the point of affecting procreation.

The criteria for distinguishing Jews, in history and in legislation, are striking in their dramatic nature. These criteria differ from era to era and from legislator to legislator, so that it is difficult to establish – as the qualification of an individual as a 'Jew' is not visible – the assignment to what is from time to time referred to as religion, ethnicity or 'race'.[11]

The criteria considered distinctive are a plurality, but they need not add up to allow classification. The *name*, which is transmitted from father to son, although it is the maternal ancestry, according to Jewish religious tradition, that connotes membership of this religion. Less relevant as a rule, but relevant according to racial laws, is the first name. The registration in the register of the Community once called the 'Israelite' 'university' now Jewish, established in a specific location.[12] Distinctive signs of cultural linguistic and geographical character

[8] Among many references see D Bidussa, E Collotti-Pischel, R Scardi, *Identità e storia degli ebrei* (Milano, Franco Angeli, 2000); M Brenner, *Breve storia degli ebrei* (Roma, Donzelli, 2009); S Shama, *La storia degli Ebrei* (Milano, Mondadori, 2014); A Foa, *Diaspora. Storia degli Ebrei nel Novecento* (Roma-Bari, Laterza, 2014); for the Italian experience, A Milano, *Storia degli ebrei in Italia* (Torino, Einaudi, 1963); R Calimani, *Storia degli ebrei italiani* (Milano, Mondadori, 2016) and the debated *Storia degli ebrei italiani sotto il fascismo* (Torino, Einaudi, 1993) by Renzo De Felice with whom Carocci, *Storia degli ebrei in Italia: dall'emancipazione a oggi* (Roma, Carocci, 2005), E Collotti, *Il fascismo e gli Ebrei. Le leggi razziali in Italia* (Roma-Bari, Laterza, 2006). For political history profiles see M olinari, *Ebrei in Italia: un problema di identità (1848–1938)* (Florence, Giuntina, 1991).

[9] E Besta, *Le persone nella storia del diritto italiano* (Padua, Cedam, 1931) 4.

[10] The history of the Marranos is also tragic in the different countries and at different times when they were received, driven out, persecuted, treated as heretics and perjurer: see D Di Cesare, *Marrani. L'altro dell'altro* (Turin, Einaudi, 2018).

[11] The inverted commas of 'race' are pragmatic, because race is an invention, its history mixed with contempt, mockery, persecution, violation of human rights and today of fundamental rights.

[12] The settlement of the Jews in Italy, particularly in Rome, predates the diaspora and the fall of Jerusalem by Titus.

are the membership of the Sephardic community, widespread in Spain and Portugal, in France and Italy, in the Mediterranean areas, or the Ashkenazi community, in the Nordic countries, Poland, Russia and Central Europe. Meanwhile, Italian Jews have an ancient origin distinct from these.

It is the religious traditions linked to the study of the Bible and the Talmud in particular that bring distinctions regarding language: Ladino, similar to Spanish, for the Sephardim and Yiddish, similar to German, for the Ashkenazis. It is a very fragmented world, in which traditions and the orientation of studies lead to the formation of groups and subgroups living together, all generically defined as 'Jews' by non-Jews as if belonging to a different religion meant homologation without differences in a classification of its own.[13]

As a rule, Jews could not own property; they could only have certain professions and some commercial activities. They could not cultivate land, they could not bear arms or engage in a military career, they could not hold public office. They were obliged to reside in ghettos where they had been established, and were locked in during the night, guarded, at their own expense, by a patrol that guarded the entrance gates.

Their mobility was justified by the activity they carried out: they were often called upon by the lords of a state or region to improve trade, to foster the development of the economic system with their funding, to start the activity of a port with their international connections. They were therefore not equated with vagabonds, and were exempt from the laws restricting transfers from one land to another. Hence the need to learn languages, the plurality of relationships, the internationality of family ties. In some respects, the life and relationships of the Jews resembled those of the nobility.

Religious reasons, often accompanied by a concern to safeguard the 'purity of the bloodline' imposed restrictive rules on marriages between Jews and non-Jews.

'Mixed' marriages, if not forbidden, were allowed with severe restrictions. Hence the separateness of Jews from other members of society, at least demographically. This separateness, the effects of which have been distorted and exaggerated by the exponents of racist culture, leads one to think and then to preach that the Jews (whose identity, moreover, can only be formally assigned) are part of a race other than the Aryan race, of an inferior rank, and are the bearers of impure blood. But the Jews are not recognisable at first sight, they do not have the features of an Indian or the dark skin of an African.

In short, historically, the impossibility of recognising them implied the display of distinguishing marks: the wheel on the shoulder, the pointed yellow

[13] The contribution of Jewish culture to the development of science and literature has been immense: see M Brunazzi and AM Fubini, *Ebraismo cultura europea del' 900* (Florence, Giuntina, 1990);M Beer and AM Foa, *Ebrei, minorities, Risorgimneto: storia, cultura, letteratura* (Rome, Viella, 2013).

hat. But the vileness and vulgarity of enigration campaigns combined with boorish forms of racism led to the spread of cartoons or caricatures linked to certain somatic characteristics that were attributed to the Jews, such as the curved nose, curly hair, and so on.

This discriminatory cultural attitude that associates a considered 'natural' inferiority with religious minority, social segregation and the condition of wandering life fades with the Enlightenment and the affirmation of natural law. The contribution of Jewish culture and some legendary figures of theologians and philosophers of the Jewish religion, especially in Germany, led to a new understanding of Judaism and its legitimisation within the multicultural community. The principles advocated in France, following the Revolution, and then some of Napoleon's measures significantly improved the legal and social status of Jews throughout Europe.

III. THE EMANCIPATION OF THE JEWS

The prohibitions fell in the Kingdom of Sardinia after the enactment of the Statuto Albertino, with a measure by Carlo Alberto a few days later. The Statute already proclaimed the principle of equality of all kingdoms.

After 1848, legislation removing the prohibitions resulted in the emancipation of the Jews, who were finally considered, formally, equal *citizens. Emancipation* also entailed *assimilation* for the Jews who converted and changed religion, but also for the Jews who, having now been admitted to civil society and to public office without prejudice, conformed to all other citizens without distinction. The distinctions that remain are those of worship, for those who are observant, and family relations, national and international. The messianic law also imposes on Jews the observance of the Sabbath feast, the prohibition of the eating of certain foods, ritual slaughter, Torah study, synagogue attendance and communal prayer.[14]

The contribution of the Jews to the development of modern society and the prosperity of the West in culture, science and the arts has been essential.

The most significant aspects of emancipation concern the historical period from the end of the eighteenth century to the end of the nineteenth century. Germany,[15] Austria and France witnessed great innovations and discoveries in all the arts and sciences. Viennese culture, from the end of the nineteenth century to the 1930s, added another important turning point to the shaping of the modern age.

[14] Molinari (n 8).

[15] A Elon, *The Pity of It All: A History of the Jews in Germany, 1743–1933* (New York, Picador USA, 2003); VR Berghahn, *Imperial Germany, 1871–1914: Economy, Society, Culture, and Politics* (New York, Berghahn, 1994) 102; Levine, *Dreamland of Humanists: Warburg, Cassirer, Panofsky, and the Hamburg School* (Chicago, The Universityof Chicago Press, 2013).

These moments of ascendancy and high regard were accompanied by serious episodes of anti-Semitism – the Dreyfus affair is symptomatic in this regard – which were a prelude to the tragedy of the *Shoah*.

As a comparison, the emancipation of women and homosexuals took a tendentially univocal path that takes place simultaneously in different areas. The emancipation of women takes place in articulated spheres from the end of World War I to the end of World War II, reaching the present day, while the emancipation of homosexuals only takes place after World War II and is still in the making. However, the emancipation of the Jews has a rapid evolution for about a century and a half, and then an equally rapid regression, which is completed with their extermination, in the Nazi and Fascist countries.

After the Reconstruction, many were convinced that the notion of race, and the fictitious distinction of men based on blood and lineage, could no longer be given a place. In reality, one had to bitterly recant: the creeping intolerance, the latency of a discriminatory subculture, and the emergence of new persecutory signs fomented regurgitations of anti-Semitism that brought the problem of 'race' back to the attention, even of jurists.

IV. THE IDEA OF 'RACE' AS A CULTURAL FACT

Historians have documented that the idea of race was born well before the discovery of America. It is true that the 'other' as such was only constructed with the discovery of the New World, but the colonisation of the territories of Africa and the Far East had begun well before the fateful date of 1492.

Ann Stoler,[16] a scholar of Dutch colonisation of the East Indies, has written with great conviction that race should never be considered merely a matter of physiology. Dutch culture is imbued with factors that distinguish Europeans from Javanese. The persecution of the Jews in the Middle Ages, wrote another scholar, Geraldine Heng,[17] should not be seen as a premonitory sign of the religious wars; it was in itself already a racial persecution. One cannot consider race merely the pseudoscientific product of the studies of doctors and biologists at the end of the nineteenth century, precisely because through religious discrimination begins a downward path to the hell of persecution. Racist thinking, practices and phenomena can thus be identified, even if they do not go by the name of race, throughout the Middle Ages. England was the first European country in which segregation of the Jews began; this is testified by the rules of the Statute of Jewery of 1275 that anticipate by almost three centuries the establishment of the first ghetto in Italy, in Venice, in 1516, and then Pope Paul IV's

[16] AL Stoler, 'Rethinking Colonial Categories: European Communities and the Boundaries of Rule' (1989) 31 *Comparative Studies in Society and History* 134.

[17] G Heng, *England and the Jews* (Cambridge, CUP, 2018).

bull establishing ghettos in the Papal States. It was also in England that the first expulsion of the Jews was decreed, again in 1275.

On the other hand, the connection between the idea of race and the idea of being subhuman, which one tends to impute to the Nazis, goes back much further, because the English considered the Irish to be subhuman and could therefore enslave them without remorse, and throughout the Christian West the fight against the Muslims was at that time considered a fight against the devil: Bernard of Clairvaux expressed it this way in writing the rule of the Templar Order.[18]

Eric Voegelin has shown that the idea of race in the modern sense originated at the end of the seventeenth century and spread in the first half of the eighteenth century – with the thought of Buffon, Herder, Blumembach and Kant himself – moving from naturalistic classifications based on skin colour and the distribution of human beings in the various regions of the world characterised by different climatic conditions.[19] The physical idea of race, still emphasised by Kant, is gradually fading away, to take on in the ninenteenth century, with the internalisation of the body and the person, an ideal and abstract meaning, associated with the finiteness of the human being and with his place within a finalistic project of history devoted to infinite progress. In the process of internalising the image of the person, man is seen as endowed with sensitivity and reason, but also as a representative of his species. Goethe and Schiller poetically illustrate his spiritual elevation over physical nature considered vulgar because it is too close to the animal state. Humboldt reverses this conception and pursues the idea of the corporeal foundation of the individual's spiritual achievements. And it is precisely the unity of spirit and body that is the basis of the theory of human races, described metaphorically in the distinction between night/day/dawn/dusk, in which the peoples of the day are the Caucasian peoples, expressing the pinnacle of humanity, then degrading in human quality as their skin colour becomes darker and darker. The peoples of the day, in which Carus also includes the Semitic peoples, are those who have performed the great human feats: they have produced a great variety of languages and achieved great things in the arts and sciences, developed means of transport, invented tools, dominated other peoples. Voegelin's conclusion is dazzling:

> [R]ace is no longer something to be studied, kept at arm's length, but a bodily and spiritual reality that includes the scholar himself: the concept of race thus concretely formed is no longer a scientific concept but a means of interpreting each person's life in its meaning, as well as the total existence of the community.[20]

[18] C Ferrini, *Alle origini del concetto di razza. Kant e la diversità umana nell'unità di specie* (Trieste, EUT Trieste, 2022).

[19] E Voegelin, *Razza. Storia di un'idea* (1933) (It trans) (Milan, Meduca Edizioni, 2006).

[20] ibid.

Alongside this line of thought is that constructed by scientific positivism, which bends Darwinian conceptions of selection due to adaptation to justify the superiority of the white race over other human races. The idea of race has now become so ingrained in mentality and culture that the 'scientific' explanation offers it a seemingly coercive justification: it obeys a law of nature; biology differentiates peoples into different races.[21] What is more, the connection between skin colour and subalternity also becomes coactive: man's social condition is conditioned by his gestation and birth. That social pyramid that in the *Ancien Régime* was determined by birth into one of the higher 'states' is now determined by genetic characteristics. Gobineau[22] therefore does not add much to what had already been achieved on the basis of the fantasies about human nature that the philosophers of the eighteenth century had indulged in.

Law offers further instruments to make these discriminations coercive:[23] it legitimises invasions, colonisations, spoliations, enslavement, and then genocides.

The history of the last five centuries can also be written under the banner of 'race wars', and it is either a history of endemic struggles between ethnic groups living within the same territorial borders or a history of wars that are an expression of colonial power and the supremacy of the European continent over other continents.[24] The enslavement of slaves and colonists is based on the diversity of skin colour, associated with linguistic and cultural subalternity dictated by European standards and their economic and social backwardness. The reduction of man to an animal, in the racists' view, also lowers his moral rectitude and elevates his aptitude for crime and vice.

V. SKIN COLOUR AND SLAVERY IN THE UNITED STATES OF AMERICA

Blacks, plundered from the coasts of Africa, the fruit of trade between Spain, England, Holland, France, Portugal and their colonies, enriched the peoples of Europe. Thanks to that trade, England populates its American colonies. It is a lucrative trade, reserved for the English and forbidden to the colonists. The occasion of the Revolution is given by the tax on tea and cotton, but behind these commodities hid human goods. Liberation from the yoke of the Mother Country, however, did not take place under the banner of freeing the slaves. On the contrary, in 1776 with the Declaration of Independence those states had

[21] G Barbujani, *The invention of races. Understanding human biodiversity* (Milan, Bompiani, 2018).

[22] MA de Gobineau, *Essai sur l'inegalité des rces humaines* (Paris, Librairie de Firmin Didot Frères, 1853).

[23] TF Gossett, *Race. The History of an Idea in America* (Oxford, OUP, 1997).

[24] R Sega, *The War of the Races* (Milan, Mursia, 1968).

recognised the freedom of whites but not of Black slaves, in spite of the fact that the proem refers to natural law principles:

> When in the course of human events the necessity arises for one people to dissolve the political ties that have bound it to another people and to assume among the powers of the earth the status of separate and equal power to which the Laws of Nature and of Nature's God entitle it, a convenient regard for the views of mankind requires that that people state the reasons why it is compelled to secede.
>
> We hold these truths to be self-evident: That all men are created equal; that they are by the Creator endowed with certain inalienable rights, that these rights are Life, Liberty, and the pursuit of Happiness; that to secure these rights governments are instituted among men which derive their just powers from the consent of the governed; that whenever any form of government tends to deny these ends, the people have a right to alter or abolish it, and to institute a new government founded on such principles, and to organise its powers in such form as seems to the people best fitted to procure their Safety and Happiness.[25]

The text of the Declaration of Independence was the product of a long dispute with the mother country. And slave ownership was a sensitive issue, involving English law and the law applied in the colonies. The colonists felt that they were considered a category marked by minority, compared to English citizens who could claim greater rights. Furthermore, English governors had used slaves to fight the colonists (W 48) and had freed and armed thousands of them to provide the necessary militia to quell riots and discontent. The connection between colonialism and slavery, both in the sense unfavourable to slaves and to colonists, had not escaped Benjamin Franklin. And it could not have escaped the observers' notice that the colonists, in order to defend their freedom and property and regain a privileged status on a par with that of English citizens, stubbornly insisted on the need to preserve slavery, and to reduce its tax burden (W 52). In addition, slaves who escaped from the colonies and took refuge in the mother country were considered free, based on a precedent set by Lord Mansfield (*Somerset v Stewart*, 1772). However, this was a misunderstanding:[26] Lord Mansfield had not declared the freedom of Blacks, but only the prohibition of exporting slaves from England to other countries. It is true that Lord Mansfield had spoken harsh words against slavery, arguing that it was a hateful condition that could not be justified on moral political grounds. And he had held that a slave brought to England and escaped from his master should not be returned to him, let alone transported to the colonies to be sold there: there was no rule in English common law imposing slavery. But the rule only applied to the Mother Country;

[25] It is debated whether Jefferson's words on equality should refer to citizenship or to individual liberties, the latter interpretation being much more implicit than the former; JN Rakove, *The Cambridge Companion to Federalist* (Cambridge, CUP, 2020).

[26] S Wiecek, 'Lord Mandsfield and the Legitimacy of Slavery in the Anglo-American World' (1974) 46 *University of Chicago Law Review* 86.

trade by English ships outside British soil was not forbidden – on the contrary, it was the subject of an exclusive right that American colonists could not enjoy.

Not even in 1781, when the first ten Amendments to the Declaration that created the Confederacy of the United States were introduced, could an understanding be reached on the freeing of slaves.

Even the Constitution of 1787, although inspired by Enlightenment principles,[27] did not include provisions concerning the freedom of slaves: it specified that the right of inviolability of the person contained in *habeas corpus* could not be suspended except for reasons of rebellion, invasion or public safety (Article 1 section IX c 3); it ensured that citizens of one state were treated equally in other states (Article 4 section II c 1); it did not recognise any title of nobility (Article1 section IX, c 8); but it did not rule on the issue of slavery. And even though the reasons for the freedom of human beings from the scourge of slavery were preached by many anti-slavery associations, the common mentality, reflected in the statutes of these associations themselves, accredited the idea of differences between 'races' and linked this difference with skin colour; in other words, even though their aim was to protect Blacks and free them from the constraints of their masters, these associations did not then address the problem of the employment of the freed slaves, who were, of course, destined to be exploited, in the factory, as 'free' men, living in a condition not much better than they would have lived on the cotton plantations (F 154).

The reasons for this deliberate omission in the Constitution and the first amendments have been the subject of an extensive literature, which has spoken of 'significant silences'.[28] The text included an obscure provision according to which:

> The Representatives shall be apportioned – the principle also applies to direct taxes – among the several States forming part of the Union in proportion to the respective number of inhabitants, to be computed by adding to the total number of free persons – including those bound by a fixed term contract, and excluding Indians not subject to taxation – three fifths of the rest of the population.
>
> (Article I, section 3)

The 'rest of the population' was the slaves. But slaves had no vote, and therefore the representatives of this fraction of the population elected to Congress were their owners (W 5). The explanation for this provision is to be found in the connection between (slave) ownership and the power of taxation. 'No taxation

[27] JO Horton, *Slavery and the Making of America* (Oxford, OUP, 2005); DB Davis, *Inhuman Bondage: The Rise and Fall of Slavery in the New World* (Oxford, OUP, 2006); I Berlin, *Many Thousands Gone: The First Two Centuries of Slavery in North America* (Cambridge, Mass, CUP, 1998).

[28] D Waldstreicher, *Slavery's Constitution: From Revolution to Ratification* (New York, Hill and Wang, 2009).

without representation' was the well-known principle according to which taxes had to be voted on by the citizens; not all, however, were admitted to vote, but only those admitted on the basis of their sex, race and census. Enjoying a numerical privilege, slave owners were better protected.

The Constitution also provided that (Article 1, section IX, c 1):

> [T]he Immigration or Importation of such Persons, as any of the States now existing shall think proper to admit, shall not be prohibited by Congress before the year 1808; but for each Person imported a Tax or Duty, not exceeding ten dollars, may be levied.

In other words, the slave trade was not prohibited to the states, as the British Crown had prohibited it to its colonies, retaining this privilege for itself. The intent of the drafters of the Constitution was therefore not the repression of slavery, but the appropriation to the Americans of the slave trade previously reserved for the Mother Country, and if anything, the concern for the preservation of white power, and thus the desirability of a limitation on the importation of excessive numbers of Blacks, who might have endangered the safety of whites. Hence the prediction that from 1808 onwards, deliberations on this matter would be resumed.

The Constitution was then to settle conflicts between a slave state and an abolitionist state, regarding the condition of the runaway slave who managed to cross the borders of the former to enter the territories of the latter, where he would find freedom. Property prevails over freedom.

The fugitive slave had to be returned; this was always for reasons of a fiscal nature:

> Whoever, subject to a fixed-term contract or to slavery in one of the States, according to the laws in force there, has taken refuge in another State, shall not, by virtue of any law or regulation in force there, be exempted from such bond, but shall, upon request, be returned to the party to whom the said bond is due.
>
> (Article 4 section II, c 3)

Historians believe that the drafters of the American Constitution were concerned with ensuring the repayment of the national debt and protecting property, which included slaves, as George Washington, James Madison and Thomas Jefferson, who, in turn, were slave owners, well knew (Berad, W 14). On the other hand, the American economy depended on slave labour: the South produced tobacco, sugar and cotton and exchanged them for manufactured goods produced in Northern factories.

In short, the problem of slavery, and its legitimacy, had arisen well before the War of Independence, and before the federal Constitution was drafted. Property protection and power sharing were vital issues on which the 13 states that had gained independence managed to compromise in Philadelphia.

The decision to free the slaves was only postponed. At the date set for 1808, the American states arrived divided. Slavery was declared illegal with the

13th and 14th Amendments, but the slave trade continued to flourish in the southern states for half a century. The problem was solved at least formally with the War of Secession.

The story was not over. A long theory of rulings by state courts, federal courts and the Supreme Court paved the difficult path to the effective abolition of slavery in the United States.

The Supreme Court played a leading role in the long march towards Black emancipation, but its attitude was not favourable to them from the beginning.

In *Plessy v Ferguson*, 163 US 537 (1896), the Court developed the argument that legitimised the segregation of Blacks (now freed) from whites, with the doctrine of 'separate but equal', which allowed for transportation for all, but separated Black passengers from white passengers by placing them in different carriages. Three years later, the principle was extended to public schools by the case *Cumming v Richmond County Board of Education*, 1175 US 528 (1899).

The problem of the legal status of Blacks was destined to drag on throughout the nineteenth century. Segregation formally ended in the mid-twentieth century with the case *Brown v Board of Education*, 347 US 483 (1954). Due to the resistance of the Southern states to abolish all discrimination, on 19 June 1964, the US Senate was forced to pass the Civil Rights Act, which radically repealed racial discrimination in America. Despite this, even today equality seems a mirage. The bloody events following the killing of George Floyd taught us that 'Black lives matter', but law enforcement does not behave in the same way with white people.

The American judiciary risks reflecting this discriminatory attitude towards Blacks in the application of algorithms to resolve legal issues. Extensive studies have shown that if mathematical formulas were used to answer questions put to judges, trying to divine the verdict on the basis of precedent, Blacks would be penalised in comparison to whites, since in the judicial record of all states, Blacks are the recipients of more serious sentences.

VI. COLONIES AND COLONIALISM

Similar problems confronted jurists with the treatment of the indigenous populations of the colonies. While slavery had already disappeared in Italy in the early nineteenth century, the question of the difference between citizens and natives of the colonies immediately arose when the country formed its first colony in Eritrea.

Legal texts dedicated to colonies distinguish 'civilised' from 'savages'.[29] The Civil Code for the Eritrean colony prepared by Vittorio Scialoja in 1908

[29] The entry Colonialism by Mondaini, (ed), *Enciclopedia Italiana* (Rome, Treccani, 1931) (now on the Treccani website, available at www.treccani.it is memorable; for the first details see the essays

distinguishes the capacity of colonists from that of the indigenous population, and forbids marriage between colonists and colonised people. The recognition of children born from relations between colonists and indigenous women is hindered; *mestizos* have no place in the system.

Equally significant is the story of the Libyan populations.

A veritable branch of law is dedicated to the legal problems opened up by the colonies, the colonial law,[30] at once an academic partition, a specialised subject of international law and administrative law, an imperialist frieze and cosmopolitan screen of a conquering action carried out with modest fortune; it is indeed a pathetic affair that characterises this period of national history, a 'colonial adventure' that shows its cracks even in the world of law.

Evidence of this is the treatment of the 'natives' in Libya.

In historical documents, in legal acts, in doctrinal elaborations, one speaks from time to time of the local population, of natives, or of Libyans; and this generically, throughout the entire period of colonisation.

Later the terminology changes, demonstrating an adjustment to the consolidation of institutions and thus of the status of individuals. But it will always be a deterrent status, polluted by racial or religious connotations. It should not be forgotten, in fact, that the changes in the Libyan framework are interconnected with the changes in the metropolitan framework: the advent of race legislation, in fact, demands differentiated but balanced treatment: in other words, Jews are discriminated against in Italy as in Libya; Muslims are discriminated against, compared to Italians, but are given a better status than Jews.

In the occupation phase, which dates from 1911 to 1919, in addition to the definition of relations with the Ottoman Empire, of which Libya was a province, the legislation prefigures the legal status of Libyans: they are defined as *Italian subjects.*

There are three criteria for the identification of natives: the place of birth; not holding Italian or other state citizenship; and descent from Italian subjects. A woman from a tribe not included in the colony acquires the status of Italian subject if she has married an Italian subject (Royal Decree 315 of 6 April 1913).[31]

Italian subjects are governed by their own personal status and enjoy civil and political rights 'in accordance with the laws that concern them' (Article 2).

With this apparently neutral formula, three conspicuous differentiations were made: the *status quo* in terms of social status was legitimised without the

published under the title 'L'Europa e gli "altri". Il diritto coloniale tra Otto e Novecento' in P Costa (ed), *Rivista Quaderni fiorentini*, XXXIII/XXXIV, 2004–2005; by Costa himself see the *Pagina introduttiva* (ibid 3ff). and 'Il fardello della civilizzazione. Metamorphosis of sovereignty in Italian colonial law' (ibid 169ff).

[30] A Vuoli, 'Il rapporto fra la metropoli e le colonie' in *Studi giuridici in onore di Santi Romano* vol III (Padua, Cedam, 1940) 267.

[31] See more extensively G Ambrosiani, 'Lo statuto dei nativi dell'Algeria e della Libia' in ibid 313.

conquest leading to the equalisation and levelling out of subjects; the pre-existing social order in the colony was maintained for political reasons of consensus and in order to invoke unrest, thus maintaining relations with the holders of tribal power. They were not put on an equal footing with Italian citizens, since they were not referred to the legislation of their homeland, but to the special laws, which properly concerned the subjects; they were granted civil and political rights to an extent that later doctrine would have considered excessive.[32] The status was closely connected with powers of self-determination and participation in councils, elective bodies with modest competences: they opted for simple consultative activities, and for this Italy was accused of impropriety in the application of the peace treaty with Turkey, signed in Lausanne in 1912.

The second phase, of consolidation of power in the colonies, which dates from 1919, is characterised by a more liberal attitude, certainly the result of the democratic ideas promoted by the American president Woodrow Wilson, but also of political calculation: the populations of the colony, stirred up by the rebels, were to be pacified with a few formal concessions. The Libyan statutes therefore reformed the system and introduced 'local Italian citizenship', a few years later called 'Libyan Italian citizenship'.

It differs from metropolitan citizenship in that it does not provide for compulsory conscription and does not subject the citizen to all the laws of the kingdom; it also the personal and inheritance status that for Muslims is a 'sacred constitution'.[33] In other words, the consecration of personal status legitimises existing social discrimination, but at the same time ensures Muslims the possibility of governing their persons, families and successions according to their beliefs, including the preservation of religion, language, principles and customs.[34]

In some provinces, there are special laws. For example, in Tripolitania, the Royal Decree of 1 June 1919 states that 'all citizens are equal before the law', citizens have their own representative bodies, elected councils have the ability to impose taxes, and competences in matters of public services; the 'local potentate' is also recognised.

The advent of the regime marks the beginning of the third phase, with the modification of electoral bodies. The authoritarian turn, sanctioned by Law no 1013 of 26 June 1927, abolishes parliaments and all other forms of autonomy; it preserves Libyan Italian citizenship, but takes a step backwards with regard to the principle of equality before the law: equality only concerns 'Libyan' Italian citizens, not Italian citizens *tout court*. The 1927 law also distinguishes Libyans according to their religion: Muslims are allowed to retain their personal and inheritance status, while Israelites retain only their personal status. The same

[32] ibid 314.
[33] ibid 320.
[34] Authors of the time linger on these aspects: see eg Catellani, *Le colonie e la Conferenza di Berlino* (Turin, UTET, 1885).

law suppressed some rights granted in 1919: the right to exercise free professions in Italy; freedom of the press and assembly; freedom of petition; the right to vote and stand for election.

The fourth, more distinctly fascist phase, heralded by the Duce's visit in March 1937, on which occasion he received the sword of Islam as a gift, as an act of submission and identity,[35] began with the Royal Decree of 9 January 1939.

From the point of view of public law, there is the incorporation of the four provinces (Tripoli, Misurata, Benghazi, Verna) into the metropolitan territory: this is the fourth shore of the Kingdom, while the condition of the Libyan Sahara remains unchanged. This entailed, in terms of legal status, the extension of the corporate union system to the four provinces; but not without discrimination, because 'the appropriate adaptations' were made, because, as Governor Italo Balbo would stress, *natura non facit saltus*.

Colonial public law became an industrious laboratory for jurists, who had to discriminate within categories that were already discriminated against, because the treatment of Libyans differed from that reserved for other colonial subjects, and the treatment of Jews differed from that reserved for them in their homeland.[36] The decree of 9 January 1939 therefore grants Libyans 'special' Italian citizenship; this is a privilege reserved for Muslim Libyans who have particular requisites of service and merit for Italy. Special citizenship guarantees certain fundamental rights, such as individual freedom, inviolability of home and property, and freedom to exercise professions.

Provision was also made to abolish the option of acquiring metropolitan citizenship: by changing their status, Libyans would have lost their personal and inheritance status, and therefore, say commentators of the time, 'the legislature wished to avoid this consequence, thus once again reaffirming its respect for the institutions to which Muslims are most jealously attached'.[37]

VII. PHYSIOGNOMY

Nature also dominates science, which, as far back as Aristotle, studies the physiological characteristics of man and associates them with ethical matters. The path is taken both in this direction and in the opposite direction, from the outside in. First, moral characters are drawn from somatic ones, then external characters are considered to correspond to given passions or spiritual

[35] G Mazzuca, *Mussolini and the Muslims. When Islam was Italy's friend* (Milan, Mondadori, 2017).

[36] M Nenna, *Principi di diritto coloniale* (Roma, Gangemi, 2011); L Martone, *Il diritto coloniale, voce dell'Enc. Treccani* (Roma, Treccani, 2012); among sources, see C Schanzer, L'acquisto delle Colonie. Diritto pubbico italiano (Roma, Loescher, 1912); and esp S Romano, *Corso di diritto coloniale* (Roma, Athenaeum, 1918).

[37] Ambrosiani (n 31) 544.

attitudes. The change occurred at the end of the eighteenth century, with the rise of the objective, positive sciences, thanks to JK Lavater's Physiognomische Fragmente of 1775–78 and GE Schulze's Psychische Anthropologie of 1819, but physiognomic science extended throughout the Middle Ages and the Renaissance.[38] Although it has been opposed by modern science, the idea that clues can be drawn from the face to define the moral status of the individual has persisted. It is one thing, however, to believe that the attitude of the face is one thing, and quite another to believe that the sign is the tell-tale of the ethos ('*cave signatos*').[39]

Even in our identity cards we indicate 'special signs': but these are signs that, through natural cause or accident, have come to rest on the face and constitute one of the criteria for recognition. Assuming a judgement from the way the individual presents himself is, however, a frequent, almost mechanical attitude. And on this aspect the anti-Semitic propaganda insisted a great deal to 'recognise the Jew', from the curly hair to the snub nose and similar nonsense.

[38] JC Lavater, GC Lichtenberg, *Lo specchio dell'anima. Pro e contro la fisiognomica, un dibattito settecentesco* (Padova, Cedam, 1991); C Righero, *Fisiognomica e alterità: dalla lettura del volto all' etica del dubbio* (Milano, Academia Press, 2014).

[39] L Corman, *Face and character. Initiation into morphopsychology* (Rome, Edizioni Mediterranee, 2003).

9

Discrimination and the Land Bond

I. THE PERSONALISTIC PRINCIPLE

'PERSONAL STATUS IS inherent in our moral individuality, like the blood flowing in our veins. It is joined to our being to such an extent that we cannot separate ourselves from it; it follows us everywhere like our shadow'. With these icastic words, François Laurent[1] described at the end of the nineteenth century a principle that we derive from Roman law and that has been passed down to us, going beyond the nineteenth and twentieth centuries. Belonging to a state today is called citizenship; under the Romans *status civitatis*: 'personal' law is one of the defining characteristics of a person, even if ordinary people perceive neither its existence nor its importance. Personal status implies that a person, wherever he may be, carries with him the rules that identify him as a human being, and as the holder of the personality rights that his system recognises.

Elsewhere in this work, we have insisted on the relationship between the individual and the land to which each of us is bound, voluntarily or only for reasons of age. In the past, the bond was even closer, often entrusted to rules that could not be waived.

In this case too, legal categories were formed slowly, as the bond with the land was established for reasons of social stability and for the protection of land ownership: whoever was born a *serf* was bound to the land, and could not leave it because he could not deprive the owner of his labour power. This subjection was also coloured by a religious content, since the servant, like other subjects, had to follow the religion of the prince. But it could happen that different cults were practised in the same region: the practice of the cult, together with social origin and status, were all distinctive factors linked to the land and the blood bond. Those who were able to move away from their land, to travel or to move elsewhere, took their personal status with them.

This situation took root with the Peace of Augsburg concluded on 25 September 1555 between Emperor Charles V and the German princes. The peace allowed the princes to choose their religious confession according to

[1] *International Civil Law* (Milan, Vallardi, 1880) I, 306.

conscience, with the obligation for their subjects to adopt the same religion, and if they did not want to abjure their faith, they had to leave the rule of the prince in whose religious choice they did not recognise themselves.

There are thus several factors that identify an individual, constituting the precipitate of a process in which several factors – historical, political, religious – contribute: personal status is linked to the *individual's origin*. And it is precisely on origin that Roman law insists to distinguish subjects. Origin is determined by the person of the father.[2]

Given the low mobility of individuals, due to economic reasons, personal security, personal ties, origin and domicile went by the wayside. They were usually national, and when a conflict arose between them, nationality, *civitas*, prevailed.[3] At the same time, whoever lived in a particular place had to observe its laws.

II. PILGRIMS, CRUSADERS, BEGGARS, TRAVELLERS, SERVANTS

The history of the Middle Ages is marked by multiple regulatory paths that shattered identities according to the position of an individual in relation to the country he crossed. Movement from one place to another was virtually unlimited because there were no borders as we know them today. Borders were only natural, rivers, lakes, mountains, while seas delimited regions, but were not an obstacle to be validated for those who had the possibility of travelling. There were no passports, only safe-conducts that allowed entry into cities.

Not everyone had the freedom of locomotion, ie to move from one place to another.

The serfs were bound to the lord's land, because they had to work it: to stray from it was to shirk their obligations. They were hereditary obligations: whoever was born a serf remained a serf for life, except for enfranchisement.

Those who were not servants could move around: knights and soldiers; merchants, who for the purchase and resale of goods moved freely from one place to another, reached fairs, settled in one place and could change it; clerics, to carry out their pastoral mission; doctors and judges, to carry out their profession, and so on.

Pilgrims travelled long routes to reach sanctuaries, or the centre of Christendom: roads built by Roman consuls and emperors branched off from Rome. Mercantile reasons had inaugurated the salt routes, religious motives had connected the major cities to centres of worship, such as Santiago de

[2] *Filius civitatem ex qua pater eius naturalem originem ducit, non domicilium sequitur*, 1, 6 § 1, Dig. Ad municip. (Fadda and Bensa, 'Notes and References to Italian Law' in B Windscheid, *Law of the Pandette, Translators' Notes to Volume I* IV (Turin, UET, 1930) 59, §35.

[3] P Costa, *Civitas. Storia della cittadinanza in Europa*, vols I–IV (Roma-Bari, Laterza, 1999).

Compostela, with its 'camino real'; religious, political and mercantile motives had promoted the Crusades.[4] People travelled on foot, like wayfarers, on horses or on mules and donkeys, like soldiers, nobles, clergymen and merchants, or in carriages, like ladies and old people.

He who had no particular reason to change places and yet set out wandering from one place to another without a fixed abode, was a poor man, a beggar. Since he only carried himself, he was not a source of profit, but if he was ever a burden or a risk to the populations where he happened to be, because of the infectious diseases he carried, the beggar was the object of limiting, penalising, discriminating rules. Only those belonging to a religious mendicant order were tolerated.

Legislation, entrusted to ordinances, by-laws, temporary measures, city statutes, distinguished the 'real' poor who could not support themselves, from the 'fake' poor, impostors, idlers, vagabonds, parasites, who were to be persecuted.

The former were taken care of by religious and secular institutions;[5] the latter by the criminal justice system.

The link with the land was thus closely linked to social role: identity was defined by provenance, and provenance was linked to status.

It is Bartolo da Sassoferrato who deals with the differences in treatment between the condemned, who are deprived of all civil rights, and therefore considered already 'dead' because they are confessed offenders, and the bandits, who were contumacious, and still endowed with the right to test. The legal capacity of the bandit 'varied not only according to the legislation of the communes or states to which he belonged, but also whether this legislation provided for it or not'.[6]

It may seem curious and surprising, but even today – in the face of free movement in our country and in European countries – in order to obtain residency in a given place, one has to go through a not simple administrative procedure, a complex bureaucratic rigmarole, due to the fact that residency in a given place implies the use of services, which are paid for by the local community, to which the person concerned reimburses taxes.

The bond of the land brings with it other bonds, or rather, other signs. Language, traditions, history and culture. These are all factors that make up the idea of nationhood.

[4] The theme is fascinating, complex and particularly significant for understanding relations between West and East: among the classics see S Runciman, *Storia delle Crociate* (Turin, Einaudi, 2014); for a revisiting of the historical account, F Cardini and A Musarra, *Il grande racconto delle Crociate* (Bologna, Il Mulino, 2019); C Tyerman, *Le guerre di Dio.Nuova storia delle Crociate* (Torino, Einaudi, 2017).

[5] M Mollat du Jordin, *I poveri nel Medioevo* (Roma-Bari, Laterza, 2001); C Albini, *Poveri e povertà nel Medioevo* (Roma, Carocci, 2016).

[6] R Trifone, *Le persone e le classi sociali nella storia del diritto italiano* (Naples, Jovene, 1931) 26ff. Lepers were also considered dead (ibid 29ff.).

III. NATION AND STATE, NATIONAL IDENTITY

Certainly the idea of nationhood is among the most ambiguous that can be conceived, and yet it is to the idea of nationhood that we owe the cementing of entire peoples, the apparent cause of revolution, upheaval, insurrection and the creation of new states.[7]

It is no coincidence that the Declaration of Human Rights of 1789 opens with the statement: 'The principle of all sovereignty resides essentially in the Nation. No body or individual can exercise authority which does not expressly emanate from it' (Article 3). The Nation here iunderstood as a true constitutional body is the source of power; the Nation replaces the divinity in the investiture of power.

Already therefore in the Enlightenment period and later with Romanticism, the Nation is drawn with the authority and colours of what is sublime, unquestionable, irrevocable. The relationship between the individual and the group, tending to encompass the collectivity, is very close: the individual is a component member of the Nation, he contributes to forming part of it and sharing its specific characters.

This is a crucial aspect in defining the idea of nationhood. Federico Chabod points out:

> To say sense of nationality is to say sense of historical individuality'. One arrives at the principle of nationhood as one arrives at affirming the principle of individuality, that is, affirming, against generalising and universalising tendencies, the principle of the particular, of the individual. For this reason, the idea of the nation arises and triumphs with the rise and triumph of that great movement of European culture known as Romanticism: sinking its first roots as early as the eighteenth century, precisely in the first precursors of the Romantic way of feeling and thinking, triumphing in full with the nineteenth century, when the sense of the individual dominates European thought.[8]

If talking about a nation means constructing an idea, a feeling, an image, this means that it is not only connected with the earth, but is populated with spiritual content. Chabod explains:

> The development of the idea of the nation thus goes hand in hand with the development of the poetics of feeling and imagination, which reacts to rationalistic schemes …; and it means, at one and the same time, the affirmation of a political idea, to which the future will fall, and of a criterion of historical evaluation, whereby history will appear, precisely, at the height of Romanticism, as the stage on which the nations will act, succeeding one another, from time to time, in carrying the torch of civilisation and in playing the part of first actor in human affairs. [It is in the

[7] C De Fiores, 'Le radici della nazione repubblicana. Fondamenti teorici e profili costituzionali' (2019) 1 *Costituzionalismo.it*.

[8] F Chabod, *L'idea di nazione* (Roma-Bari, Laterza, 1998) 17.

> discovery of this national soul that the great novelty of the idea of the nation in the late 18th and nineteenth centuries consists; it is in the recognition of the indelible moral and spiritual peculiarities of each people that the fruit of the pre-Romantic and Romantic experience lies.[9]

However, the idea of nation, constructed in the eighteenth century, is marginal in Enlightenment thought, which is cosmopolitan by nature. It became strong with the birth of unitary states, and in the nineteenth century, with the distinction between state and nation, one tending to appropriate the other and the other to evade the former.

Constructing nation-states therefore requires constructing the notion of state and the notion of nation. Each geopolitical area has its own conception of the one and the other, depending on whether the state wants to incorporate one or more nations, and whether a nation wants to transcend state borders or distinguish itself from other nations within the same state borders. PS Mancini had defined the state as the 'legal order of the nation'.

But the problems are many: the Industrial Revolution causes urbanism, impoverishes and depopulates local communities, creates masses in need of identity and integration.

Geographical configuration is therefore not enough to build the nation; culture, traditions and a sense of belonging are needed.[10]

[9] ibid 21.

[10] G Mazzini, *Dell'unità italiana*, in *Scritti editi ed inediti*, III (Imola, Galeati, 1906); PS Mancini, *Della nazionalità come fondamento del diritto delle genti* (1885) in *Diritto internazionale. Prelezioni* (Napoli, Jovene, 1879); F Ruffini, *Il principio di nazionalità in G. Mazzini e in P. S. Mancini* (Milano, SEI, 1917); V Gioberti, *Della nazionalità italiana* (Livorno, Berlinghieri, 1847); already in *Il gesuita moderno*, V (*Documenti*), no 30; G Pisanelli, *Lo stato e la nazionalità* (Napoli, Università di Napoli, 1862); A Gemelli, *Principio di nazionalità e amor di patria nella dottrina cattolica*, 3rd edn (Turin, 1918); F Meinecke, *Cosmopolitismo e Stato nazionale* (1907) (It trans, Firenze, La Nuova Italia, 1975) vol 2; S Panunzio, *Popolo, Nazione, Stato* (Florence, La Nuova Italia, 1933).

10

Registry Identity

I. THE SURNAME: BIRTH OF A SIGN OF DISTINCTION

ACCORDING TO HISTORIANS, the use of the surname, in the modern sense, as connoting a person with a family name, originated in the early Middle Ages. These were usages dictated by the management of acquired power – as in the case of aristocrats – or by the need to distinguish individuals bearing the same pre-name, normally chosen on the basis of the names of saints marked on the calendar. In practice, cases of homonymy were frequent, and to distinguish individuals one had to resort to nicknames, either connected to physical features, derived from the places where they lived or assigned to their family. Nicknames, physical features, or even the trade exercised tended to become consolidated over time and thus became the family name[1] and passed on to descendants. Hence also the appearance on public deeds, parish registers, tax collectors' registers, of a name accompanying the first name; in common parlance, this family name is called the *surname*.

Almost everywhere, the formation of the surname takes place by tradition; customs are the essential legal source for the attribution and transmission of the surname. As a rule, the transmission is patrilineal, but there are states or regions, such as Spain and Portugal and their colonies, where the maternal surname is indicated alongside the paternal surname. In the succession of degrees, the double surname is always chosen with regard to the paternal surname of the father and mother.

In legal language, a surname is called a first *name*, and the term we colloquially call a first name (or given name) is called a *prename*.

The right to a name is also born from uses: the legal system provides remedies for the defence of the name from usurpations, from undue use, from the competitive or derogatory use that others make of it. The juridical construction of the right to a name is rather late, and the juridical construction of the category to which the right to a name belongs – personality rights – was only born between the end of the nineteenth century and the beginning of the twentieth century.

[1] A Lefebvre-Teillard, *Le nom: droit et histoire* (Paris, PUF, 1990) 21–27, 29, 33.

There is a connection between first name and family name, such that the son does not bear his father's first name but a different one, often his grandfather's first name, thus skipping a generation.

As a family name, for natural children, born out of wedlock, until the Napoleonic Code of 1804, both customary and canonical rules protected the child and gave him the name (colloquially, the surname) of his father if he was known.

In addition to being closely connected to family ties, the name is linked to the land (*nom de seigneurie*) (p.75); for nobles, the name of the land is maintained even if the fief is lost. Alongside the name for nobles is the noble title and the signs of nobility, the 'arms', which the meticulous and complex science of heraldry provides for.

However, each region, city or state follows its own traditions. Hence the impossibility of dictating a uniform naming discipline.

Scholars of anthroponomy explain the different traditions.

In Italy, as early as the twelfth century, a connotation derived from the family, the *consorteria*, the corporation to which it belonged was added to the proper name.[2] Names are used to distinguish individuals, for the allocation of land and their registration in the land register, in the survey for the census, or for military conscription, or to banish an individual from society. Bartolo, Baldo, Rolandino are the medieval jurists who explain the rules applied to the name, to meet the requirements of civil law and canon law. The core of the discipline is always family membership, whether of low or high lineage.

The different connotations of an individual are bound together. The right to the name is protected together with the coat of arms, the seal, the family tree. If the name originates from tradition, the right to the name is shaped by the intervention of jurists; this fundamental characteristic of the individual tends to become a sort of cage that the person carries: the right to the name is imprescriptible and inalienable. Over the centuries, the name loses its connection with territorial origin and is handed down for other reasons, which are connected with the status held[3] and matrilineal descent.[4] However, the territorial origin may emerge not only from the name of the territory, but also from the onomastics typical of the regions in which the person was born. The name is a clue to phenomena of immigration, repopulation, transfer: think of the Albanian names in Calabria or the Lombard names throughout the South or the proper names of the inhabitants of Monferrato found in Sicily.[5]

It also happens that there are curious juxtapositions of surname and first name: in Corsica, after Pasquale Paoli's revolution, the short-lived independence

[2] F Spagnesi, *Person, noble dimension, name* (Pisa, ETS, 2018) 145.
[3] R Bizzocchi, *I cognomi degli italiani. Una storia di mille anni* (Roma-Bari, Laterza, 2014) 259.
[4] ibid 45.
[5] ibid 249.

and the subjugation to France – changes that took place at the end of the 1860s – many inhabitants kept their Genoese and Pisan surnames alongside a French first name.

The research of scholars of surnames go back as far as the Middle Ages, mainly analysing notarial documents, phonetic variants, transcription errors, and often multiple expressions to identify the same individual.

Transmission to descendants ensures the continuity of the name. The name is constant, but in a context in which there is not yet an administrative organisation aimed at registering names, it is possible to change it by one's own will. Since immutability is a guarantee of the certainty and stability of legal ties, it was precisely in the Middle Ages that rules began to be introduced to prevent name changes, which debtors resorted to fraudulently in order to escape their creditors, criminals to evade official orders and bans, and serfs to shake off the bond with the land that prevented them from freedom of movement. Since the Justinian Code did not set insuperable limits (*De mutatione nominis*, 9.25), it was mainly the municipal statutes that laid down restrictions.

The aggregation of families into groups served to increase their power; so that the heads of families could lose their original surnames to take on that of the most powerful family. And the authorities could also assign a surname coercively: as was the case with the grouping of noble Genoese families into *hotels* reorganised by Andrea Doria in 1528. The assignment of a name therefore also served to distinguish the noble from the commoner, the master from the servant.

The registration of individuals existing in the territory at a given time fulfils public and social needs. The authority makes use of it to train its militia, but above all for tax reasons. However, the owner who frees the servant is exempt from the relevant tax.[6]

The name is also a sign of wealth: the commoner, who is part of the indistinct mass, uses only the pre-name, the merchant the name of his place of origin,[7] the nobleman uses as predicate the name of the land of which he is feudal lord.

The name often suffers the fate of families, disrupted by events beyond the individual's control, as happens with plagues that cause the death of millions of people, their relocation to areas unaffected by the disease, and their aggregation into other families. It often characterises families that took refuge in hospitable regions because they were persecuted for religious reasons, as is the case with the French names still possessed by the descendants of the Waldensians, who fled to Piedmont's valleys to escape the Provençal persecutions of the Middle Ages, and likewise for the Albanians in Calabria and Sicily.

[6] Bizzocchi (n 3) 61.

[7] The fortunes of the surnames of 14th–18th century Italian merchants in Polish anthroponymy. In the extensive literature on surnames see M Alinei and F Benozzo, *Dizionario etimologico-sematico dei cognomi itaiani* (Savona, Pendragon, 2017).

Noble marriages led to the accumulation of several surnames. Sometimes these names became extinct due to women becoming nuns or the destination of male children to religious or military life.

The history of names changed radically with the preparation of parish registers decided by decrees approved by the Council of Trent in 1563 and with the demographic, cadastral and fiscal organisation prepared by the civil authorities. The latter also included believers of religions other than Catholic, for whom there was no provision for registration in the parish registers where baptisms and marriages were recorded. The *Rituale romanum* of 1614 introduced the registration of confirmation, communion, extreme unction and then deaths: the registers 'of souls' documented the imparting of the sacraments and thus made it possible to monitor the observance of the religious precepts of each believer.[8]

Registers were not carefully kept. It was not until the eighteenth century that surnames were more rigorously recorded in civil registers; property, the first source of wealth, favoured the scriptural technique of the taxman, the land registry, the definition of boundaries and the presumed calculation of incomes. In the nineteenth century, laws took over this registry function, but the transmission of names continued to be the result – and will continue to be so – of customary rules.

In short, since the Middle Ages, names have been formed in a completely free and erratic manner; however, once formed, names become unchangeable and their embedding lasts for centuries. Scholars describe this long process in a series of measures of the civil and ecclesiastical authorities in the last three centuries of the *Ancien Régime*:[9] parish priests, notaries, civil servants all contribute to forming this enormous mass of data.

As mentioned above, even before the Council of Trent, civil authorities had begun to register individuals existing in the territory. With the French Revolution, this function became essentially public. Registers and thus civil status records belong to the state.

During the debate on the Civil Code before the Tribunate, Siméon recognised the diligence of parish priests in compiling the registers now appropriated by the civil authority:

> The revolution found the civil status registers in the hands of the curates. It was quite natural that the same individuals from whom one went to ask for blessings and prayers at the time of birth, marriage, and death, should note the dates, and draw

[8] R Trifone, *Le persone e le classi sociali nella storia del diritto Italiano* (Napoli, Jovene, 1939) 42ff explains that Emanuele Filiberto obliged court secretaries and parish priests to keep birth registers; civil registers, introduced by the Revolutionary Constituent Assembly, were then definitively imposed by the Napoleonic Civil Code in Art 34ff.; with the Restoration, the registers returned to the parish priests (ibid 43).

[9] ibid 90ff.

> up the minutes ... It must be confessed that they were well and faithfully kept by individuals, whose ministry required instruction and scrupulous probity.

At the end of the eighteenth century, however, secularisation was not yet complete. Louis XVI himself, in 1787, by restoring civil rights to Protestants, wanted to reaffirm the pre-eminence of the Catholic religion to which alone were reserved the rights and honours of public worship. In commenting on the historical development of civil status acts François Laurent, a professor at the University of Ghent and one of the best-known commentators on the Civil Code, emphasises how the intolerance of French Catholics was such that Louis XVI's edict was harshly opposed when it appeared. So much so that the liberating force of the Revolution invested even the acts of the civil state in the name of the principle of equality. 'The citizen,' said Muraire, 'belongs to the fatherland, independently of any religion' (L II 9). The intervention of the civil authority, however, did not limit the expression of worship by citizens, who could continue to celebrate baptisms, confirmations, communions, marriages and extreme unction without any restrictions (L 12).

We owe to Le Chapelier, one of the most famous deputies of the National Assembly, the new formulation of the rules on the names of French citizens, resulting from the abolition of the three states, and in particular the abolition of the nobility, coats of arms and all aristocratic symbols. Indeed, the law of 23 July 1790 proposed by Le Chapelier states in Article 1 that 'aucun citoyen ne pourra prende que le vrai nom de sa famille'.

'The true name of his family' is an equivocal formula to which jurists try to give an unambiguous meaning: family name is the name attributed to the head of the family, by custom and patrilineal descent; the 'truth' of the name implies that the name has not been altered or obscured by the noble predicate.

The 'real family name' was linked to geographical origin, but many kept their acquired name, such as the La Fayette or Mirabeau families.[10] As uncertainties persisted, in 1792 the Convention was forced to order the compilation of a register of names, ie to establish the 'civil status' in which 'heretics', ie the Cathars, Waldensians, Albigensians, and followers of Pierre de Bruys, could finally be registered.[11] The law of 14 November 1793 completes the discipline by leaving people free to choose their own first name; the following year, the Convention intervenes again, stipulating that everyone must bear the name assigned to them in the birth certificate. These rules are reproduced by Napoleon in the Civil Code which, wishing to regulate the rights and duties of citizens, cannot fail to deal with civil status records (Tit II L I); these are public registers subject to administrative rules issued by the local authority, ie the mayor. Special laws followed over the years concerning foreign Jews who settled in the territories of

[10] ibid 250.
[11] ibid 25.

the republic and were obliged to accompany their pre-name with a surname if they did not have one (Imperial Decree 20 July 1808);[12] to avoid confusion, it was stipulated that the surname could not be taken from the Old Testament or the town of origin. However, this prescription is not respected: many French Jewish surnames are derived from the Bible and many from the region from which the family came.

Toullier speaks of the right to a name when describing the ways of acquiring property, commenting on Napoleon's Code civil (sixth edition). In a society in which the entire system revolves around the right to property – the 'terrible right' according to the revolutionary connotation – even a person's name is part of the ownership universe. The name becomes both an object of 'ownership' of the individual and also a tool used by the police.

In the nineteenth century, it was jurisprudence that set the rules on the recognition of the name assigned by custom to an individual. And the rule followed by the French courts does not entrust proof to testimony, nor to notarial documents, but to the signature: only the signing of a deed, expressing its formation and its authenticity, can establish whether the name the individual bears is the 'true' one (LT 146).

In Italy, the regulation of civil status records follows Napoleon's conquests: the Civil Code, translated into Italian following the proclamation of the Viceroyalty of Italy in 1806, stipulates that the birth must be reported within three days of the birth: the birth record must indicate the day, time and place of the birth, the sex of the child and the names given, the names, surnames, occupation and domicile of the father and mother, and that of the witnesses (Article 57). For foundlings, the choice of name and surname is up to the person who found them (Article 58). The father's surname is in any case that derived from custom; customary rules are therefore followed.

After the fall of Napoleon, surname identification in the pre-unification states followed different rules.

The first Italian Civil Code makes no mention of the discipline of the name.

Orphans who had no known family connection received their names from the person who found them, or from the registrar, or from the parish priest. Fancy in the choice of an orphan's surname is one of the curiosities of anthroponomy studies. It often reveals a malevolent attitude aimed at perpetuating the dark origins of the unfortunates, on whom ignominious surnames are imposed. There are names that reproduce the name of the institution where the foundlings were taken in, names typical of a locality, names that allude to geographical origin, names that reflect the condition of the foundling, and so on.

[12] This was not the case with Italian Jews, whose family names refer to the towns where they lived or from which they arrived in Italy.

II. VICISSITUDES OF THE SURNAME

The situation described above remained unchanged for almost two centuries. It is no longer the effect of secularisation, but of the rights of liberty, in particular the principle of equality between men and women, that drives state legislators to change the millenary tradition entrusted to custom and to alter the attribution of the surname.

France is once again the leading experience.

In 2002, Law No 2002-304 of 4 March, which came into force on 5 March 2005, introduced the principle that the family name, ie the surname, can be chosen by the parents when registering the birth from among three possible options: either the father's surname, or the mother's surname, or the association of the two surnames; the double surname is not transmissible per se, however; the prohibition is imposed for practical reasons, the aggregation of many surnames that drag on from one generation to the next would lead to inefficiency and inconvenience.

In Italy, a similar text has only been approved by the Chamber of Deputies, so the parliamentary process is awaiting completion. The text would resolve once and for all the issue of the surname, which, entrusted to tradition, perpetuates a past insensitive to the principle of gender equality.

It is precisely in accordance with this principle that the right of the child to keep its mother's surname has been established in case law. The Constitutional Court has ruled that at the time of birth parents may register their child with a double surname, giving precedence to the paternal surname; if there is no agreement, the traditional rule is followed.[13] And the Court of Cassation has ruled that in special situations, a child who has developed his personality in a milieu where he is known by his mother's surname may keep it, if he is interested, if that surname was given to him first; he is therefore not obliged to add his father's surname to it, provided that the father recognised it after the mother.[14]

From the moment of registration, the name – consisting of first name and surname – can no longer be changed. As seen above, surname-isation was the result of the requalification of the individual: the individual is no longer an amorphous monad in the anonymous crowd, but has his own personality expressed by his name. The name is a sign of freedom: it is no coincidence that the Italian Constitution, like other constitutional texts, recognises in the name an essential connotation of the person, and protects the name as a fundamental right together with legal capacity (Article 22). This is to avoid the horrors of the past: the exchange of a name for a number in concentration camps, its substitution if of foreign origin. We must not forget that in Italy, even the name has been

[13] Judgment of 21 December 2016 No 286.
[14] Order of 2017 No 17139.

the subject of troubled legislation, due to the racial laws and a distorted use of the principle of nationality.

With the acquisition of the provinces of Trieste and Gorizia, Dalmatia and Istria, the 'Italianisation' of the surname was imposed on the new citizens in the years following the First World War.

III. SURNAMES IN EUROPE

It has already been said that the French legal system, by the accidents of history, has been a guide to the discipline of the name in Italy, subject of course to local traditions.

The Austrian General Civil Code of 1811 deferred to the legislature the power to establish the acquisition and transmission of the surname; in 1816 the provision applied to the Italian provinces. The choice obviously intertwined the regulation of the name with that of family relations. With regard to the powers exercised by parents over their children, § 146 in fact provides that 'the children shall take on the surname and coats of arms of their father, and participate in all other rights of the family and the father's status, which are not merely personal'. The surname could be changed if certain conditions were met.[15]

In Great Britain, regulation of the surname follows rules that are partly similar to those of the two models examined. Here, the situation reflects its political history, which brings with it different legal rules in England, Scotland, Wales and Ireland in which very pronounced local traditions have been preserved, to which the autonomy of the Isle of Man is added; the different religions practised on the islands have influenced these traditions. The appearance of surnames also dates back to the Middle Ages; the urbanisation caused by the first Industrial Revolution, in the second half of the eighteenth century, led to a mixture of surnames, especially in the big cities.

English historians emphasise the difficulties encountered in researching the origins of surnames, the variety of which is down to the diversity of languages and dialects spoken in the various regions, the movements of populations, epidemics that caused the disappearance of already established surnames, and the concentration of surnames in the Lancashire or Yorkshire countryside.

It is interesting to note, however, that even in these islands the origin of surnames has the same characteristics as on the Continent: surnames derive from pre-names, from the occupations they perform, from nicknames, from localities, or from family relationships. The variety of surnames increased with trade, and with sojourns in other countries such as Normandy, Flanders and the Netherlands, from which the English returned with modified or newly created

[15] See the circular of 1 July 1826.

surnames; and given the close relations with France, including central and southern France, surnames of French importation were very frequent. In addition to political upheavals and trade relations, religious persecution also played its part. What makes this interesting is that civil registers flanked parish registers much earlier than on the continent: surnames were recorded in the Public Record Office, which replaced the notarial records from which surnames were usually extracted in searches on the continent. Foreigners were issued a 'letter' identifying them with their denounced name (*letter of denunciation*); surnames were noted on patent rolls (*rotuli litterarum patentiae*) as early as 1201. Obviously, censuses and land surveys also helped to fix the surnames of the inhabitants.

Typical local surnames make it possible to observe mass movements to and from Ireland or Scotland, although the Anglicisation of Gaelic surnames over the centuries tends to obscure these transitions. In the counties, the proportions of surname categories also vary from time to time determined by location, trades practised, nicknames, and so on: historical research indicates that in Lancashire toponyms prevail, in Shropshire nicknames prevail, in Surrey occupations prevail.[16]

Surname inheritance began around the year 1000: after the Battle of Hastings in 1066, the Norman nobles brought their names and titles to the conquered island. Hence the confirmation that surnames are linked to the status held, and the land owned, both carefully recorded for dynastic, hereditary and tax reasons. The serfs did not have a surname – they had no reason to register it, they were not part of documentary acts – so that in the lower classes surnames tend to be perpetuated from 1350 until the sixteenth century.

The late adoption of the surname affects entire countries, such as Wales, where it did not appear until after the sixteenth century, and presents constants in the diction or registration, such as the final 's', indicating the derivation from a family, or the final 'son' that is a suffix of the pre-name. Surnames beginning with 'Mac' became widespread in Scotland, connoting membership of a clan, also identified through the colours of the flag reproduced in coats of arms and robes.

Many names are derived from Latin, as Latin was the official language in which documents were formed.

Women only acquired their husband's name from the sixteenth century onwards.

Noble titles, followed by the predicate connected with the land owned or administered, are closely connected with the discipline of land ownership, coats of arms with the heraldic rules that originated with the patents of nobility.

In Germany, too, the origin of surnames does not differ from the deep-rooted traditions in other continental European countries.

[16] J Moss, *Great British Family Names and Their History* (London, Pen and Sword History, 2019).

IV. THE SURNAMES OF THE JEWS

Persecuted for centuries in most European states – bearers of a millennial history of restrictions and deprivation, deportations and migrations (the *Story of the Wandering Jew*[17] is symptomatic in this regard) – even in the regulation of surnames, the Jews are subject to prescriptions and directives. Each state provides its own, and it varies from country to country. Unlike other religions, the Jews are subject to a special discipline, which follows their condition through the centuries. Being forced to live in cramped quarters, and since the sixteenth century obliged to live in ghettos, they did not need special signs to recognise themselves, so that many did not have a patronymic. It was only with the establishment of civil registers that Jews were also obliged to add a surname (and thus the family name) to their pre-name. Hence the use of 'speaking' names, ie names that for various reasons make it possible to trace their origin because they are transmitted from family to family, following the customs of the states in which they live or move. The surname is transmitted by paternal line, while membership of the Jewish religion is transmitted by maternal line. The recurrence of particular names does not exclude coincidence with Christian names, so that the name alone is not a sure indication that a particular person belongs to the Jewish religion. Historians have documented the fallacy of the thesis of Samuele Schaerf, who in 1925 wrote a book listing the names of Italian Jews.[18] That book became one of the tools used by the Nazis and Fascists to search for Jews who had gone into hiding to escape persecution and to send them to extermination camps.[19]

Many Jewish names derive from place names, as, moreover – as has been said – happens with the names of Christians. Others derive from patronymics turned into surnames, and still others reproduce physical, moral or intellectual characteristics, as has been seen to be the case with many surnames. Only surnames that reflect liturgical offices can be considered typically Jewish.

In the uncertainty of identifying Jews by the surname they bore, the racial laws did not miss the opportunity to dictate rules on the matter: the law of 13 July 1939 ordered Jews who had changed their name to take back their original name, and non-Jewish Italian citizens who had a name similar to a Jewish name were allowed to change their name, subject to proof of their 'Aryan-ness' (l. 13 July 1939, no 1055, l. 28 September 1940, no 1459).[20]

[17] Bizzocchi (n 3) ch 42 written by L Luzzati.

[18] Luzzati (ibid) 499; and see G Resta and V Zeno-Zencovich, *Le leggi razziali.Passato/presente* (Rome, RomaTrePress, 2015) 77ff.

[19] For the publishing house Israel, Florence, 1925.

[20] For further study see G Resta, *I nomi ebraici e le leggi razziali: modelli a confronto* (Rome, RomaGTrePress, 2019); and the proceedings of the conference of Italia Judaica, on *Gli ebrei in Italia dalla segregazione alla emancipazione*, Tel Aviv, 1986 and Rome, 1989.

V. SIGNS, COATS OF ARMS, DOCUMENTS

Until a centralised system for registering individuals was established in the various states, when individuals were pulled out of the crowd so that an 'identity' could be assigned to them, the criteria for identifying a person were very limited. The first and simplest was the portrait. Portraits by painters of distinction were reserved for the higher social categories. For the other categories, the portrait, or a sketch, was used to satisfy public interests, and was used by the person concerned for travel; it was also used by the public force to track down wanted persons, to signal dangerous individuals; portraits had an infamous representation for the populace: the drawn effigy had repugnant or threatening expressions to arouse reactions of horror and fear.

Since better image reproduction systems were not available, the individual would add the name, and, if available, the family coat of arms and arms, to the portrait.[21]

To authenticate a writing, a seal (with family arms or initials) was used in addition to the signature. Depending on the function of the deed, either the seal of the person making the declaration or referred to in the writing (eg in a will) was affixed, or the seal of the person who had formed the document, usually the seal of the notary for private deeds, or that of the authority for travel documents. The seal reproduced the coat of arms impressed on the sealing wax, in different colours.

In the fourteenth and fifteenth centuries, trademarks also began to be used to authenticate the origin or quality of a product. Among jurists, Bartolo da Sassoferrato excels in his treatment of signs. In his *De insigniis et armis* he is the first to illustrate, with his usual acuity, the function of these distinctive signs and their discipline.[22]

Bartolo specifies that anyone could bear a coat of arms and use it for identification purposes. The use granted by the sovereign could be enjoyed in perpetuity by descendants. The 'coat of arms' could depict simple colours, bands, quarters, geometric designs, animals, fruit, flowers, tools, and anything that alluded to the surname it was intended to represent; in this case, the coat of arms depicted an 'enterprise'.

The marks that were connected to an individual could also consist of badges used to identify couriers, guards, office-holders.[23] These badges were used to enter and leave towns; they were also issued to provide proof of payment of tolls upon entry or transit, to transport goods, to confirm the authenticity of travel documents. They also marked individuals as belonging to special

[21] V Groebner, *Storia dell'identità personale e della sua certificazione* (Bellinzona, Casagrande, 2008) 40ff.

[22] Reprinted by Hoepli, Milan, 1998.

[23] Groebner (n 21) 47.

categories, such as pilgrims, beggars, the needy, and members of confraternities. They were also worn on clothing. Sometimes it was compulsory to wear them: men were required to wear a yellow badge and usually a pointed hat, while women were required to wear different types of clothing or hair styles.[24]

The coat of arms was not separate from the portrait, and served to make an individual recognisable by providing the recipient with several distinctive signs. The coat of arms followed the individual from the cradle to the grave: this is how one can 'read' the splendid floor of St John's Cathedral in Malta, made up of the Knights' sumptuous tombstones from the various regional lodges in which those who had been admitted to the Order as noblemen were grouped.[25]

Although the coat of arms was not necessarily a sign of nobility, it was mainly used in battle and in the uniforms of knights, and soldiers in general, in flags and banners, in arms in the proper sense, both to display the noble title and to be recognised, the face being covered by the helmet.

Marks on the body – initials, cuts and scars, mutilations, writing on the skin – were also widespread. 'The body was the physical seat of the Self.'[26] The body is at the same time the personification of the individual, the embodiment of his soul and intellect, as taught by scholars of physiognomy and great physicians such as Vesalius.[27]

Yes, the signs of the body can be an instrument of communication, persecution, investigation of feelings, and so on. The integrity of the body takes on symbolic significance in the connection between the physical figure and its mystical transfiguration. The skin was memory.[28] It was also the sign of belonging to a religious belief, in the fourteenth and fifteenth centuries. Or the sign of ownership, where slavery was permitted.[29]

In addition to the marks on the body, clothes, weapons and so on, the identification of the person is done later with personal documents.

The history of the identification document traces this technique back to centuries closer to us, starting in the sixteenth century. They are always travel documents, tax documents, religious documents. They presuppose that the bearer and the addressee know how to read, and are based on a primordial

[24] The literature on the subject is vast:A Borst, *Forme di vita nel Medioevo* (Naples,Guida, 1988); N Guglielmi, *Il Medioevo degli ultini.Emarginazione e marginalità nei secoli XI–XIV* (Naples, Città Nuova, 2001); on the suntary laws see F Boldrini, *Per la storia delle leggi suntuarie in Italia nei secoli XV–XVI. Il Tractatus de ornatu mulierum di Orfeo Cancellieri* (Milano, Monduzzi, 2019).

[25] The literature is vast: C Donati, *L'idea di nobiltà in Italia: secoli XIV–XVIII* (Roma-Bari, Laterza, 1995); F Cardini, *Il guerriero e il cavaliere. L'uomo medievale* (Roma-Bari, Laterza, 2001); F Cardini, *Alle origini della cavalleria medievale* (Bologna, Il Mulino, 2014).

[26] Groebner (n 21) 93.

[27] On physiognomy see below; M Bragagnolo, 'Fisiognomic e profezia nel pensiero giuridico tra Cinque e Seicento' (2018) 21 *Laboratoire Italien.*

[28] Groebner (n 21) 101.

[29] ibid 108.

local or central organisation, which issues them in canonical formulas, possibly asseverated by a seal certifying their authenticity.[30]

The identity document comes long after the other identifying marks. But it carries with it, as an onerous burden, this symbolic history: it is a pass-pass, a safe-conduct, a passport, almost a password often associated with the payment of sums of money, of tips, of payments and has nothing to do with the commercial documents, invented more or less in the same period, Renaissance or seventeenth century, such as the bill of lading, the letter of exchange and similar.[31]

[30] ibid 207.

[31] G Melis, *Documenti per la storia economica dei secoli XIII–XVI* (Florence, Olschki, 1972); V Piergiovanni, *Norme, scienza e pratica giuridica tra Genova e l'Occidente medievale e moderno* (Genoa, ECIG, 2003).

11

The Subject of Law

I. THE GEOMETRY OF CONCEPTS

IN THE NINETEENTH century, an era in which legal analysis was populated with abstract concepts by their very nature, and subtle distinctions were gradually refined by the culture handed down from studies of Roman law, a number of questions arose, dictated by the rigour of legal logic: since man cannot be the object of rights, how can one justify the exercise of a right over the body, the name, the image? And again, when we speak of the rights of the person, are we talking about a multiplicity of distinct rights or a single right with many representations?

It was the German science of the second half of the century that took on the task of resolving these questions, but both raised debates and polemics, which did not lead to clear solutions; in the different legal systems there are varied answers, sometimes reflected in legal provisions, other times created by case law.

Usually one describes this path with three terms hat represent the crescendo of rights that accumulate on the person: *from the individual*, considered as an anonymous monad within a collectivity to the *subject of law*, holder of certain essential rights, to the *person* understood as the individual endowed with guarantees and recognitions, prerogatives and fundamental rights, irrepressible, imprescriptible, inalienable.

It is a useful itinerary, didactically effective because it plumbs historical periods constructed in such a way that the path is a progressive expansion of the role that the individual acquires within society. But it is one thing to recognise rights, quite another to use the terminology of legal language, which uses concepts developed with the aid of technology.

In other words, that path is more complex than how it is represented succinctly and simply.

As we have seen, the term *persona* was already used by Gaius, in the second century AD, but its meaning is quite different from the one it has today, when we speak of it as the terminal landing place of a journey that has lasted two millennia. It has already been said that persona was the mask, that is, it was the way in which the individual was portrayed in the world of law; but that mask included both freemen and freedmen and slaves, the father of the family, the wife-mother, and the children of full age and underage; each of these had a role and therefore rights and duties, in a spectrum that went from a maximum dimension – the rights of the *pater familias* – to a minimum dimension – the rights of the slave.

The rights of the person are thus the rights granted to the individual in correlation with his role. *Personal rights are* the rights that are instituted between persons, whereas rights *over things* are the rights that are instituted between a person and a thing. If the slave is regarded as a person *dimidiate*, and Gaius even speaks of it as a 'thing',[1] this means that the expression 'person' was initially not clearly defined in the rational universe, but had an eminently practical meaning. Its meaning was gradually refined when the concepts used by the great jurists of the Classical and Byzantine eras, ie in the centuries following the second century AD, were refined. And, as historians tell us, since when the legal notion of person has used Christian theological terminology. The whole problematic of the 'person' referring to the divinity, to the Trinity, originated with Tertullian shortly after Gaius, and was then elaborated by Augustine, Thomas Aquinas, and then received more in-depth analysis during the Middle Ages, until it exploded in the Renaissance. The anthropocentric conception of the universe that ousts the theocentric one exalts the difference between man, in flesh and blood, in his materiality and individuality linked to his earthly life, and person, who continues to be the mask imposed by law on the individual.

In the centuries that followed, the separation between philosophical and legal thought was consummated. The philosophical path of the individual/person binomial is quite intriguing. Studies of the history of philosophy give us wonderful frescoes painted by Hobbes, Locke, Spinoza, Leibnitz, Kant, Hegel and Marx. Likewise, in the nineteenth century, studies of sociology, anthropology, psychology. But while scholars from other disciplines ventured into the terrain of law, it rarely happened that jurists appropriated the categories and experiences of philosophers and other social scientists.

In order to understand the way in which law views man as a subject of law and then as a person in the modern sense, one must go back to the roots of normative concepts and formulae as created and transmitted by legal culture.[2]

[1] A Schiavone, *At the Origins of Bourgeois Law. Hegel v. Savigny* (Roma-Bari, Laterza, 1984).

[2] In the United States, there is debate as to whether law can be considered a cultural factor: PS Berman, *The Enduring Connections Between Law and Culture: Reviewing Lawrence Rosen, Law as Culture, and Oscar Chase, Law, Culture, and Ritual* (2009) 57 *American Journal of Comparative Law* 101 and more generally, N Irti, *La cultura del diritto civile* (Torino, Giappichelli, 1990); P Grossi, *Il diritto in una società che cambia* (Bologna, Il Mulino, 2017); P Grossi, *L'ordine giuridico medievale* (Roma-Bari, Laterza, 2006); P Grossi, *Prima lezione di diritto* (Roma-Bari, Laterza, 2003); P Grossi, *Ritorno al diritto* (Roma-Bari, Laterza, 2015); P Grossi, *L'Europa del diritto* (Roma-Bari, Laterza, 2007); P Grossi, *L'invenzione del diritto* (Roma-Bari, Laterza, 2017); MR Ferrarese, *Diritto sconfinato. Legal inventiveness and spaces in the global world* (Roma-Bari, Laterza, 2006) 24ff; MR Ferrarese, *Le istituzioni della globalizzazione. Diritto e diritti nella società transnazionale* (Bologna, Il Mulino, 2000).

II. THE SUBJECT OF LAW IN THE PANDECTIST SCHOOL

There was therefore a need to return to an organic and unitary concept a notion that is by nature elusive and ambiguous.

For the reconstruction of the notion of 'person', scholars[3] start from the text of the Pandette. Civil law was imbued with that culture until the 1970s. Today's civil law is left with the task of ascertaining how much of its terminology, concepts and reasoning has remained intact, how much has been transferred or misrepresented, and how much has settled into our way of thinking to such an extent that it is difficult to reconstruct the heritage of the past.[4] The civilist is faced with a complex path: going back in time to the origins of the terms and concepts used in the works of the Pandectists, and analysing the translations and reflections that those concepts and terms have had in our experience. The second path is impassable, because the nineteenth- and twentieth-century sources do not critically reflect the Pandectist influence, as they are so steeped in it that they identify with it. The fact that Glueck's *Commentary on the Pandette*, written at the end of the eighteenth century, was published in Italian a century later, with an extraordinary intellectual effort and with such an invigorating concourse of wits as to make it relevant today, and that the Italian translations of the works of Savigny and Windscheid, who had collected the seeds, spread throughout Europe without any temporal reference and without any critical apparatus, except for the extraordinary commentary by Fadda and Bensa, suggests many things: that that cultural operation was not considered by its authors, Vittorio Scialoja, Filippo Serafini and Pietro Cogliolo, as an anachronistic manipulation, nor as an anti-historical superimposition of sources, but as the current source of civil law; and, that in that season of law studies, the dissociation between the logical structure of the rules and their actual application could be carried out without prejudice to the understanding of the past and the present.

On the contrary. In the Preface to Glueck's undated Italian translation – almost as if it were a monument, a milestone that is outside of history and stands untouched by time – Serafini and Cogliolo do not bother to justify their choice but consider it natural that the 'favourable conditions' and the 'renewed desire to return to ancient greatness' have reinvigorated legal studies,[5] particularly of Roman law, which was to be considered a life-giving force in

[3] See the essays collected in *Quaderni fiorentini*, no XXXII (Milan, 2003).

[4] For a first horizon of problems see P Grossi, *Scienza giuridica italiana. Un profilo storico (1860–1950)* (Milan, Giuffré, 2000); B Montanari (ed), *La dottrina giuridica italiana alla fine del XX secolo. Un bilancio* (Milan, Giuffré, 1998); G Alpa, *La cultura delle regole. Storia del diritto civile italiano* (Roma-Bari, Laterza, 2000).

[5] F Serafini and P Cogliolo (eds), *Commentario alle Pandette di F Glueck* (1791) It trans C Ferrini (Milan, Vallardi, 1888–1909).

legal thought. This 'reawakening' – they say – also echoed through daily legal practice,

> where judgments and memoirs abandoned the old baggage of empty formulas and common phrases, in order to apply the purity of principles and the results of science to the concrete case, thus eschewing the crude logical commentary of the articles of the code.[6]

The apparatus of notes accompanying the text serves to create a 'beneficial union between Roman law and domestic law', with the aim of drawing on the supreme ideal of science, namely 'a single common law'.

After describing the general principles on laws, Glueck deals with the Gaian tripartition of private law into 'persons, things, actions'. The object of private law is 'the mortal actions of citizens in their private relations'.[7] The rights and duties of men, which arise from their 'private relations', depend on the 'subjective qualities of persons'. These qualities are related to *status*; men's rights are not independent of things; they are not autonomous and have no value in themselves.[8] In turn, *status* depends on man's physical qualities and political or moral relations. In short, Glueck takes up the Roman tradition, arranging it in concepts and assumptions. As for the origin of man according to his physical condition, he distinguishes men (not 'persons') into 'born' and 'unborn'.[9] This is followed by the distinction of men with respect to sex, freedom, age, and so on.

Taking the analysis to a greater degree of abstraction, Savigny links the conception of persons to 'legal relations', these are placed within the general conception of the sources of current Roman law.[10] 'Person' is not an individual in the flesh but a complex of relationships.

The legal relationship is defined as 'a sphere of independent dominion of the individual will', in which law is expressed in the subjective sense, ie the power of the will that reigns with consent.[11] Savigny is opposed to the idea of an innate right that man would have over himself; the rights attributed to the 'person' are acquired; one person's rights over another person cannot

[6] ibid vi.

[7] Glueck (n 5) 473.

[8] As Hugo argued in *Histoire du droit romain Paris* (Paris, Librairie de jurisprudence, 1825).

[9] The unborn may not yet have been conceived or may be in the embryonic state, but neither the unconceived nor the foetuses are considered men in the proper sense. Embryos are considered part of the womb. Abortion was punished because it was considered an infringement of the father's rights, and the pregnant woman was subjected neither to torture nor to punishment for fear that she would lose her child. In this regard, the editors observe that the proposition *nasciturus pro iam nato habetur* was first expounded by Julian with the aim of grouping all the cases in which a provision in favour of the unborn was relevant in a single principle, without, however, implying that the unborn child was considered to have rights.

[10] The *Sistema del diritto romano attuale* was published beginning with the first three volumes in Berlin in 1840; translations into Italian soon began, the most scientifically correct of which was the one offered by Vittorio Scialoja for the Unione Tipografica Editrice (Turin, 1886).

[11] Savigny (n 10) vol I, 36, and 335.

be constituted to the point of annihilating their will and thus their freedom; only 'obligations' can be constituted. The person is part of a family, but the relationships he establishes with family members only partly fall within the realm of obligations; the empire of the will is expressed in the realm of property law, in which real rights and obligatory rights are distinguished. From family relations Savigny derives two concepts: 'representation' in property acquisitions – which corresponds to the position of the person within the family and thus to the relations of *potestas*, *manus*, *mancipium* – and 'legal capacity', which is connected with *statuses* and *capitis deminutio*. However, unlike Hugo, who regarded legal capacity as emerging from family *statuses*, Savigny observes that *statuses* deriving from public law, inherent in freedom, are also components of it.[12]

The treatment of the 'person' therefore follows from its framing in the 'legal relationship', which consists of the relationship of a person with another person.[13] The person is thus the 'subject of a legal relationship', which may relate to another person or to all citizens. The person is a subject of law, and subjects of law can only be persons; the subject of law coincides with man.[14]

And it is here that one grasps the turning point Savigny imprinted on the legal culture of his time: since – geometrically speaking – man is a person, the person is the holder of the legal relationship, insofar as endowed with 'legal capacity', and therefore every man is in the abstract 'capable of law', but 'the primitive concept of person can be modified by positive law in two ways, limiting and extending'. Positive law can limit legal capacity, as well as attribute it in full to artificial persons, such as legal persons.[15] Savigny attributes to 'artificial' operations the creation of the legal person, an abstract entity that lives only in the world of law, and fails to realise that legal capacity is also an abstract notion, and that the reduction of the person to a complex of legal relations, with the possibility of limiting his legal capacity, allows for the 'justification' of any limitation on the ownership of rights, provided it is provided for by the legal system.

Legal capacity is linked to the three *statuses* (*libertatis*, *civitatis*, *familiae*). In coeval law, the family relationship remains; other limitations, the result of modern law, are added. Savigny examines the Code Napoléon and the authors from whom the compilers of the Code drew inspiration[16] and deals in particular with the 'civil death' with which the French revolutionary laws affected emigrants, converting it into the loss of citizenship. Civil death concerned those condemned to death and those sentenced to the most serious punishments; civil death was accompanied by the limitations on legal capacity resulting from

[12] ibid 396ff.
[13] ibid vol II, 1.
[14] ibid vol II, 2.
[15] ibid vol II, 2.
[16] ibid vol II, 160.

'infamy',[17] an accessory penalty to criminal punishment. Among the limitations of legal capacity, Savigny also includes those due to 'religious causes': the limitations concerning pagans, Jews, heretics and apostates are therefore due to the Christian emperors; with regard to the period contemporary with him, Savigny recalls the prohibition of marriage between Christians and Jews. This prohibition was lifted with the confederation act (*Bundesakte*) of 1815, in which legal capacity was granted to all without limitation; for the Jews, ad hoc provisions were introduced concerning the enjoyment of civil rights.[18,19]

It is therefore true that Savigny does not deny every person legal capacity, but he does not consider it an innate right. By returning its boundaries to positive law, he leaves man, covered by this mask of law called the *person*, at the mercy of ordinary law.

What emerges is a 'pure legal concept' of the person, which legitimises every economic exploitation and every legislative aberration. What is 'imposed' by the legislator cannot be criticised on the level of political expediency but only on the level of legal rationality.

A pupil of Savigny, Puchta also relies on the will to describe concepts concerning the person.[20] 'Law makes a man a person, and determines his activity as such'; 'personality is the possibility of a legal will, as a quality of a subject' – and this is expressed in terms of 'capacity for law'; law distinguishes persons into classes, graduating for each of them this capacity; every right is a power over an object, which is subject to the legal will; the object of law can be things or persons, but over persons the right cannot be full. Up to this point, Savigny's ideas are taken up, in a less precise and argued manner.

But Puchta believes in the existence of a 'right on one's own person, in which the will immediately refers to itself':[21] it is the 'legal power to be a person, the *right of personality*'. The system of rights begins with the system of legal relations; the right belongs to man as the subject of the will, but it is a will that belongs to all men despite their natural inequality. Law does not give equal importance to all natural inequalities, but only to the authority of one person over another 'which gives legal character to natural differences'. The path of law is thus directed towards an ideal of perfection that is realised in the future equality of all, in spite of natural inequalities.[22]

[17] ibid vol II, 180ff.

[18] ibid vol II, 239.

[19] On the concept of *status* and *capitis deminutio* Savigny sets out in vol II, App VI, 439ff philological and conceptual criticisms of the Roman sources and their commentators. But, having dealt with legal persons, he returns to the problem of the connection between legal relationship and person, this time understood not only as a man, but as a subject of law, a concept that also encompasses the legal person. The connection is constituted by an 'act' (eg contract, will) or by a 'fact', as well as, of course, by legal relations under public law.

[20] G Puchta, *Corso delle Istituzioni presso il popolo romano* (1841); It trans edited by Turchirulo (Naples, All'insegna del Diogene, 1854).

[21] ibid.

[22] ibid lxxiv.

How different this approach is from Savigny's, although deriving from the same Romanist matrix! And how much more appreciable in its realistic concreteness, and in painting the role of law.

Equally concise but along the same lines as Savigny is the thought of Arndts.[23] The 'person' in the legal sense is every individual who 'is or can be subjugated to rights'; this quality constitutes *his personality*, ie his 'legal capacity'; legal capacity belongs to the 'natural' person – but objective law can place limitations on it (eg certain limitations on the patrimonial rights of the Jews and marriage bans on them[24]) – and to the legal person. Arndts theorises the general law of personality as a receptacle for subjective rights and makes legal capacity correspond to *statuses*. As we approach the end of the nineteenth and the beginning of the twentieth century, the notions become more refined, the legal language sharper, the conceptual abstraction reaches its peak. Dernburg[25] a contemporary of Windscheid, publishes a treatise on Pandette that spreads rapidly in Italy; he is icastic on the point: 'juridically capable *or subjective of the right or person* is one who can have rights: capable is one who can dispose of an independent share in the goods of life'. Legal capacity is a prerequisite for rights, but is itself an important right.[26] It is distinct from the capacity to act, which means the capacity to perform legally recognised acts and is distinguished into the capacity to conclude legal transactions and the capacity to commit offences. Legal subjectivities are natural persons and legal persons, ie social organisations with independent legal capacity. In the world of law, rights cannot exist without a subject, because those that are constituted on the unborn child relate to a hoped-for future person. Legal capacity begins with birth and the rights of the unborn child are limited to succession relations. This is followed by a discussion of the limitations of legal capacity.

To close this review – in which, as we have seen, the only partially dissonant voice is that of Puchta – one can profitably reread the pages of Windscheid.[27] He places the treatment of the person within the framework of the treatment of law in general. He disputes Puchta's thesis on the existence of a general right of personality, the receptacle of rights to one's own person: in his conception, the 'will of man, in and of itself, can … be thought of as the decisive norm for one's own person'; the right consists in the extrinsic expression of the 'faculty of will'. In this sense person is the subject of law: 'the person, whose will is declared

[23] *Trattato delle Pandette, Prima versione italiana sulla nona tedesca di Filippo Serafini*, 3rd edn (Bologna, 1877) 47.

[24] ibid 62.

[25] *Pandette* (1884), It trans by Francesco Bernardino Cicala from 6th edn, vol. I, General Part (Turin, 1906) 126.

[26] ibid 127, fn 3.

[27] Pandette, 1st It trans by Carlo Fadda and Emilio Bensa, from the last German edn, vol I, Part I, (Turin, 1902) 177ff.

decisive, is the subject of law'.[28] Person is man, the man who exerts a will. Man 'is capable of being a subject of rights and obligations, of being a legal subject; he is capable of law from his birth'.[29] Following the Roman sources, Windscheid discusses the differences between men 'relevant to law' (and not, as Puchta sharply wrote, 'constructed' by law, ie by jurists): age, sex, health, etc, including limitations of a religious nature; and he points out that the Jews were granted equal rights by the law of the German Empire of 1869.[30]

In the face of this mighty elaboration of the concepts that envelop man and make him a person relevant to law insofar as he is endowed with capacity and will, Italian doctrine adapts. The formal perspective prevails over every aspect – natural, social, economic – and the person becomes a 'legal phenomenon'.

Legal phenomena consist of two elements: the material element and the formal element; the material element is given by the external factual situation, the formal element is given by the set of rules that allow the external fact to be qualified in legal terms, to which the legal effects and consequences of them are linked.[31] In turn, the factual situation comprises, in a broad sense, the material conditions, and, in a narrower sense, the object to which the qualification is addressed; the transition from the factual situation to its qualification thus postulates a selection of the factual elements, which verifies their subsistence, completeness, integrity and defects.

In this context, 'subjects' constitute the qualifying prerequisites of the case[32] – they are its 'subjective presuppositions' – and when the case has produced its effects, the effects are referred directly to the subjects, who are 'automatically "legitimised" in the legal situations in which those consequences are resolved'.[33]

The qualification process comprises two moments: relevance and effectiveness. Relevance marks the step in which the extra-legal entity penetrates the system of legal phenomena. In turn, consequences are distinguished into personal – if they are inherent to the quality of the person – and patrimonial – if they are inherent to the legal sphere of the subject, ie his assets; the former therefore include *status* and capacity to act. The subject, thus deciphered, thus becomes a 'legal fact'.

Man, as an extra-legal material substratum, was a founding and essential factor of the legal case: hence the definition of a legal subject as a case resulting

[28] ibid 206.
[29] ibid 215.
[30] ibid 222.
[31] For a reconstruction of this issue, with references to its Germanic doctrinal sources see A Falzea, *Il soggetto nel sistema dei fenomeni giuridici* (Milan, Giiffré, 1939) 4ff.
[32] ibid 19.
[33] ibid 20.

from the composition of a factual element existing in the extra-legal reality and the normative qualification.[34] In this sense the natural person is

> constituted by the synthesis of a material substratum (physical-psychic organism) endowed with the requisites … [provided for by the Civil Code],[35] which constitute as many prerequisites for the qualification of the subjective (individual) fact and the formal recognition, with which the quality of person in the legal sense is attributed to this factual substratum.[36]

The logical consequence of these premises is that man can qualify as a subject of law not because of his ethical-psychological characteristics nor his social relations, 'but only by virtue of formal recognition by the legal system'.

The subject of law is a 'point of subjective legitimation of legal consequences', and personality and capacity for legitimation are not qualities of the subject but the form and prerequisite of all the legal qualities that can be conferred on the person.[37]

From a formal point of view, therefore, limitations can be placed on legal capacity that, in the world of forms, appear legitimate.[38]

III. RIGHTS OVER ONE'S OWN PERSON AND THE ENUMERATION OF PERSONALITY RIGHTS

At the end of the nineteenth century, the panorama of law built around the person was therefore very jagged. The progressive abstractions made by jurists over the centuries meant that civil law scholars never spoke of man, but of the subject of law. And when one approaches law as the subject of law or the person as the subject of law, many distinctions are made: the person becomes a cluster of concepts, reflecting the many meanings in which the adjective 'personal' can be declined.

The rights of *the person* see their dimension expand or shrink, depending on whether they include family rights and the rights of obligations.

It is then discussed whether rights can be given over a *person*: in modern times, the rights of one person over another should be outlawed, considered outdated and no longer tenable, because slavery and serfdom are now a sign of the past. Serfdom has turned into a contract in which one party voluntarily submits to the commands of the other by putting its labour power at his disposal. This issue, however, is set aside. What the jurists of the late nineteenth

[34] ibid 60.

[35] The author refers to Art 724 of the Civil Code of 1865, which included among the incapacities for succession those who were not born *viable*.

[36] Falzea (n 31) 62.

[37] ibid 75.

[38] ibid 75.

century were interested in was whether it was possible to conceive in the abstract that the person had rights over himself. There is no consensus on the existence of a *right over one's own person*.[39]

Alongside the right over the body (whether a subject's property right over his own body can be admitted) are rights concerning the qualities of the person. These rights presuppose, in the conceptual construction of the jurists of the time, *personality*, a general right, the presupposition of every right, which, as Fadda and Bensa write in their commentary on the Pandette of Windscheid,[40] is the element that pervades every private right and is contained in each of them: it is nothing other than legal capacity, the possibility of having rights.

Until then, the person is discussed as the complex of legal relations, and as the holder of a right, legal capacity, to be the holder of other rights. Personhood is identified with capacity. And capacity is not an innate right; it does not precede the order of the state, but is the product of it.

Alongside this dimension, however, is a new perspective. Among the various rights that a person has, one discovers the rights to the body, the right to a name, the right to an image.

In the elaboration of the general doctrines of civil law, Francesco Ferrara Sr gave his masterly interpretation, which was to become dominant: this 'new species of private rights' is called *personality rights*. Ferrara traces them to the works of a German author who had remained on the fringes of the Pandectist orientation, Otto von Gierke.

Picking up on Gierke, Ferrara points out that these rights were unknown in Roman law, because it was only at the end of the nineteenth century that they 'came to develop and acquire their own individuality, and claim their place in the legal system'.[41]

The elaboration of these rights still oscillates between a unitary and a pluralistic conception – 'an unenclosed set of rights'. But while the unitary theory is confused with legal personality, the pluralistic theory can be broadened to include rights to intangible goods, such as copyright, trademarks, etc. Personality rights correspond to the qualities of the person that must be defended in relations with others: personality rights are 'powers identified in favour of the person, tending to the protection of certain personal goods'.[42] They are absolute personal rights of exclusion. Enumerating them, they are the right to personal integrity (which includes the right of ownership over detached body parts), the right to personal liberty, the right to honour, the right to one's own image, the right to one's name.[43]

[39] The young Adolfo Ravà, right at the beginning of the 20th century, shows how unreasonable and inconsistent a right over one's own body exercised by a person who is that body is.

[40] Vol I (Turin, UTET, 1902) 601.

[41] F Ferrara Sr, *Trattato di diritto civile italiano. Dottrine generali* (Rome, Athenaeum, 1921) (anastatic reprint by the University of Camerino, Naples, 1985).

[42] ibid 397.

[43] ibid 398ff.

This arrangement seasons the abstract theoretical construction with factual data emerging from the concrete reality of the time will have the future for itself.

It penetrates even the most accredited manuals.

Exemplary in its clarity, and in the use of the term, is the treatment by Biagio Brugi, professor emeritus of the University of Padua and professor at the University of Pisa,[44] who dedicates a chapter of his successful handbook to these themes. The title refers to the 'subject of the legal relationship', the subtitle bears the words 'personality in general. Personality and capacity to act'; the text illustrates the (physical) person 'that is, man as he is endowed with personality, by virtue of his own nature'. And he succinctly recalls the historical development of man's personality, considered by Roman law not in the abstract but with regard to his status. He dwells above all on the *status libertatis*, considering it now obsolete, on the status *familiae*, which is now regulated by family law, and on the *status civitatis*, which is replaced by nationality and recalls (a rare occurrence among scholars of Roman law and civil law) Article 24 of the Albertine Statute, which had formally equalised all citizens. Brugi then indicates the distinguishing criteria of persons, no longer linked to conditions of nature (sex, age, health) or social conditions (religion, profession) and even name and legal seat. He then adds: 'The concept of personality is so broad and abstract that it includes the most varied and concrete rights … It can be said that man's personality is the source of all his rights'. Name, image, physical integrity, etc, referred to as *personality rights*, are considered particular aspects of personality.

Roberto De Ruggiero, a full professor at the University of Rome, also begins the discourse on personality by entitling the chapter on 'natural persons', equating personality with legal subjectivity[45] and specifies: 'personality is not in itself a subjective right, but the source and presupposition of all subjective rights … But there are some, complex and of manifold content, which constitute, as it were, the primary cause of all other particular rights'.[46] Enumerated here are the right to liberty, the right to be able to establish property relations with others, the right to test and create family relations, the right to name, image and personal integrity.

In the notes to the text[47] De Ruggiero dwells on the Project of Book I of the Civil Code reform, identifying these rights, and recalling some problems that were still open at the time, such as the criminal protection of integrity, the prohibition for the doctor to administer drugs to the patient even when the latter 'has begged for them to stop unbearable physical pain', and the right to report news and criticism, which prevailed over the right to image.

[44] Ist.dir.civ., 4th edn (Milan, 1923).
[45] Ist.dir.civ.,VII (Messina, 1934).
[46] ibid 329.
[47] ibid 330 and 331.

The personality of man is considered, on the one hand, to be a synonym for legal capacity, the capacity to be the holder of rights and duties, and, on the other hand, as a set of rights pertaining to man as such. It is then discussed whether these rights pertain to man by nature, or whether they depend on the laws of the state.

There are flashes of freedom, which stand out against the formalist culture.

Legal historians dedicated to the person go beyond legal forms to penetrate the reality of life.[48]

In the 'carthae' of liberty and franchise between the tenth and twelfth centuries, Sergio Mochi Onory was able to read 'the result of concrete bargains between certain social groups and the lord or prince'; and how there is 'no innate right: every right is recognised as a consequence of a bargain … In the Middle Ages there is no enunciation of principles': Mochi first carefully studied the freedom charters, their diffusion and the increase in number, in the substance of the concessions, in the enlargement of the recipients. He described the slow evolutionary process that saw the emergence of the people as the subject of law, the addressee of the legal norm, and highlighted how the first and simplest limit to the lord's coercion was recourse to the 'bona et justa consuetudo'. It is also his merit to have grasped how in medieval charters 'the existence of legal capacity is always presupposed, if in concrete terms the individual rights that derive from it are admitted, listed and specified in detail'.

The topic was original for those years in Italy (1935–40) and bears witness to a strong political interest. In *Studi sulle origini storiche dei diritti essenziali della persona* (*Studies on the historical origins of the essential rights of the person*), Mochi Onory devotes his attention 'to the time when the rights of liberty began to find a legal guarantee after centuries of illegality and arbitrariness' moved by the 'painful realisation of how the human personality was then trampled upon in several respects'.[49]

It was in this period that a direction was born that has been little studied, and sometimes resurfaces even in the writings of private scholars, which theorises the category of the *essential* rights of the person; those that would later be, with more solid theory construction, called human rights and fundamental rights.

The philosophers of law are divided between the naturalistic and Christian, the idealistic Crocian and the idealistic Gentilian orientation; there are still neo-Kantians, formalist legal positivists who find in the form the detachment from social-political ideas they do not share, and social-communist jurists now reduced to silence and the bush.

[48] Three works stand out in this period: Besta's manual, Trifone's monograph, Mochi Onory's monograph.

[49] U Nicolini, 'Fonti canonistiche dell'idea moderna dello Stato' in *Rivista di storia del diritto italiano*, XXIV (1951) 234.

Many scholars tend to see the person as a unicum that reproduces itself in all human beings, endowed with autonomy and freedom, and with rights linked to its nature.

Even before the drafting of the regulatory text that would lead to the approval of Book I of the Civil Code, doctrine and jurisprudence introduced the expression 'personality rights' into legal language. Thus, in Italian legal culture there is a bipartition between authors who continue to reason about personality in terms of legal capacity, that is, the capacity to be the holder of rights and duties, and authors who build on the concept of 'personality' a series of rights that are its specification.

On the contrary, the law subservient to power is concerned with emphasising the differences between people: it is a sexist, classist law, which legitimises servitude, especially of colonised natives; it is a racist law, which under the guise of demographic studies conceals a thought that codifies the very concept of race and racial distinctions, which are the premise for discrimination, hatred, repression, persecution. They prepare and accompany the intervention of the legislature. It is a crescendo of increasingly stringent measures that find a humus of favour – if not indifference – in the Italian population. The Roman and Aryan origins of the Italians are a falsification in which many jurists show faith.

Fulvio Maroi studies the genesis of those rights that he calls 'essential personal rights' or 'personality rights'. Originating from the limitation of the state's position vis-à-vis the citizen, they are addressed

> in two directions: the first concerns rights as a mainly political and publicistic reference … and developed in the modern and contemporary ages; the second refers to rights with a more private content, the emergence of which can be traced back to the late Middle Ages.[50]

We are now in 1938, on the threshold of codification. The rights of the person are barely sketched out. The concepts used by jurists, in particular civil law scholars, are conceptual abstractions. Law is dominated by legal positivism; only the norms in force mark out the person's way of being. There is no shortage of philosophers advocating a more modern natural lawism.

IV. THE POSITION OF CATHOLIC LEGAL PHILOSOPHY ON THE THRESHOLD OF CIVIL CODIFICATION

On the threshold of the new civil codification, the Catholic Church's position on the place of the individual within the legal system was informed by an all-encompassing and unitary conception of the *person*. The legal aspect was considered the least significant, of course, compared to the theological, moral,

[50] GS Pene Vidari, 'Legal history and essential rights of the person: the medieval beginnings' in GS Pene Vidari, *I diritti della persona nella storia delle istituzioni* (Turin, Giappichelli, 1991) 9.

philosophical and social aspects. But there is no doubt that the connotation of the human being as a 'person' rather than a mere individual or subject of law could only be the expression of an 'all-round' vision, far richer and more multifaceted than the abstract definitions offered by civil law or public law, which necessarily belonged to a non-religious but secular conception of law. Behind the person stood the medieval and modern theological tradition, the conception of man as the image of God, as the bearer of a body and as the host of a soul, the configuration of the body as the receptacle of the Holy Sacraments, the mystery of the Trinity composed of 'three equal and distinct persons', and the social doctrine of the Church introduced by the encyclical *Rerum Novarum* established the relationship of the individual with property and profit, and the role of the individual in associations and the Church.

In the 1917 Code of Canon Law, the abstract definitions of the jurists re-emerged, ignoring the debate on the nature of the Indians, the legitimisation of slavery, the fight against heresies and anything else that might appear to be 'contrary to nature'. The past is in the past we look to the future with anxiety to organise the legal differentiation of people and their functions according to a rigid legal order.

Book I is dedicated to the general norms, ie the sources; Book II is dedicated to the persons, and sees at the base of the canonical order the *clerics*, at its summit the Roman Pontiff, and gradually descending through the grades of the hierarchy, the Curia with the Sacred Congregations, the Tribunals and Offices, the Papal Legates, the Patriarchs, the Primates and the Metropolitans, the Apostolic Vicars and Prefects, the Apostolic Administrators, the inferior Prelates, and then the Bishops, the Canons, the Parish Priests, the Vicars of the Parish Priests, the Rectors, and then the Religious Orders, the Confessors, the Chaplains and the Novices, and finally the associations in which those who are Catholics can serve.

This hierarchical conception does not forget the 'faithful'. In fact, in the provision with which the Book on Persons opens, it is specified that

> in the Church with *baptism one becomes a person* with duties and rights, as long as one does not obstruct or censure. A person is a major from the age of 21; before that he is a minor. He is considered pubescent from the completed fourteenth year if male, from the twelfth if female. An impubescent before the full seven years is called a child and is considered irresponsible: so is one who habitually lacks the use of reason. The major has the full exercise of his rights: the minor, not opposing the right, depends on his parents or guardians (Can. 87–89).

Clerics, religious and laity are the categories into which all those who entered the Church as baptised can be placed according to their role. But, as has been said, the rules, from the first enunciation, then flow towards the composition of the hierarchical structure of the Church.

The law, however, is left with very little space compared to the richness of Christian thought. Catholic legal philosophers are therefore faced with the alternative: either ignore the meta-legal context, or incorporate the debate on the meaning of the person into Catholic thought.

Following the second horn of the dilemma, Guido Gonella, a student of Giorgio Del Vecchio, published a very learned work in the series of the Institute of Philosophy of Law at the University of Rome dedicated to *La persona nella filosofia del diritto*.[51] The year of publication is crucial because it coincides with the year of the promulgation of Book I of the Civil Code, with the enactment of the racial laws, and with the elaboration of personality rights that enlivened the doctrine of civil law at that time.

Gonella followed in the footsteps of his Master, who had anticipated the treatment of the rights of the person in a famous lecture given in Ferrara in 1904. On that occasion, the thesis he expounded concerned human personality in the philosophy of law. The person is the substratum of natural law. 'In the human person [is to be found] the absolute criterion of every value and the metaphysical *prius* of the truth of law',[52] Del Vecchio said; and in his historical excursus from the Greek philosophers to contemporary thinkers – passing through Rousseau, Kant and Fichte and arriving at positive law – he had criticised legal formalism on the basis of which only the rights recognised by the legislator exist, seeing in this an impoverishment of legal science.

In the very first pages of the book Gonella makes it clear that 'the legal concept of person is subordinate to the philosophical concept'.[53] He therefore does not deal with canon law, nor with the social doctrine of the Church, but compares the philosophical concept – reconstructed according to philosophy in its historical development, particularly medieval philosophy, and Thomist philosophy in particular – with the juridical concept, which he sees made explicit in the concept of subject of law and subjective right.[54] And he polemises with Francesco Ferrara Sr, who had distinguished in the notion of person the physical-anthropological sense of man, the theological-philosophical sense of rational being, the juridical sense of juridical function or capacity.[55] This was because, as he saw it, the theological conception (which concerns man's relationship with God) could not be confused with the philosophical and moral conception (which sees man as the principle of the moral world and therefore

[51] G Gonella, *La persona nella filosofia del diritto* (Milan, Giuffrè, 1938) 262; the series was directed by Giorgio Del Vecchio, who, as a Jew, despite having converted to Catholicism, was persecuted, and as a result of the racial laws had to leave the chair of the Faculty of Law and the chair of Philosophy of Law; he managed to save himself, hiding with his wife, thanks to the generous assistance of his student and Roman religious institutes, which offered him providential hospitality.

[52] G Del Vecchio, *Diritto e personalità umana nella storia del pensiero* (Bologna, Tip.Università, 1904).

[53] ibid 4. It is no coincidence that the opening quotation is taken from the Summa Theologica of Thomas Aquinas: 'Persona significat id quod est perfectissimum in tota natura, scilicet subsistens in rationali natura' (I,q. 29, a.3).

[54] ibid 4.

[55] F Ferrara Sr, *Theory of Legal Persons* (Turin, UTET, 1915) 336.

of freedom), and the anthropological conception could not be confused with the juridical one, because it constitutes its presupposition. What is more, all these aspects make up the unity of the person, and show how miserable and misleading the technical-legal conception of the person is. Hence the division of his thought into three fundamental aspects: metaphysics, ethics, and law, understood as the complex of the legal aspects of the person.

It is a courageous discourse both for the era in which it is proposed and for the opposing front against which it is measured: a front in which the advocates of legal positivism, the advocates of institutionalism, and the advocates of statist and corporatist law are seen as allies.

Among the legal positivists Gonella criticises the major exponent of this orientation, Hans Kelsen, who considers the person 'as the metaphorical expression of the objective validity of a normative order', that is, as the centre of convergence of acts that may be imputed to him. He criticises Croce, as representing one wing of the institutionalist orientation, because he sees the person as an (abstract) process of actions; he ignores corporate statism, but also the Code of Canon Law. Christian philosophy stands out in the two central parts of the work, dedicated to metaphysics and ethics, as premises for the philosophy of law. In the reconstruction of the metaphysical dimension, Gonella emphasises the substantiality, individuality, naturalness and rationality of the person, taking the thought of Boethius, St Augustine and St Thomas,[56] the philosophers of the Renaissance, modern and contemporary philosophers, among whom the thought of Jacques Maritain stands out. Indeed, after World War II, the *integral man* will become the foundation of the non-traditional Catholic philosophical conception.[57] In the development of ethical profiles, Gonella constructs the Kantian concept of freedom, its connections with the will (of Hobbes and Hegel), and with self-limitation. Particular emphasis – and this aspect of Gonella's thought is significant in the stormy times in which it is formulated – is placed in the 'theologism of the person', in the conception of the person not as a means but as an end. There is no lack of discussion of the issues examined at two conferences on moral philosophy, one held in Rome in 1926, and the other in France in 1937, where, with reference to the role of the person in the family and school education, the person was seen as 'in danger'.

The legal aspects of the person are illustrated in the third part, with which the work concludes. These are interesting pages because they are steeped in legal humanism, for which the birth of man is the *birth of the person*.[58] The person, seen as a subject with rights (of freedom, of attributes), is not regarded as a monad, but as the holder of a role within the community and the state.

[56] Dialogue with Descartes, Locke, Leibniz, Wolf, exponents of historicism, phenomenalism, materialism.

[57] J Maritain, *Humanisme integral* (Paris, Cerf, 1936).

[58] ibid 167.

Only at this point does Gonella, having constructed the philosophical context in which to examine legal concepts, turn to the category of the person and personality rights. It is precisely by moving from the idea of the person as an *end* that he arrives at an appreciation of the Jheringian theory of the purpose of law as the *preservation of the person*, in other words 'the preservation of the person is a moral duty'.[59] And yet his conception of the person goes beyond Jhering's theory: the person is the affirmation of law, but is also its *limit*.[60]

Hence the criticism of modern law, which unifies the concepts of personhood and capacity, taking a step backwards compared to Roman law, in which even the slave, although in a state of subjection, retained a glimmer of personhood.

As an appendix to his work Gonella includes an essay on 'personality and religiosity'. And precisely in portraying the Christian conception of the person he evokes two terms that will appear in the first norms of the Republican Constitution: *dignity* and *solidarity*. He writes in this regard:

> It can be concluded that the influence of Christianity in positively affirming the dignity of the person and the duty of solidarity (ie the duty of respect for the social person) has been no less considerable than the influence of Christian theology and metaphysics in deepening the metaphysical conception of the person.[61]

Citing Cicala,[62] he claims under the armour of Christianity 'the unity (identity) of the moral dignity of all men of whatever race or civilisation', with all individual differences, a unity that is reconciled with the unity of the law, and exalts the individuality and freedom of the person.[63]

V. THE PERSON IN FASCIST IDEOLOGY AND IN BOOK I OF THE CIVIL CODE (1938)

The Draft of Book I prepared by the Royal Commission for the Reform of the Codes – chaired by Vittorio Scialoja – was published in 1931, and approved in 1936, following the reworking by the ministerial commission, under the direction of Arrigo Solmi, then Minister of Justice.

In illustrating the new provisions, the Royal Commission's report (on p 34) outlines the framework of the subject matter: 'until now, it has been left to doctrine and jurisprudence to define the nature of the right to a name and to regulate its defence'. The draft starts from the principle that there is a right to a name based on human personality, a right that is private in nature, with aspects

[59] ibid 172.
[60] ibid 173.
[61] ibid 260.
[62] ibid 261.
[63] ibid 262.

of public law, that does not merely connote the individuality of each person, but is 'an expression of the moral and material life of a person in all his family and social relations'. Recalling the orientation of the Court of Cassation that erects the name to an absolute right that cannot be renounced and is non-negotiable, the name becomes an expression 'of the personal qualities of intellect, probity of the individual as such and of his position as a citizen and as an element of the family order'.

Solmi himself in 1938 hastened the final approval of the preparatory text and its introduction into the legal system with some modifications; and so with the precept according to which 'every person has the right to the name attributed to him by law' (Article 6) Book I of the Civil Code opened.

When presenting the text of the Civil Code to the King, the new Minister Guardasigilli Dino Grandi is very laconic, limiting himself to emphasising 'the principle that every person has the right to the name attributed to him by law'. The commentary on Article 10 is more diffuse, concerning the abuse of the right to another person's image, coordinated by copyright. It is precisely this fragment of the Report that confirms what has been said so far: the civil code 'must contain the complete regulation of *personality rights*' (No 23).

And so at the end of 1938 the right to physical integrity, the right to a name and a pseudonym, and the right to the image, which concerns the physical image as reproduced by the new techniques of photography and cinema (Articles 5–10) are codified as absolute subjective rights of the person; other rights, to honour and reputation, are then derived from criminal law.

The ideas that civil science had developed in the late 1930s thus penetrated the new Civil Code. Among the jurists who contributed to the construction of the discipline of natural persons was Fulvio Maroi. Although politically neutral, personality rights did not fail to prompt the reflections of jurists who supported the Regime. The essay that Maroi published in the *Monitore dei Tribunali* in 1941 is significant;[64] it is entitled *La codificazione fascista del diritto civile.*

In these pages, Maroi outlines the institutes he dealt with in his work as a codifier. They reproduce the speech he gave at the Institute of Political and Social Sciences in Budapest on 24 August 1940. The beginning of the speech starts with the history of Magyar agrarian law. Then, illustrating the lines of the new Italian codification, directed at expressing a 'new social order', Maroi takes care to emphasise that the rules intended to take the place of the old discipline are not dissociated from the origins of Roman law – a Roman law understood, here, not as Domat and Pothier understood it, but rather as the jurists of his time, Scialoja, Bonfante, Riccobono, studied it; a Roman law 'guardian of European civilisation', an idea that Maroi links to Koschaker's essay, published in 1938.

[64] F Maroi, *La codificazione fascista del diritto civile* (1941) *Monitore dei Tribunali* 63.

Having recalled the new conception of general principles, expressed in the 'prelegislation', Maroi describes the progress of the legislation, compared to the previous codification. For natural persons, for example, he emphasises its more organic discipline, based on rules 'of a mandatory and cogent nature', and highlights its publicist purposes. Maroi emphasises that the Civil Code, by placing among its first provisions those dedicated to natural persons and personality rights, tends to protect the person in his individual sphere. Quoting Giovanni Gentile[65] he therefore excludes that 'there could ever be a day when the individual is completely resolved in the State, because on that day there would no longer be the individual, but there would not be the State either'.[66]

It is worth expanding on the discipline of natural persons, because Maroi makes it the subject of the first commentary to the new Civil Code, edited by Mariano d'Amelio and published immediately after its promulgation.[67]

Here we see another peculiarity of civil law studies: continuity. The war, the fall of the Regime, the advent of a new state order, the Republic and the Constitution, offer neither rethinks nor breaks with the past. Law passes over all these upheavals without a quiver or a perplexity.

It is no coincidence that in the first commentary to Book I of the new Civil Code edited by the President of the Court of Cassation, Mariano d'Amelio, the analysis of the provisions (Articles 1–10) devoted to legal capacity and personality rights is still entrusted to Fulvio Maroi.

In commenting on Articles 1–10 of the Civil Code, Maroi points out that the capacity recognised in the conceived person is neither 'an anticipation of' personality nor a legal fiction, but rather the suspension of a position that creates a state of 'expectation'.[68] With regard to the capacity to work, he emphasises the social function of this provision. On the right to a name and other personality rights, he takes up what was mentioned at the Hungarian conference. The footnotes accompany the text with cultured references to the various sources to which his multifaceted spirit and vast erudition drove him. And he returns to his studies on

[65] F Maroi, 'Individuo e Ststo' (1933) *Giornale critico della filosofia* 214.

[66] ibid 66. As for the family, while making some concessions to the mentality of the time, Maroi tends to emphasise the modern aspects of the discipline. He emphasises how one of the legislative purposes was to bring the civil order closer to the canonical one; how the rules on family patrimony must be understood in their economic-social meaning; how these purposes emerge from the regulation of the recognition of a legal *status* to children born out of wedlock, who are ensured a 'more dignified family and social life', rescuing them – he says – 'from mortality, unemployment, debauchery and early delinquency'. Likewise for the search for paternity, the extension of which is precisely within the scope of these aims, attributed to the 'fascist ethic'. More lukewarm is his appreciation for the new law of succession, which seems to him – as is true, after all – too close to the Justinian and Christian tradition. Nevertheless, among the most relevant innovations, in the wake of social aims, he points to the improved treatment of the surviving spouse, the protection of the interests of co-heirs, and the heir's responsibility for the debts of the deceased.

[67] F Maroi, *Civil Code*. Book I. Persons and Family, now in *Scritti giuridici* (Milan, Giuffré, 1956) vol I, 203–31.

[68] ibid 209.

Religious Elements in Archaic Roman Law[69] to remind the reader that the term 'person', now used with unconscious naturalness in colloquial jargon and legal vocabulary, has a fascinating ancestry because it 'has a mystical-religious meaning'; 'persona' in fact was the mask that was affixed to the face of the deceased or an heirloom depicting his somatic features to preserve his memory by his loved ones; in short, 'it was the double of the deceased, … the mystical refraction of his ego'. Hence the heir's responsibility for the deceased's debts, given the almost physical continuity between one and the other. These considerations are then developed in a broader context in *The Human Personality. Glosse di un giurista al libro di un medico*, in the context of a paper offered to the Roman Centre for Comparison and Synthesis in 1947.

The pages of the Commentary hold other surprises. As is well known, Article 1 of the Civil Code originally included a third paragraph, repealed with the fall of the Regime, which dealt with limitations to legal capacity determined by racial affiliation. The *status* of the Jews was marked by this classification, later fortunately repudiated. The Civil Code, which acted as the 'glue' of the special sector laws, and thus also of the racial laws, therefore bore the mark.[70]

Maroi makes an aseptic reading of the provisions: he does not criticise them, but does not extol their purpose, as other illustrious jurists of the time did. He does, however, recall a notation according to which

> the concept of belonging to the Aryan race cannot be for the code any different from that which inspires legislation for the defence of the race. It is not so much a biological or anthropological concept as a political and juridical one whose concrete determination is given by special laws or by the competent organs of the State.[71]

Thus declined, personality rights enter the workshop of civil law in which doctrine and jurisprudence prepare to rework them, dividing the tasks: doctrine takes care of the dogmatic profiles, jurisprudence by solving practical cases adapts them to the palpitating reality and from time to time shapes and updates them. But neither one nor the other reaches unambiguous conclusions.

In the meantime, however, since personality rights can register a very significant point in their favour, namely the legislature's recognition within the Civil Code, their life can proceed swiftly, overcoming the doubts of part of the doctrine. And the separation in the text between legal capacity (as the normative

[69] F Maroi, 'Religious Elements in Archaic Roman Law' (1933) *Archivio Giuridico* 89.

[70] It must also be said that most jurists ignored the racial laws; others even supported them, making their own contribution to the discriminatory policy.

[71] Maroi (n 69) 213. Maroi advocated an idea of 'race' as a cultural and historical fact: this can be deduced from another essay, included in the *Scritti giuridici*, on *Difesa della stirpe e diritto rurale*, which appeared in 1938. In spite of the tenor of the title, which might sound sinister today, the essay is all about the historical descent of the original Italian model from the Romans and the peoples of the Medieval Age, a model that unites – anthropologically and culturally speaking – the cultivator of the land with the legislation that concerns him.

expression of the general right of personality as the foundation of the subject's rights) and individual personality rights is now a definitive landing place. In other words, the two approaches that had emerged with some uncertainty at the end of the nineteenth century and then taken root in the following decades find their own composition, resulting in a separate codification.

And Maroi, in defining the lexical meaning of *person*, points out that personality rights constitute a category unknown to the Romans.[72]

VI. MARRIAGE AS A 'REMEDY AGAINST CONCUPISCENCE' IN CANON LAW AND THE HUSBAND'S RIGHTS OVER HIS WIFE'S BODY IN CIVIL LAW

The person in the family is another segment of the life of law that is worth examining. Here, according to the mentality of the time, and not only in the canons of the Regime, the roles of the man (husband and father) and the woman (wife and mother) are well established. The husband/father is the head of the family. The woman, relegated to an ancillary role, provides for her offspring. The emblematic conception of the woman is the discrimination on the 'marital debt'.

Twenty years after the promulgation of the 1937 Code of Canon Law and in the immediacy of the drafting of Book I of the Civil Code, one of the greatest scholars of canon law and ecclesiastical law, Arturo Carlo Jemolo, published a valuable work, *Il matrimonio (Marriage)*, intended for the treatise directed by Filippo Vassalli, followed shortly afterwards by the book on *Il matrimonio nel diritto canonico* (*Marriage in Canon Law*).[73]

Jemolo questions, among many problematic points, a particular aspect concerning the consent of the *nubendi* and the values expressed in the matrimonial act considered from the point of view of civil law (secular) and in the sacrament from the point of view of the Christian religion. For various reasons, neither one nor the other gives entry to sentiments: civil law, because the celebration is an administrative act; canon law, because among the aspects that determine consent and can be considered relevant for the purposes of its annulment (love, esteem, affection, recognition in a common life project) are not taken into account. Neither requires that the marriage, in order to be valid, must be consummated. Unlike civil marriage, however, religious marriage sees offspring as one of the *bona* of the sacrament.[74]

[72] F Maroi, *Commentary on Article 5 in Civil Code*, Commentary directed by M D'Amelio (Florence, Barbera, 1940) 97ff.

[73] *Dal Concilio di Trento al Codice del 1917, 1941*, rist inalt (Bologna, Il Mulino, 1993) with a preface by Jean Gaudemet, 122ff.

[74] To tell the truth, Fascism's demographic policy also looked favourably on families with large offspring.

Some scholars, more prosaically as it were, question the husband's right to demand sexual relations with his wife. And they discuss the configuration of this relationship, defined as a *power of subjection of the wife to the husband.*

Imaginative and determined as ever, Francesco Carnelutti even argued that it was a right *in rem*, a servitude exercised by the husband over his wife's body. Pio Fedele, more discreet, configured it as a right of claim (!).[75] Civil law has always had problems defining the legal aspects of the body, which cannot be considered a thing, nor obviously a sacred object, nor even, per se, a person. It has also had problems defining the relationship of the individual with his own body, as emerged from the late-nineteenth-century debate on the rights to be exercised over one's own person, just as it ended up banishing the idea of a property right that one subject can exercise over another.

Filippo Vassalli found the time – in a difficult wartime period – to write a very fine work, *Del Ius in corpus, del debitum coniugale e della servitù d'amore, ovverosia la dogmatica ludicra.*[76] It has been said that this work traces a historical excursus 'made possible by its rich legal and literary library, not lacking in rarities' (such as *Les arrêts d'amour* by Martial d'Auvergne, fifteenth century). In this very serious essay, which has been compared to those of Montaigne, under the surface of an ironic, sharp and crystal-clear prose, in which Varron's satirical vein is combined with a bitter Horatian smile, Vassalli notes 'the despondency into which the ius in corpus has fallen',[77] and reiterates his civilised vision of law as an instrument for the elevation and not the conditioning of man, branding as jest the crude exercises that reduce the person to 'pure bodily expression devoid of all humanity'.

In later elaborations, the formalism of jurists emerges in all its aridity, even when dealing with issues involving the person in his affective dimension. To 'appease, at least to a certain extent, the jurist's conscience', Vincenzo Del Giudice, still in the early 1960s, 20 years after the civil codification and 40 after the canonical codification, takes refuge in the history of ideas, recalling religious precepts and Thomistic theology, to establish when relations between spouses must take place, what effects are to be had on marriage in the event of impotence (*generandi* and *coeundi*), whether a marriage in which not so much procreation but the possibility of intercourse is excluded is admissible (the answer was positive); and gives life advice to elderly couples.[78] In other words,

> the body, despite the legislature's reticence, remained … at the centre of the matrimonial institution insofar as it was implicitly the object of rights and duties since it

[75] F Carnelutti, 'Reply on marriage' (1943) *Il Foro Italiano*; P Fedele 'Postilla' (1943) *Archivio di diritto ecclesiastico.*

[76] Rome 1944 (reprinted with readings by S Caprioli (Bologna, Forni editore, 2001) with reflections by P Rescigno.

[77] V Filippo, *Del Ius in corpus*, del debito coniugale e della servitù d'amore (Rome, Bardi, 1944) 43.

[78] V Del Giudice, *Error condicionis and the ends of marriage* (1962) *Jus canonicum* 111.

was an essential means of realising the traditional aims of marriage: the generation of offspring and a remedy against moral debauchery.[79]

VII. TOWARDS THE REFORM OF THE CIVIL CODE AND GENERAL PERSONALITY LAW

For a long time in the doctrine of civil law, the furrow remained deep between the proponents of the natural law in force, who find Giorgio Del Vecchio as their coryphaeus,[80] and the proponents of legal positivism, among whom Mario Allara stands out,[81] who do not consider personality rights inherent to human nature, but simply the result of civil laws. Adriano De Cupis, who has dedicated his entire life's work to this subject, adheres to the first direction,[82] and qualifies them as *essential rights*, taking up a phrase by Adolfo Ravà.[83] He correctly distinguishes between the person, as a human being, personality, as the person's way of being, legal personality or legal capacity, which is the prerequisite for subjective rights, and personality rights, which are their explication.[84]

De Cupis's viewpoint, perfectly framed in the Civil Code, is nevertheless narrow: he criticises the constitutional text because he considers it to be an expression of jusformalism or, if properly interpreted, the driving force behind the legal protection of the person.

It is therefore in positive law – in the opinion of the proponents of the critical direction of actualised natural lawism – that one must find the way to defend the person also from the state, from the authority, and thus build him that armour that allows him to express his personality, to enjoy freedoms, to be able to contribute, remaining himself and with all his qualities, to social life, in accordance with the principles of equality and solidarity.

It is understood that personality rights can be named, ie find their source in individual provisions of the Civil Code or special law. But in the years following the new formulation of personality rights with the 1942 Code, the doctrine began to question whether a general personality right could be derived from these provisions, not fragmented, but unified in the category of person.

It is precisely by considering the place of the person in the Constitution that the meaning of the 'constitutionalisation of personality rights' can be coherently understood.

[79] MS Testuzza, 'Marriage and codes. The ambiguous status of corporeity' (2013) 42 *Quad fiorentini* 281ff.

[80] *Natural law in force* (Rome, Athenaeum,1951) 22.

[81] M.Allara, *Le nozioni fondamentali del diritto civile*, vol I, IV (Turin, Giappichelli, 1953) 645.

[82] *I diritti della personalità* (Milan, Giuffré, 1950).

[83] *Istituzioni di diritto privato* (Milan, Giuffré, 1938) 152ff.

[84] See now the new edition of that volume (Milan, Giuffré, 1982) 25.

12

The Constitutional Revolution. From the Subject to the Person

I. THE PERSON IN THE ITALIAN CONSTITUTION OF 1948

THE CONSTITUTION RESERVES many rules for the protection of the person: civil rights, freedom rights, the various aspects of personality are fundamental points of the Constitutional Charter and thus of the legal system as a whole.

Its model was the Weimar Constitution of 1919.

An expression of the power established in Germany after the disastrous end of World War I and the collapse of the Prussian Empire, the Constitution approved in Weimar is inspired by a social-democratic conception. Aspects that are relevant to our discussion include: the use of the concept of fundamental principles as an expression of the *law of nations* (Article 4);[1] the use of the concept of *fundamental rights*, only recognised for Germans, who are equal 'before the law' (Article 109); the affirmation of the principle of equality between the sexes, established 'as a rule'; the abolition of privileges linked to birth or class membership; the preservation of noble titles as part of the name. This Constitution uses the expression 'person' with regard to personal freedom, which is inviolable; the provision applies to everyone, there are no privileges for citizens in this area; the home and correspondence are also inviolable (Articles 114, 115 and 117); everyone has access to public office. The rights concerning 'collective life' (Article 119ff) include the protection of the rights of illegitimate children, which are equal to those of legitimate children (Article 121) and marriage, which is the foundation of the family and the nation; equality between the sexes is ensured within it (Article 119).

[1] The *ius gentium* of the Romans evolved into natural law: J Bederman, *International Law in Antiquity* (Cambridge, CUP, 2011); P Catalano, *Linee del sistema sovrannazionale romano*, vol I (Turin, Giappichelli, 1965); for a recent interpretation, M Bettini, 'Human Rights and the Classical World' in M Flores, T Groppi, R Pisillo Mazzeschi (eds), *Diritti umani. Cultura dei diritti e dignità della persona nell'epoca della globalizzazione*, Dictionary (Turin, UTET, 2007) 402; G Pugliese, 'Notazioni storiche sui diritti umani' in S Caprioli, F Treggiari (eds), *Diritti umani e civiltà giuridica* (Perugia, Università, 1992) 19ff; FP Casavola, *I Diritti Umani* (Padua, Cedam, 1997).

The Weimar Constitution enumerates the fundamental freedoms in detail and for the first time in a constitutional text associates the notion of *obligation with the* right to property (Article 153). In addition, the text refers to the *common good*, that consideration of the use and utility of goods seen in a public dimension that in our Constitution has taken the name of *social function*.

Many of these formulae have been taken up in the text of the Italian Constitution of 1948, in the Basic Law of Bonn of 1949, and also in the European Charter of Fundamental Rights of 2000, to which the Lisbon Treaty of 2009 gave legally binding effects.

These formulae represent a synthesis of ethical values, give substance to aspirations for social justice, and prefigure the establishment of an ordered and prosperous society. The legal construction of the roles of men and women, the transformation of the individual into a person, is not a literary game; in legal texts, words carry enormous weight, because rules, behaviour, sanctions derive from them. Although declamatory, these constitutions were the fruit of bitter struggles, sacrifices and mourning. That is why each of them is surrounded by an aura of nobility and it is an ethical purpose to preserve their memory and historical weight.

In this sense, the norms with which the text of the Italian Constitution opens are emblematic. Article 1, which founds the legal system on work as an instrument of man's elevation and the object of duties of solidarity that every individual, as a member of the Republic, must fulfil; work is the justifying source of wealth. Article 2, which protects the individual, both as a single person and in the formations where his or her personality takes place: these are the social formations, such as the family, associations, groups, work communities, etc, in which the individual lives, matures and carries out his or her life experience; the legal system prevents any action aimed at repressing or damaging his or her personality; the person is also protected within the family.

The state undertakes to protect the individual in his or her economic and social relations, ensuring formal equality in relation to other subjects and providing for the removal of obstacles that impede the development of the personality for social reasons: the meaning of Article 3(1)–(2) of the Constitution, which enshrines the principle of equality, must be understood in terms of protecting the individual.

Protection of the individual does not, of course, mean protection or preservation of privileged positions; rather, it means balancing the interests of the individual with those of the community.

Freedom and authority are thus the binomial in which the protection of the individual must be placed. A binomial that, over the centuries, has been variously resolved now in favour of the individual, now in favour of the state.

The Constitution guarantees rights that it defines as inviolable (Articles 2 and 13ff); protected in the head of each person; in return, each person is required to fulfil duties of political, economic and social solidarity.

The guarantee of the person is therefore extensive: in addition to personal freedom, the Constitution protects the inviolability of the home and correspondence, freedom of movement and residence, freedom of association, freedom of religious profession and freedom to express one's thoughts; and then the right to health, and the freedoms of groups, of which the individual is a member (Articles 39, 49, 17, 18 and 19).

The Constitutional Court has made extensive use of Article 2 of the Constitution, often in connection with Article 3. The person is thus understood not in an abstract way, but in a concrete way, with regard to the needs of biological life and associative life. The direct application of constitutional law to relations between private individuals has forced the observance of principles that protect the person also in economic and social relations.

It is a complex experience, and a very extensive one.

II. THE CONSTITUTIONAL PLOT

The constitutional dictate, as has already been pointed out, is rich in references to the person as such (for whom Articles 2, 3 and 22 of the Constitution apply) and for the provisions that presuppose the 'value of the person' and confirm the existence of a general principle aimed at protecting the person (Articles 9, 13–27, 29–31, 32, 33, 34, 35–40 and 41–54). On the one hand, the person is considered as such; on the other hand as homo *oeconomicus* and as *homo socialis*.[2]

Since the late 1960s, civil law doctrine has been reinterpreting the rules of the Civil Code and special legislation by informing the interpretation of the value of the person.

The legal-formal dimension in which reflection is placed today still oscillates, as it did for personality rights in the first half of the twentieth century, between two antithetical positions: legal positivist and legal naturalist. According to the formalist and statist wing, civil liberties are exclusively those enumerated in the text of the Constitution, ie personal liberty, inviolability of the home, freedom of movement, assembly, association, worship, manifestation of thought, legal capacity, citizenship, name, taxation, judicial protection, the right to asylum, the personality of punishment, the personal responsibility of public officials and employees (Articles 13–28 of the Constitution). According to the natural

[2] In the constitutional text, the terminological qualification of the person, the mention of which places the reference in the context of individual cases, is varied and very rich. A lexical analysis alone reveals how many legally relevant situations are prefigured by the constituents, and how the person is at the heart of the fundamental legal framework itself. From time to time he is considered as a member of an entity (such as the people), as a member of the political organisation (voter, elected), as part of the administrative organisation (official, employee, dependent), and above all in family roles (spouse, parent, child, minor), social roles (citizen, foreigner), professional roles (worker, professor, lawyer, magistrate, military, police officer), including consideration of economic conditions (not wealthy, indigent) and conditions of marginality (minor, disabled, handicapped).

law wing, these provisions are the epiphany of the values that underlie every civil and democratic consortium, and their normative content is enriched, in their interpretation and application, by precisely those values, even if not made explicit, that refer to the person, human solidarity, protection from interference by public powers, and so on.

The formalist position finds it difficult to give meaning to Article 2 of the Constitution, since it is too broad and generic, and tends to consider it as a norm of reference, a 'closed' norm that finds specification in all the others that have regard to specific individual rights,[3] and points out the danger of a naturalistic interpretation of the legislation, detached from the formal datum and therefore susceptible to giving entry to the arbitrariness of the interpreter, to a living law that escapes the control of legality and rationality.

The natural law position holds that the Constitution has codified principles that are incumbent on the individual/person as a natural being, recognising rights that the person already possesses as such and that the state must only guarantee but not assign.[4]

Between these extremes are conceptions with different nuances, moving from the assumption that Article 2 is an 'open' text, interwoven with the values shared by the social conscience,[5] destined to make the system 'fluid', informed by a mild right,[6] by the plurality of rights,[7] distinguished between rights-claims, and rights-opportunities (in which merit, author-responsibility, private initiative emerge[8]); this provision becomes the keystone of the Constitution and the foundation of the *right to have rights.*[9]

From the perspective of effectiveness, we can calculate the real substance of these provisions and measure the distance between the 'letter' and the reality of the constitutional provisions.[10]

[3] A Pace, 'From Citizens' Rights to Fundamental Human Rights' (2010) *Associazione Italiana di Diritto Comparato* 1.

[4] F Todescan, *Le radici teologiche del giusnaturalismo laico. Il problema della secolarizzazione nel pensiero giuridico del sec. XVII* (Padua, Cedam, 2014).

[5] A Baldassarre, '*Privacy*' *e Costituzione* (Rome, Bulzoni, 1974).

[6] G Zagrebelsky, *Il diritto mite* (Turin, Einaudi, 1992).

[7] N Bobbio, *L'età dei diritti* (Turin, Einaudi, 1992).

[8] G Amato and A Barbrera, *Manuale di diritto pubblico* (Bologna, Il Mulino, 1993).

[9] S Rodotà, *Il diritto di avere diritti* (Roma-Bari, Laterza, 2013).

[10] In the various experiences, the issue of personal rights is frayed along certain basic lines. Wherever 'strong' constitutional protection has taken root, the rights of the person find their foundation – as a normative referent – in the constitutional texts, in their jurisprudential elaborations by the constitutional courts and in doctrinal elaborations: this is the case in the German experience (see eg P Haeberle, *Le libertà fondamentali nello Stato costituzionale,* partial Italian translation (Rome, Carocci, 1993); R Alexy, *Theorie der Grundrechte* (Frankfurt, 1986; Italian translation Bologna, Il Mulino, 2012). Where the constitutional relevance of the dimension of the person is less strong, because the normative referents are more appreciated in their political than in their legal-formal valence, the issue is placed in the sphere of public freedoms, as is the case with the French experience: M Frangi, *Constitution et droit privé* (Aix Marseille, Paris, 1992). The Italian experience is in an intermediate position: on the one hand, it lacks the theoretical-dogmatic construction of fundamental rights; on the other hand, the contribution of private law scholars has ensured that

Articles 2 and 3 of the Constitution have served to create new personal rights: alongside legal capacity, physical identity and citizenship, the right to *privacy* was created, ie the right to keep information concerning one's private life confidential, the right to protection from computerised collection of personal data, the right to personal identity, ie the right to prevent or repress any misrepresentation by third parties of the values one believes in and professes, the right to sexual identity, ie the right to change one's sex when for physiological or psychological reasons a subject belongs or feels that he belongs to a sex other than the one attributed to him at birth, the right to health (elaborated in the connection of these norms with Article 32), ie the right to obtain adequate care, and to prevent or repress any behaviour, private or public, that is dangerous to health, the right to a healthy environment (elaborated in the connection of these norms with Articles 9 and 32).

More problematic are the subjective positions concerning bioethics matters: the right to preserve one's genetic heritage, the right to procreation (now recognised for adult couples of different sexes, married or cohabiting, of childbearing age, by law no 40/2004), the right to know one's ethnic origins and possible hereditary diseases, the right to sterilisation, the right to prevent therapeutic treatment, the rights of the embryo and animals. Equally problematic, and even more debated, are other freedoms, such as sexual freedom, understood in the sense of choice and practice of inherent or acquired sexual orientation, and the techniques for repressing sexual violence against weak subjects (women and minors).

Rights must be balanced against each other.

The right to honour, reputation, and personal identity conflict with the freedom of the press (sometimes turned into abuse), which should not prevail over the rights of the individual, because, beyond the right of correction, it is very difficult to prevent or hinder the circulation of news disseminated through the *mass media* that are detrimental to personality rights, and once the damage has been caused, its reparation, even in numerical terms, is never completely satisfactory.[11]

The general provision with which Article 22 of the Constitution expresses itself required clarification and delimitation, which in the course of the debate in the Constituent Assembly was limited to citizenship, and not to legal

the subject of individual freedoms can be brought within the general principle of protection of the person, *pursuant to* Article 2 of the Constitution, so that personality rights have also found space and protection within it. In addition to these directions, there is the supranational direction that promotes the protection of human rights. For a reconsideration of these issues see, for all, A Pizzorusso in A Pizzorusso, R Romboli, U Breccia, A De Vita, *Persone fisiche, Comm. cod. civ.* (Bologna, Zanichelli, 1988) 16ff.

[11] Jurisprudence is oscillating, moving from the journalist's decalogue, which is more protective of the person, to the almost unconditional protection of freedom of reporting and satire: on this point G Alpa and G Resta, *Le persone fisiche e i diritti della personalità* (Turin, UTET, 2019).

capacity and the name.[12] Precisely because the provision lays down a prohibition on deprivation that extends to everyone ('no one may be deprived …'), at least for legal capacity and the name it was considered that this prohibition operates indiscriminately as legal capacity and name are intrinsic qualities of the person as such. An exception is made for legal capacity inherent in the exercise of public rights;[13] but legal capacity in the strict sense and name are guaranteed both by Articles 2 and 3 of the Constitution and, *a fortiori*, by Article 22. It responds to a logical requirement, even before it responds to a precise political choice, to assign to Article 22 a role that strengthens rather than restricts the guarantees for the protection of these aspects of the person: because, otherwise, what is promised in Articles 2 and 3 would be contradicted by the limitations introduced shortly afterwards by Article 22, understood in the sense of legitimising restrictions and disallowances.

The fact that the provision contains the phrase 'for political reasons' poses two further orders of problems, which are, however, easily solved. In the first place, the phrase must be understood in a broad sense: restrictions may not be introduced whether they are connected to political affiliation or to any other assessment in which a political opinion or orientation or connected to the public interests of the community may have an impact; furthermore, the phrase is not valid to allow limitations or restrictions dictated by reasons other than 'political' ones, since that very specification is to specify that 'not even' for political reasons such restrictions would be admissible. The limitation and the warning to the legislature therefore remain firm and intact.

The expression 'legal capacity' must be understood in the philological-historical sense and in the current sense. When the text of Article 22 was drafted, the Constituent Fathers brought their cultural background to the drafting, reasoning and expressing themselves with the legal categories then employed: these were the categories coeval with the drafting of the Civil Code discussed above. Today, the expression 'legal capacity' must be understood in a broad sense: encompassing all aspects of the person, and all the rights and duties, the subjective situations, of which he is the holder per se. Reductions in capacity will therefore not be admissible; if the distinction between legal capacity and capacity to act is accepted, limitations to the latter will be admissible only where they do not conflict with the nature and dignity of the person and the principle of equality.

This also applies to the name.

In the case of citizenship, Article 10 of the Constitution is taken into consideration, as well as the discipline of ordinary law in which some limitations are still maintained, with regard to the foreigner and with regard to

[12] U De Siervo, *Commentario della Costituzione* (di Branca ed) *Rapporti civili* Art. 22–23 (Bologna-Roma, Laterza, 1978) 5ff.

[13] ibid 8.

loss for having served in favour of other states. However, the current discipline of citizenship (unlike the 1912 law) is largely inspired by the constitutional dictate.[14]

III. EQUALITY, DIFFERENCES AND THE PRINCIPLE OF RATIONALITY

The immense literature on the principle of equality, as celebrated in the Italian Constitution (Article 3, paragraphs 1 and 2) has posed the problem of differences: indeed, just as the text recites, this literature has started from an indisputable observation that is assumed as an ineliminable fact. Differences exist, but they must not affect the legal treatment of individuals. 'Equal treatment' with respect to natural, political, religious, social differences. Differences must not result, in other words, in discrimination.

Today, reflection on the principle of equality is very sophisticated. It does not stop at equal treatment, nor does it demand homologation of the person to his peers and the environment in which he lives.

In other words, there is an insistence on the 'rationality' of differences. Equal 'social dignity' and 'equal legal dignity'[15] are guaranteed to all, but the legislature may depart from or derogate from them on reasonable grounds. It is admitted that the legislature may discriminate against categories of social formations, but not against individuals belonging to them.

The reading of Article 3 of the Italian Constitution legitimises differentiations: 'the law is equally differentiated[16] because it must treat equal situations equally and different situations (equally rational) differently'.

The principle of equality stands as a limit for the legislator, the public administration, and private individuals:

(a) to the legislature, so that the Italian Constitutional Court, in reviewing the rationality of the unequal treatment, can ascertain whether the conditions

[14] For a more in-depth analysis of these issues see G Alpa, *Status and Capacity. The legal construction of individual differences* (Roma-Bari, Laterza, 1993).

[15] A faithful and acute mirror of the prerogatives and duties contained in the Constitution is the work by Barile, *Diritti dell'uomo e libertà fondamentali* (Bologna, IlMulino, 1984), to which reference is made without the need for further bibliographical references. Ideality, utopia, the concrete operation of human rights in the international order are illustrated by Cassese, *I diritti umani nel mondo contemporaneo* (Roma-Bari, Laterza, 1988). An overall picture of this issue in the French experience is the work of A Heymann-Doat, *Libertés publiques et droits de l'homme* (Paris, Dalloz, 1990). Reflection on equality, civil rights and social justice has also invested French culture. The essays discussing the theses of J Rawls collected in the volume AA.VV., *Individue et justice sociale,* with a preface by F Terré (Paris, Dalloz, 1988); in the volume *La force du droit*, (Paris, Bourez, 1991), and in A Renaut and L Sosoe, *Philosophie du droit* (Paris, PUF, 1991), in which much space is given to the 'deconstructivist' theses of the subject of law, and both Arendt's right to difference and the reappearance of racial prejudice, as documented by PATaguiet, in *La force du préjujé. Essai sur le racisme et ses doubles* (Paris, Gallimard, 1988) 203ff.

[16] ibid 75. The Bill of Rights is continuously 'rewritten' by doctrine and jurisprudence, ie by interpreters: for an accurate documentation see B. Ackermann, *We the People*, vol I, *Foundations* (Cambridge, Mass, Harvard UniversityPress, 1992).

for discriminating exist and whether the differential standardisation is reasonable;

(b) to the public administration, as discrimination entails an unlimited application of discretionary powers (thus preventing abuses and excesses);

(c) to private individuals, so that in the context of their relations the exceptions to the prohibition of discrimination are not perpetuated, which, being banned by fundamental law, could not be legitimised under the shield of private autonomy.

This aspect is highly relevant because in civil law doctrine, the direct applicability of Article 3 of the Constitution to relations between private individuals is debated. For example, it is considered legitimate for the statute of a private association not to admit candidates on the grounds of race, sex, language, ideological, religious, trade union or sexual orientation, while it would not be admissible to discriminate against them if they already have the *status* of a member. Discrimination in the choice of counterpart, eg in rental contracts, but not in employment contracts, is considered possible.

The answers given to these questions are not convincing. It is said that within the association the individual is protected in all his prerogatives; but from outside the individual cannot claim not to be discriminated against by the members. It is said that the landlord can entrust his property to whomever he likes, and thus also choose the tenant on the basis of 'race'.

For contractual relations, it is necessary to ascertain the relevance of the discrimination: the power of refusal, which in the Civil Code finds a mention and a limit only in the context of services provided under a monopoly regime, may find another limit in Article 3 itself if it is justified by referring to one of the seven parameters codified by the same Article 3.[17]

Wisely, the legislator does not trust the direct jurisprudential application of Article 3 to private relations and between private individuals and the public administration. Therefore, it has reaffirmed the prohibition of discrimination in some fundamental laws. The technique is always the same: assuming different cases, or differentiated parameters, the prohibition of discrimination is laid down. Examples of this are: the Workers' Statute (1970); the Military Discipline Act (1984); the law ratifying the European Convention on Databases (1990); the Consolidation Act of the provisions governing immigration and the rules on the condition of foreigners (legislative decree no 286/1998), which banned all forms of discrimination on grounds of nationality, religion, race or ethnicity; Directive 2000/43/EC (transposed into our legal system by legislative decree no 215/2003), which prohibited discrimination on the grounds of racial or ethnic origin; Directive 2000/78/EC (transposed into Italian law

[17] On these issues see E Navarretta, 'L'evoluzione dell'autonomia contrattuale fra ideologie e principi' (2014) 43 *Quaderni fiorentini* 589; G Alpa and G Conte (eds), *Diritti e libertà fondamentali nei rapporti contrattuali* (Padua, Cedam, 2018).

by legislative decree no 216/2003), which established a series of measures for equal treatment in employment and occupation, prohibiting discrimination on the grounds of religion or belief, disability, age or sexual orientation; Law No 76/2006, which introduced specific provisions for the judicial protection of disabled persons suffering discrimination.

It must also be considered, from the point of view of legislative technique, that the prohibition fulfils a preventive role, discouraging conflicting initiatives; whereas the interpretation of Article 3 entails a weaker binding scope in any case.

The interpretation of Article 3 raises at least two further questions: is the list of parameters of differentiation exhaustive? It does not include, for example, ethical conventions; nor does it include sexual orientation; can the parameters be enriched by interpretation?

The second question concerns precisely the choice of individual parameters: how is the 'nature of things' understood by the constituent legislator, the ordinary legislator, constitutional and ordinary judges and other interpreters?

For example, how is the assumption of the parameter 'race' to be understood? As the acknowledgement of the existence of anthropological currents that distinguish men from a physical point of view; or as a datum referring to other experiences (discrimination against Blacks); or as a datum of Italian historical experience (anti-Semitic discrimination)? In other words, is the parameter 'race' taken as a factually existing and therefore legally relevant but non-discriminatory distinguishing datum, or as a datum derived from the collective imagination that can degenerate and therefore needs to be kept in check to avoid persecution? Would it not be better to speak of 'ethnicity'?[18]

What about 'personal conditions' or social conditions? Can personal conditions cover the handicapped, the elderly, the sick, drug addicts? Or do we only take into consideration the hypotheses that conform to the natural evolution of age, health or random biological deficiencies, but do not extend to the deteriorating conditions in which the individual places himself by an act of will (drug addicts, so-called 'at-risk subjects' of AIDS)? Again. What social *statuses* were the constituent legislator thinking of when he dictated the rule? And how should they be understood today, in a country that is socially so different from the one after the Second World War?

As can be seen, there are many questions that have been answered by jurists in an interlocutory or even unsatisfactory manner.[19]

These questions are not answered in jurisprudence.

[18] On the racial question in the USA see also R Polenberg, *One Nation Divisible: Class, Race and Ethnicity in the U.S. since 1938* (London, Penguin, 1991). On the cultural construction of race in the French experience see T Todorov, *Noi e gli altri* (Turin, Einaudi, 1991).

[19] See Schiavone's recent insightful reflection on these issues: *Eguaglianza.Una nuova vision sul filo della storia* (Turin, Einaudi, 2019).

The organic collections of case law on equality[20] highlight above all the problems of a formal nature that emerge and are resolved in the judgement of constitutionality; the Constitutional Court's use of the so-called *tertium comparationis*, ie the parameter of comparison between the interests defended by the challenged law, the constitutional regulation and the rule or principle of the system with which the challenged regulation is in contrast: and also the parameter of reasonableness that justifies, or condemns, the derogation to equality.

When it comes to discrimination, the most widespread case law concerns criminal law, labour, public and private, the social security sector, procedural law or issues concerning the principle of formal equality; there are very few issues concerning equality in the substantive sense.[21]

Two words stand out in the constitutional text that, when combined with the term 'person', give it a special connotation. These two words are *solidarity* and *dignity*.

IV. THE PRINCIPLE OF SOLIDARITY

'Solidarity' is an expression found by way of exception in normative terminology. It tends to occur more frequently in constitutional texts than

[20] I refer to B Caravita's reconstruction, in *Commentario breve alla Costituzione*, edited by V Crisafulli and L Paladin (Padua, Cedam, 1990), Art 3 Italian Constitution, and to the repertory of maxims edited by G Pescatore, F Felicetti, and G Marziale, *Costituzione e leggi sul processo costituzionale e sui referendum* (Milan, Giuffré, 1984), Art 3 Italian Constitution. Further indications are in *L'interpretazione giudiziaria della Convenzione europea dei diritti dell'uomo*, edited by Facchin (Padua, Cedam, 1988); V Pocar, 'Diritti umani e diritti dei viventi. Una riflessione sociologica' (1991) I *Sociologia del Diritto* 67, where one can also read MV De Giorgi's essay, 'Modelli giuridici dell'eguaglianza e dell'equità' 20. On the notion of equality see the precise observations of R Guastini, 'La grammatica di "eguaglianza"' (1992) *Lavoro e Diritto* 205ff.

[21] The Italian Court of Cassation has pointed out that 'with regard to the termination of employment due to age limits for workers in the entertainment industry belonging to the categories of dancers, the transitional regulations set forth in Article 3, paragraph 7, of legislative decree no. 64 of 2010, converted, with amendments, into law no. 100 of 2010, introduce discrimination based on gender in that it differentiates the maximum retirement age set for women (forty-six years of age) and men (fifty-two years of age), in law no. 100 of 2010, introduces a discrimination based on sex where it diversifies the maximum retirement age set for women (forty-six years) and for men (fifty-two); it follows that the rule in conflict with Article 14, paragraph 1, letter c) of directive 2006/54/EC cannot be directly applied, without the need to raise an issue of constitutionality'. The case dealt with by the Constitutional Court was different, which found illegitimate Article 1(3)(g), second sentence, limited to the words 'and to the relative duration' and Article 10(20 of Provincial Law no 12 of Bolzano of 2011 in that 'the provincial legislator has ... used the fact of qualified residence to diversify the access of foreigners to services exceeding the limits of the essential intended for study support, both school and university' and this criterion contrasts with the principles of reasonableness and equality, resulting in violation of Article 3 of the Constitution. Finally, again purely by way of example, the Court of Justice of the European Union has specified that the legitimacy 'of a difference of treatment based on religion or belief is subject to the objectively verifiable existence of a direct link between the requirement for the performance of the work activity imposed by the employer and the activity in question'; this 'requirement' must be 'as required by Article 4(2) of Directive 2000/78, "essential, legitimate and justified"'.

in lower-ranking laws: constitutions codify the tables of values on which the legal system is based and outline the guidelines to be followed by the ordinary legislator, they also identify the freedoms of individuals and the fundamental rights of citizens; solidarity, as a general value, thus finds its natural home in the basic norms of a legal system.

A less rare mention of this term is to be found in the constitutions immediately following the Second World War: in the wake of the greatest massacre in history, of the atrocities perpetrated in particular by the Nazis and the militias of the Republic of Salò on combatants, resistance fighters, dissidents, ethnic minorities, and the defenceless population itself, the reference to solidarity in the text of the fundamental laws sounds like a condemnation of the past, a warning to the present, a commitment to the future. The reference to solidarity is also a bar to exasperated individualism, which tramples on the dignity of the individual and ignores feelings of brotherhood and mutual support between people, between citizens, between social categories; it also sounds like a lesson to future generations, so that they may learn from the mistakes recorded in history and pass on this lofty message.

Solidarity is considered a strong value in the Italian Constitution: it already appears at the beginning, in Article 2, where inviolable human rights are recognised and guaranteed, protected both for the individual person and in reference to social groups; 'rights' are matched by 'duties', and the duty stated first is precisely the duty of solidarity; it then recurs – implicitly – where the right and duty to work is prescribed and the contribution of citizens to the material or spiritual progress of society is prescribed (Article 4); solidarity is expressed to the weak categories, in the Republic's commitment to remove economic and social obstacles that limit the freedom and equality of citizens, the development of the individual and the participation of workers in the political, economic and social organisation of the country (Article 3, paragraph 2); solidarity is offered to foreigners exercising their right to asylum (Article 10); and where it repudiates war as an instrument of offence against the freedom of other peoples; this is in function of peace and justice among nations (Article 11); or where it protects religious freedom, exercised individually and in association; it manifests itself to needy (and 'numerous': Article 31), and to families who have to provide for the school education of minors (Article 34, paragraph 3); solidarity is expressed to emigrants and protecting the work of Italians abroad, to working women (Article 37), to those unable to work and individual workers so that they may have a dignified existence (Article 38) as well as to the disabled and handicapped (Article 38, paragraph 3), and so on. The expression therefore appears among the duties: and it is not a daring juxtaposition to call to mind the French revolutionary constitutions that break with the past, and precisely introduce the category of 'duty' which is very different from the category of 'subjection' to privilege proper to the *Ancien Regime*.

The text proposed by the subcommittee mentioned economic and spiritual solidarity (precisely in the sense of the 'security' of the French revolutionary constitutions): and it was understood as 'the necessary sociality of all persons who are destined to complement and perfect each other'. Solidarity is thus the expression of socialisation from communities such as family, territorial, professional, religious, etc., and finally the state.

In the universal charters of rights, solidarity is not mentioned expressly, but is a value suffused in both the 1948 Declaration and the 1950 European Convention, where the duties and responsibilities of individuals are recalled.

Comparison with other modern constitutions only enhances the organic and comprehensive design of the Italian Constitution. On the one hand, in fact, the majority of constitutions maintain the individualistic structure of nineteenth-century origin, and thus concern themselves with claiming spaces of freedom and guarantees of protection for the individual, but not with demanding his solidarity in favour of other citizens. Solidarity is not even mentioned in the constitutions of Belgium and the Netherlands; on the other hand, even in the most recent texts, the value of solidarity is relegated to the background.

In the preamble of the French Constitution of 1946, for example, solidarity is placed alongside the equality of all French people in the face of the burdens of national disasters; but nothing is said about the duties and development of the personality or other requirements for cooperation or collaboration by individuals and groups.

In the Bonn Basic Law of 1949, innate rights are protected but there is no mention of duties of solidarity; a large group of parliamentarians also proposed an amendment to the text of Article 2 to include the formula that every person is called upon to show love of neighbour and a sense of solidarity (§ 2a).

The Irish Constitution (of 1937), on the other hand, stands out, devoting ample attention to the relationship between individuals and the bonds of solidarity that the Republic intends to promote and strengthen. In this text – which was born with a markedly confessional qualification (the preamble opens with the invocation to the Holy Trinity, in whose name and in the name of Jesus Christ, the Constitution is adopted) – there are recurring mentions of charity, forms of protection of individual rights and concerns related to greater social justice (see eg Article 43(1)(2), regarding property, the guiding principles of social policy, and so on).

It would therefore seem that the principle of solidarity is peculiar to confessional constitutions or constitutions that have arisen, like the Italian one, from compromise between different political forces.

More recent constitutions, including secular ones, appear more sensitive to this aspect of human coexistence.

The Portuguese Constitution of 1976 is particularly diffuse on the right to work and workers' rights, consumers' rights and the social security system, about which it mentions solidarity; but this concern also emerges from the provisions on housing, health, etc. The Spanish Constitution of 1978 promotes favourable conditions for social and economic progress and for a fair distribution of regional income as well as for maintaining a public social security system; it also protects not only fundamental social rights, but also the rights of consumers and users, the *handicapped, the* marginalised.

Being a generic, allusive, evocative expression, solidarity is specified with objectification: now it refers to economic relations, now to social or family relations. Its meaning, however, still retains imprecise and blurred contours. And yet, logically, even before legally, solidarity implies:

(i) an inter-individual relationship, not being able to give solidarity with or for oneself (self-love is, on the other hand, an expression of individualism, separateness, self-defence);
(ii) a relationship between equals, by economic and social conditions, by elective affinities, by belonging to classes, categories, religions, ethnicities, cultures, languages; which implies reciprocity, cooperation, defence against external aggregations; or
(iii) an unequal relationship, if established with the other who suffers, who is more disadvantaged, who is more uncultured.

Solidarity thus implies duality or plurality of subjects and thus of relationships; it implies above all the recognition of individual otherness or group otherness; again, an internal solidarity (within the group, category, etc) and an external solidarity (to the group, category, etc); it may involve a horizontal relationship, between individuals and between groups, or a vertical relationship, between individuals and groups and the state.

As for the relationship with the other, it may be individual or social; as for its manifestation, it may be spontaneous or coercive; as for the modalities of expression, it may concern political relations (pluralism, tolerance, collaboration), religious relations (protection of minorities), social relations (in family relations, man-woman relations, rich-poor relations), economic relations (in fair relations between employers and workers, between businesses and consumers, etc).

Historically speaking, the immediate modern reference to the content of solidarity is found in the works and theses of the natural lawyers: at the very moment when the Hobbesian *homo homini lupus is* overcome, and a framework of ideal values is outlined in which the individual-person is considered, as such, *sui iuris*, solidarity is affirmed for the other than oneself, considered as an equal to oneself; obviously, with all the nuances and curvatures dictated by the mentality and culture of the jurist and the historical-social environment in which he operates.

The problem affects *ab imis* the very meaning of society, and thus connotes the foundations of public law. But it also affects civil law.

Among the civil law scholars is Jean Domat who, in the mid-seventeenth century, felt the influence of his friend Pascal, and enunciates the decalogue of friendship at the very opening of his *Lois civiles*.

At the beginning of the *Lois civiles*, he indicates the sources of bonds, distinguishing a first type, which relates to natural bonds (marriage, kinship, affinity) and a second type, which includes voluntary bonds and those independent of the will. Alongside these bonds, he identifies another species of bond 'which unites men more closely than any other commitment, apart from marriage and birth: it is the bond of friendship'. The meaning of 'friendship' in this context goes beyond the election of two persons, but implies that of solidarity: the bonds of friendship are multiplied, 'by succour that each one procures from the persons who are adherents of his friends'.[22] Friendship implies reciprocity and is a consequence of commitment. Domat again distinguishes between friendship dictated by self-love, which undoubtedly seeks its own interest, and friendship born of the love of the highest good, which seeks the common good of both. The characters common to both types are reciprocity and freedom. And it is precisely thanks to freedom, which implies absence of sanction, that these bonds can be attenuated, dissolved, re-established without any legal consequences, since these bonds do not fall within the scope of civil law.

As we can see, Domat does not arrive at the conception of friendship-solidarity understood as a true obligation: it is a bond that remains outside the juridical dimension; although narrow, his conception identifies individual friendship and friendship *in incertam personam*, ie solidarity towards those in need (friendship dictated by the highest good).

Solidarity, understood in the sense of fraternity, emerges strongly in the revolutionary climate.

There is no proclamation of 'duties' in the Declaration of Rights: Thomas Paine justifies this omission by arguing that it is not an omission, every right having its correlated duty.[23] The rights of the individual are then summarised in Marat's brilliant prose in this way: the premise is that 'the civil rights of every individual are, indeed, nothing but his natural rights counterbalanced by those of other individuals and limited where they would thus begin to infringe them'. Respect for the rights of others, however, is seen from a utilitarian perspective: respect is motivated by 'securing the peaceful enjoyment' of one's own rights.

The listing of civil rights is an anticipation of the text of the Declaration: personal security, individual liberty, and ownership of property are listed.[24]

Apparently the formula reproduces Locke's tetralogy.[25] The friend of the people would seem here to propose a manifesto of the most inveterate individualism; but solidarity penetrates it through the guarantee of property: property

[22] *Le leggi civili disposte nel loro ordine naturale*, I (1723) It trans (Pavia, Bizzoni, 1825) 56.
[23] See *Rights of Men* (London, Penguin, 1987) 114.
[24] J-P Marat, *Projet de déclaration des droits de l'homme et du citoyen, suivi d'un plan de Constitution juste, sage et libre* (Paris, 1789) 11ff.
[25] S Rials, *La déclaration des droits de l'homme et du citoyen* (Paris, Etude Poche, 1988) 382.

and labour are the pair that supports the edifice of the citizen's rights. This is because – Marat[26] explains – society must ensure, for those who are poor and can only dispose of their labour, 'sustenance, which to feed, clothe and inhabit conveniently'.

However, solidarity is expressed vertically: it affects the relationship between the individual (citizen) and the state; others are regarded as monads, not as a community.

The transition to the communitarian conception of society will occur with the advent of the Jacobins, and the Constitution of 1793. But the community will be identified with the state and there will be a shift from exaggerated individualism to a dangerous statolatry.[27]

On the other hand, it could only be this way: in a revolutionary political and social environment in which the tragic dilemma between proclaiming and allowing the exercise of fundamental rights, and thus also of the right to associate, and limiting some of these rights in order to save the state from probable destabilisation by *clubs*, corporations, companies, is resolved[28] in the second horn of the dilemma: a proclamation of solidarity could not be expected to invest the separate bodies of the state. Solidarity could only be indirect, that is, passing through the state.

This, however, is the strand from which 'fraternity', as a fundamental principle of the French Revolution, derives.

The expression *fraternité* has gone down in history as the mythical emblem of revolutionary values, associated with 'liberty' and 'equality' in the famous triad that connoted citizens' rights. However, the fraternity did not appear in legal texts at the same time as the other two, but was added later.

The reasons for the addition are to be found in the political moment that suggests its inclusion. In truth, the expression glimpses in some marginal provision, such as in the penultimate paragraph of Title I, already in the Constitution of 1791, regarding the introduction of national holidays in memory of the Revolution; there the reason for the provision is stated, which consists in 'maintaining fraternity between citizens and binding them to the Constitution, the Fatherland, the Laws'. It is clear that fraternity here means 'fraternising', allowing individuals to make friends, to rejoice together; at the same time, it also means a political instrument to strengthen the patriotic spirit, nourished by revolutionary certainties, and necessary to fight the enemies of the Revolution, inside and outside the country.

But it is with 1793, as mentioned above, that the expression takes on a different and more meaningful meaning. In the draft declaration of rights drafted by Robespierre on 24 April 1793, fraternity indicates a universal value: men of

[26] ibid 43.
[27] ibid 398.
[28] H Burstin, 'A legislative itinerary: Le Chapelier laws 1791' in H Burstin (ed), *French Revolution: the force of ideas, the force of things* (Milan, Guerini, 1990) 76.

all countries are recognised as brothers and the different peoples 'must help each other according to their power, like citizens of the same state'. Fraternity also plays an important role in relations between private individuals, where in negotiations the new laws require the parties to behave according to good faith.[29]

Robespierre himself is the inventor of the triad 'liberty, equality, fraternity': the term appears for the first time in a draft decree that he prepared as early as 5 December 1790, foreseeing the defence of man and citizen, and proposing that the three words be written on the chest and drapes of the national guard.[30] After the fall of the monarchy, and the proclamation of the republic, the expression becomes the message that France addresses to all oppressed peoples: fraternity thus becomes synonymous with 'sovereignty of the people'; it does not only concern the cement of the French nation, complementing Robespierre's conception of fatherland, but becomes a universal political message.[31] Hence, again, the push for the liberation of the colonies, and the debate on the legitimacy of slavery.

In the Constitution of 24 June 1793, fraternity is indeed not mentioned, but its contents surface where it speaks of liberty ('do not do unto others as you would not have them do unto you': Article 6); while security is understood as the 'protection granted by society to each of its members for the preservation of the person, his rights and his property' (Article 8).

Just as it is not mentioned in the Declaration of Rights and Duties that preceded the French Constitution of 22 August 1795 (the so-called Constitution of the third year of the French Republic) in which, however, it is confused with security, which is defined no longer in the claim that the citizen can assert against the state in an active intervention in his defence, but, reversing the relationship, as 'the result of the concurrence of all to ensure the rights of each' (Article 4). In other words, the citizen must not wait inertly for the public apparatus to take action and provide for his needs, but must himself take a diligent part and contribute to building and nurturing a better society. This is, once the regime of privileges is overthrown, everyone must take action to build the new society.

In the French Constitution of 1795, 'duties' as well as human rights appear in a fundamental text for the first time. The duties include the precepts 'do not do unto others as you would not have them do unto you' and 'always do unto others as you would have them do unto you' (Article 2); it specifies that 'he is not a good citizen who is not a good son, a good father, a good brother, a good

[29] D Corradini, 'Il processo costituzionale nella Francia rivoluzionaria e il diritto privato' in G Cattaneo (ed), *Diritto e Stato nella filosofia della Rivoluzione francese* (Milan, Giuffré, 1992) 202.

[30] F Gauthier, *Triomphe et mort du droit naturel en Révolution, 1789-1802* (Paris, Syllepse, 1992) 137.

[31] ibid 141.

friend, a good spouse' (Article 4); it adds that 'he is not a good man who does not frankly and religiously observe the laws' (Article 5).

Here fraternity, and solidarity, though blurred in their physiognomy, present a content of duty: it is the duty to be active, to do good, which for the first time appears in a normative text. Domat, which is not surprising in a Jansenist, had treated it as a non-civil obligation; having broken the individualist arc linking the *Ancien Regime* to the Revolution, the obligation to cooperate is introduced into the normative dictate. And the discourse no longer concerns man's feelings, but his responsibilities in the face of the state's legitimate demands.

As can be seen, in the seventeenth and eighteenth centuries, and again at the beginning of the nineteenth century, solidarity entered the field. Admittedly, this is a nuance: that there is continuity between fraternity and solidarity, and therefore homogeneity of values, is unquestionable; but as already noted, brotherhood and friendship still appear to be carved in an individualist dimension, while solidarity immediately evokes a community dimension.

This was a short-lived season: with Napoleon's coming to power and the proclamation of the Empire, solidarity-fraternity disappears. In the civil codes of the nineteenth century, the term is ignored: but this is not so surprising, as economic liberalism is more selfish, a symbol appropriate to a bourgeois and classist political and social structure. Not only that: solidarity is a value that tends not to have a patrimonial content, because it recalls friendly relations, spontaneously assumed commitments, absence of correspondence, while those codes are concerned with dictating rules to private individuals considered either as owners or as traders; the discipline of property and exchanges is antithetical to generosity and gratuitousness, it views economically unproductive operations with suspicion, it eliminates constraints, abolishes claims to cooperation; individualism is its nourishment.

The Restoration completes this – as is well known – descending path.

Instead, solidarity resurfaces in the Constitution of 4 October 1848; in the preamble, in Article III, it is finally proclaimed that the French Republic 'has Liberty, Equality and Fraternity as its principles' (to which is added: 'and has the family, work, property and public order as its basis').

In this liberal-socialist Constitution, the expression fraternity is the subject of troubled discussion. In the first draft (which Tocqueville, Coquerel and Lamennais, among others, had worked on) it was not explicitly mentioned; however, the Constitution proper was preceded by a declaration of 'duties' and 'rights' (note the inversion); Article 1 of the declaration dealt with the duties 'of man in society', among which was the *pratique fraternelle* in the maxim: 'do not do unto others what you would not have them do unto you; what you would have men do for you, do for them'. At the end of the day, elevated to a duty, we have an enriched content of solidarity, because to the evangelical-Kantian maxim (do not do unto others … , ie do not treat others as means, but as ends) ie the negative command, is added the positive command, which implies the activation of a behaviour of solidarity. The body of the Constitution then contains other principles that will be considered in the drafting of the Italian Constitution, such as the right to work, the connection between property and work, and so on.[32]

The second draft, only a few weeks later, is authored by Thiers and Cremieux, among others. Here, they discuss whether it is appropriate to have a preamble preceding the constitutional discipline; and having resolved the question positively, fraternity appears there along with liberty and equality; the three values are called 'dogmas'. Finally, in the text of 28 October 1848, the three values are qualified as 'principles'.

Fraternity – now understood as solidarity – re-emerged at the end of the century, again by socialists and Catholics: political socialism and legal socialism on the one hand, and cooperation and assistance on the other, became the pillars of contemporary forms of solidarity.

The end of the century saw the first theorisations of solidarity as it is understood in the contemporary sense: Leon Bourgeois, responding to Guyot's criticism that society is nothing more than the aggregate of individuals, points out that rights and duties are certainly instituted among men, but not between men and 'society', which could not be assumed to be a body equated to a man: men are aggregated among themselves as 'associated with a common work and obliged to one another by the requirement of a common purpose'.[33]

Therefore, the positive law will have to take into account the burdens of this association, distributing the assets and costs fairly.

No longer the theory of the social contract, but the theory of the quasi-contract (where constraints rest neither on negotiation nor on correspondence) seems the most appropriate legal-political reference for those who want to chart a middle course between individualism and socialism.

The history of the turn of the century records – as is well known – important social upheavals that are based on solidarity: the struggles of the working class to obtain more humane working conditions and a wage that guarantees survival; the emergence of parties and trade unions advocating egalitarian and socialist ideas in the political life of all countries; the commitment of Catholics in assistance and education works. Solidarity is a message of brotherhood, of charity, of connection that is understood quite differently by lay people and Catholics: the former understand it as *esprit de corps* (class struggle, solidarity within the class), the latter as an expression of charity towards the weakest individuals. Fraternity has become an irrepressible value, political in nature but also juridical. It has been keenly observed that 'it is not a liberal principle, but a Catholic or socialist one';[34] or even a Freemason one, since, 'Christian

[32] P Craveri, *Genesis of a Constitution. Liberty and Socialism in the Constitutional Debate of 1848 in France* (Naples, Guida, 1985) 72ff.

[33] *La solidarité* (Paris, 1902) 87, now in F Worms (ed), *Droits de l'homme et philosophie. Une anthologie* (Paris, Edition du CNRS, 1993) 386–87.

[34] A Martinelli, 'I princìpi della Rivoluzione francese e la società moderna' in A Martinelli, M Salvati and S Veca, *Progetto 89* (Milan, Il Saggiatore, 1989) 74.

solidarism stands as an alternative to trade union and cooperative organisation of socialist inspiration'.[35]

The exponents of legal socialism, from Menger to Gianturco to Cimbali, appropriated it, and so did the forces of the left, politically more active, at that stage, than the Catholic forces.

In the current civil codes, solidarity is ignored: in ours it is a product of corporate ideology, and must therefore be replaced with the notion of solidarity derived from the constitutional text.

The Italian interpreter therefore has at his disposal a constitutional text rich in references and cues and a civil code stingy with solidaristic thrusts. An operation of direct application of constitutional norms to relations between private individuals is therefore necessary.

Faced with such an organic framework, however, the jurisprudential application of Article 2 of the Constitution, which is very explicit in terms of duties of solidarity, reveals disappointing operational results. The rule appears very marginal both with respect to the application of the other rules contained in this provision and with respect to the other provisions referred to therein.

At the end of the day, either the duty of solidarity is understood as compulsory acquiescence to the suspension of procedural deadlines dictated by calamitous events[36] or as a substitutive duty of the public administration (or public bodies) in the case of protection of public order and arrest in flagrante,[37] or as a duty of contribution in the case of pension payments,[38] or as a duty of contribution to urbanisation charges,[39] or as a duty of information.[40]

Far more stimulating is the use of the principle in civil law.

Civilists rediscover solidarity, re-evaluating the direct application of the Constitution to relations between private individuals and making use of the general clauses referring to good faith, fairness and equity. Its application is proposed in matters of property where proprietary individualism is contrasted with the conception of the social function of property; in matters of economic activities, where market freedom is contrasted with the social utility of economic initiative; in contractual freedom, where the protection of the weaker contracting party is opposed to the bargaining power of the company, both in the employment sector and in the consumption and savings sectors; in matters of tort, where greater importance is given to the person and to the quantification of the damage, the theory of business risk is favoured and an attempt is made to overcome the principle of typicality of the hypotheses of omissive fault.[41]

[35] ibid 83.
[36] Italian Constitutional Court, No 47/1969.
[37] Italian Constitutional Court, No 89/1970.
[38] Italian Constitutional Court, No 35/1981 and Constitutional Court, No 173/2018.
[39] Italian Constitutional Court, No 127/1983.
[40] Italian Constitutional Court, no. 364/1988.
[41] See, for all, S Rodotà, *Il diritto privato nella società moderna* (Bologna, Il Mulino, 1980).

But why elevate solidarity to a juridical rule, that is, to a binding and coercive norm? Why is there a need to remove solidarity from the world of non-juridical relationships, from the world of spontaneous and friendly action, from the world of chance and caprice? The answer, at once banal and simple, is quickly said: because solidarity is a peculiar feature of modern and civilised societies, inspired by the protection of the other, of the different, of the marginalised; but it is a feature that tends to be submerged, when not eradicated, by the individualism (or worse, the selfishness) inherent in human nature. Homo *homini lupus* is a historical truth, unsurpassed and perhaps unsurpassable. And it is precisely to temper this natural urge, to preserve social cohesion itself, to elevate brute coexistence to civilised coexistence, that solidarity must not only be recognised but also imposed as a value and a principle.

Elevating solidarity to a principle of law means making the 'solidarity' act or behaviour compulsory. As long as the law binds the legislator, there are no problems: he is the interpreter of the social conscience and, to the extent that this is required by the drive towards greater social equality and is permitted by the economic and political situation, he intervenes from time to time in favour of the weak, marginalised, discriminated categories. The construction of the so-called welfare state responds to these needs; the re-fluxing of the social conscience towards individualism, selfishness, brutal competition, accompanied by the tendency towards the privatisation of services, private and optional welfare and assistance, provokes the dismantling of the welfare state and the search not for general models of justice but for separate and graduated spheres of justice.

Solidarity is thus – in this publicist perspective – both a limit to individual action dictated by social reasons and an obligation (assumed by the legislator himself but also imposed on individuals) to work for the realisation of fairer social relations and more humane living conditions.

Interventions in favour of health, housing, the environment, consumption and savings are also dictated by reasons of solidarity.

The concept of solidarity professed by the Church emerges clearly from the text of the Catechism, given in Rome by John Paul II on 11 October 1992. The expression is used quite frequently in different contexts. It moves from the basic solidarity, dictated by the common fatherhood of all creatures, according to the Franciscan laude (§ 344) it insists on the unity of the human race, united by the same origin, the divine creation (§ 361) and emphasises that human solidarity combined with charity is a law that ensures brotherhood among men; solidarity is based on the communion of saints (§ 953). Above all, emphasis is placed on 'human' solidarity in the indication of the tasks of Catholic man in the social sphere (§ 1939) where the principle of solidarity 'also designated by the name of friendship or social charity is a direct requirement of human and Christian fraternity'. Solidarity – also in this sense – is manifested in the distribution of goods and remuneration for work (§ 1940): the commitment is not just individual, it is not just casual, but presupposes the promotion of a 'more just social order', obviously to be achieved peacefully (with 'negotiated' solutions). Solidarity understood in this way comes close to the meaning enshrined in the Italian Constitution. Again: solidarity is not only vertical, but also horizontal (the poor must be in solidarity with each other, entrepreneurs must be in solidarity with each other: § 1941). In other words, solidarity is connected with equality, dignity, brotherhood, social justice.

This lesson and this commitment are echoed at the international level with regard to justice and solidarity between nations: the lack of solidarity impedes the development of less advanced countries, allows the imposition of abusive if not usurious financial systems, unequal trade relations, the prevarication of rich nations over the poor, and so on.

A teaching and commitment reaffirmed in the encyclical *Veritatis splendor* of 6 August 1993 where solidarity goes hand in hand with the humiliation of peoples whose human rights have been violated (§ 98) and is a value of renewal, associated with justice, honesty and transparency. Solidarity imposes respect for minorities (§ 99) and correct behaviour, such as reprobation of theft, fair pay, fair trade, prohibition of appropriation of a company's social assets, etc (§ 100).

The two souls of solidarity have been preserved to this day: on the one hand horizontal solidarity, the result of the initiative of the individual in favour of his or her own group or weaker groups; an initiative dictated by charity (in the Catholic sense) or by the common struggle against capitalist exploitation (in the socialist sense); on the other hand vertical solidarity, ie the contribution required by the state from each citizen to sustain social coexistence: personal benefits, taxation, restrictions on property and economic initiative, and so on, in order to operate a redistribution that relieves the hardships of the less well-off and establishes equitable social relations.

V. THE PRINCIPLE OF DIGNITY

The word 'dignity' appears at the beginning of the Constitution (Article 3(1)) in the sense of 'social dignity' – the equality of which, together with equality before the law, is guaranteed to all citizens – and again in the context of the provisions dedicated to economic relations with regard to remuneration for work, which must ensure a free and dignified existence for the worker and his family (Article 36), and in the area of limits to the exercise of economic activities, where it is provided that economic initiative may not be detrimental to security, freedom and human dignity (Article 41(2)).

In its conceptual elaboration, this term is evidently connected, in the eyes of Italian jurists, to freedoms, equality and therefore to the inviolable rights of the person, of which the Constitution always makes usbergo in the opening provision enshrined in Article 2.[42]

The systematic placement of this expression and the adjectives that are attached to it should not mislead. Even though 'dignity' is explicitly mentioned in Article 3 of the Constitution and in the other provisions referred to in an apparently circumscribed manner, its inclusion in the text has not obscured the universally shared conception of Italian jurists, coming from different backgrounds and intent on cultivating different sectors of the legal system, civil law, labour law, constitutional law, criminal law, procedural law, and so on, in the sense that the dignity of the person is considered the basis of inviolable rights and therefore the basis of the entire legal system. And it is a significant fact that since 1956 the Constitutional Court has invoked it in at least 100 pronouncements and that in the jurisprudence of the Court of Cassation it is invoked in thousands of pronouncements in the field of labour law, personality rights, family relations, but also environmental law, the right to health, in the field of criminal trial law and even in the field of deontological control of the intellectual professions.[43]

Although used so frequently, one should not believe that the term appears in all constitutions of the Western world. On the contrary. In the US federal Constitution it is only a value, whereas it is an explicitly guaranteed right in the Constitutions of Montana, Illinois, Louisiana and Puerto Rico. In the Canadian Constitution it is only a value. In the South African Constitution it is a value and a right, but a limited one. In Israel, dignity is a constitutionally guaranteed right but is not considered an absolute value. It is a relative right, which fractures into many other rights (life, freedom of expression, privacy, etc) that are balanced, and often contradictory to each other, and it is not a right that operates retroactively.[44]

The German Constitution stands out and differentiates itself among them all, because in that text, which opens in Article 1 with the codification of dignity, this concept is considered an absolute, *intangible* value, not just inviolable, as National Constitutions (eg Italian and German) and the European Charter of Fundamental Rights preach: therefore it is not subject to limits or balancing in the application of other personal rights. In this sense, the highest appreciation

[42] In comparative treatments of experiences on both sides of the Atlantic, the debate is heated: G Kateb, *Human Dignity* (Cambridge, Mass, Harvard University Press, 2011); J Waldron, *Dignity, Ranks & Rights* (Oxford, OUP, 2012); M Rosen, *Dignity. History and Meaning* (Harvad Mass., Harvard University Press, 2012); S Moyn, *Human Rights and the Uses of History* (London and New York, Verso Books, 2014).

[43] G Alpa, 'Dignity' (1999) II *Nuova Giurisprudenza Civile Commentate* and G Alpa, *Solidarity. A Normative Principle* (Alphen and der Rhijn, Wolters Kluwer, 2023).

[44] A Barak, *Human Dignity. The Constitutional Value and the Constitutional Right* (Cambridge, CUP, 2015).

of this value can be found in the legal system of a country that wants to remember its tragic past and make amends for its criminal history.[45]

Etymologically speaking, the expression must be understood in its historical development,[46] because behind this sign/symbol lie many meanings that are coloured in a varied manner depending on the context and era in which the term is used. Today, it is understood as the essential element of the new conception of the person, a sort of 'anthropology of *homo dignus*',[47] which connotes the way in which man is to be considered as the bearer of values, protected therefore from threats to life, health and freedom, and as an end, not a means, by other men. It is precisely for this reason that when jurists reason on the meaning of this term, they recall its complex philosophical history, which starts even from Cicero, passes through the doctrine of the Fathers of the Church, finds ample treatment in the writings of St Thomas Aquinas, is the subject of a treatise by Pico della Mirandola, and then finds its most luxuriant season in Humanism and in the roots of seventeenth-century natural law.[48] From there it comes back to life, as the conception of man changes in the eighteenth,[49] nineteenth and twentieth centuries.[50]

It is evident that its interpenetration with the individual carves out its contours, because it reflects the conception of the individual considered in the dimension of space and time proper to those who expound it. We cannot therefore confuse the values on which Greco-Roman culture and natural rights as understood in Platonic and Aristotelian philosophy were based with the values of the medieval era and those of the Renaissance and then the Enlightenment. On the former, the pages of Leo Strauss remain unsurpassed, in a work reprinted several times, also in Italy,[51] in which he distinguishes the ancient and aristocratic conception of natural rights from the modern conception of natural rights. For human rights in medieval legal civilisation, it is sufficient to refer to the dialogue between Paolo Grossi and Brian Thierny,[52] which established a

[45] For all see J Habermas, *Morals, Law, Politics* (Turin, Einaudi, 1992); R Alexy, *Theory of Fundamental Rights* (Bologna, Il Mulino, 2012); P Ridola, *Comparative Law and European Constitutional Law* (Turin, Giappichrelli, 2010).

[46] C. McCrudden, *Human Dignity and Judicial Interpretation of Human Rights* (Oxford, OUP, 2008).

[47] To use Rodotà's expression, 'Antropologia dell'homo dignus' (2013) 2 civilistica.com 1; by S Rodotà see also *Il diritto di avere diritti* (Roma-Bari, Laterza, 2013); *Solidarietà .Una utopia necessaria* (Roma-Bari, Laterza, 2015).

[48] GM Flick, *Elogio della dignità* (Vatican City, Libreria editrice vaticana, 2015); P Becchi, *Il principio dignità umana* (Brescia, Morcelliana, 2013); Ridola (n 45) 80ff.

[49] V Ferrone, *Storia dei diritti dell'uomo* (Roma-Bari, Laterza, 2015).

[50] S Rodotà, *Dal soggetto alla persona* (Naples, Edizioni scientifiche, 2007); P Zatti, 'Note sulla "semantica della dignità"' in M Furlan (ed), *Bioetica e dignità umana. Interpretazioni a confronto a partire dalla Convenzione di Oviedo* (Milan, Giuffré, 2009) 95ff and *Maschere del diritto volti della vita* (Milan, Giuffré, 2009).

[51] L Strauss, *Natural Law and History* (Chicago, University of Chicago Press, 1965).

[52] Resumed in the essays collected by S Chignola and G Duso, *Sui concetti giuridici e politici della Costituzione dell'Europa* (Milan, Franco Angeli, 2005).

direct thread between Ockham, Grotius and Windscheid on the origin of individual rights, passing through Roman law, canon law and the construction of the category of 'subjective right'. It is worth emphasising that it is precisely the dignity of man that is evoked by St Thomas as an emblem of man's rationality ('*magnae dignitatis est in rationali creatura subsistere*'[53]), and to the dignity of man is dedicated the discourse of Pico della Mirandola, who, in *De hominis dignitate*, sees the recognisability of man compared to beasts in 'God clothed in human flesh', in the wise and pious contemplative spirit proper to man as such. The connection between dignity and religiosity, or rather between dignity and the profession of a religion, is at the heart of Spinoza's reflection.[54] Scholars of the Enlightenment, the seventeenth- and eighteenth-century Revolutions, Kantian thought and its epigones would have much to say about the dignity and values of the person.[55] It is therefore important that the Lisbon Treaty, and now the consolidated version of the Treaty on European Union, bear this imprint, this sort of chrism reflecting the history of humanity in the West, with universalist aspirations.

VI. DIGNITY IN THE CASE LAW OF THE ITALIAN CONSTITUTIONAL COURT AND THE ITALIAN SUPREME COURT

The provision, in several provisions of the Italian Constitutional Charter, of the principle of guaranteeing and protecting the dignity of the person has recorded, as already highlighted, a very extensive application by the Constitutional Court. In a voluminous notebook edited by the Constitutional Court itself[56] are collected the numerous rulings – amounting to more than 100 – in which the judges of the Constitutional Court have made use of the principle of human dignity, with regard to the treatment of foreigners, discrimination on the grounds of sex – in particular, the treatment of women in the family, in the employment relationship, in political elections, discrimination on the grounds of language, religious freedom, opinions, personal conditions, with particular reference to compulsory health treatment, the right to be treated, the disabled, juvenile status, the condition of prisoners and discrimination in the workplace.

[53] See B Tierney, The Idea of Natural Rights. Studies on Natural Rights, Natural Law and Church Law 1150–1625 (Atlanta, Scholars Press, 1997) reviewd by P Grossi, in *Zeitschrift der Savigny-Stiftung für Rechtsgeschichte: Kanonistische Abteilung*, available at doi.org/10.7767/zrgka.2000.86.1.554. They both discuss St Thomas's ideas, expressed in *Summa theologica*, I, quaestio 29, 3, 2 (Studio Domenicano, Bologna, 2014).

[54] Strauss (n 51).

[55] Ferrone (n 49).

[56] M Bellocci and M Passaglia (eds), *The Dignity of Man as a Constitutional Principle*, in *Quaderni* (Rome, 2007). But see also P Zuddas, *La pari dignità sociale a tre dimensioni* (Padova, Cedam, 2019).

The principle of dignity is also increasingly used by the Court of Cassation. In civil matters, the ruling by the Court of Cassation on 11 November 2008 no 26972, concerning compensation for non-asset damage, gave rise to many doubts, not so much because of the new classification of the items of damage (a classification that could be appreciated) but because the Court held that such damage is compensable in cases provided for by law as a crime, in cases provided for by special law, in cases of injury to 'inviolable rights' provided for by the Constitution; human rights guaranteed by the ECHR are not equated to this category. This constitutionally oriented interpretation of Articles 2043 and 2059 of the Civil Code was reaffirmed in a case of demotion by judgment No 2352 of 2 February 2010.

On the level of effects, it is easy to verify how, in our legal system, the rules concerning the legal position of 'non-citizens', which affect both the principle of dignity, the principle of equality, and the principle of equal opportunities, are widely censured; how the rulings that violate the principle of equality in the application of the rules implementing the directives on non-discrimination are censured; how the rulings on the principle of informed consent, on the other hand, are appreciable.

The Court of Cassation has proven itself in directly applying the principle of dignity to relations between private individuals. An analysis of recent rulings confirms this positive assessment. In the balancing act between the right to exercise economic initiative and the protection of personality rights – first and foremost the dignity of the person – it has reaffirmed the primacy of dignity, safeguarding the confidentiality of the person concerned by dealing with commercial information and not freedom of expression.[57]

And even in the matter of freedom of the press, dignity constitutes a limit to its exercise if done in a detrimental form, because this freedom must conform to the social utility of the information, to the truth (objective or even only putative) of the facts set out, to the civil form, respectful of the person portrayed. If it does not conform to these canons, the exercise of the right of the press may constitute a civil offence even if it does not constitute a crime.[58] In particular, on the subject of the right to be forgotten, jurisprudence has consistently affirmed that 'it is always the public interest that justifies the violation of that aspect of dignity – confidentiality that is defined as the right to be forgotten':

> [T]he journalist who intends to report on an event involving judicial implications at a distance of time from the time of acquisition of the news, has a stringent obligation, by reason of the natural and by no means foreseeable course of the case, to complete and then update the verification of the soundness of the news at the time of its circulation, using the previous regulatory sources, or any other suitable available.[59]

[57] Italian Court of Cassation, 23 January 2014, no 1361.
[58] Italian Court of Cassation, 18 October 1984, no 5259.
[59] Italian Criminal Court of Cassation, 8 January 2015, no 13941.

Particularly significant, because it concerns one of the essential aspects of today's life, ie the use of databases by means of IT tools, is judgment no 18981 rendered on 8 August 2013, on the basis of which:

> [T]he law also protects data that are already public or published, since the person who carries out processing operations on such information, from their juxtaposition, comparison, examination, analysis, conjunction, relationship or intersection, can obtain further information and, therefore, an 'added informative value', which cannot be extracted from the data considered in isolation, potentially damaging to the dignity of the person concerned (pursuant to Article 3, first paragraph, first part, and Article 2 of the Constitution), to be considered pre-eminent with respect to private economic initiative which, according to Article 41 of the Constitution, cannot be carried out in such a way as to cause the data subject to be subject to the protection of his dignity, cannot be carried out in such a way as to harm human dignity.

In any case, the protection of the person, in all its aspects, is the aim that the Court identifies in Article 2 of the Constitution, which refers to the inviolable rights of man.[60]

Another important case involving first the Italian Court of Cassation and then the Constitutional Court concerned the massacre of civilians by German troops during WW2. Leaving aside questions of international law and agreements between Italy and Germany, both courts held that limits could not be imposed on the national order when the value of human dignity was compromised.

First of all, the United Sections of the Italian Court of Cassation, in Judgment No 14199 of 29 May 2008, specified that the customary rule of international law, which imposes on states the obligation to abstain from exercising their jurisdictional power for acts *iure imperii*, is not unconditional in character but encounters a limit in the recognition of the absolute primacy of the fundamental values of freedom and dignity of the human person.

Then the same Constitutional Court, with a ruling whose decision was very tormented, concerning the compensation of damages of Italian citizens deported to concentration camps by the German armed forces during WW2, admitted the responsibility of the German state, overcoming the principle of immunity.[61] The premise is that:

> [T]he fundamental principles of the constitutional order and the inalienable rights of the person constitute a 'limit to the entry … of the generally recognised international norms to which the Italian legal system conforms according to Article 10, first paragraph, of the Constitution' (judgments n. 48 of 1979 and n. 73 of 2001) and operate as a 'limit to the entry … of the generally recognised international norms to which the Italian legal system conforms according to Article 10, first paragraph, of the Constitution' (judgments n. 48 of 1979 and n. 73 of 2001) and operate as 'counter-balances' to the entry of European Union norms (ex plurimis: judgments

[60] Italian Court of cassation, 10 May 2001, no 6507.
[61] Constitutional Court, judgment no 238 of 2014.

> no 183 of 1973, no 170 of 1984, no 232 of 1989, no 168 of 1991, no 284 of 2007), as well as limits to the entry of the norms implementing the Lateran Pacts and the Concordat (judgments no. 18 of 1982, no. 32, no. 31 and no. 30 of 1971). They represent, in other words, the identifying and inalienable elements of the constitutional order, for this reason also exempt from constitutional revision (Articles 138 and 139 of the Constitution: thus in Judgment No 1146 of 1988) .... The referring judge has not by chance jointly indicated Articles 2 and 24 of the Constitution, which are inextricably linked in the assessment of constitutional legitimacy requested of this Court. The first is the substantive rule placed, among the fundamental principles of the Constitutional Charter, to protect the inviolability of the fundamental rights of the person, among which, in this case conferred as a primary right, dignity. The second is also to safeguard the dignity of the person, protecting his right to have access to justice to assert his inviolable right.[62]

Hence the illegitimacy of the Italian judge's obligation to apply Law No 5 of 2013, which would require him to respect the immunity of the foreign state.

Recently, there have been pronouncements of the jurisprudence of legitimacy concerning the principle of equal dignity of spouses;[63] dignity of workers and the lawfulness of controls carried out by the employer.[64] Of particular importance is the ruling of the Court of Genoa, according to which, in accordance with the right to equal social dignity and non-discrimination, it constitutes

> disadvantageous and discriminatory treatment that of a municipality that imposes – on persons without fixed abode coming from African Asian and South American countries – the obligation to undergo a health check, the content of which is uncertain, or, failing that, to be denied access to the municipal territory and/or to the relevant reception facilities, a treatment that is borne exclusively or almost entirely by the social group characterised by non-Italian citizenship and belonging to a non-European ethnic group.[65]

VII. THE FUNCTION OF 'DIGNITY'

Here then, from a formal point of view, are the issues currently under discussion: whether 'dignity' is in our system only a value, a value and also a right, or whether it is even a 'super-right'. According to the most widespread orientation, inviolable rights are indivisible and must be balanced against each other; dignity is the very basis of rights and cannot be appreciated only from a subjective point of view, but is also relevant from an objective, ie relational, point of view, in the relations that the person establishes with other citizens.

[62] Constitutional Court, judgment no 238 of 2014.
[63] Italian Court of cassation, 23 July 2008, no 20296.
[64] Italian Court of cassation, 3 November 2016, no 22313.
[65] Tribunal of Genoa, 28 July 2017, available at www.iusexplorer.it.

One can also entertain the idea[66] that dignity should be understood as a *status* in the modern (or rather, postmodern) sense because it refers to every man as such and wherever he may be. In any case, precisely because of its substantial content, it cannot be used in a rhetorical or merely exorbitant sense, but in a functional sense. On this the courts converge, using texts explicitly or implicitly inclusive of the term, in the context of their various competences, they make very wide use of it.

Written texts are important, but even more important are the decisions of judges operating at different levels and with different competences. This is because where there are no written texts, the protection of fundamental rights takes place – in modern Western democracies – on the basis of common principles and shared values; and even if the so-called Even if the so-called Bill of Rights is not contained in a written constitution, or derived from a constitutional custom, or refer to a law that we would define as ordinary, such as the UK Human Rights Act (of 1999), it is then up to the judges, in their delicate work supported by the lawyers (who fight for the defence of fundamental rights, promote their guarantee in court, argue in their defence pleadings to persuade the judge, appeal against decisions deemed insensitive to human rights) to give real consistency to the written and unwritten rules that govern our societies. More. Even where there are written texts, fundamental rights are now entrusted to the judges, so much so that a colloquium held at the Sorbonne in May 2008 spoke of the dignity '*saisie par les juges*', ie, appropriated by judges in Europe.[67] The colloquium followed another seminar organised in Limoges in November 2004[68] in which dignity had been examined in the framework of justice and ethics, and thus of the fundamental aspects of the person, as enriched by (but also exposed to the dangers of) biological and computer technologies.

VIII. THE EUROPEAN CONVENTION. DIGNITY AND HUMAN RIGHTS

The attention that must be paid to the European Convention on Human Rights is not out of place, both because the Strasbourg Court has primacy in the construction of human rights in their modern sense, and because the violation of human rights is unfortunately also a frequent practice in the EU Member States despite the fact that their constitutions enshrine the values of the individual.

The jurisprudence of the Strasbourg Court, which must be read according to the criteria of English case law,[69] as the judges who create it themselves

[66] Waldron (n 42).

[67] A Crue, 'La dignité saisie par les juges en Europe' (23 May 2008, Pathéon Sorbonne).

[68] *Justice, étique et dignité* (Limoges, 2004).

[69] In this sense, see G Zagrebelsky, 'La giurisprudenza casistica della Corte europea dei diritti dell'uomo. Fact and law in the light of precedent'; G Alpa (ed), *The Essence of Democracy. I diritti umani e il ruolo dell'avvocatura* (Rome, Carocci, 2010) 205ff.

suggest, is indeed very extensive. The Court has elaborated the meaning of the rights recognised by the Convention but has also 'dialogued' with national judges. What is more, the Court has had the merit of 'dialoguing' with national judges and thus the concrete, direct application of the principles enshrined in the Convention has promoted their knowledge and respect to a much greater extent than if they had been entrusted only to the – albeit tireless – initiative of the Strasbourg judges.

Extensive research conducted in some EU countries on the application of the principles contained in the ECHR by national judges has shown that, although these countries already had a constitution guaranteeing fundamental rights, the application of the ECHR had disruptive effects.[70] Given the results, there are authors who consider the Strasbourg Court to be the constitutional court of Europe. On the other hand, looking at the numerous rulings condemning the Italian state, this statement is not entirely peregrine.

There are many cases that have caused an uproar, such as those concerning due process, which even led the Italian legislator to amend the text of the Italian Constitution (Article 111) and to introduce a specific remedy for the compensation of damages suffered by victims of delays in the administration of justice (the so-called Pinto Law, as amended and supplemented by Law Decree No 83/2012, converted by Law No 134/2012, the so-called 'Crescitalia Decree'), or such as those on acquisitive occupation, which led the legislator to amend the rules on expropriation and to recognise an adequate compensation for acquisitive occupation in order to better protect the right to property.

Cases concerning the infringement of the ECHR by Italy have different objects: eg the conviction for unjust detention of a Venezuelan migrant extradited from Greece (*Gallardo Sanchez v Italy*); the conviction for not commuting the prison sentence with house arrest to a detainee who was in very serious health conditions (*Contrada v Italy*); the conviction for three same-sex couples who were prevented from forming a family in the form of civil union or marriage (*Oliari v Italy*).

However, the transposition of the ECHR principles is not unequivocal and the Italian Constitutional Court has developed the theory of 'counter-limits', so that 'in the event of a conflict between a domestic rule and a rule of the European Convention, the common national court must … proceed to an interpretation of the former in conformity with the conventional one', but the rule of the ECHR does not have direct application and therefore, if it is found to be in conflict, the court must raise a question of constitutionality with reference to Articles 10 and 117 of the Constitution.

In Judgment No 317 of 2009 on the defendant in absentia, the Court took the reasoning a step further, stating that the application of the ECHR standards

[70] H Keller and A Stone Sweet (eds), *A Europe of Rights. The Impact of ECHR on National Legal Systems* (Oxford, OUP, 2008).

must result in a 'plus of protection' for the entire system of fundamental rights, so that

> the ECHR standard, at the moment in which it supplements the first paragraph of Article 117 of the Constitution, takes its place in the system of sources, with all that follows in terms of interpretation and balancing, which are the ordinary operations to which this Court is called upon in all its judgments from this it reaffirms its rank in the system of sources, with all that follows in terms of interpretation and balancing, which are the ordinary operations to which this Court is called in all judgments within its jurisdiction.

IX. DIGNITY AND FUNDAMENTAL RIGHTS IN THE JURISPRUDENCE OF THE EUROPEAN COURT OF JUSTICE

The preamble of the European Charter of Fundamental Rights opens with a declination of the founding characteristics of the Union, refers to its 'spiritual and moral heritage', to its 'indivisible and universal values' and – in specifying these values – refers to expressions typical of modern constitutionalism: human dignity, freedom, equality, solidarity. These values constitute as many chapters into which the text of the Charter is divided, together with citizenship and justice.[71]

The preamble adds that the Union is based on 'principles of democracy and the rule of law', creating an area of 'freedom, security and justice'. Each term can be qualified as a value, but also as a principle and as a subjective right, and in any case has marked the legal culture of the West.[72] However, each of them has received different chrisms: in the triad of liberty, equality and solidarity (or fraternity) we recognise the ideal emblems of the French Revolution, and thus the fall of the *Ancien Régime* and the disappearance of the *statuses* that cemented the social orders.[73]

For their part, democracy and the 'rule of law' – the 'Rule of Law' of the English experience[74] – connote the modern way of organising political, economic and social life. Over all these emblems stands *dignity*, *human dignity*, which immediately evokes the role of the *person* in the legal system and thus stands at the centre of the entire system, acting as a pillar of the European legal system. Of it, the Charter says that it 'is inviolable' and 'must be respected and protected'.[75]

[71] P Stein and P Shand, *The Common Values of the West* (Milan, Giuffré, 1970) 3ff.

[72] ibid 15ff.

[73] See for all G Tarello, *Storia della cultura giuridica moderna. Assolutismo e codificazione del diritto* (Bologna, Il Mulino, 1998); P Grossi, *L'Europa del diritto* (Roma-Bari, Laterza, 2009); G Alpa and M Andenas, *Fondamenti del diritto privato europeo* (Milano, Giuffré, 2005).

[74] Lord T Bingham, *The Rule of Law* (London, Penguin, 2010).

[75] For the first references see P Ridola, 'La dignità dell'uomo e il 'principio libertà' nella cultura costituzionale europea' in P Ridola, *Diritto comparato e diritto costituzionale europeo* (Torino,

The Court of Justice has promoted the enforcement of fundamental rights within the limits of its competences – and started to apply the Nice Charter since 2001 even though it did not yet have legal force.

Particularly significant cases are *Kreil* (2000), *Schmidberger* (2003), *Omega* (2004), *KB* (2004), the terrorism case (2005), *Richards* (2006), *Tadao Maruko* (2008).

Case 148/13 discussed whether a non-European citizen who, if returned to his country of origin, would have suffered restrictions on his personal liberty and as a homosexual could be deported. The Court held that repatriation was not permissible in light of Article 4(3)(c) of Council Directive 2004/83/EC of 29 April 2004 on minimum standards for the qualification and status of third country nationals or stateless persons as refugees or as persons who otherwise need international protection and the content of the protection granted and Article 13(3)(a) of Council Directive 2005/85/EC of 1 December 2005 on minimum standards on procedures in Member States for granting and withdrawing refugee *status*. And in Case 571/10, the Court ruled that national law, if aimed at preserving anti-discriminatory treatment, must be disapplied.

The solutions proposed by the Court cannot always be considered 'progressive' in the sense of affirming protection at all costs. In other words, the orientation of the Court can sometimes appear oscillating, and perhaps open to criticism, as was the case with the non-accession of the European Union to the Convention on Human Rights on the basis of an opinion (the second) of a negative tenor delivered by the Court of Justice.[76]

However, fundamental rights are taken seriously and are 'in action'. Therefore, the categories configured for domestic constitutional rights and law of jurisprudential origin can also be applied to fundamental rights.

The Europe of law has turned into the Europe of rights, and now into the Europe of courts.

But the doctrine has warned the interpreter, who might be tickled by the idea of lengthening the catalogue of rights or systematising rights in a mechanical manner.

However, even at this level of analysis, and in this area, the diatribe between *ius litigatoris* and *ius constitutionis* has opened up. In other words, the question is whether one should give protection to the right and thus create the remedy (*ubi ius, ibi remedium*) or whether one should give entry to the remedy to protect the right (*ubi remedium, ibi ius*).

Giappichelli, 2010) 77ff; G Resta, *Dignità, persone, mercati* (Torino, Giappichelli, 2014); and for a general discussion, McCudden (ed), *Understanding Human Dignity* (Oxford, OUP, 2013); on the European Convention on Human Rights see in particular M Gerars and M Fleuren (eds), *Implementation of the European Convention on Human Rights and of the judgements of the ECHR in national case-law. A comparative analysis* (Cambridge, CUP, 2014).

[76] Opinion 2/13 of 14 December 2014.

X. THE LISBON TREATY

The Treaty of Lisbon, amending the Treaty on European Union and the Treaty establishing the European Community, was signed on 13 December 2007 and entered into force on 1 December 2009. There are three qualifying points in particular that concern the issue at hand: the preamble, Article 2 and Article 6, to which one should then add, in the reconstruction of the legal framework, the provisions of the European Charter of Fundamental Rights, which deal with freedoms, equality, solidarity, citizenship and justice. Much has been written about the Charter, and also about its adventurous paths;[77] little has been written about the Lisbon Treaty by private law scholars, despite its enormous political and legal relevance at the same time. Only constitutional and EU law studies are exceptions to this rule.

From our perspective, the preamble of the treaty is already evocative, because it recalls – by way of 'inspiration' and thus as an interpretive guide to the text – 'the cultural, religious and humanist heritage of Europe, from which the universal values of the inviolable and inalienable rights of the person, freedom, democracy, equality and the rule of law have developed'. It is easy to see in these words the answer, modernised and polished, to the crucial question posed to the commission that was to draft the text of the European Charter, concerning the Christian, or Judeo-Christian, or Enlightenment, or secular roots of Europe.

In the preamble, it is also easy to register the fungibility of the terms used, since rights are considered values, inviolable and inalienable rights are equated with the fundamental rights guaranteed by the European Charter, dignity is not mentioned but hovers when freedom, democracy and equality are evoked. The original version already confirmed the signatory states' 'attachment' to 'the principles of liberty, democracy and respect for human rights and fundamental freedoms and the rule of law' and referred to the principles of the 1961 European Social Charter and the 1989 Charter of the Rights of Workers, but this additional clarification now takes on greater significance.

In turn, Article 2 reaffirms that 'the Union is founded on the values of respect for human dignity, freedom, democracy, equality, the rule of law and respect for human rights, including the rights of persons belonging to minorities'. It adds: 'These values are common to the Member States in a society characterised by pluralism, non-discrimination, tolerance, justice, solidarity and equality between women and men'. This clarification sums up the meaning of 'dignity' as a value, as a substratum of freedom and democracy, as a yardstick of equality, as a support for solidarity and justice. What concerns the EU legislator, however, is the principle of unity in diversity, of cultural pluralism, of equal treatment of

[77] The political path is described by R Cangelosi, *Il ventennio costituzionale dell'Unione Europea* (Venice, Morcelliana, 2009).

men and women, of protection of minorities, and thus non-discrimination and tolerance. These are non-emphatic formulas that hint, on the one hand, at the meaning of European citizenship and, on the other, at the problems underlying a union of peoples that was initially planned only for economic purposes and now needs to be strengthened in its political dimension.

The use of the term 'tolerance', which appears a little weak compared to the strongly egalitarian imprint of the formulas quoted, may perhaps raise perplexity, but it is clear that these are calibrated, mediated, carefully screened expressions.

A quick note can also be made of Article 4, which states respect for the equality of Member States before the treaties and especially their 'national identity'. This is where the debate on the approval of the Lisbon Treaty and the discussion on the German Constitutional Court's ruling on the relationship between the Treaty and domestic constitutional law came in; the ruling, of 30 June 2009, placed the reservation of sovereignty, the reservation of constitutional identity and the reservation of the national configuration of public space.

National constitutions, in this perspective, are considered a founding element of the identity of an order and thus of a people; as jurists, we can also agree with this, although it is reasonable to wonder whether the common person is aware of this aspect and whether he recognises himself, from an identity perspective, in his or her own constitution rather than in mere citizenship or other connotative factors, such as language, traditions and customs, homeland history, and so on.

More problematic is Article 6, where there is the unresolved problem of drafting a European constitution and we see not so much a balancing act, but, in my view, a conflict between the Nice Charter and the treaties. This is because it says there that the Union 'recognises the rights, freedoms and principles set out in the Charter of Fundamental Rights of the European Union … , which has the same legal value as the Treaties', thus not yet giving the Charter a pre-eminent role, as if it were the constitution of the Community order; it recognises the European Convention on Human Rights, in the form of an accession, and thus emphasises the conventional nature of that text; it specifies, however, that 'fundamental rights, guaranteed by the Convention … resulting from the constitutional traditions common to the Member States, form part of the law of the Union as general principles'.

Certainly the provisions of the Nice Charter are general principles; they coincide – though not completely – with the provisions of the Rome Convention. There is therefore a need for a balancing of principles carried out by the interpreters, in particular by the (Luxembourg and Strasbourg) courts, which now have partly competing competences. Moreover, since they are general principles, according to the theory of sources, they should be considered as prevailing over all other principles contained in EU legislation. Therefore, whether they are contained in the consolidated Treaty, or in the Nice Charter, or in the Convention (in the transposition of its contents of conventional origin to the level of general principles of the Community order), these values, from dignity on down, are all inviolable, fundamental, human rights and constitute the pivot of the entire Community order.

However, this perspective is not shared by many, starting with scholars of EU international law and domestic constitutional law. But neither are the courts, constitutional and supreme.

Finally, it should be noted that, during three seminars organised by the Consiglio Nazionale Forense on this topic – one dedicated to European citizenship, the other to fundamental rights and the third to the Lisbon Treaty – the speakers discussed the titles under which these topics were presented. It does not seem so, but even the title is an indication of a perspective or even a stance. The question arose, for instance, whether one should speak of fundamental rights 'in' the Lisbon Treaty, or of fundamental rights 'and' the Lisbon Treaty.

Fundamental rights are a category in their own right, disengaged from the normative texts and, at most, recognised and guaranteed by them, or they live in so far as they are included in the normative texts. This is the problem that has been agitated for so long in national experiences concerning rights 'recognised and guaranteed' by written constitutions. The *habeas corpus* introduced at Community level by the Nice Charter, as reconfirmed on 12 December 2007 in Strasbourg, has been released from the Treaty, but, according to some, this operation would have a positive effect, because its visibility and use by citizens would increase. However, it would not be possible to bring an infringement action against a state that violated these fundamental rights, because the action is limited to the violation of the Treaty; the Charter does not extend the jurisdiction of national courts; accession to the ECHR should increase the protection of human rights; but the violation of a fundamental right by a state could legitimise the individual to bring an action before the Court of Justice. The fact that fundamental rights are common implies that they are doubly guaranteed, at EU level and at national level. Thus, 'multi-level' protection is established.'

XI. THE CHARTER OF FUNDAMENTAL RIGHTS OF THE EUROPEAN UNION AND THE RIGHTS OF THE INDIVIDUAL

The Charter of Rights approved in Nice in a certain sense extends and updates the rights of the individual. For example, it provides for the right to respect for private life (Article 8), which Italian *case law* had built on Article 2 of the Constitution. This right – understood as the right to *privacy* – is not provided for in the written Constitution, but is the result of a hermeneutic process that started around the 1960s. But the Nice Charter adds to this right another right, relating to the protection of personal data (Article 8). Until 1996, this right was in its infancy in Italy, and was enshrined in the 1996 Data Protection Act No 675 and then in the Consolidated Text on Personal Data and most recently in the European Regulation 2016/679 (GDPR) which became enforceable on 25 May 2018. Elevating this right to the rank of constitutionally guaranteed rights is thus further progress towards a modern statute of personal rights. In the same way, the Nice Charter, by recognising the right to form a family (Article 9), goes beyond the Italian constitutional dictate that considers the family as a natural society founded on marriage, and recognises to the de facto family only a relevance as a social formation where the personality of the individual develops (Article 2). The Nice text not only includes in the fundamental rights of the person the right to form a family not based on marriage, but is open to the recognition of families formed by persons of the same sex, a factuality now regulated in our legal system by Law No 76 of 20 May 2016. Also with regard to the principles of equality and non-discrimination (Articles 20–26), the Nice Charter expands the rights of the person as recognised and guaranteed in the Italian Constitution, because it inserts the prohibition of discrimination based on skin colour, genetic characteristics, birth, *disability*, sexual orientation. In addition, the Nice Charter makes explicit rights that can only be derived from the text of the Italian Constitution with an accurate hermeneutic interpretation, such as the rights of the child (Article 24), of the elderly (Article 25) and of the weak (Article 26). Then there are the provisions concerning the protection of the environment (Article 37) and consumers (Article 38). For the protection of the environment, the Italian Constitution already provides for a provision (Article 9 concerning the landscape) which, as a result of an extensive interpretation, has been applied to limit the rights of the owner and to compensate for the damage suffered by individuals and communities due to pollution. But the word 'consumer' is ignored in the Italian Constitution, and is acquired in the jurists' vocabulary, as well as in the pronouncements of the Courts of every order and degree, due to the Community interventions on the subject.[78]

There are several cases that can be recalled to clarify the lines of this guideline, which admits the direct application of fundamental rights but with some limitations, each time corrected according to the law considered and the case brought to the Court's attention. The distinction between the direct application of fundamental rights and the exclusion of the direct application of principles remains firm.

On 22 May 2014, judgment C-356/12 was filed in *Wolfgang Glatzel v Freistaat Bayern*, concerning the competent authority's refusal to issue a driving licence due to a visual defect in one of the plaintiff's eyes. The principle invoked was that of 'non-discrimination'. The Court decided the question for a preliminary ruling raised by the German court by stating that the minimum visual acuity thresholds

[78] On this point, we return below.

for the issue of C1 and C1E licences provided for in Directive 2006/126/EC are in conformity with Articles 20, 21 and 26 of the Charter (respectively, 'Equality before the law', 'Non-discrimination' and 'Integration of persons with disabilities').

The judgment is interesting because it deals with rights inherent to social relations and treats them as equivalent to the fundamental rights on freedoms, suggesting that there is no ranking of fundamental rights and that social rights do not enjoy differentiated and lesser protection than other rights. But it leaves intact the distinction between fundamental rights and principles. The distinction was reiterated in the *Association Médiation sociale* case (C-176/12) in which, again with regard to rights relating to information and consultation of workers, the Court, responding to a question raised by the French Court of Cassation, specified that it is possible to disapply rules of national law that are contrary to directives even if the problem arises in the context of relations between private individuals.

The *Mangold* case concerning the principle of non-discrimination on grounds of age in employment contracts (Case C-144/04 of 22 November 2005) remains fundamental. On that occasion the Court specified that the principle of non-discrimination on grounds of age must 'be regarded as a general principle of Community law'. Where national legislation falls within the scope of the latter, as is the case with Paragraph 14(3) of the TzBfG, as amended by the 2002 Law, as a measure implementing Directive 1999/70 … , the Court, when giving a preliminary ruling, must provide all the elements of interpretation necessary for the national court to assess whether that legislation complies with that principle … Consequently, compliance with the general principle of equal treatment, in particular on grounds of age, does not depend, as such, on the expiry of the period allowed to the Member States to transpose a directive intended to establish a general framework for combating discrimination on grounds of age, in particular as regards the organisation of the appropriate means of redress, the burden of proof, protection against retaliation, social dialogue, positive action and other specific measures implementing such a directive. That being so, it is for the national court, before which a dispute is brought challenging the principle of non-discrimination on grounds of age, to ensure, within the ambit of its jurisdiction, the legal protection which Community law confers on individuals, guaranteeing its full effectiveness and disapplying any provision of national law to the contrary. Having regard to all of the foregoing, the answer to the second and third questions is that Community law and, in particular, Article 6(1) of Directive 2000/78 must be interpreted as precluding national legislation such as that at issue in the main proceedings, which authorises, without restriction, unless there is a close connection with a previous employment contract of indefinite duration concluded with the same employer, the conclusion of fixed-term employment contracts where the worker has reached the age of 52.

It is therefore the task of the national court to ensure the full effectiveness of the general principle of non-discrimination on grounds of age by disapplying any contrary provision of national law, even when the period for transposition of that directive has not yet expired.

Finally, the reports drawn up annually since 2010 by the European Commission and the Court of Justice on the protection of fundamental rights are valuable.

In its judgment of 26 February 2013, in Case C-617/10, *Åkerberg Fransson*, the Court of Justice provided explanations on the interpretation of Article 51 of the Charter of Fundamental Rights, with reference to the question of its scope of application vis-à-vis the Member States, and expressed its views on the role of national judgments in relation to the Charter. In particular, the Court confirmed that

> the case law … concerning the extent to which the actions of the Member States must comply with the requirements flowing from the fundamental rights guaranteed in the legal order of the Union' and stated that 'since the fundamental rights guaranteed by the Charter must be respected when national legislation falls within the scope of Union law, there can be no cases falling within the scope of Union law without those fundamental rights being applicable [; the] applicability of Union law implies that of the fundamental rights guaranteed by the Charter.

As regards the role of the national court in the event of national provisions contrary to the Charter, the Court noted that, according to settled case law,

> the national court entrusted with the application, within the scope of its jurisdiction, of the rules of European Union law is under an obligation to ensure that those rules are fully effective by disapplying, where appropriate on its own initiative, any conflicting provision of national law, even if subsequent, without having to request or await its prior removal by legislative or any other constitutional procedure.

13

The Fight against Discrimination and Today's Law

I. THE PROTECTION OF WOMEN

THE LONG JOURNEY towards equality only began after the Second World War: in 1946 women were granted the right to vote in the referendum on the form of government; and finally in 1948 attained the right to vote in general elections.

The right to equality is proclaimed in Articles 3, 37 and 51 of the Constitution.

This is seen most clearly in the world of work.

In 1950, the law on the protection of mothers was passed; in 1956 the law on equal pay; in 1958 the law on domestic work; in 1963 access to the professions and the judiciary was liberalised; in 1971 the law on the protection of mothers was improved; in 1973 the law on home work was passed; and in 1977 the law on equal treatment of men and women in employment.

The body of labour provisions is collected in the Code of equal opportunities between men and women, pursuant to Article 6 of Law No 246 of 28 November 2005 (Legislative Decree No 198 of 11 April 2006).

The Code provides for the general principle of equal opportunities, equal opportunity policies, the establishment of the Commission for Equal Opportunities between Men and Women and the National Committee for the implementation of the principles of equal treatment and equal opportunities between men and women workers, and the prohibition of discrimination. Positive actions are envisaged for the promotion of equal opportunities.

Law No 120 of 12 July 2011 introduced provisions on financial intermediation, with the aim of protecting gender equality in access to the management and control bodies of companies listed on regulated markets and in public companies.

From work to family.

The 1975 reform re-evaluated the role of women in the family, finally implementing the principle of legal and moral equality of spouses.

The emancipation of women also passed through the legitimisation of the de facto family, since it was precisely because of the woman's inferior position that she was considered morally objectionable if she entered into an affectionate relationship with a man outside of marriage (her own or the man's), and received no protection, except in cases of exception, at the time of the dissolution of the relationship or even during the course of the relationship. If children were born of the relationship, they were considered illegitimate, and *statu* limitations also applied to them.

The de facto family was opposed because it was not founded on marriage.

Very often, in a neutral way, the expressions 'cohabitation more uxorio' ('para-marital cohabitation') is used, where reference is not made to the presence of children (an unnecessary but almost obvious addition when speaking of a 'family') but particularly to the custom of life in common, carried out with similar (or identical) manners, behaviour and attitudes to those of the spouses.

If one then used the expression 'free union', which became popular in the doctrine of the end of the last century and the first decades of this one, to allude to a phenomenon informed by characters of freedom, of fragility, of easy dissolution, entirely entrusted to the intangible will of the individual member of the group: to a phenomenon, that is, which intends to exhaust itself, as it does, in the sphere of private autonomy, and which does not tolerate the intervention of the state (ie the intervention of the legislator, or of the judge) because this intervention would end up distorting its authentic essence.

Finally, if one wished to negatively connote the phenomenon, one used expressions such as 'concubinage', 'adulterous cohabitation', 'extramarital cohabitation', 'cohabitation outside marriage', 'non-family'; this was precisely to signal that one was not only outside the institution, and therefore outside the law, but also outside the social order, outside the values recognised by all, and therefore fell within the sphere of what was illicit, abnormal, and therefore reprehensible and to blame.[1]

Changes in social relations have meant that cohabitation between persons of different sexes has become widespread and now constitutes a significant presence within family models. Hence the need to establish the regime of those who prefer not to enter into marriage but to behave as if they were spouses, and the regime of those who wish to register their position in order to acquire additional benefits over and above those already known to jurisprudence, and the special regime that the law now grants to those who, belonging to the same sex, cohabit united by affectionate relations. De facto cohabitation may in fact concern persons of different sexes and persons of the same sex. The latter hypothesis was regulated along with the regularisation of the de facto family of a traditional nature by Law No 76 of 2016.

It is worthwhile, however, to refer to the earlier situation in order to understand how the phenomenon of cohabitation more uxorio was legally qualified.

[1] According to statistics, de facto families in Italy almost tripled in 10 years, from 192,000 in 1995 to 555,000 in 2005. In 2022 the number of non-married families amounts to approximately 12 million out of 25 million families in total.

It is possible to briefly review the rules that directly concern de facto families: one may recall Law Decree No 1276 of 27 October 1918, which recognised the retirement treatment of the 'betrothed' of a deceased soldier, if there was a declaration of intention to marry; the Civil Code (Article 74) (Article 2 of Presidential Decree No 136 of 31 January 1958, defines a family for registry purposes as a group of persons bound by emotional ties and cohabiting, who normally provide for their needs by pooling all or part of their income; Article 317 bis of the Civil Code introduced by the reform of family law, according to which if the child is recognised by both parents, the exercise of parental authority is jointly vested in both of them if they are cohabiting; Article 324 of the Civil Code, according to which the parents exercising parental authority have joint legal usufruct over the child's property; Article 148 of the Civil Code concerning the concurrence of parents in family burdens; ; Article 1 of Law No 405 of 29 June 1975, on the establishment of family advisory centres, lists among those entitled to assistance not only 'individuals' or 'families' but also 'couples'; Article 5 of Law No 194 of 22 May 1978 on the social protection of maternity and the voluntary interruption of pregnancy (ie the law on abortion) provides for the participation in the procedure of the person indicated as the father of the conceived child.

Even if it is difficult to argue that these norms alone are sufficient to give a comprehensive overview of the legal significance of the de facto family, they are not insignificant normative references.

Two types of intervention must be distinguished: intervention that brings disadvantages to cohabitees; and intervention that brings them advantages. Often the model sentences by which the de facto family is recognised as legally relevant are, in essence, undermined by a penalisation of cohabitation.

Favourable interventions are very rare, and, for the most part, carried out in more recent years. They can be classified as follows:

- pronouncements extending the provisions of the regulations on the duration of the lease for residential use (so-called extension of leases) or on succession in the lease, to de facto cohabitees.[2] Worthy of note in this connection is the ruling of the Constitutional Court (of the 'additive' type) recognising the legitimacy of Article 6(1) of law 27 July 1978, no 392 (the law on equitable rent) 'in the part in which it provides that, in the event of the tenant's death, the more uxorio cohabitee is among the successors in title to the lease' and the illegitimacy of Article 6 in the part in which it provides for the succession in the lease to the tenant who has ceased cohabitation more uxorio, in favour of the former cohabitee, when there are natural offspring.[3] However, the illegitimacy was not declared on the grounds of unequal treatment between the legitimate family and the natural family (on the contrary, the Court is

[2] Tribunal of Geneva 12 March 1979, in *Giur. mer*, 1979, I, 912 (with some contrary precedent).
[3] Judgment 7 April 1988, no 404, in *Foro it*, 1988, I, c 2515.

keen to specify that the condition of the spouse remains 'in any case different from that of the cohabitee more uxorio'), but on the grounds of the violation of Article 47 of the Constitution, which establishes a subjective right to housing;

- pronouncements allowing damages to the cohabiting partner if the other partner who is a debtor is killed in an accident;[4]
- rulings extending insurance benefits (in particular, hospital care) to cohabitees of the insured person;[5]
- pronouncements that consider valid the registration of a property to the cohabitee, carried out in the course of the cohabitation, considering it as the payment of a patrimonial entity compensating for the work performed;[6]
- pronouncements that ignore cohabitation more uxorio in order to qualify the woman as head of the household and grant her higher remuneration.[7]

It is also useful to recall the ruling of the European Court of Justice, which recognised the relevance of the de facto bond established by the worker with his cohabitees, and thus held that

> a Member State that allows the unmarried partner of its national, who is not himself a national, to reside on its territory must grant the same benefit to the unmarried partner of the worker who is a national of another Member State and who is employed on its territory.[8]

Recent case law tends to equate de facto cohabitation with matrimonial cohabitation in certain respects.

First of all, it was considered that a cohabiting couple is stable when the cohabitation has lasted for at least two years,[9] while a long engagement was ruled out as a more uxorio cohabitation.[10]

While not considering that the provisions of Article 143 of the Civil Code may be extended analogically tout court to the de facto family, the judges nevertheless show particular regard for the cohabitee (usually the woman) who is in a weaker economic situation.

It has therefore been held that the contribution made by one of the cohabitees to the other for the running of the family ménage during the course of the cohabitation is legally relevant;[11] that the constitution of a gratuitous usufruct in favour of the cohabitee is legitimate, also in order to compensate

[4] Tribunal of Verona 3 December 1980, in *Resp civ prev*, 1981 74.
[5] Tribunal of Geneva 17 December 1979, in *Dir fam pers*, 1981, 159.
[6] Tribunal of Bari 21 January 1977, in *Giur it*, 1978, I, 2, c 254.
[7] Cass 9 April 1971, no 1053, in *Temi*, 1973, 57.
[8] Judgment 17 April 1986, in *Foro it*, 1987, IV, c 293.
[9] Tribunal of Brescia 10 April 2003.
[10] Tribunal of Milan 13 July 2001.
[11] Tribunal of Turin 11 June 2002.

his contribution to family life;[12] that the heirs of the deceased cohabitee are not entitled to recover sums contributed by the deceased cohabitee to the other cohabitee in the course of their common life, provided that the sums are not disproportionate[13] that it is possible to give the cohabitee – to whom the children are entrusted after the termination of the cohabitation – the right to live in the family home, even if it is owned by the other cohabitee;[14] that it is possible to give the survivor's pension to the cohabitee,[15] even if the wife is still alive, if the latter is in a more favourable economic situation than the other.

On the other hand, it is excluded that the cohabitee is entitled to maintenance or alimony,[16] and that he may succeed to the lease.[17] While it is controversial whether the divorce allowance can be kept[18] or not[19] if, after the divorce, the former assignee spouse has established a more uxorio cohabitation with another person.[20]

This is the situation offered by the jurisprudential framework (due to the creativity of the case aw, before the new law was introduced). The legislature has not clarified whether the situation thus described continues even in the presence of the new law, ie whether the new law is intended only for cohabitees who have registered their partnership.

II. THE LEGITIMACY OF COHABITATION BETWEEN PERSONS OF DIFFERENT SEXES AND COHABITATION BETWEEN PERSONS OF THE SAME SEX

Law No 76 of 2016 gives a definition (precisely normative) of cohabitation, subjective in the sense that 'de facto cohabitees' means two persons of full age who are permanently united by bonds of affection and mutual moral and material assistance, not bound by relationships of kinship, affinity or adoption, by

[12] Tribunal of Savona 7 March 2001.
[13] Tribunal of Monza 18 November 1999.
[14] Court of Cassation 26 May 2004, no 11975.
[15] Court of Cassation 10 October 2003, no 15148.
[16] Court of Cassation 10 October 2003, no 15148.
[17] Constitutional Court, 11 June 2003, no 204.
[18] Court of Cassation 8 August 2003, no 11975.
[19] Court of Cassation 12 December 2003, no 19042.
[20] Mere occasional cohabitation is certainly not (Court of Cassation 25 November 2010, No 23968). The Constitutional Court has recently held that the current discipline that only contemplates marriage between a man and a woman cannot be censured for violation of the Constitution (Constitutional Court 14 April 2010, no 138 and 22 July 2010, no 276). The Italian Court of Cassation, according to Art 2 of the Italian Constitution considers legally relevant a stable and lasting formation (two partners living together) in which the personality of the individual can be expressed, if it is the expression of a free and conscious existential choice, which is qualified by the full assumption of the risk to the relationship and, therefore, excludes any residual form of post-marital solidarity with the previous spouse, who must be considered definitively exempt from the obligation to pay the divorce allowance' (7 February 2023, no 3645).

marriage or by a civil partnership (c 36). The objective profile is determined by the registry declaration that cohabitees are required to make in order for their stable cohabitation to be ascertained.

If, on the other hand, the cohabitees do not take advantage of this legislation, they are considered to be participants in a free union. As pointed out, prior to the approval of the law in question, the members of the de facto family based on free union were in any case recognised certain rights and imposed certain obligations and prohibitions. The law now in force does not take a position on this point, and therefore individuals who, while cohabiting, do not bother to register their cohabitation should not be denied the rights recognised to them by case law. However, these were only different-sex couples living '*more uxorio*'. The application of the law, the elaborations of doctrine and the practice of jurisprudence must therefore resolve two problems: whether to recognise cohabitees who have not made the declaration as having any rights and whether these rights can be extended to same-sex cohabitees who are not in a civil partnership or have not declare their cohabitation.

It is not possible to accept the argument that (declared) cohabitation may also concern two persons living together, of different sexes or of the same sex (eg two distant relatives, two friends, two school or university friends, two colleagues between whom it is not possible to recognise an affective bond as a couple: the 'couple' to which the law refers is a social formation (eg Article 2) assimilated to marriage it is not simply a numerical entity.

De facto cohabitees who have made the declaration and are thus a registered couple are recognised rights specifically listed by law; given the detailed and meticulous list, it must be assumed that these are the only recognised rights:

(a) The same rights as to a spouse in cases provided for in the prison regulations.
(b) In the event of illness or hospitalisation, the reciprocal right of visit, assistance and access to personal information, in accordance with the rules governing the organisation of public, private or contracted hospital or care facilities for spouses and family members.
(c) The right to designate the other cohabitee as his representative with full or limited powers in the event of illness leading to incapacity, for decisions on health matters; in the event of death, with regard to organ donation, arrangements for the treatment of the body and funeral celebrations.
(d) In the event of the death of the owner of the house of common residence, the right of the surviving de facto cohabitee to continue to live in the same dwelling for two years or for a period equal to the cohabitation if longer than two years, and in any case not longer than five years. And the right to continue to live in the joint residence for a period of not less than three years if the surviving cohabitee's minor children or disabled children are living in the same dwelling; this right ceases, however, if the surviving cohabitee ceases to live permanently in the joint residence or decides to marry, enter into a civil partnership or establish a new de facto cohabitation.

(e) In the event of the death of the tenant or the tenant's withdrawal from the lease of the house of common residence, the right to succeed to the tenant.
(f) The de facto cohabitee who works on a permanent basis in the other cohabitee's business is entitled to share in the profits of the family business and the assets acquired with them, as well as in the increase of the business, including goodwill, commensurate with the work performed. The right of participation does not apply if there is a partnership or employment relationship between the cohabitees (Article 230b).
(g) The right to be appointed guardian, curator or support administrator, if the other party is declared disqualified or incapacitated under applicable law or if the requirements of Article 404 of the Civil Code are met.
(h) In the event of the death of the cohabitee resulting from the wrongful act of a third party, the same criteria as those applied to the compensation of the surviving spouse shall apply when determining the damages to be paid to the surviving party.
(i) In the event of the death of one of the cohabitees, the surviving cohabitee (as provided by paragraphs 42 et seq of Law No 76/2016) is entitled to continue to live in the same house for two years (or for three if there are minor or disabled children of the surviving cohabitee) or for a period equal to the cohabitation, if longer, and in any case not longer than five years. In the event of the tenant's death, the surviving cohabitee may succeed him in the lease of the house of common residence.

No other rights accrue, in the absence of testamentary provisions, to the surviving cohabitee.

Up to this point, the legal rights, some of which, as seen when describing the situation of de facto cohabitees (of different sexes) prior to the introduction of the law, had already been consolidated by consistent case law.

The cohabitees may, however, extend the range of rights (and obligations) arising from cohabitation by concluding an agreement that the law calls a cohabitation contract (c 50). The text of the law is clear, so paraphrasing it may suffice.

The 'contract', its amendments and its termination are drawn up in writing, under penalty of nullity, by public deed or private deed with an authenticated signature by a notary public or a lawyer who certify its compliance with mandatory rules and public order. The enforceability of the contract against third parties is obtained by transmitting the deed to the municipality of residence and its 'registration in the registry office'.

The contract may contain:

(a) an indication of residence;
(b) the modalities of contribution to the necessities of life in common, in relation to each person's substance and capacity for professional or household work;

(c) the community of property regime set out in Section III of Chapter VI of Title VI of Book I of the Civil Code (provided for marriage); the property regime chosen in the cohabitation contract may be modified at any time during the course of the cohabitation.

The cohabitation contract may not be subject to terms or conditions. If the parties insert terms or conditions, they are deemed not to have been attached.

The cohabitation contract is affected by irremediable nullity, which can be enforced by anyone with an interest in it if it is concluded:

(a) in the presence of a marriage bond, civil partnership or other cohabitation contract;
(b) if the conditions of cohabitation are not met;
(c) by a person under the age of 18;
(d) by a judicially disqualified person;
(e) in case of conviction for the offence referred to in Article 88 of the Civil Code.

The effects of the cohabitation contract shall remain suspended pending judicial disqualification proceedings or in the event of committal for trial or precautionary measures ordered for the offence referred to in Article 88 of the Civil Code, until an acquittal sentence is pronounced.

The cohabitation contract is terminated by:

(a) agreement of the parties;
(b) unilateral termination;
(c) whether a marriage or civil partnership between the cohabitees or between a cohabitee and another person has taken place since its conclusion;
(d) death of one of the contracting parties.

Termination of the cohabitation contract by agreement of the parties or by unilateral termination must be in writing. If the cohabitation contract provides for the community of property ownership regime, its termination determines the dissolution of the community of property and the provisions of Section III of Chapter VI of Title VI of Book I of the Civil Code shall apply, in so far as they are compatible. In any case, the notary's jurisdiction for deeds of transfer of rights in rem in immovable property, however arising from the cohabitation contract, shall remain unaffected.

In the case of a unilateral withdrawal from a cohabitation contract the deed by which the withdrawal is exercised must be received and authenticated by the qualified professional who receives or authenticates the deed, who shall, in addition to the formalities referred to in paragraph 52, be bound to serve a copy of it on the other contracting party at the address stated in the contract. Where the family home is at the sole disposal of the withdrawing party, the declaration of withdrawal shall, on penalty of nullity, contain the period, not less than 90 days, allow to the cohabitee to leave the home.

The law lays down other rules on the cohabitation 'contract', in addition to those mentioned above concerning the modalities of conclusion, form, nullity and termination.

In the event of the termination of de facto cohabitation, the court establishes the right of the cohabitee to receive alimony from the other cohabitee if he is in a state of need and is unable to provide for his own maintenance. In such cases, alimony is awarded for a period proportional to the duration of the cohabitation and in the amount determined pursuant to Article 438(2) of the Civil Code. For the purposes of determining the order of the obligors pursuant to Article 433 of the Civil Code, the maintenance obligation of the cohabitee referred to in this paragraph shall be fulfilled with priority over the siblings.

The common national law of the contracting parties shall apply to cohabitation contracts. The law of the place where the cohabitation is principally located applies to parties of different nationalities. This is without prejudice to the national, European and international rules that regulate the case of multiple nationality (Article 30 l. 31.5.1995 No 218).

The cohabitation 'contract' is a typical transaction, and therefore neither the rules on marriage nor the rules on civil unions can be applied analogically to it. This is because the will of the cohabitees is clear: the choice made is in the sense of the type indicated and not any other way of constituting the family group. Since the law, as pointed out at the outset, mentions the contract (and not the agreement), one may wonder whether, in addition to the specifically formulated rules, the general rules on contracts may be applied, insofar as they are compatible with the nature of the act considered.[21]

III. TOLERANCE OF THE DIFFERENT

As mentioned, protection against discrimination on grounds of sex is indirectly guaranteed by Article 3 of the Constitution and by Article 14 of the European Charter of Human Rights. Sexual orientation as a criterion for identifying persons and thus discriminating against them is, on the other hand, explicitly spoken of in closing in Article 21 of the European Charter of Fundamental Rights.

The topic, in all its facets, is discussed extensively in court rulings.

The Court of Justice has dealt with this mainly in regard to labour relations.[22]

[21] M Tamponi, *Del convivere. La società post-familiare* (Milano, Giuffré, 2018); L Balestra, *La famiglia di fatto* (Padova, Cedam, 2004).

[22] When two grounds for discrimination – homosexuality and refugee status – arise together, the question arises as to whether detailed information can be requested at the time of entry in the course of the medical examinations provided for in the entry procedure. The answer of the Court of Justice is negative. The question was examined to decide the dispute between the Ministry of Immigration from Asia and X, Y and Z. In that case, the Court held that the immigrant applicants who would be punished as criminals because they had a 'different' sexual orientation in their country of origin

The jurisprudence of the European Court of Human Rights is extensive, concerning rights of liberty and security, respect for private and family life, and sometimes the cultural and social identity of the claimants. It is a controversial jurisprudence, which, according to the Court's practice, is bound to the fact rather than to principles, to the national context rather than to the established guidelines of the constitutional courts, and it is therefore difficult to envisage uniform models of judgement.

The case of *Hamalainen v Finland* is emblematic in this regard.[23] This case concerned a person who had changed sex and therefore wished to amend her civil registration data. Since in Finland, at the time the matter was examined, a regulation had come into force that legitimised same-sex civil unions, the Court held that the appeal should not be allowed because the change of sex would not affect family relationships.

The Court first examined the arguments that the Finnish courts had put forward in order to reject the application, by denying that there was infringement of the applicant's right to privacy and the right to form a family. It then examined with great care the legislation in force in the Council of Europe Member States on 'marriage' or civil partnership of same-sex couples, concluding that the refusal to carry out the sex rectification on the identity card would not harm the applicant.

But it could be argued that by doing so, the applicant was forced to carry the stigma of gender reassignment, whereas if she had been allowed to change her biographical data, she could have formed a new life as a 'wife' instead of as a cohabitant of her partner.

Gender identity has also raised questions about the legitimacy of surgeries deemed necessary to identify the sex of a newborn child. The Council of Europe (EDC) condemned this practice in Resolution No 1952 of 2013. National courts have applied Article 8 of the ECHR to deem the imposition of sex-rectification surgery unlawful. The example brought by the *Handbook on anti-discrimination discipline* published by the European Agency for Fundamental Rights (FRA)[24] is a judgment of the Justice of the Peace of Athens (No 418/2016) that ruled in this sense. The Italian Constitutional Court came to the same solution.

The European Court of Human Rights has applied Article 8 on the protection of privacy and the right to found a family extensively.

In an earlier case, the Court had gone so far – again taking into account the guidelines expressed by national legislators – as to allow the adoption of a child by an applicant who was legally cohabiting with a person of the same sex and had held that the refusal by the national court was the expression of a discriminatory act (*EB v France*[25]).

were entitled to refugee status and that it was not necessary to examine whether they had committed acts expressive of their orientation.

[23] ECHR No 37379/09.

[24] Fundamental Rights Agency, *Handbook of European non-discrimination law* (Brussels, 2018).

[25] ECHR, No 43546/02.

Some cases decided by the Court concerned Italy.

The refusal of a residency permit to the partner of an Italian citizen – made when the regulation of same-sex unions was not yet in force in Italy – was considered an act in breach of Article 8 of the ECHR. The case (*Taddeucci and Mc Call v Italy*[26]) was decided taking into account the determinations of several supranational bodies. The explanatory statement refers to Recommendation 1470 (2000) of the Parliamentary Assembly of the Council of Europe (PACE) concerning the situation of different people in matters of asylum and immigration.[27] The Court also cited the determination of the European Commission on Sexual Orientation Law (ECSOL).[28]

The conclusions reached by the Strasbourg judges are that

> it is precisely the lack of the possibility for same-sex couples to have access to a form of legal recognition [at the time Law No 16 of 2016 had not yet been enacted] that placed the applicants in a different situation from that of an unmarried heterosexual couple … Even supposing that at the time at issue the Convention did not oblige

[26] ECHR, No 51362/09.

[27] 'The Assembly recalls and reaffirms the principles of its Recommendation 924 (1981) on discrimination against homosexuals, its Recommendation 1236 (1994) on the right to asylum and its Recommendation 1327 (1997) on the protection and enhancement of the human rights of refugees and asylum seekers in Europe. Furthermore, the Assembly is aware that the refusal of most Member States to recognise a right of residence for members of same-sex couples with dual nationality is the cause of very painful situations for many same-sex couples, who may be separated because of this and forced to live in two different countries. He considers that the rules applicable to couples in immigration matters should not distinguish between homosexual and heterosexual relationships. Therefore, a document proving the existence of an established relationship, other than a marriage certificate, should be admissible among the documents required to obtain the right of residence in the case of same-sex couples.'

[28] '78. ECSOL firstly indicates that an analysis of EU law shows the importance of prioritising relationships and family reunification as freedom of movement must be exercised under objective conditions of freedom and dignity. Thus, according to ESCOL, the Member States must at least facilitate the entry and residence of same-sex partners in the host country by seeking to identify the consequences that a refusal to issue a residence permit might have in practice on the private and family life of the persons concerned. 79. ECSOL then presented a comparative law study on the possibility for same-sex partners to obtain a residence permit in host countries. This study covered the legislation of 32 Member States of the Council of Europe (Germany, Austria, Belgium, Bosnia-Herzegovina, Bulgaria, Cyprus, Czech Republic, Denmark, Spain, Estonia, Finland, France, Georgia, Greece, Hungary, Iceland, Ireland, Italy, Latvia, Liechtenstein, Luxembourg, Malta, Netherlands, Norway, Poland, Portugal, Romania, Russia, Serbia, Sweden and Switzerland). This results in: that at least 24 states do not discriminate on the grounds of sexual orientation when issuing residence permits and provide mechanisms to do so (while leaving, in some cases, a margin of appreciation to the competent national authorities); that 22 states recognise, at least to some extent, the right to a residence permit for unmarried same-sex partners who have not entered into a registered civil partnership; that some courts have held that when a formal union, in particular a marriage, cannot be registered in the country of origin, a duly proven stable relationship may lead to a residence permit being issued by the authorities; that indirect discrimination may result from not treating different situations differently (eg refusing to recognise the existence of legal obstacles to marriage for same-sex partners); that the courts of some states recognised that, in the area of immigration of de facto same-sex partners, the Convention had played a role in protecting the private and family life of the persons concerned; that a European consensus is emerging in immigration matters, which wants same-sex unions to be considered "family life".'

> the Government to provide, for persons of the same sex in a stable and serious relationship, the possibility of concluding a civil partnership or a registered partnership attesting to their status and guaranteeing them certain essential rights, this cannot in any way affect the finding that, unlike a heterosexual couple, the second applicant had no legal means in Italy of being recognised as a 'family member' of the first applicant and thus being able to benefit from a residence permit for family reasons.

The European Court of Human Rights then held that the Austrian legislation, which at the time did not allow the cohabitee to be able to take over as a party to the lease established with the landlord in the event of the partner's death, violated Article 14 on discrimination (*Karner v Austria*[29,30]).

The European Committee for Social Rights (ECSR) within the Council of Europe has also examined issues concerning the repression of homosexuality. In a case in which school programmes aimed at informing students about sexual and reproductive health were found to have discriminatory content, it condemned the state for violating human rights[31] (*Interights v Croatia*).

Similar decisions and measures have been taken for discrimination due to disability, age, and so on.[32]

IV. THE INFLUENCE OF THE US MODEL

By common consent, in the United States the rights of the different have been recognised as a priority. It is not, of course, a matter of special rights reserved for those who manifest such a sexual orientation, but of the recognition of the freedom to exercise fundamental rights that are guaranteed to all persons, without distinction of treatment based on sexual orientation. In other words, recognition results in the removal of a prohibition that is discriminatory. However, it has a meaning beyond the mere application of the principle of equality in a formal sense; it has a moral meaning, because it does not discriminate against homosexuals, and it has a value meaning, because it affirms their human 'dignity' on a par with other individuals.

Recognition took place in several stages, through a path built on individual landmark cases decided by the Supreme Court.[33]

[29] EDU Court No 40016/98.

[30] 'The aim of protecting the family in the traditional sense is rather abstract and a broad variety of concrete measures may be used to implement it. In cases in which the margin of appreciation afforded to states is narrow, as is the position where there is a difference in treatment based on sex or sexual orientation, the principle of proportionality does not merely require that the measure chosen is in principle suited for realising the aim sought. It must also be shown that it was necessary in order to achieve that aim to exclude certain categories of people – in this instance persons living in a homosexual relationship – from the scope of application of section 14 of the Rent Act. The Court cannot see that the Government have advanced any arguments that would allow such a conclusion.'

[31] CEDS, Order No 45/2007.

[32] See the cases reported by the Handbook (n 24) 199ff.

[33] United States Court of Appeals, Ninth Circuit, 12 April 1957, 241 F.2d 772 (9th Cir 1957).

The first case concerned freedom of the press, and thus freedom of expression. At issue was whether a periodical, published in the Los Angeles area, entitled *One: The Homosexual Magazine*, could be put up for distribution. The State Postal Authority had deemed it obscene and banned its distribution. The Court of Appeal upheld the legitimacy of the measure in a learned and articulate ruling. Examining the contents of the magazine, it pointed out that an article can be considered

> vulgar, offensive and indecent, even if it is not considered as such by a particular group of individuals constituting a small segment of the population, because their social and moral standards are below those of the general community. Social standards are determined by the general community and not by a stronger or weaker minority.

The Supreme Court changed its previous orientation and affirmed the opposite principle, simply ruling on the admissibility of reviewing the case.

The decision is considered a milestone in the fight against discrimination because it was adopted in the late 1950s, at a time when American society was highly intolerant of gays. It is a pronouncement that also resulted in an important affirmation of freedom of the press and *free speech*, which are protected by the First Amendment of the US Constitution.[34]

Much more involved is the decision in *Baker v Nelson*[35] in which the Court addressed the issue of same-sex marriage for the first time. The case stemmed from a dispute in which the Minnesota Supreme Court had ruled that the appellants had the right to be united in marriage, being of the same sex.

In crucial passages, the Minnesota Court had acknowledged that marriage should be considered one of man's civil rights, fundamental to his existence and survival; it had also recalled precedents in which the prohibition of 'interracial' marriage had been removed by recourse to the Fourteenth Amendment, which excludes the possibility of placing limits on 'interracial' marriage choices. It had argued, however, that common sense and the correct meaning of the constitutional text 'did not permit distinctions of race to be equated with distinctions of sex'. In other words, precedents that liberalised marriage between persons of a different 'race' could not be invoked to legitimise same-sex marriage.

The persons concerned appealed to the Supreme Court invoking their right to marry, demanding the removal of discriminatory prohibitions (on the basis of the Fourteenth Amendment) and invoking the protection of their right to privacy, on the basis of the Nineth Amendment, which, as mentioned above, refers to the protection of *other rights* not specifically provided for.

[34] 'Amendment I. Congress shall make no law respecting an establishment of religion, or prohibiting the free exercise thereof; or abridging the freedom of speech, or of the press; or the right of the people peaceably to assemble, and to petition the government for a redress of grievances.'

[35] *Baker v Nelson*, 409 810 (US 1972).

The decision was very controversial, and was taken by a narrow majority (5:4). The Court defined the right to marry as one of the fundamental freedoms and held that same-sex marriage did not differ in this respect from opposite-sex marriage. The opposing arguments – expressed by the conservative Justices, then in a minority on the Court – point to reasoning pertaining to legislative policy, with Justice Roberts holding that it was up to state legislatures to decide whether or not to allow same-sex marriage on the basis of the will of their constituents, while Justice Scalia observed that the right to marry between persons of the same sex was not provided for in the text of the Constitution. Justice Thomas also voted against, arguing that such a radical choice was for the legislature and not the judiciary; and Justice Alito held that the legislative choice should be left to the states. The outcome, however, although a favourable decision on the merits, was negative for reasons of procedural law.

The Supreme Court's orientation is emerging in favour of homosexual behaviour, but it is still a long way off. In 1986, another piece was added to this chronology with the case of *Bowers v Hardwick*[36] in which the Court held that a Georgia law aimed at repressing acts of sodomy (by whomever and with whomever they were committed) was contrary to the Constitution, despite the fact that the competent Court of Appeal had held to the contrary. This was because this crime was codified in the legislation of many states. However, the Court took a step forward in the defence of the rights of the different, describing as laughable some of the arguments used to condemn these acts, eg that the prohibition was deeply rooted in the history of the country or that it was inherent in an ordered liberty. This is because the Constitution does not protect the right of homosexuals to engage in acts of sodomy. In any case, the Court ruled that sodomy laws should be repealed on moral grounds.

Even more relevant is the decision in the 1996 *Romer v Evans* case[37] in which the Court upheld an amendment to the Colorado State Constitution that offered protection to those discriminated against because of their sexual orientation in the allocation of public housing, employment, school services, private leases, health and welfare services, and in general economic transactions. The principle of formal equality was to be interpreted in the sense that those belonging to weak or discriminated against groups were to be specifically protected by law.

It is clear that the composition of the Court, decided by presidential appointment, affects its decisions, so that when the majority of the judges are conservative, traditions weigh more heavily than innovations, and the views of the majority over the rights of the minority. This can be seen in 1996 with the *Boy Scouts of America v Dale* case in which the Court held that the exclusion of a scoutmaster from the association because news had spread that he was an activist in the gay community, an exclusion contrary to respect for sexual

[36] *Bowers v Hardwick*, 478 US 186 (1986).
[37] *Romer v Evans*, 517 US 620 (1996).

orientations, even if minority, could not imply his readmission, because freedom of association had to be protected.

The Court overcame state legislation prohibiting same-sex sexual relations between even consenting adults with its ruling in *Lawrence v Texas* in 2003.[38] In other words, the state cannot intrude into the private lives of citizens to the extent of prohibiting acts that are considered immoral by the majority – provided, of course, that these are acts performed between consenting adults. Here again, the reference is to a right that is not explicitly provided for in the Constitution, and yet deserving of protection.

In more recent cases, the Court has spoken out unequivocally in favour of gays. In the 2013 *United States v Windsor* case,[39] the issue was whether a woman who had been married to another woman in Canada, her spouse having subsequently died, could benefit from tax exemptions on assets received as an inheritance from her spouse. The judges' discourse directly affects same-sex marriage, in particular the legal definition of marriage offered by the Defense of Marriage Act (of 1996), which referred to the union of a man and a woman who become husband and wife. The judges, by a majority, considered that marriage entails responsibilities as well as rights, and therefore the dignity and integrity of the person are involved. Hence the conclusion that a law that infringes the principle of equality cannot be considered to be in conformity with the Constitution.

In *Obergefell v Hodges*[40] the Court returned to the subject, holding that definitions of marriage that have discriminatory content must be repealed. Once again, the values of dignity and autonomy are invoked. While recognising that marriage is a pillar of the social order and a fundamental right in the constitutional system, it cannot become an instrument of discrimination, which can lead to the humiliation of children born to same-sex couples. The First Amendment, which protects everyone's religious views and beliefs, does not prevent those with different views from observing and teaching them. But that does not mean that the rights of those living with another person of the same sex should not also be taken into account. On the other hand, the judges emphasise (again, in a majority decision) that

> marriage has undergone an increasing evolution from its traditional origins. Marriages agreed upon by the parents of the spouses have been abolished, the husband's right to dispose of his wife's property has been abolished, the ban on contraceptives and the prohibition of 'inter-racial' marriages have been lifted, and there is therefore no reason to hesitate in recognising the rights of persons of the same sex who wish to marry, given the intense debate, research and contributions produced on the subject. The legislative process in a democracy is the vehicle for change, but the courts must intervene when fundamental rights are violated.

[38] 539 US 558 (2003).
[39] 570 US 744 (2013).
[40] 576 US (2015).

Here too, the dissenting judges appealed to the distinction of powers, arguing that such an important decision could only have been adopted by a parliament and not be the result of 'judicial activism', and that the will of an elite few could not be expected to impose the will of the many. Furthermore, that the Constitution does not prevent states from adopting their own definitions of marriage, nor could judges impose on states their views on how they should operate. This decision concluded the very long process that the Court – under Justice Kennedy's leadership – followed to reach the desired result. With this decision, the Court allowed the United States to join the 22 other countries that had already recognised same-sex marriage.[41]

This is the context of one of the latest decisions to create a lot of stir, concerning the refusal of a pastry chef to prepare a wedding cake for the marriage of two persons of the same sex.

Since the Colorado state judges had held that the refusal should be qualified as a violation of the civil rights law prohibiting discrimination based on sexual orientation, the confectioner had appealed to the Supreme Court. The case may seem trivial, but it is significant because it shows how fundamental rights can be violated even in the simplest cases.

The Court had in recent years changed its composition, and so had its political orientation, the majority of judges now being conservative. Consequently, when the discussion opened on the solution to be given to the case, arguments of equal weight were put forward: on the one hand the just protection of minority rights; on the other the right to express one's own opinions and religious beliefs, even if expressed in the context of commercial relations. By a majority, therefore, the Court ruled in favour of the confectioner's refusal to bake the wedding cake.

With regard to the registration of marriage between two same-sex partners, the Court held that the 'family' is neutral, and therefore its citizens cannot be denied the right to marry outside the family with persons of the same sex. The case concerned a Lithuanian citizen (11 January 2019).

V. EFFECTIVE PROTECTION AND HOMOPHOBIA

Those different on the basis of sexual orientation still experience resistance to change in relations between private individuals and difficulties in the recognition of rights in the courts. This delay in implementing the principle of dignity and EU directives is amply documented in the reports of the EU Fundamental Rights Agency. Significant, on the other hand, is the jurisprudence of the

[41] Argentina, Belgium, Brazil, Canada, Denmark, the United Kingdom (except for Northern Ireland), Finland, France, French Guiana, Greenland, Iceland, Ireland, Luxembourg, Mexico, the Netherlands, New Zealand, Norway, Portugal, South Africa, Spain, Sweden and Uruguay.

Court of Justice, which has deemed as anti-discriminatory not only the direct violation of protective legislation, but also the mere possibility of discrimination occurring, as is the case when discriminatory intent is made explicit.

The *Feryn* case[42] is emblematic in this respect. The question was to what extent previous discriminatory facts (public declaration of directly discriminatory selection criteria) constituted 'facts from which it may be presumed that there has been direct or indirect discrimination' within the meaning of Article 8(1) of Directive 2000/43. The owner of the company Feryn, in Belgium, had stated in a television interview that if his customers expressed a preference for his products because they were manufactured by local workers, he would refuse to hire non-native workers. An association for the defence of human rights had sued the entrepreneur for violation of the discipline aimed at penalising discrimination. The Court ruled that

> public statements by which an employer makes it known that, as part of its recruitment policy, it will not recruit employees of a certain ethnic or racial origin are sufficient to give rise to a presumption of the existence of a recruitment policy which is directly discriminatory within the meaning of Article 8(1) of Directive 2000/43. It is therefore for that employer to prove that there has been no breach of the principle of equal treatment. It may do so by showing that the actual recruitment practice of the undertaking does not correspond to those statements. It is for the referring court to verify that the facts alleged are established and to assess whether the evidence adduced in support of that employer's assertions that it did not breach the principle of equal treatment is sufficient.

A similar principle was affirmed in a case in which an Italian lawyer had declared during a radio broadcast that he would not allow homosexual associates to practise in his office.[43] The case arose following a lawsuit by a legal association for the protection of LGBTI rights (Lenford Network) and in the first instance, with a judgment of the Court of Bergamo, and in the second instance, with a judgment of the Court of Appeal of Brescia, the lawyer had been convicted. The Court of Cassation eferred the question to the Court of Justice for a preliminary ruling, raising some issues that were not easy to resolve: whether the association had legal standing to assert the rights of a potentially discriminated category and to ask for compensation in its favour, whether the anti-discrimination discipline on employment could also be applied to the manifestation of thought. More precisely, whether the anti-discrimination discipline could be applied even in the absence of an employment contract, and in itself could restrict freedom of thought.

With respect to the *Feyn* case, the Court of Cassation, in its interlocutory order, specified that there it was a declaration in which the criteria for

[42] ECJ, Sec 2, 10 July 2008 – C-54/07.
[43] Court of Justice, 23 April 2020, Case C-507/18.

recruitment that the company would respect were succinctly set out, excluding allogenes, which was not the case here. Another case, *Associatia Accept*,[44] involved statements made by a shareholder of a team concerning a football player that was supposed to be acquired by the team; the recruitment then did not take place, due to the reporting in the press of those statements. Again, the negotiations were ongoing and thus the opportunity for work was concrete, whereas in the present case it was merely a matter of stated intentions for the future.

The Court of Justice therefore had to balance two rights: freedom of expression and the right not to be discriminated against. The arguments used by Advocate General,[45] which concluded for the condemnation of the lawyer and the establishment of the association's legal standing, were widespread and precise. The Court, in a more concise decision, followed the precedent concerning the Accept Association and the Advocate General's orientation, holding that the lack of an ongoing selection procedure, in this case, was not in itself decisive in determining whether the statements made were in breach of the principle of employment discrimination. The Court acknowledged that 'undoubtedly freedom of expression, as an essential foundation of a democratic and pluralist society reflecting the values on which the Union is founded, under Article 2 TEU, constitutes a fundamental right guaranteed by Article 11 of the Charter'.[46] However, it specified that

> freedom of expression is not an absolute right and its exercise may be subject to limitations. Limitations derive from the law and from the principle of proportionality, and meet the general requirements of the protection of the rights and freedoms of others.

On the other question concerning the legitimacy of associations, the Court referred to the national legislator.

VI. CIVIL UNIONS

The long journey of fundamental rights, which also involved the forms of aggregation of individuals, promoted the recognition of same-sex partnerships, and thanks to the extended protection of fundamental rights, unions between people could be sealed with a stronger bond.[47] In spite of the fact that the interested parties and a large part of public opinion had called for full recognition – ie for marriage to be available to same-sex couples – a median position prevailed in Parliament, whereby the union was regulated by equating

[44] Court of Justice, 25 April 2013, C-81/12.
[45] Eleanor Sharpston, 31 October 2019.
[46] Court of Justice 6 September 2011, C-163/10.
[47] CM Bianca, *Le unioni civili e le convivenze* (Turin, Giappichelli, 2018).

it to marriage, but without using this term, evoking not only an institution ennobled by an august tradition, but also the principles laid down in Articles 7, 8, 29, 30 and 31 of the Constitution, which refer to civil marriage or religious marriage with civil effects contracted by persons of a different sex. Recognition has been helped by earlier case law, which, on the basis of the doctrine's proposals, broadened the boundaries of Article 2 of the Constitution to include, among social formations, cohabitations not based on marriage, including those involving persons of the same sex. Account was also taken of the provisions of the European Convention on Human Rights and the European Charter of Fundamental Rights, both with regard to the right to form a family and with regard to the protection of dignity, personal identity and sexual orientation and the prohibition of discrimination.

The legislature (by Law No 76 of 20 May 2016) has given cohabitation between persons of the same sex who wish to form a family the same-sex civil union, instead of marriage. This means that a same-sex civil union is a social entity inside which the members may develop their personality (according Article 2 of the Italian Constitution); the same entity could qualify as a 'natural society'. Natural society is not only the society intended for procreation, but it is the society formed by people according to their way of being and their perception of 'nature'.

It was not necessary, because it was shared by all, but it seemed useful (both politically and for exegetical purposes) to emphasise in the opening of the text (Article 1 of Law No 76 of 2016) to recognise the civil union between persons of the same sex as a social formation within the meaning of Articles 2 and 3 of the Constitution.

A civil partnership is subjectively defined through the declaration made before the civil registrar in the presence of two witnesses. Registration is carried out in the civil registrar's archive. The members of the union must have reached the age of majority (whereas there are exceptions for marriage: see Article 84 of the Civil Code).

Not all people living together create a 'civil partnership'. A civil partnership between persons of the same sex is relevant for the law only if it is certified by a document attesting to the constitution of the partnership, which must contain the personal data of the parties, an indication of their matrimonial status and residence, as well as the personal data and residence of the witnesses (c 9).

By declaration to the registrar, the parties may agree to take a common surname for the duration of the same-sex civil partnership, choosing it from among their surnames. The party may put before or after the common surname their own surname, if different, by making a declaration to the registrar (c 10).

Most of the provisions regulating civil unions take over the discipline of marriage, but the legislative choice to specifically identify the provisions applicable to this social formation, without providing for a general reference to the discipline of the code, implies that the provisions on marriage cannot be extended interpretatively or applied analogically to civil unions. In other words, the regime of civil unions is based on the rules formulated in the text of the law under consideration, and on the normative references explicitly referred to the Civil Code or special laws.

In fact, Article 1(19) of the aforementioned law provides that the provisions of Title XIII of Book I of the Civil Code, as well as Articles 116(1), 146, 2647, 2653(1),(4) and 2659 of the Civil Code apply to civil partnerships between persons of the same sex. Further, c 20 states that

> for the sole purpose of ensuring the effectiveness of the protection of rights and the full performance of the obligations arising from the same-sex civil partnership, the provisions referring to marriage and the provisions containing the words 'spouse', 'spouses' or equivalent terms, wherever they occur in laws, acts having the force of law, regulations, administrative acts and collective agreements, shall also apply to each of the parties to the same-sex civil partnership. The provision referred to in the preceding sentence does not apply to the provisions of the Civil Code that are not expressly referred to in this law, nor to the provisions of Law 184 of 4 May 1983. This shall be without prejudice to what is provided for and allowed in the matter of adoption under the regulations in force. Paragraph 21 provides that 'the provisions of Chapter III and Chapter X of Title I, Title II and Chapter II and Chapter Va *of* Title IV of Book Two of the Civil Code shall apply to the parties to a civil partnership between persons of the same sex'.

The grounds for preventing the establishment of same-sex civil unions are as follows:

(a) the existence, for one of the parties, of a marriage bond or a civil partnership between persons of the same sex; but not a civil partnership contract, nor a declared cohabitation;
(b) the disqualification of one of the parties by reason of insanity; if the application for disqualification is only made, the public prosecutor may request that the constitution of the civil partnership be suspended; in this case, the proceedings may not take place until the judgment ruling on the application has become final;
(c) the existence between the parties of the relationships referred to in Article 87(1) of the Civil Code (kinship, affinity, adoption); an uncle and nephew and an aunt and niece may also not enter into a civil partnership between persons of the same sex; the provisions of Article 87 shall apply;
(d) the final conviction of a party for murder committed or attempted against a person who is married or civilly united with the other party; if only an indictment or conviction at first or second instance or a precautionary measure has been ordered, the constitution of the same-sex civil partnership is suspended until an acquittal.

The existence of one of the grounds for impediment entails the nullity of the same-sex civil partnership. Articles 65 and 68 (remarriage and nullity of remarriage) and the provisions of Articles 119, 120, 123, 125, 126, 127, 128, 129 and 129 bis of the Civil Code (disqualification and incapacity) apply to same-sex civil partnerships.

A civil partnership constituted in violation of one of the impeding causes, or in violation of Article 68 of the Civil Code, may be challenged by each of the parties to the civil partnership, the next of kin, the public prosecutor and all those who have a legitimate and current interest in challenging it. A civil partnership formed by one party during the absence of the other may not be challenged as long as the absence lasts.

Violence is also a ground for avoidance of the contract when the threatened harm relates to the person or property of the other party to the civil union constituted by the contracting party or a descendant or ascendant of that party.

A civil partnership may be challenged by the party whose consent has been extorted by violence or determined by exceptionally serious fear caused by causes external to the party. It may also be challenged by the party whose consent was given as a result of a mistake as to the identity of the person or an essential mistake as to personal qualities of the other party. The action may not be brought if there has been cohabitation for one year after the violence or the causes which gave rise to the fear have ceased or the mistake has been discovered. Mistake as to personal qualities is essential if, having regard to the circumstances of the other party, it is established that that party would not have given its consent if it had known exactly what those circumstances were and provided that the mistake relates to:

(a) the existence of a physical or mental illness such as to prevent the performance of life in common;
(b) the circumstances referred to in Article 122(3)(2), (3) and (4) of the Civil Code.

The party may at any time challenge the marriage or civil partnership of the other party. If the nullity of the first civil partnership is contested, this issue must be adjudicated beforehand.

With the constitution of a civil partnership between persons of the same sex, the parties acquire the same rights and assume the same duties; a mutual obligation to moral and material assistance and cohabitation derives from the civil partnership. Both parties are obliged, each according to their substance and their capacity for professional and household work, to contribute to the common needs (c 11). The parties agree among themselves on the direction of family life and fix the common residence; each party has the power to implement the agreed direction (para 12).

Unlike marriage (Article 143 of the Civil Code), there is no obligation of fidelity.

The matrimonial regime of a civil partnership between persons of the same sex, in the absence of a different property agreement, is community of property. Articles 162, 163, 164 and 166 of the Civil Code shall apply with regard to form, modification, simulation and capacity to enter into property agreements. The parties may not derogate from either the rights or the duties provided by law as a result of the civil partnership. The provisions of Sections II, III, IV, V and VI of Chapter VI of Title VI of Book One of the Civil Code shall apply (c 13).

When the conduct of the party to the civil partnership causes serious harm to the physical or moral integrity or freedom of the other party, the judge, upon request of a party, may adopt by decree one or more of the measures referred to in Article 342 ter of the Civil Code.

When choosing the support administrator, the protective judge prefers, where possible, the party to the same-sex civil partnership. Interdiction or incapacitation may also be initiated by the party to the civil partnership, who may apply for revocation when the cause ceases to exist.

In the event of the death of the employee, the allowances indicated in Articles 2118 and 2120 of the Civil Code must also be paid to the party to the civil union.

The statute of limitations remains suspended between the parties to the civil union.

The provisions of Title XIII of Book I of the Civil Code (discipline of alimony) and Articles 116(1), 146, 2647, 2653(1)(4) and 2659 of the Civil Code apply to same-sex civil partnerships.

The death or declaration of presumed death of one of the parties to the civil union determines its dissolution.

A civil partnership is also dissolved in the cases provided for in Article 3(1) and (2)(a), (c), (d) and (e) of Law 898 of 1 December 1970 (divorce).

The civil partnership is also dissolved when the parties have manifested, even separately, their will to dissolve it before the civil registrar. In such a case, the application for dissolution of the civil partnership is made three months after the date of the manifestation of the will to dissolve the partnership (Article 25).

The gender rectification ruling determines the dissolution of the same-sex civil partnership. This means that if the members of the now dissolved union wished to continue living together, they could choose to live together in a free union, or in a declared cohabitation, or enter into marriage.

The civil partnership between persons of the same sex is automatically established upon the rectification of sex, if the spouses have expressed the will not to dissolve the marriage or cease its civil effects. This provision relates directly to the case that was the subject of sentence No 170 of 2014 of the Constitutional Court and the related case decided by the Court of Cassation. This is a special case of conversion of the nullity of the shop.

The same provisions that apply to spouses in matters of legitimate succession apply to the party to the civil partnership (see para 21 of Law No 76/2016).

VII. THE DISCUSSION ON THE CONCEPT OF 'RACE'

Despite the scientific clarification of the inconsistency and unfoundedness of the concept of 'race', the word is not only widespread but continues to underpin aberrant political positions and give rise to serious episodes of racism: bloody deeds, physical and moral aggression, constant incitement to racial hatred prove that fascism and nazism, as a movement of grim and dangerous thought, are never really dead. Hence the multiplication of occasions to renew the condemnation of every episode of intolerance, and the heartfelt remembrance – the constant presence of memory – of so many innocent people persecuted because of their religion, their ethnicity, their diversity.

As a result many people have formed the conviction that it is no longer appropriate to speak of races, and the fear that using this ominous and meaningless term when referring to mankind may lead to the belief that they really exist, with all the consequences that are before our eyes.

The Superior Council of the Magistracy convened a seminar to commemorate those persecuted by the racial laws, collecting the papers of the participants in a volume entitled *Race and Injustice*.[48] The President Emeritus of the Constitutional Court, Gaetano Silvestri presented a report on 'The term "race" in the Constitution', which sparked a heated debate between those who, like the speaker, believed that in order to remember the past and to avert inauspicious returns, it is appropriate for the term to remain engraved in the Constitution, and those who instead would like to erase it forever, and believe that it should not be present in the Constitution. Both positions are remarkable. The fact that other equally august texts, such as the Convention on Human Rights and the Charter of Fundamental Rights, speak of race means that the memory must be preserved in legislative texts as a warning to anyone who wants to conform to the principles of a civilised and democratic society. Only when the forms of persecution, including verbal ones, that make use of this term have disappeared can it be erased.

VIII. LANGUAGE OF HATRED. THE PAST THAT DOES NOT PASS

The succession of terrorist attacks over the last few years in Europe are a source of concern for parliaments and governments, but also for individuals living in democratically based societies. These are phenomena that transcend the imagination and escape possible prophecies, which, however, while constituting the bloody extreme to which blind aversion to all that is different from oneself can lead, they are nothing more than the extreme expression of attitudes and the instrumentalisation of ideas reflected on different continents through the communications of political groups cloaked in self-styled religious beliefs, the discriminatory activities of intolerant factions, movements and sects, and proclamations with the dissemination of images inspired by principles of intolerance, revenge, hatred and intolerance. Actions are preceded by ideas, and reinforce those ideas in their concretisation into historical facts. What is more,

[48] Rome, Publications of the Constitutional Court, 2018.

information systems, which complement traditional communication systems and virtual contact systems that bring together the most disparate people, located anywhere, only serve to increase the levels of communication and irrepressibly multiply their harmful and frightening effects.

They are a sign that under the superficial guise of controllable conflicts of opinion and civilised debates, ideas repudiated by the advent of the democratic rule of law are being passed on. But it is not just a matter of apparent or self-styled religious wars or nostalgia for political totalitarianism.

The twentieth century marked in this respect perhaps the lowest level of cruelty and dehumanisation that history has recorded. But these tragic events that mark the history of mankind found support in large swathes of public opinion and were fostered by the legal construction of the identity of persons or groups, which for centuries consolidated and justified the minority of persons and groups, and tolerated attitudes of contempt, hatred and marginalization.[49]

In short, with much sadness, but also with great indignation, we must note that the situation has not changed in contemporary societies, but has only found new forms of expression and the effrontery to re-emerge in all its violence.

In 2017 at the Portico d'Ottavia (the space in the Rome ghetto where on 16 October 1943 the Nazis rounded up more than 1,000 Jews who had not been able to go into hiding and deported them to the extermination camps), an exhibition on anti-Semitic propaganda in Germany and Italy in the late 1930s was on display.[50] On display were newspapers and magazines, as well as furnishings, drawings, cartoons that depicted the members of the 'accursed race' in the most disgusting fashions, with persuasive tones, jokes and familiar language, precisely because the consensus of the majority had to be cultivated and strengthened in order to politically and socially legitimise the anti-Semitic campaign and the resulting measures. But in addition to the exhibition of the first editions of *Mein Kampf* and ssues of the magazine *La difesa della razza*, for the first time the techniques of the filmic image were highlighted, the news footage transmitted in cinemas, designed with extreme finesse to captivate and almost magically envelop the spectator, who, without critical reflexes, swallowed words, insults, mockery formulated against the non-Aryan race. The first techniques of mass communication were premonitory of the advent and use of the new technologies, which today have developed rapidly with the rise of social networks.

These phenomena have strengthened and multiplied on the web: the random aggregations that take place through the network bring together and unite subjects once linked to a territory, and now scattered across the virtual world, the network acting as a multiplier, almost as if it were a 'bass drum' that

[49] eg, for the beginning of discrimination against Jews in the Roman Empire see Morwood, *Adriano* (Bologna, 2013); Mereu, *Storia dell'intolleranza in Europa* (Milan, 2000); Corm, *Contro il conflitto di civiltà* (Milan, 2016).

[50] M Pezzetti and S Berger, *La razza nemica. La propaganda antisemita nazista e fascista* (Rome, Gangemi, 2017).

emphasises signals and actions, and at the same time encourages anonymity and therefore impunity.

In the face of this bleak and worrying scenario, jurists have reacted both by expressing the orientation of the institutions to which they are attached and in their social function as defenders of rights and thus as protectors of discriminated minorities, of weak categories that are not adequately protected, of individuals who are endangered or are indicated as bearers of disvalues or act as symbols of oppressed and mocked status.

The twenty-first century has thus begun under the banner of the continuity of the 'short century'. It has not been able to defeat the subversive, intolerant, discriminatory movements, nor repudiate the atrocities committed in the past century because of the ideas that supported them.

Obviously, these phenomena did not only affect the Jews, but all minorities, united by skin colour, ethnic origins, minority languages or dialects, sexual orientation, beliefs, religious sentiments, political ideals and trade unions, all signs and symbols that connoted people considered different from those belonging to the majority. In order to appear more persuasive, those who spread ideas with hate language do not hesitate to make distorted use of history, from Holocaust deniers to statue-bashers. But it one thing to pull down the statue of the tyrant – as happened in the cities of Italy at the fall of Mussolini – with which the symbols of dictatorship in the yearning for freedom were to be done away with; it is quite another to attribute predatory and genocidal sentiments to historical figures, such as Christopher Columbus, who had other intentions and other roles.

Those who believe in the democratic rule of law, in a modern and inclusive Rule of Law, continue to use the tools of reason, the arguments of dialogue and persuasion rather than retaliate or fight with the same weapons against the disrupters of communities who, on the contrary, yearn for peace, justice and prosperity.

The fight against hate speech encounters many difficulties determined by the absence of a global agreement on the protection of the individual, and clashes with the impotence of the law (whether derived from a constituted authority or from conventional sources) and the courts (whether national or international). We cannot give up the fight, in the name of a changing and uncontrollable world order, as Henry Kissinger argues, nor resign ourselves to the clash of civilisations, as Samuel P Hungtinton teaches; nor can we ignore the fact that what is happening harms not only contemporaries but also future generations.

A. The Limits of Legal Discourse

What about the jurists? How can the jurists contribute – aside from the creators of the law, the judges who apply it, and above all the lawyers who fight personally and at their own risk with their petitions and pleadings – to react against the abuse of the rights of individuals and groups?

We must first of all clear the field of the limits often placed on this discourse: there are those who consider the phenomena in question to be the product of social media and information technology, those who consider legal models inspired by different historical origins, different visions of reality, different ways of reacting to the current situation to be incompatible with each other, those who still reduce the phenomenon to 'language', neglecting to see that aversion and intolerance are also communicated through other and varied forms of expression.

The first limitation – prejudice – is the idea that it is only with the advent of the Internet that the problem arose, and therefore by operating in this medium, it is possible to prevent or solve these phenomena. But this is debunked by the very events that unfold before our eyes: while it is true that the recruitment of jihadists takes place mainly through Internet channels, that the planning of terrorist attacks is planned and coordinated through the Internet, and that the 'creed' presented as legitimising these events is spread mainly through the Internet, this does not mean that we should consider the Internet a dangerous system, nor that these events would not have taken place if this 'bass drum' had not been available. The Internet is merely a powerful and barely controllable medium that emphasises the harmful effects of those attitudes.

The second limitation is the fact that those who believe in the rights of the individual do not agree on the legal qualification of the phenomenon. Nor have they found a satisfactory definition of the words with which it is expressed. The documents drawn up by the most representative institutions have tried to reach a lowest common denominator in order to overcome this obstacle.

But the most difficult limit to overcome is inherent in the legal framework itself.

In the Western world, two extreme models of reaction can be briefly distinguished: the European model, which is based on the balancing of fundamental rights and therefore legitimises limitations on freedom of expression; and the American model, which, on the other hand, does not place any limits on freedom of expression and hence considers hate speech legitimate: this not so much because it approves of its contents and aims, but because it considers that repressing it would imply the violation of the very foundation of democratic society, which undermines the autonomy of the individual, the legitimacy of his actions, and the tolerability of the harm inflicted by it.

So, balanced freedom versus maximum freedom.

The dilemma is difficult to solve: should we consider that freedom of expression in and of itself does not tolerate any limitation, or should we consider that freedom of expression cannot go so far as to undermine the dignity of a person, a group, a community or a people? And if values are to be balanced, can a hierarchy be established between them?

B. Freedom of Expression and Fundamental Rights. The Italian Model

We can overcome these problems by thinking in models and trying to find a common language, a common direction, a common project.

If one were to interpret literally Article 21 of the Italian Constitution according to which everyone – not only citizens – has 'the right to express their thoughts freely by word, writing and any other means of dissemination' (c 1) and that 'the press cannot be subject to authorisation or censorship' (c 2) it might appear that the Italian legal model follows the same rubric as the US model, in which no limits are allowed to the expression of opinions, and therefore expressions of hatred, contempt, incitement to action and so on would also be allowed without limits. And yet what belies this is the wording of Article 21, which places the first prohibition, common decency, with a reservation of the law for detailed regulation. 'Common decency' is a general clause which tracks the evolution of common feeling, the orientations and behaviour of the citizens. The jurisprudence applying this limit has therefore shifted as morality – sexual morality, in particular – acquired new contours, tending to be more lax.

But there are other limits, dictated by the protected interests of the Constitution, and therefore of *equal* rank to freedom of expression: honour, privacy, religious sentiment, the interest in the administration of justice, the duty of loyalty, to the institutions, the prestige of the institutions, the defence of the homeland, state security, public order, health and maternity, the interest of minors, etc. All these limits have been the subject of interpretation by the Constitutional Court, and correspond to a large body of constitutional case law that has used the method of *balancing conflicting interests*, aimed at establishing which of them should prevail.

The jurisprudence of the Supreme Court of Cassation has taken the same line, which, with rulings on civil and criminal matters, has adapted to the interpretative directives of the Constitutional Court, following the method of *balancing interests*.

These limitations also apply to the right of criticism: eg sentence of the Court of Cassation no 5788 of 15/06/1994 held that:

> The right to express one's own thought provided for by Article 21, first paragraph, of the Italian Constitution, in addition to meeting the limits placed on the protection of the rights and freedoms of others by other provisions of the same Constitution, must be coordinated with the various interests of public and constitutional rank protected by special laws, such as the right to freedom of expression, in addition to meeting the limits set to protect the rights and freedoms of others by other provisions of the same Constitution, must be coordinated with the various public and constitutional interests protected by special laws, such as the regulation of the profession of lawyer and procurator laid down by Royal Decree Law no. 1578 of 27 November 1933; whose Article 38 of which, affirming the disciplinary sanctionability of conduct inconsistent with professional dignity and decorum, is also

applicable with regard to expressions of the professional (in the present case, criticism of the bureaucratic red tape of the Social Security Fund) which, although not directly relating to the exercise of the profession and leaving aside the provisions of the criminal law on offence to the honour and reputation of persons, are capable – according to a judgment entrusted to the professional association – of adversely affecting the prestige and dignity of the legal profession.

But the cases are varied; on another occasion, with regard to respect for the religious sentiment of the individual, the Court of Cassation, in judgment no 7468 of 23 March 2017, specified that:

> It must be excluded that the organisation of a single artistic performance can, in itself, constitute a violation of the personal sentiment religious of a single citizen and be sanctioned by the law with the recognition of a claim for compensation not only because there is clearly no objective connection between the former and the latter, but also because the requirement of unjust damage cannot be recognised, the programming of an artistic event being an expression of a freedom guaranteed by the Constitution.

(In the case in point, the Supreme Court ruled out the liability of the organising body of an artistic event for having hosted, within its premises, a show considered contrary to the principles of the Catholic religion, for infringement of the individual right of religious freedom.)

With regard to the individual's feeling of honour and reputation, the principle can be found in a large body of case law, according to which (Court of Cassation judgment no 17211 of 27 August 2015):

> The legitimate exercise of the rights of chronicle and journalistic criticism is conditioned by the limit, in addition to truth and public interest, of continence, understood as formal correctness of the exposition and not exceeding what is strictly necessary for the public interest, so as to guarantee chronicle and criticism are not manifested by means and modalities detrimental to the fundamental rights to honour and reputation, so that, with regard to a television broadcast, the modalities of communication used are relevant, where a peculiar combination of images and sound has been realised, such as to be transmodifying the aforementioned limit.

(In the case in point, the Supreme Court held that a television report on the phenomenon of female sex tourism in Jamaica was exorbitant: the image of the plaintiff, who was not a public figure, had been combined with a soundtrack to imply that her presence 'in loco' was aimed at seeking easy sexual encounters.)

Precisely with reference to the comparative assessment of interests, judgment no 45051 of 17 July 2009 by the Supreme Court of Cassation in criminal cases established that:

> On the subject of defamation by means of 'mass media' – it being understood that the freedom of the press, expression of the right to manifest thought sanctioned by Article 21 of the Constitution, entails the compression of the legal assets of confidentiality, of the honour and reputation, which, moreover, also have constitutional dignity, pursuant to Articles 2 and 3 of the Constitution. – the reference at a distance,

> in the so-called television talk show, of the development of judicial police investigations, allowed in a historical key of the event as well as criticism of the work of the investigators, implies that the ethical obligation of the journalist must be measured against criteria of even greater rigour than the ordinary, in the sense that, where the public interest in the relative propagation persists or is revived – which, in this case, must be balanced with the right to oblivion – and historical or artistic reconstruction requirements require it, the news must be accompanied by the necessary warning that the investigative theses remained at the level of mere working hypothesis, have not found any confirmation or have even been decisively refuted by the subsequent investigative development, as it is incumbent on the journalist the legal duty to provide complete information and to carry out, for that purpose, all the checks necessary to verify the results of a given investigation.

And since the problem of limitations on freedom of expression in the press or in television and theatrical works is often taken as an example by various commentators to assess their admissibility, consider this case decided by the Court of Cassation in its judgment no 8959 of 3 July 1997:

> For the purposes of the distinction between the offences referred to in Articles 527 and 726 of the Criminal Code, the notions of obscene and modesty do not refer to a concept considered in itself, but to the context and the manner in which the acts or objects are performed or displayed. The discretional criterion is to be found in the more specific content of the crime of 'obscene acts', which refers to 'sexual decency', with respect to that complex of ethical-social rules, which require each person to abstain from anything that may offend the collective feeling of the most elementary constitutionality It follows that full nudity – considering the average feeling of the community and the values of the social conscience and the reactions of the average normal man – takes on different values. It may be included in the special cause of exclusion of obscenity (Article 529 of the Criminal Code) – as, for example, in sex education lessons or in cinematographic or theatrical works – or it may be an expression of individual freedom or derive from health convictions or a particularly uninhibited costume. If practised on a secluded beach frequented only by naturists, it is criminally irrelevant; whereas it is not so in a seaside resort crowded with variously clothed subjects. In particular, the exhibition of the genitals (unlike the exhibition of the naked breast, which no longer constitutes an offence) – apart from the exceptions mentioned – constitutes the offence of obscene acts, since it is aimed at satisfying the 'libido'.

Satire is also subject to limitations, as we are reminded by an accurate order of the Court of Cassation, which, in Order No 21235 of 17 September 2013, specified that:

> The satire constitutes a corrosive and often merciless modality of the right to criticism, so that, unlike the news, it is subtracted from the obligation to report true facts, as it expresses by means of paradox and surreal metaphor an ironic judgement on a fact, albeit subject to the limit of the continence and functionality of the expressions or images with respect to the social or political denunciation purpose pursued. Consequently, in the formulation of the critical judgment, expressions of any kind may be used, even those damaging to the reputation of others, provided that they are

instrumentally linked to the manifestation of a reasoned dissent from the opinion or conduct targeted and do not result in a gratuitous and destructive attack on the honour and reputation of the person concerned, since the exemption provided for in Article. 51 of the Criminal Code in cases of attribution of unlawful or morally dishonourable conduct, of vulgar or repugnant juxtapositions, of deformation of the image in such a way as to arouse contempt of the person and ridicule of his public image. (In the present case, the limits of the right to satire were deemed to have been exceeded, as a person was indicated as having been wrongfully accused of having received money or other benefits from the disposal of toxic waste, whereas he – although actually involved in criminal proceedings against others – had never taken on such a role) (Defendant Grillo)

And cartoons are also subject to assessment, if they are such as to harm the honour or reputation of a person: eg, Court of Cassation Judgment No 4993 of 29 May 1996 stated that:

> The right to satire, guaranteed by Art. 9, 21 and 33 of the Constitution, may be exercised only within the limits of the causal consistency between the quality of the public dimension of the character made the subject of the satire and the artistic – expressive content of the satire itself with the consequence that, although characterised by its caricature and desecration purposes, which allow it not to faithfully respect the truth of the facts it cannot be subjugated to a merely denigrating purpose (in the present case, the Court of Cassation held correct the grounds of the judgment on the merits that had considered defamatory a cartoon that, in a newspaper, illustrated a fact constituting a crime falsely attributed to a well-known political figure in an article published in the same newspaper, reproducing, with a caricature, the character himself dressed as a thief in order to make more immediate the perception, in the reader, of the connection between this character and the episode referred to in the article). (Plaintiff Craxi)

Not even a person's public role – even in the case of holding public office – can constitute an exemption if the right to satire is abused. The Court of Cassation in its Judgment No 37706 of 23 May 2013 stated that:

> On the subject of defamation in the press, for the purposes of recognition of the exemption provided for by Article 51 of the Criminal Code, if the article contains a criticism formulated in a manner peculiar to satire, if the article contains a criticism formulated in the manner typical of satire, the judge, in assessing the requirement of continence, must take into account the essentially symbolic and paradoxical language of the satirical writing, with respect to which the usual standard of correctness of expression cannot be applied, remaining, however, the limit of respect for fundamental values, which must be considered exceeded when the public person, in addition to the ridicule of his image, is exposed to contempt.

It is evident, then, that freedom of expression cannot be considered – in our legal system – at the top of a pyramid where everything is permitted. In particular, the limit of the protection of personal values, which we could summarise in terms of *dignity*, requires continence.

C. The Pyramid of Hatred in Italy

The Chamber of Deputies, in consideration of the phenomena of anti-Semitism, racism, reaction to immigration and hatred towards minorities that have been recorded in our country even recently, set up the Jo Cox Committee, named after the British MP murdered during the referendum campaign for Brexit. The Committee, at the conclusion of its work, set out 56 recommendations to prevent and counteract hatred, addressing them to the relevant actors: Government, regulatory and supervisory authorities, EU institutions, supranational organisations, the media, journalists' associations and trade unions, and all other actors. The recommendations fell into the following main areas:

1) closing serious gaps in the collection and analysis of data on hate phenomena at national and supranational levels, particularly with regard to sexism;
2) promoting a national strategy to combat hate in all its forms, articulated in specific action plans to combat discrimination of individual groups, and implement the National Roma, Sinti and Travellers Inclusion Strategy;
3) approving some important bills pending before the Houses of Parliament, including those on citizenship and the fight against homophobia and transphobia;
4) including sexist hate speech in hate and discrimination legislation;
5) penalising hate campaigns (public insults, defamation or threats) against persons or groups;
6) evaluating, based on the experiences of other countries and protecting freedom of information on the Internet, the possibility of
    a) demanding self-regulation of platforms in order to remove online hate speech;
    b) establishing the joint and several legal liability of providers and social networking platforms and oblige them to remove content reported as harmful by users as soon as possible;
7) requiring social network platforms to set up offices with adequate human resources to receive reports and promptly remove hate speech, including by activating alerts on online pages and toll-free numbers available to users;
8) strengthening the mandate of the UNAR (National Anti-Racial Discrimination Office) in the direction of greater autonomy, also by configuring it as an independent authority;
9) empowering influential institutional and political figures in the public debate by adopting regulatory mechanisms to combat hate speech;
10) improving victims' knowledge of their rights and enabling organisations active in the fight against hate speech to become civil parties in court;
11) implementing and disseminating knowledge of the regulations set out in Law No 71 of 2017 on bullying;

12) strengthening gender and citizenship education in schools, aimed at the objectives of respect, intercultural and inter-religious openness and combating intolerance and racism;
13) supporting and promoting no-hate blogs and activists or publications that promote counter-narrative and information campaigns against hate speech, especially in the non-profit world of schools and universities;
14) countering stereotypes and racism by raising awareness and empowering the media, especially online, to avoid hate speech, including unfounded, false and defamatory news;
15) providing for the establishment of a jury to guarantee the fairness of information, as also envisaged by bills submitted in this and previous legislatures, and urge the professional association and the journalists' union on the control of professional ethics.

D. European Union Law

On the basis of the principles set out above, the configuration of manifestations of thought that are directed at infringing the fundamental rights of a person, or of a group, or of a community, and as such deemed to infringe fundamental rights and therefore to be prosecuted, is clear.

Particularly significant in this regard have been the measures of EU bodies. Among the many pronouncements, it is worth mentioning the Resolution of 23 November 2016 on the Union's communication strategy for countering third-party propaganda that may be harmful to democracy, the rule of law and respect for human rights and fundamental freedoms.

The premises of the Resolution summarise the entire path taken by the Bodies of the Union and the other institutions combating war propaganda or hate speech on racial and religious grounds, inciting hostile actions against minorities, as well as freedom of expression, freedom of the press and freedom of journalists as exemptions from liability and exculpatory in the application of limits and sanctions.

In fact, the preamble refers to many measures:

[T]he resolution of 2 April 2009 on European conscience and totalitarianism,

- the Strasbourg/Kehl Summit Declaration, adopted by NATO on 4 April 2009, on the occasion of NATO's 60th anniversary,
- the resolution of 11 December 2012 on 'A strategy of digital freedom in EU foreign policy',
- the Foreign Affairs Council conclusions on combating terrorism of 9 February 2015,
- the conclusions of the European Council of 19 and 20 March 2015,

- the Council Conclusions on the EU Regional Strategy for Syria and Iraq and the Threat posed by ISIS/Daesh of 16 March 2015, which were reconfirmed by the Foreign Affairs Council on 23 May 2016,
- the report of the Vice-President of the Commission/High Representative of the Union for Foreign Affairs and Security Policy (VP/HR) of 18 May 2015, entitled 'The EU in a Changing Global Context – A More Connected, Contested and Complex World', and the ongoing work on a new EU Strategy for Global Security,
- the resolution of 10 June 2015 on the state of EU-Russia relations,
- the EU Action Plan on Strategic Communication (ref. Ares (2015) 2608242 of 22 June 2015),
- the resolution of 9 July 2015 on the review of the European Neighbourhood Policy(4),
- the declaration of the NATO summit in Wales on 5 September 2014,
- the resolution of 25 November 2015 on the prevention of radicalisation and recruitment of European citizens by terrorist organisations,
- The Communication from the Commission to the European Parliament, the Council, the European Economic and Social Committee and the Committee of the Regions of 28 April 2015 entitled 'European Security Agenda' (COM(2015)0185),
- the Joint Communication from the Commission and the High Representative of the Union for Foreign Affairs and Security Policy to the European Parliament and the Council of 6 April 2016 entitled 'Joint Framework for Countering Hybrid Threats: the EU response' (JOIN(2016)0018),
- the Communication from the Commission to the European Parliament, the European Council and the Council of 20 April 2016 entitled 'Implementing the European Security Agenda to combat terrorism and prepare the ground for the Security Union' (COM(2016)0230).

This is an impressive piece of work that recalls the most recent documents, but presupposes the Parliament resolution on homophobia of 18 January 2006, the Council of Europe resolution on combating racism and xenophobia No 919 of 2008, and other documents compiled as far back as the late 1990s.

The resolution concludes with invitations to the Member States to take action to cut off ISIS/Daesh access to funding and resources and to promote this principle in EU external action, emphasising the need to expose the true nature of ISIS/Daesh and to repudiate its ideological legitimisation. In addition, it:

> 20. Call on the EU and its Member States to take consistent, EU-wide action against hate speech systematically promoted by intolerant and extremist preachers through sermons, books, TV shows, the Internet and all other media that can create a breeding ground for terrorist organisations such as ISIS/Daesh and Al-Qaeda;
>
> 21. Stresses the importance for the EU and the Member States to cooperate with social media service providers to counter ISIS/Daesh propaganda spread via social media;

> 22. Stresses that Islamist terrorist organisations, especially ISIS/Daesh and Al-Qaeda, are engaged in active disinformation campaigns aimed at undermining European values and interests; highlights, in this regard, the importance of a specific strategy to counter anti-EU Islamist propaganda and disinformation;
>
> 23. Stresses that unbiased, reliable and objective reporting and fact-based information flows regarding developments in EU countries would prevent the spread of propaganda fuelled by third parties;

It also describes its strategy to counter propaganda:

> 24. Welcomes the Strategic Communication Action Plan; welcomes the Joint Communication on the 'Joint Framework for Countering Hybrid Threats' and calls for the immediate approval and implementation of its recommendations; stresses that the proposed actions require the cooperation and coordination of all relevant actors at national and EU level is of the opinion that only a comprehensive approach can lead to a successful outcome of the EU's efforts; calls on the Member States holding the rotating EU Presidency to always include strategic communications in the framework of their programme, in order to ensure continuity of work on the matter welcomes the initiatives and achievements of the Latvian Presidency in this regard; calls on the VP/HR to ensure frequent communication at the political level with the Member States with a view to better coordination of EU actions; stresses that cooperation between the EU and NATO in the field of strategic communication should be substantially strengthened; welcomes the intention of the Slovak Presidency to organise a conference on totalitarianism on the occasion of the European Day of Remembrance for the victims of totalitarian regimes;
>
> 25. Calls on the relevant EU institutions and authorities to closely monitor the sources of funding for anti-European propaganda;
>
> 26. Stresses the need for more funding to support media freedom in the European Neighbourhood Policy (ENP) countries under the EU's instruments in support of democracy; calls, in this regard, on the Commission to ensure full use of existing instruments, such as the European Instrument for Democracy and Human Rights (EIDHR), the ENP, the Eastern Partnership Media Freedom Watch and the European Endowment for Democracy (EED), for the protection of media freedom and pluralism;
>
> 27. Notes the enormous resources devoted to propaganda activities by Russia and the possible impact of hostile propaganda on decision-making processes in the EU, as well as its detrimental effect on public trust, openness and democracy; commends the considerable work done by the EU Strategic Communication Task Force therefore calls for the EU Strategic Communication Task Force to be strengthened by transforming it into a fully-fledged unit within the EEAS, responsible for the Eastern and Southern Neighbourhood, with adequate staffing and budgetary resources, possibly through the creation of an additional budget line dedicated to it calls for enhanced cooperation between the intelligence services of the Member States with a view to assessing the influence of third countries seeking to undermine the EU's democratic foundations and values; calls, in the context of the strategic communication, for closer cooperation between the European Parliament and the EEAS, including through the use of Parliament's analytical tools and the intelligence offices in the Member States;

28. Reiterates that it is essential for the EU to continue to actively promote respect for fundamental rights and freedoms through its external actions; considers that support for freedom of expression and assembly, the right of access to information and the independence of the media in neighbouring countries should be the main thread running through the EU's initiatives to counter propaganda;

29. Stresses the need to strengthen pluralism, objectivity, impartiality and independence of the media within the EU and in its neighbourhood, including non-state actors, for example by supporting journalists and developing capacity-building programmes for media actors fostering partnerships and information exchange networks, such as content sharing platforms, media research, training and mobility opportunities for journalists and internships in EU-based media, to facilitate the exchange of good practices;

It stresses the important role of teaching quality journalism and related training within and outside the EU in order to produce quality journalistic analysis and high editorial standards; stating that the promotion of the EU values of freedom of the press and freedom of expression and media pluralism includes support for persecuted or imprisoned journalists and human rights defenders in third countries:

31. Supports closer cooperation between EU institutions, the European Endowment for Democracy (EED), the Organisation for Security and Cooperation in Europe (OSCE), the Council of Europe and Member States in order to avoid duplication and ensure synergy in similar initiatives;

It expresses its dismay at the serious problems relating to the independence and freedom of the media in some EU Member States, as reported by international organisations such as Reporters Without Borders; calls on the EU and the Member States to take appropriate measures to improve the existing situation in the media, so as to ensure that the credibility of the EU's external action in support of the freedom, impartiality and independence of the media is also guaranteed:

33. Calls on the Task Force on Communication, strengthened as proposed, to put online, using the Twitter account @EUvsDisInfo, a site aimed at the general public that brings together the various tools for detecting disinformation, explains how they work and serves as a link between the many civil society initiatives in this regard;

34. Affirms that an efficient communication strategy must include local communities in discussions on EU actions, foster people-to-people contacts and properly consider cultural and social exchanges as key platforms for combating prejudices of local populations; recalls that, in this perspective, EU delegations must maintain direct contact with local stakeholders at grassroots level and civil society representatives;

35. Emphasises that incitement to hatred, violence or war cannot 'hide' behind freedom of expression; encourages legal initiatives in this regard, with a view to taking greater responsibility for disinformation;

36. Stresses the importance of ensuring effective and coherent communication of EU policies, both internally and externally, and of providing targeted communication to

specific regions, including access to information in local languages; welcomes, in this context, the launch of the EEAS website in Russian as a first step in the right direction and encourages translation of the site into other languages, such as Arabic and Turkish;

37. Stresses the responsibility of the Member States to actively, preventively and in a spirit of cooperation counter hostile information campaigns, or those contrary to their interests, conducted on their territory; urges the governments of the Member States to develop their own strategic communication capabilities;

38. Calls on each Member State to make the two weekly newsletters of the EU Task Force on Strategic Communication (The Disinformation Digest and The Disinformation Review) available to its citizens in order to raise awareness of propaganda methods used by third parties;

39. Insists on the difference between propaganda and criticism;

40. Emphasises that although not all criticism of the EU or its policies, particularly in the context of political expression, is necessarily propaganda or disinformation, instances of manipulation or support linked to third countries and intended to fuel and exacerbate such criticism give rise to doubts as to the reliability of the messages in question;

41. Stresses that, while it is necessary to take a stand against anti-EU propaganda and disinformation by third countries, this should not, on the other hand, call into question the importance of having a constructive relationship with third countries and making them strategic partners in addressing common challenges;

42. Welcomes the adoption of the Action Plan on Strategic Communication and the establishment of the East StratCom team within the European External Action Service (EEAS) with the aim of communicating EU policies and countering anti-EU propaganda and disinformation; calls for strategic communication to be further intensified considers that the efficiency and transparency of the work of the East StratCom team should be further improved; calls on the EEAS to develop criteria to measure the efficiency of its work; stresses the importance of ensuring that the East StratCom team is adequately funded and staffed;

It also notes that the 'Disinformation Review' published by the StratCom Task Force must comply with the criteria set out in the International Federation of Journalists' Declaration of Principles on the Conduct of Journalists; stresses that the 'Disinformation Review' must be drafted in an appropriate manner, without resorting to offensive language or value judgments; and calls on the East StratCom Task Force to review the criteria followed in drafting the 'Disinformation Review':

44. Believes that an effective strategy to counter anti-EU propaganda could consist in taking measures to provide a targeted audience with appropriate and interesting information on EU activities, European values and other issues of public interest, and points out that modern technologies and social networks could be used for such purposes;

45. Calls on the Commission to pursue certain legal initiatives in order to increase its effectiveness and accountability in countering disinformation and propaganda, and

to use the mid-term review of the European Neighbourhood Instrument to promote the strengthening of media resilience as a strategic priority calls on the Commission to carry out a thorough review of the efficiency of existing EU financial instruments and to come forward with a proposal for a comprehensive and flexible solution that can provide direct support to independent press, think tanks and NGOs, especially in the target group's native language, and allow additional resources to be channelled to organisations with the capacity to do so, such as the European Endowment for Democracy, while reducing financial flows to support individuals or bodies engaged in strategic communication activities or incitement to hatred and violence calls on the Commission to carry out a thorough audit of the efficiency of certain EU-funded large-scale media projects, such as Euronews;

46. Emphasises the importance of online media awareness, education and media literacy in the EU and neighbourhood, with a view to empowering citizens to critically analyse media content in order to identify propaganda; stresses, in this regard, the importance of strengthening knowledge at all levels of the education system emphasises the need to engage people in active citizenship to develop their awareness as media consumers; highlights the central role of online tools, especially social media, where the dissemination of false information and the launching of disinformation campaigns are easier and often encounter no obstacles recalls that countering propaganda with other propaganda is counterproductive, and understands, therefore, that the EU as a whole and the Member States taken individually can only combat third-party propaganda by rejecting disinformation campaigns and making positive use of messages and information, recalling the need to develop a truly effective strategy, which should be differentiated and adapted to the nature of the actors disseminating information through propaganda; recognises that the financial crisis and the advance of new forms of digital media have posed major challenges for quality journalism;

47. Expresses concern about the use of social media and online platforms for criminal incitement to hatred and violence, and urges Member States to adapt and update their legislation to address ongoing developments, or to fully implement and enforce existing legislation on incitement to hatred, both online and offline; affirms the need for greater cooperation in this regard with online platforms and leading Internet and media companies;

48. Calls on the Member States to provide and guarantee the necessary framework for quality journalism and variety of information by counteracting media concentration, which has a negative impact on media pluralism;

49. Points out that media education provides knowledge and skills and enables citizens to exercise their right to freedom of expression, to critically analyse media content and to react to disinformation; therefore emphasises the need to raise awareness of the risks of disinformation through media literacy initiatives at all levels, including through a European information campaign on media, journalistic and editorial ethics, and by promoting greater cooperation with social platforms and joint initiatives to tackle incitement to hatred and violence and online discrimination;

50. Notes that no soft power strategy can succeed without cultural diplomacy and the promotion of intercultural dialogue between and within countries, in the EU and outside the EU; therefore encourages long-term public and cultural diplomatic

actions and initiatives, such as scholarships and exchange programmes for students and young professionals, including initiatives to support intercultural dialogue, strengthen cultural ties with the EU, promote common heritage and cultural ties, and provide adequate training for EU delegation and EEAS staff to equip them with appropriate intercultural skills;

51. Believes that the public media should set an example of how to provide unbiased and objective information, in accordance with best practices and ethics of journalism;

52. Stresses the need to pay special attention to new technologies – including the dissemination of digital content, mobile communications, online media and social networks, including those of a regional nature – which facilitate the dissemination of information, as well as increased awareness, about European values enshrined in the Treaties recalls that such communications must be of a high standard, contain concrete best practices and highlight the EU's impact on third countries, including EU humanitarian assistance, as well as the opportunities and benefits of closer association and cooperation with the EU for third-country nationals, in particular young people, such as visa-free travel or capacity-building, mobility and exchange programmes, where applicable;

53. Stresses the need to ensure that the new ENP portal, currently being developed under the OPEN Neighbourhood programme, not only brings together content aimed at expert communities, but also contains a section specifically designed for a wider audience; considers that the portal should include a section on the Eastern Partnership, bringing together information on initiatives that are currently fragmented among numerous sites;

54. Highlights the potential of popular culture and educational entertainment as tools for expressing shared human values and communicating European policies;

55. Emphasises its support for initiatives such as the Baltic Centre for Media Excellence in Riga, the NATO Strategic Communications Centre of Excellence (NATO StratCom COE) or the European Radicalisation Awareness Network Centre of Excellence; emphasises the need to make use of their findings and analysis, as well as to strengthen the EU's analytical capacities at all levels calls on the Commission and the Member States to initiate similar projects, to take care of the training of journalists, to support independent media outlets and media diversity, to encourage networking and cooperation between media and think tanks, as well as the exchange of best practices and information in these areas;

56. Condemns the continued repression of independent media, journalists and civil society activists in Russia and the occupied territories, including Crimea following its illegal annexation; points out that since 1999 dozens of journalists have been killed, disappeared without trace or been imprisoned in Russia; calls on the Commission and the Member States to strengthen the protection of journalists in Russia and in the EU neighbourhood, as well as to support Russian civil society and invest in people-to-people contacts; calls for the immediate release of journalists notes that the EU is strengthening relations with its Eastern partners and other neighbouring regions while keeping communication channels with Russia open; recognises that the greatest obstacle to Russian disinformation campaigns would be the existence of independent and free media within Russia itself considers that achieving this should be the EU's goal; calls for special attention and sufficient resources to be devoted to pluralism

in the media, local media, investigative journalism and media in foreign languages, especially Russian, Arabic, Farsi, Turkish and Urdu as well as other languages spoken by populations vulnerable to propaganda;

57. Supports the communication campaigns conducted by relevant actors in Syria, Iraq and the region (as well as in the countries of origin of foreign fighters) to discredit the ideology of ISIS/Daesh, denounce human rights violations perpetrated by it and combat violent extremism and incitement to hatred, including by other groups in the region calls on the EU and its Member States, in their dialogue with MENA countries, to emphasise that good governance, accountability, transparency, the rule of law and respect for human rights are essential prerequisites for protecting these societies from the spread of intolerant and violent ideologies that inspire terrorist organisations such as ISIS/Daesh and Al-Qaeda stresses, in the face of the growing terrorist threat from ISIS/Daesh and other international terrorist organisations, the need to strengthen cooperation on security issues with countries that have a long track record in countering terrorism.

E. Dignity as the Foundation of Freedoms and Rights

In the comparative assessment of the interests at stake, particular importance is attached to the Charter of Fundamental Rights in which the *dignity* of the person – and thus of the communities and minorities to which the person belongs, or with which he identifies – is considered the pillar on which the entire European order rests.

The provision, in several provisions of our Constitutional Charter, of the principle of guaranteeing and protecting the dignity of the person has recorded, as already highlighted, a very extensive application by the Constitutional Court. In a voluminous notebook edited by the Constitutional Court itself[51] are more than 100 rulings in which the judges of the Constitutional Court has made use of the principle of human dignity, with regard to the treatment of foreigners, discrimination on the grounds of sex – in particular, the treatment of women in the family, in the employment relationship, in political elections, discrimination on the grounds of language, religious freedom, opinions, personal conditions, with particular reference to compulsory health treatment, the right to be treated, the disabled, juvenile status, the condition of prisoners, and discrimination in the workplace.

Each of these areas merits an in-depth discussion, but as the issues relate to areas that will be examined later in correspondence with similar provisions in the European Charter of Fundamental Rights, it is appropriate to refrain from doing so in this context and to refer to the subsequent discussions.

The principle of dignity is also increasingly used by the Court of Cassation. This is a remarkable fact, because unlike the Constitutional Court, which

[51] M Bellocci and P Passaglia (eds), *The Dignity of Man as a Constitutional Principle* (Rome, Quaderni, 2007).

syndicates laws on the basis of rules enshrined in the Basic Charter, the Court of Cassation deals in civil matters with relationships established between private individuals respectively. In criminal matters, dignity constitutes a limit to criminal prosecution and its consequences. In civil matters, the Court of Cassation's ruling of 11 November 2008 no 26972 on compensation for non-pecuniary damage gave rise to many doubts, not so much because of the new classification of the items of damage (a classification that could be appreciated), but because the Court held that such damage is compensable in cases provided for by law as a crime, in cases provided for by special law, in cases of injury to 'inviolable rights' provided for by the Constitution; human rights guaranteed by the ECHR are not equated to this category. This constitutionally oriented interpretation of Articles 2043 and 2059 of the Civil Code was reaffirmed in a case of demotion by judgment No 2352 of 2 February 2010.

On the level of effects, it is easy to verify how, in our legal system, the rules concerning the legal position of the 'non-citizen' are widely censurable, which affect both the principle of dignity and the principle of equality, as well as the principle of equal opportunities; how censurable are the pronouncements that violate the principle of equality in the application of the norms implementing the directives on non-discrimination; how appreciable, instead, are the pronouncements on the principle of informed consent.

The Court of Cassation has proven itself in directly applying the principle of dignity to relations between private individuals. An analysis of the most recent measures confirms this positive assessment.

Returning to non-asset damage, the Court held that

> the general category of non-asset damage – which relates to the injury of interests inherent to the person not connoted by exchange value – has a composite nature, articulated in a series of aspects (or items) having a merely descriptive function, such as non-material damage (identifiable in the soulache or inner suffering suffered by the victim of the wrongful act, or in the injury caused to dignity or moral integrity, as the maximum expression of human dignity), the biological one (understood as the damage to health) and the existential one (consisting of the disruption of the injured party's life habits), which – if they occur cumulatively – must be taken into account when settling the damages, in accordance with the principle of the entirety of the compensation, without this being precluded by the unitary nature of the settlement, which is considered violated only when the same aspect (or item) is calculated twice (or more) on the basis of different, merely formal, denominations. In balancing the right to the exercise of economic initiative and the protection of personality rights – first and foremost the dignity of the person – it reaffirmed the primacy of dignity, safeguarding the confidentiality of the interested party since it is a matter of commercial information and not of freedom of expression.

And even in the matter of freedom of the press, dignity constitutes a limit to its exercise if done in an injurious form, as stated by the Court of Cassation:

> The right to the press, ie the freedom to disseminate news and commentary through the press, enshrined in principle in Article 21 of the Constitution. And regulated by

> the law of 8 February 1948 no. 47, is legitimate when the following three conditions are met a) social usefulness of the information; b) truth (objective or even only putative, provided that it is the result of serious and diligent research) of the facts reported, which is not met when, although the individual facts reported are true, other facts, so closely related to the former as to completely change their meaning, are fraudulently or even only negligently withheld; C) a 'civil' form of reporting and assessment of the facts, ie not exceeding the informative purpose to be achieved, marked by serene objectivity at least in the sense of excluding any preconceived disparaging intent and, in any case, respectful of that minimum dignity to which even the most reprehensible person is always entitled, so that trivial offence or offence to the most human feelings is never permitted. The form of criticism is not civilised when it is not marked by loyal clarity, ie when the journalist resorts to clever subtexts, suggestive juxtapositions, a disproportionately scandalised and indignant tone or, in any case, the artificial and systematic dramatisation with which neutral news is reported, or outright insinuations. In such cases, the exercise of the right to print may constitute a civil offence even if it does not constitute a crime. (Judgment of 18.10.1984, no 5259.)

Particularly significant, because it concerns one of the essential aspects of today's life, the use of databases by means of IT tools, is the ruling rendered by the Court of Cassation on 8 August 2013, no 18981, according to which

> the law also protects data that are already public or published, since the person who carries out processing operations on such information, from their juxtaposition, comparison, examination, analysis, conjunction, relationship or intersection, may obtain further information and, therefore, an 'added informative value', which cannot be extracted from the data considered in isolation, potentially damaging to the dignity of the person concerned (pursuant to Articles 3, first paragraph, first part, and 2 Const.), to be considered pre-eminent with respect to private economic initiative which, according to Article 41 Const, cannot be carried out in such a way as to harm human dignity. In the case in point, the Court of Appeal upheld the judgment rejecting the objection lodged against a decision of the Data Protection Authority, which had ordered a company entrusted with compiling 'dossiers' for commercial purposes to prohibit it from continuing to associate with certain persons the information concerning the bankruptcy of a limited liability company, on whose board of directors the persons concerned had sat at a time prior to the declaration of insolvency, since the information in question exceeded the purposes of the information, in the absence of any assumption of personal liability on the part of the persons concerned.

In any case, the protection of the person, in all its aspects, is the aim that the court identifies in Article 2 of the Constitution, which refers to the inviolable rights of man (Court of Cassation judgment of 10 July 2001, no 6507):

> On the subject of personality rights human, there exists a true and proper perfect subjective right to personal reputation also outside the hypotheses expressly provided for by ordinary law, which is to be framed in the system of constitutional protection of the person human, drawing in the Constitution its normative foundation (Constitutional Court 184/1986, 479/87), in particular in art. 2 (as well as in art. 3, which refers to the dignity social) and in the recognition of the inviolable rights of the

> person. Article 2 of the Constitution, in affirming the constitutional relevance of the human person in all its aspects, implies that the interpreter, in the search for spaces to protect the person, is legitimised to construct all subjective positions suitable to guarantee, on the ground of the positive legal system, every projection of the person in the social reality, within the limits in which it is a consequence of the protection of the inviolable rights of man, both as an individual and in the social formations in which his personality is expressed. The express reference to the person as an individual certainly represents a valid regulatory basis for giving consistency as a right to the subject's reputation, in correlation also with the primary objective of protecting 'the full development of the person human ', referred to in Article 3 of the Constitutional Constitution (implicitly on this point Constitutional Court, 3 February 1994, no. 13). In fact, within the sphere of human personality rights, with a constitutional basis, the right to image, name, honour, reputation, privacy are but individual aspects of the constitutional relevance that the person, in its unity, has acquired in the system of the Constitution. They are therefore homogeneous rights, the protected good being unique.

An important case involving both the Court of Cassation and later the Constitutional Court concerned the massacre of civilians by German troops during WW2. Both courts held that limits could not be imposed on the national order when the value of human dignity was compromised.

First of all, the Unified Sections of the Court of Cassation, in its judgment of 29 May 2008, no 14199 of 29 May 2008, stated that:

> On the subject of the recognition of foreign judgments, the judgment of the Supreme Court of Cassation of Greece ordering the Federal Republic of Germany to pay the costs of proceedings in a successful claim for compensation brought by the heirs of the victims of a massacre of civilians carried out by the German armed forces on Greek territory during the Second World War cannot be considered contrary to domestic public policy, since the customary rule of international law, which requires States to abstain from exercising their jurisdictional power over acts 'in the name of the State', is not applicable to the recognition of foreign judgments, which imposes on States the obligation to refrain from exercising their jurisdictional power in respect of acts 'iure imperii', is not unconditional in nature but is limited by the recognition of the absolute primacy of the fundamental values of liberty and dignity of the person human and, consequently, it cannot be invoked in the presence of conduct by the foreign State of such gravity as to constitute crimes against humanity inasmuch as it is detrimental to those universal values of respect for human dignity dignity that transcend the interests of individual State communities.

Then the Constitutional Court itself followed with a ruling whose decision was highly tormented, concerning the compensation of Italian citizens deported to concentration camps by the German armed forces during the last war.

The premise is that the fundamental principles of the constitutional order and the inalienable rights of the person constitute a

> limit to the entry … of the generally recognised international norms to which the Italian legal system conforms according to article 10, paragraph 1 of the

Constitution' (judgments n. 48 of 1979 and n. 73 of 2001) and operate as 'counter-limits' to the entry of the norms of the European Union (ex plurimis: judgments n. 183 of 1973, n. 170 of 1984, n. 232 of 1989, n. 168 of 1991, n. 284 of 2007), as well as limits to the entry of the norms of execution of the Lateran Pacts and the Concordat (judgments n. 48 of 1979 and n. 73 of 2001). of 1984, no. 232 of 1989, no. 168 of 1991, no. 284 of 2007), as well as limiting the entry of the rules implementing the Lateran Pacts and the Concordat (judgments no. 18 of 1982, no. 32, no. 31 and no. 30 of 1971). They represent, in other words, the identifying and inalienable elements of the constitutional order, for this very reason also exempt from constitutional revision (articles 138 and 139 of the Constitution: thus in sentence no. 1146 of 1988) (…) The referring judge has not by chance jointly indicated articles 2 and 24 of the Constitution, which are inextricably linked in the assessment of constitutional legitimacy requested of this Court. The first is the substantive rule placed, among the fundamental principles of the Constitutional Charter, to protect the inviolability of the fundamental rights of the person, among which, in this case conferred as a primary right, dignity. The second is also to safeguard the dignity of the person, protecting his right to have access to justice to assert his inviolable right. Hence the illegitimacy of the Italian judge's obligation to apply law no. 5 of 2013, which would require him to respect the immunity of the foreign State.

F. The ECHR and the Court EDU

The European Court of Human Rights has been very active in this area.

The European Convention on Human Rights does not speak of dignity, but places the person at the centre of any legal system. Therefore it cannot but consider the protection of the person as preponderant over freedom of expression. From this point of view, the European Court of Human Rights has ruled in many cases.

As is its custom, the Court does not enunciate general principles, but assesseson a case-by-case basis. A very thorough research prepared by Tarlach McGonagle of the Institute for Information Law has reviewed the many rulings by which the European Court of Human Rights has examined cases submitted to it in recent years.

The provision that comes into consideration, among others, in the reasoning of the judgments, concerns freedom of expression. For mere reconnaissance purposes, the text is reproduced:

> Everyone has the right to freedom of expression. This right shall include freedom to hold opinions and to receive or impart information or ideas without interference by public authority and regardless of frontiers. This Article does not prevent States from subjecting broadcasting, film or television undertakings to a licensing regime. 2. The exercise of these freedoms, insofar as it carries with it duties and responsibilities, may be subject to such formalities, conditions, restrictions or penalties as are prescribed by law and are necessary in a democratic society in the interests of national security, territorial integrity or public safety, for the defence of law and order and the

prevention of crime, for the protection of health or morals, for the protection of the reputation or rights of others, for preventing the disclosure of confidential information or for securing the authority and impartiality of the judiciary.

As mentioned above, there are many rulings by the European Court of Human Rights on hate speech.

One of the first cases, which the relevant doctrine considers eminent (*Handyside v UK*[52]), concerned the publication of a book by a publisher (by the name of Handyside) whose series had included several publications by communist authors, and had now published a book for schools (*The Red School Book*) in which, among other things, the fundamental aspects of adult sexual life were briefly dealt with, a didactic introduction referring pupils to more in-depth scientific literature for more information. Although circulated in many countries, the book had been seized in the United Kingdom because it was considered obscene on the basis of the legislation then in force. Having gone through all levels of jurisdiction, the publisher had appealed to the European Court of Human Rights, which, in a very detailed decision, held that there was no violation of Article 10 of the Convention on Freedom of Expression, and that no 'obscenity' could be found in the information given to readers, even if they were minors.

The point concerned the concept of 'obscenity' (on the other hand, at the very opening of our discourse, reference was also made to censorship as a limitation of freedom of expression). and in this regard we read:

> It is not possible to find in the domestic law of the various Contracting States a uniform European conception of morals. The view taken by their respective laws of the requirements of morals varies from time to time and from place to place, especially in our era which is characterised by a rapid and far-reaching evolution of opinions on the subject. By reason of their direct and continuous contact with the vital forces of their countries, State authorities are in principle in a better position than the international judge to give an opinion on the exact content of these requirements as well as on the 'necessity' of a 'restriction' or 'penalty' intended to meet them.

However, the Court has never ruled that militant language in favour of racism, xenophobia or anti-Semitism, or denialism, could be protected by Article 10.

Although without defining it, the Court found *hate speech* to be contrary to Article 10 in four cases decided against Turkey in 1999. It also emphasised that the media had become a tool for spreading hate speech and promoting violence.[53]

The Court, the protector of freedoms and democracy, is well aware that any restriction on freedom of opinion, expression, or the press can undermine democracy, and yet, when it comes not only to passages describing facts, or

[52] Application no 5493/72, ECHR, 7 December 1976.
[53] Application no. 23927/94, ECHR, 8 July 1999.

information and mere ideas that may appear embarrassing or impact on public opinion, but expressions that encompass hatred and appreciation of violence, those expressions may be prohibited.

It would be easier to understand the Court's assessments if it had proceeded to define hate speech; but having not done so, the meaning of this expression must be taken from the context. This can be understood in the decision that found a television campaign promoting racist and xenophobic ideas unacceptable to a democratic society (*Jersild v Denmark*[54]).

Despite the fact that the journalist had defended himself by claiming that he had distanced himself from the interviewees' statements, the Court held that:

> [T]he reasons adduced in support of the applicant's conviction and sentence were not sufficient to establish convincingly that the interference thereby occasioned with the enjoyment of his right to freedom of expression was 'necessary in a democratic society'; in particular the means employed were disproportionate to the aim of protecting 'the reputation or rights of others.

In another case (*Norwood v UK*[55]), a journalist had launched an aggressive attack against the multitude of Muslims living in the UK, and called for their expulsion. The Court held that this was an act of terrorism.

But the Court assesses a case-by-case basis the incidence of the words, symbols or images used on to ascertain whether it is *necessary* in order to safeguard democracy in a society founded on the rule of law to allow expressions that may offend, harm honour or otherwise violently criticise minority groups, or to prohibit them because they challenge the very values that freedom of expression is intended to save.

For example, in *Vajnai v Hungary*,[56] Vajnai had participated in a demonstration in Hungary, organised near a statue of the recently defeated communist regime, and displayed a red star on his jacket. The court held that prohibiting the display of the red star was not a necessary measure to protect democracy. The perspicuous reasoning states that:

> As regards the link between the prohibition on displaying the red star and the offensive totalitarian ideology underlying that symbol, the Court emphasises that, however troublesome the potential dissemination of that ideology may be, that cannot be the only reason justifying its restriction by means of a criminal sanction. Indeed, it is not possible to equate with dangerous propaganda a symbol that could have had different meanings in the context of the present case, in which it was displayed by a leader of a political party with no known totalitarian ambitions. However, Section 269/B of the Hungarian Criminal Code does not require proof that the actual display amounts to propaganda of totalitarianism. On the contrary, mere ostentation is unquestionably considered to be such unless it is for scientific, artistic, educational or informative

[54] Application no 15890/89, ECHR, 23 September 1994.
[55] no 23131/03, ECHR, 16 November 2004.
[56] Application no 6061/10, ECHR, 23 September 2014.

purposes (see paragraph 41, supra, in fine). For the Court, this indiscriminate nature of the prohibition supports the finding that it is unacceptably broad. 57. The Court is of course aware that the systematic use of terror to consolidate the communist regime in several countries, including Hungary, remains a serious scar in the mind and heart of Europe. The Court recognises that the display of a symbol that was omnipresent during the reign of such regimes may create unease among victims of the past and their relatives, who may rightly find such displays disrespectful. It considers, however, that such sentiments, however understandable, cannot by themselves place limits on freedom of expression. Given the well-known guarantees that the Republic of Hungary provided legally, morally and materially to the victims of communism, such emotions cannot be regarded as rational fears. In the Court's opinion, a legal system that applies restrictions on human rights in order to satisfy the dictates of public opinion – real or imagined – cannot be considered as meeting the imperative social needs recognised in a democratic society, since society must remain rational in its judgement. To hold otherwise would be to subject freedom of speech and opinion to the veto of censorship. 58. The foregoing considerations are sufficient to enable the Court to conclude that the applicant's conviction for merely wearing a red star cannot be regarded as meeting a 'compelling social need'. Moreover, the extent to which his conduct was sanctioned, even if relatively minor, belongs to the sphere of criminal law, a sphere which carries the most serious consequences. The Court does not consider that the sanction was proportionate to the legitimate aim pursued. It follows that the interference with the applicant's freedom of expression cannot be justified under Article 10 § 2 of the Convention.

The ECHR is therefore sensitive to the protection of freedom of expression, but demonstrates its limits when it is not necessary to safeguard it because this freedom would conflict with interests, values, rights, which are inherent to the human person or the security or democracy of a society.

Thus, there are rulings on racial hate speech (*Vona v Hungary*[57]) targeting public demonstrations against Roma. However, in another case where the applicant, individually, had felt offended by the use in some publications of the Turkish expression translating the word 'Roma', it held that there was no violation of Article 10 (*Aksu v Turkey*[58]).

Similarly, in a highly controversial judgment, the Court held that a racist electoral campaign did not violate Article 10 (*Féret v Belgium*[59]) precisely because the albeit violent expressions had been used in the course of an electoral competition and thus in a context in which public opinion could democratically assess whether or not they were excessive.

On the contrary, in the case of a journalist who had approved an attack in France against American imperialism (*Leroy v France*[60]), the Court held that violence of expression was an attack on democracy). Similarly, in the 1979 case

[57] Application no 35943/10, ECHR, 9 July 2013.
[58] Applications nos 4149/04 and 41029/04, ECHR, 15 March 2012.
[59] Application no 15615/07, ECHR, 16 July 2009.
[60] Application no 36109/03, ECHR, 2 October 2018.

Glimmerveen and Hagenbeek v The Netherlands,[61] the purity of the Dutch 'race' was preached.

As for religious hatred, the Court, also through the instrument of inadmissibility (which often indirectly implies that the contested measure is justified) has struck down speeches praising the Islamic victory over the infidels (*Hizb Ut-Tahrir and others v Germany*[62]). A similar judgment arose in *Gündüz v Turkey*.[63]

The Court has also spoken out in favour of the protection of minorities with regard to sexual orientation (*Vejdeland and others v Sweden*[64]) and in favour of the condemnation of anti-Semitism, including with regard to denialism (*Garaudy v France*[65]) and the use of gas chambers for the destruction of the Jews (*Honsik v Austria*[66]).

G. The Impact of EDU Court Rulings on Italian Case Law

The judgments of the European Court of Human Rights are relevant for the application of domestic law. Some rulings of the Supreme Court have referred to them to define the new concept of moral damage.

Judgments Nos 348 and 349 of 2007 clarify the scope and effects of the limit of compliance with the constraints deriving from international obligations, provided for by Article 117(1) of the Constitution as a limit for state and regional legislative power, with reference to the provisions of the ECHR. Preliminarily, the Court clarifies that the common judge does not have the power to disapply the domestic legislative norm held to be in contrast with a rule of the ECHR, since 'the alleged incompatibility between the two presents itself as a question of constitutional legitimacy, due to a possible violation of Article 117, first paragraph, of the Constitution, which is the exclusive competence of the judge of laws'. This, however,

> does not mean that the norms of the ECHR, as interpreted by the Strasbourg Court, acquire the force of constitutional norms and are therefore immune from this Court's review of constitutional legitimacy. Precisely because they are norms that supplement the constitutional parameter, but still remain at a sub-constitutional level, it is necessary for them to be in conformity with the Constitution. The particular nature of the same norms, which are different from both community norms and concordat norms, means that the scrutiny of constitutionality cannot be limited to the possible infringement of fundamental principles and rights or supreme principles, but must

[61] Application Nos 8348/78 and 8406/78, ECHR, 8 September 2020.
[62] Application no 31098/08, ECHR, 12 June 2012.
[63] Application no 35071/97, ECHR, 14 June 2004.
[64] no. 1813/07, ECHR, 9 February 2002.
[65] Application no 65831/0124, ECHR, June 2006.
[66] Application no 25062/94, ECHR, 28 October 1997.

> extend to any profile of contrast between the 'interposed norms' and the constitutional ones.

Article 117(1) of the Constitution does not allow 'attributing constitutional rank to the norms contained in international agreements, which are the subject of an ordinary law of adaptation, as is the case with the norms of the Cedu', but it does determine

> the obligation of the ordinary legislator to respect these norms, with the consequence that the national norm that is incompatible with the norm of the Cedu and therefore with the international obligations referred to in Article 117, first paragraph, violates this constitutional parameter.

The provisions of the ECHR become, therefore, 'interposed norms' in the judgement of constitutional legitimacy in relation to the parameter of international obligations provided for in Article 117(1) of the Italian Constitution.

However, the Constitutional Court has also been cooperative, sometimes conforming and sometimes deviating from the orientation of the ECHR.

As the former President Franco Gallo wrote:[67]

> The Italian constitutional jurisprudence has certainly not been insensitive to the problems of the reception of ECHR jurisprudence in our legal system and has, in fact, elaborated a number of principles governing this reception. I will briefly recall the two most important ones.
>
> The first is basic and is directly based on the ECHR itself (Article 32(1) of the Convention). According to this principle, the domestic judge, in order to ascertain whether there is a conflict between the national rules and the ECHR rules, must take into account the latter only in the meaning attributed to them by the ECHR Court[68] and, in any case, must interpret the national legislation in a manner consistent with the ECHR.[69] There is no need to dwell on this. Instead, I will deal with the second principle that has been created by the Court's jurisprudence. According to this principle, the common court must, in any event, refer to the Constitutional Court the review of the compatibility of the domestic law with the ECHR, raising a question of constitutional legitimacy before it for that purpose.
>
> While confirming the non-independence of the interpretation of the Convention provided by the Strasbourg Court, the Constitutional Court thus reserves to itself the possibility – in addition to checking the conformity of the ECHR rules with the Constitution – also of 'assessing how and to what extent the product of the

[67] Report, 12 April 2013, available at www.cortecostituzionale.it/documenti/relazioni_annuali/RelazioneGallo_20130412.pdf.

[68] The content of the convention and the obligations arising from it is essentially that which is drawn from the case law that the European Court of Human Rights has developed over the years (Judgments Nos 257, 236, 187, 181 and 113 of 2011, 93 of 2010, 311 and 239 of 2009, 39 of 2008, 349 and 348 of 2007; Order No 180 of 2011).

[69] On pain of inadmissibility of the question of constitutionality, where such an attempt is not rendered impossible by the textual constraint of the *littera legis* and where no living law contrary to the interpretation conforming to the ECHR has been formed: Judgments Nos 236, 113, 80 and Judgments of 2011; 196, 138 and 87 of 2010; 317, 311 and 239 of 2009; 39 of 2008.

interpretation of the European Court fits into the Italian constitutional order'. This assessment is resolved, in particular, 111 by the Constitutional Court's appreciation of the 'European case law consolidated on the conferring norm', which allows it to respect its substance and, at the same time, also to take into account the peculiarities of the legal system in which the conventional norm is destined to be inserted' as an interposed norm.[70]

To this necessary finding of formal 'non-incompatibility' between conventional law and the Constitution, Judgment No. 317 of 2009 added a further important condition of a substantive order: namely, that 'the overall result of the integration of the system's guarantees must be positive, in the sense that the impact of the individual ECHR norm on Italian legislation must result in an added protection for the entire [national] system of fundamental rights'.

By requesting this 'plus of protection', the Constitutional Court is therefore prepared for an open confrontation with EU and international jurisprudences, not retreating into nationalistic logic, but reconfirming its willingness to go beyond the very principle of sovereignty of the political constitution when this serves to broaden the protection of the rights of the individual.

H. The Rulings of the Court of Justice

Although freedom of expression is taken up by the European Charter of Fundamental Rights in Article 11, it has not been the subject of many ECJ rulings. We do, however, find important stances in the material that can be found. On one of the rare occasions when the Court has had occasion to deal with the subject, the Luxembourg judges formulated a definition of freedom of expression and its limits. In the *Connolly* case[71] (in which an EU official was highly critical of the euro system) we read that:

> Fundamental rights form an integral part of the general principles of law whose observance the Court ensures. To this end, the Court is guided by the constitutional traditions common to the Member States and by the indications provided by international treaties on the protection of human rights to which the Member States have cooperated or acceded. The European Convention on Human Rights is of particular significance in this regard. These principles have been incorporated in Article 6(2) EU.

The Court refers to the case law of the Court of Human Rights and states that

> freedom of expression constitutes one of the essential foundations of a democratic society, one of the basic conditions for the progress of that society and for the full development of each individual person. Subject to Article 10(2) of the European Convention on Human Rights, freedom of expression applies not only to 'information'

[70] Judgments Nos 236, 113, 80 and 2011; 196, 138 and 87 of 2010; 3 I 7 of 2009; 349 and 348 of 2007.

[71] *Connolly*, C-274/99.

> or 'ideas' that are favourably received or regarded as inoffensive or indifferent, but also to such information or ideas that disturb, shock or disturb. Freedom of expression may be subject to the limitations provided for in Article 10(2) of the Convention, which must, however, be interpreted restrictively. The adjective 'necessary' in Article 10(2) implies an overriding social need and, while it is true that the Contracting States enjoy a certain discretion in assessing whether such a need exists, it is also true that the interference must be proportionate to the legitimate aim pursued and that the reasons invoked by the national authorities to justify it must be relevant and sufficient. Moreover, any prior restriction requires special scrutiny. Moreover, the restrictions must be provided for by rules formulated in a sufficiently precise manner to enable the persons concerned to adapt their conduct, having recourse, where appropriate, to the advice of trained advisers.

Despite this general premise, however, the Court held that the sanctions imposed on an employee who had severely criticised the Euro system were not unlawful because they violated the relationship of trust between employer and employee.

Regarding personal data, in the *Google Spain* case,[72] the Court affirmed the right to oblivion, later incorporated in the Regulation that replaced the EU Directive on personal data banks: it therefore assessed the right to personal identity and the protection of the individual in the hope of privacy as prevailing over the right to be informed through the freedom of the press and of reproduction on the web of news published by newspapers.

Apart from other rulings that have compared freedom of expression with the freedom to produce services, the most debated and still unregulated issue concerns whistleblowing and business secrecy.

I. The Debate between Proponents and Critics of Hate Speech

The most interesting debate on *hate speech* has not taken place within European culture, but in the relations between European culture or the countries influenced by European culture and US culture. In particular, I would like to refer to the positions of Robert Post and Robert Kahn on the one hand and Jeremy Waldron and Karl Loewenstein on the other, although the topic has been the subject of a very extensive literature, which cannot be taken into account for the purposes of this work.

The debate on hate speech has found nourishment in the diaspora of intellectuals of Jewish origin or bearers of democratic ideas who were forced to take refuge abroad to avoid being persecuted in countries that were dominated by totalitarian regimes in the 1930s (this was the case in almost all of Europe,

[72] Judgment of the Court (Grand Chamber), 13 May 2014. *Google Spain SL and Google Inc. v Agencia Española de Protección de Datos (AEPD) and Mario Costeja González*. Request for a preliminary ruling from the Audiencia Nacional.

except in the Scandinavian countries). The emigration of European intellectuals, which gave rise to a great contribution of thought in England, France, the United States and South America, enriched the cultural level of host countries and reinvigorated the democratic values on which they were founded. Emblematic, in fact, is the personal story of Karl Loewenstein, who repeatedly published books and essays on militant democracy, in which he highlighted the foundations of democracy overwhelmed by totalitarian regimes.[73]

Freedom of expression thus becomes, on the one hand, the bulwark of democracy, because it is repressed in totalitarian regimes that tend to stifle all forms of dissent; on the other hand, if it is directed against individuals or groups, with violent forms of hatred, contempt, defamation, it becomes a danger to democracy. Hence the need to place limits on this right.

Antony Lewis, together with other eminent American jurists and political philosophers, continues to maintain that the very First Amendment of the American Constitution is the guarantee of freedom of expression, which must be understood in an absolute way.[74] Thus, this freedom must also include those whom we do not appreciate because they are bearers of illiberal, when not fascist, ideas. But the Supreme Court, as early as 1952, held *in Beauharnais v Illinois*[75] that defamation of groups – in that case it was a campaign against Blacks – cannot be protected by the First Amendment. But in the case of *New York v Sullivan*,[76] the Court ruled that the publication of information about public figures could constitute a violation of the constitutional principle. Here prevails – again upholding democratic principles – the right of citizens to have access to data, information, stances, concerning individuals who stand for election, or hold public office, and thus must be enabled to evaluate their actions and act accordingly.

In this regard, Jeremy Waldron, who has written one of the most interesting books on hate speech, and on the models that compare and clash in different Western countries, believes that Lewis's thesis can be overcome by having recourse to the protection of dignity, understood as the status of persons, which is inalienable and irrepressible.

The political philosopher Ed Baker argued that autonomy must be granted to individuals, who, if they want express their extremist ideas, must be free to do so, obviously exposing themselves to criticism from those who do not share their positions. Waldron also raises the issue of solidarity with regard to Baker: in a community, autonomy of expression cannot be taken to the limit of undermining solidarity, because it undermines social coexistence.

[73] Amherst College, Publications, Karl Loewenstein Papers, Collection, Identifier MA 00206.

[74] A Lewis, *Freedom for the Thought That We Hate: A Biography of the First Amendment* (New York, Basic Books, 2010).

[75] *Beauharnais v Illinois*, 343 US 250 (1952).

[76] *New York Times Co v Sullivan*, 376 US 254 (1964).

For his part, Ronald Dworkin reasons in terms of 'legitimacy': the rules that sanction hate speech collide with other equally legitimate rules. But it is clear that the order consists of conflicting rules, and that it is up to an ordered society to coordinate them and assign them a hierarchy, in defence of the common good.

Robert Post points out that hate speech is often not an expression of self-determination, but rather the effect of intense psychological suggestion work by the media, so that those who engage in hateful expressions to target individuals or groups belonging to minorities are not free. On the other hand, the First Amendment cannot be allowed to become the shield for every aggression that puts the values of democracy at stake.

Finally, Jeremy Waldron, precisely by recalling the requirements of an 'ordered' society and the protection of people's dignity, proposes a comparative evaluation of the interests at stake that saves freedom of expression but places the necessary limits on it to safeguard precisely the cohesion (through the inclusion of minorities) of the social base and respect – which is a different attitude from the 'tolerance' of individuals.[77]

[77] For bibliographical references see R Petrilli, *Hate Speech, L'odio nel discorso pubblico. Politica, media, società* (Roma, Round Robin, 2020); M Hertz and P Molnar, *The Content and Context of Hate Speech* (Cambridge, CUP, 2012).

14

Citizenship. Plurality of Meanings

I. CULTURAL IDENTITY AND 'CITIZENSHIP'

UNTIL A FEW years ago, the notions of being a citizen and having citizenship had unambiguous meanings: they concerned 'the belonging of a subject to a state' and thus the discipline of citizenship concerned the relations between the citizen and the state. Today, it is a more complex matter; the terms must be decoded according to their contexts.

We speak of 'European citizenship' to emphasise the legal status, ie the set of rights and duties (*status*), of those who belong to an EU Member State. It is, for the time being, a political notion because there are no Community rules for conferring European citizenship; however, fundamental rights, social rights and political rights are recognised for citizens of the Member States, as are duties of solidarity, intervention and abstention.

We speak of 'local citizenship' because, following the reform of local authorities (law no 142 of 1990), the statutes of municipalities, provinces and metropolitan cities recognise the rights of individuals to participate, as individuals and as members of associations, groups and communities, in the governance of public affairs, the rights to use services, and the rights inherent in the performance of their personalities at local level; these rights, in line with the discretionary choices of the statutes, may be recognised not only for Italian citizens of full age, but also for minors and foreigners.

There is still talk of 'universal citizenship' (as proposed by Norbert Elias)[1] to affirm that in modern societies, individuals must be recognised as having a fundamental core of rights, enabling them to live safe from abuse and in a civilised manner.

One speaks of 'economic and social citizenship' when referring, according to sociologist Theodore Marshall, to the living conditions of an individual within a community. Today, we look at the individual as a holder of fundamental rights and as a holder of rights within the market.[2]

[1] *Power and civilisation. The civilisation process* (Bologna, Il Mulino, 2010).

[2] T Marshall, *Citizenship and Social Class* (Turin, Einaudi, 1975). According to the ISTAT report, as of 1 January 2019, the estimated population of Italy is 60,391,000; the population of Italian citizens has decreased to 55,157,000, while foreign residents amount to 5,234,000 and represent 8.7% of the total population.

As for citizenship in the traditional sense of the term, Law no 91 of 5-2-1992 (New regulations on citizenship) reformulated the entire discipline, which was already contained in the fundamental law of 1912. The acquisition of Italian citizenship can take place through different legal facts:

- by family ties (*jus sanguinis*), because the child of a citizen father or mother is a citizen by birth;
- by birth or discovery in the territory of the Republic;
- birth in the territory alone is not sufficient, as both parents must be unknown or stateless;
- for recognition or judicial declaration of filiation during the child's minority;
- for adoption of a foreign child;
- by filiation from a father or mother who were Italian citizens, or by second-degree direct descent, if the foreigner or stateless person performs military service for the Italian state, or is employed in public service by the state, or on reaching the age of majority has resided in the Republic for at least two years and, in all these cases, declares that he wishes to acquire Italian nationality;
- a foreigner with 'refugee' *status* is treated as a stateless person but is not obliged to perform military service;
- by marriage: foreigners who are the spouses of Italian nationals obtain nationality, following a request presented to the prefect of the place of residence of the interested party, or, if residing abroad, to the competent consular authority, if they can simultaneously satisfy the conditions laid down by law: legal residency in Italian territory for at least two years following the marriage or, alternatively, for foreigners residing abroad, the elapse of three years from the date of the marriage between the foreigner and the national; these terms are halved in the presence of children born to the spouses; persistence of the marriage bond; absence of legal separation; absence of criminal convictions for offences against the international and internal personality of the state and against the political rights of citizens; absence of criminal convictions for non-culpable offences for which a sentence of no less than three years is stipulated absence of criminal convictions for non-political offences, with a prison sentence of more than one year, imposed by foreign judicial authorities with a sentence recognised in Italy; absence of proven reasons relating to the security of the Republic) and if there has been residency in Italy for at least one year of marriage (in the presence of offspring), or for at least two years (in the absence of offspring). Furthermore, the minimum duration of the marriage required for a foreign spouse residing abroad to acquire nationality remains unchanged (three years) in the case of marriage without offspring, and is halved (18 months) in the case of marriage with offspring (modifications introduced by the so-called 'security package', Law no 94/2009, Art 1, § 11.

A foreigner who was born in Italy and has resided there without interruption until reaching the age of majority may acquire nationality within a year of reaching the age of majority, if he so requests; civil registrars are required to inform the interested party of the possibility of exercising this right by the time he reaches the age of 18. Failing this, the right may also be exercised after that date. The so-called 'del fare' decree-law (dl no 69/2013, Article 33) introduced a provision to simplify the procedure for the acquisition of citizenship for foreigners born in Italy, according to which, for the purposes of Article 4(2) of Law no 91/1992, the interested party is not responsible for any failure to comply with the requirements attributable to his parents or the public administration offices and he may prove that he meets the requirements with any other appropriate documentation.

Similarly, a foreigner who has been resident in Italy for at least 10 years (if a non-EU citizen) or for at least four years (if a citizen of an EU Member State), or who has served, including abroad, for at least five years in the service of the state, or who has been legally resident in the territory of the Republic for at least five years, may apply for citizenship and acquire it by concession by decree of the President of the Republic.

The Italian law also regulates other, less frequent cases (rendering of services, exceptional interest of the state, adoption of foreigners of age).

The citizen may renounce citizenship if he resides abroad. He loses his nationality when he has taken up a public office or public position abroad and has not renounced it at the invitation of the Italian Government, or when he has taken up a public office or performed military service for a foreign state, or when he has voluntarily acquired the nationality of the state in question, when these circumstances occur during a state of war with it. Citizenship may be re-acquired if declared, under certain circumstances (in particular, Articles 13 and 17 of Law No 91/1992).

The citizenship reform (Law No 132/2018 converting Decree-Law No 113/2018) introduced new rules on the acquisition and revocation of citizenship, amending and supplementing Law No 91/1992; in particular, the acquisition of citizenship by marriage (Article 5) and by concession by law (Article 9). In particular, the acquisition of nationality by marriage (Article 5) and by concession by law (Article 9) is conditional on the interested party's adequate knowledge of the Italian language, not inferior to level B1 of the Common European Framework of Reference for Languages (CEFR). It may be acquired by so-called naturalisation (Article 9). A new hypothesis is provided for the revocation of nationality in the case of a final sentence for crimes committed for the purposes of terrorism and subversion of the constitutional order, for which the law provides for a minimum of five years' or a maximum of 10 years' imprisonment. In this case, the revocation is adopted by decree of the President of the Republic, on the proposal of the Minister of the Interior, within three years of the final passage of the conviction.

II. THE FOREIGNER AND THE STATELESS PERSON

Being a citizen or non-citizen, ie a foreigner, entails, depending on the type of relationship, the enjoyment or otherwise of the rights reserved by law for this status.

Fundamental rights are also recognised in respect of foreigners (Articles 2 and 3) to whom all constitutional provisions apply, in which no distinction is made and no position of protection is noted for citizens alone. The foreigner is entitled to the enjoyment of the 'civil rights' attributed to the citizen (Article 16). The expression 'civil rights' comes from the discipline transmitted by tradition, with language (now in disuse) aimed at distinguishing between positions that concern private relations and positions that concern relations with the state. In reality, these are powers that have as their object the lawfulness of testing (until the nineteenth-century codifications, immovable property belonging to a foreigner who died in Italian states was acquired by the state by virtue of the right of *albinaggio*); matrimonial freedom (foreigners may marry citizens); contractual freedom; commercial freedom; freedom to carry out work activities; judicial protection.

This regime is particularly liberal, even though it is subject to the condition of reciprocity (which does not operate for functional protection, which is guaranteed to all).

This condition does not apply to citizens of EU Member States; it is precisely through EU law that the freedom of movement of persons, services, goods, and capital has been proclaimed.[3]

Stateless, on the other hand, is the person whom no state considers as its citizen. As far as 'civil rights' are concerned, the stateless person is equated with a citizen.

III. CITIZENSHIP IN PUBLIC LAW

In a general sense, 'citizenship' means the condition within a legal system that is reserved for a natural person by virtue of his membership of the state of which the system is an expression. This formula must be specified from the point of view of public law, international law and private law:

(i) In public law, citizenship summarises a person's relationship with the state, ie the rights he has towards the state and the duties to which he is subject. It is a question, as regards the active situations, of the right of incumbency, ie the right to reside in the territory of the state; political rights (active and passive electoral rights); the right to access public offices; the

[3] F Toriello, *La condizione dello straniero. Profili di diritto comparato e comunitario* (Padua, Cedam, 1997).

right to maintenance and social assistance; as regards the passive situations, the duty to perform military service, the duty to pay taxes, the duty of loyalty; alongside these rights and duties, we must also consider the rights and duties that are guaranteed or imposed on citizens alone in the Constitution.

(ii) In international law, there is the right of diplomatic protection, to be granted to the citizen when he is abroad, and the duty of admission.

(iii) In private law citizenship is one of the elements of the legal condition of the person, his status.

The Italian Constitutional Court has on many occasions dealt with the legal status of foreigners, applying, whenever possible, the principles that put their rights in certain areas on an equal footing with citizens, and resorting to the principle of equality, even though this is reserved by the Constitution for citizens. The Court has extended to foreigners not only the application of the provisions on fundamental rights, but also the provisions of special social legislation. The fact that individuals were 'foreigners' did not imply their *deminutio* as persons – instead their dignity had to be safeguarded – and thus the legitimacy of discriminatory choices by the Italian legislature.

Among its decisions,[4] the Court has affirmed the right to an accompaniment allowance (Judgment No 306 of 2008); the right to an incapacity pension (Judgment No 11 of 2009); the right to a monthly disability allowance (Judgment No 187 of 2010); the right to health and essential therapies (Order No 197 of 2013); the right to pharmaceutical assistance and general practitioner services (Judgment No 299 of 2010); and the right to use public and private services without discrimination (Judgment No 8 of 2011). These are just a few of the most significant decisions, two of which are particularly noteworthy: the first generally concerns the treatment of foreigners in the light of the application of fundamental rights; the second emphasises the difference in status between citizens and foreigners with regard to the attachability of wages. The first one (sentence no 61 of 2011) concerned certain provisions of Campania Law no 6 of 8 February 2010 introduced for the social, economic and cultural inclusion of foreigners present in Campania. Given the breadth of the profiles considered, the ruling stands out not only for the pen of its drafter (Paolo Grossi) but also for the distinctions it introduces precisely by safeguarding some fundamental rights and deeming the discrimination of foreigners with respect to citizens to be reasonable for other legal situations.

From a general point of view, the judgment specifies that

> public intervention concerning foreigners cannot be limited to the mere control of their entry and stay in the national territory, but must necessarily consider other

[4] M Fierro, *Prestazioni sociali e cittadinanza* (Rome, Constitutional Court, 2016).

> areas – from social assistance to education, from health to housing – which involve multiple normative competences, some attributed to the State, others to the Regions (judgments n. 156 of 2006, n. 300 of 2005). All the more so since the foreigner is the holder of all the fundamental rights that the Constitution recognises as being due to the person (Judgment No 148 of 2008)'.

The Court endorses the general provision contained in legislative decree no 286 of 1998, according to which

> A foreigner, however present at the border or in the territory of the State, shall be recognised the fundamental human rights provided by the rules of domestic law, by the international conventions in force and by the generally recognised principles of international law. Art. 3, paragraph 5, provides that 'Within the scope of their respective powers and budgetary allocations, the regions, provinces, municipalities and other local authorities shall adopt measures concurrent with the pursuit of the objective of removing the obstacles that in fact prevent the full recognition of the rights and interests recognised for foreigners in the territory of the State, with particular regard to those relating to housing, language and social integration, in compliance with the fundamental rights of the human person'.

The Court – in declaring unfounded or inadmissible the questions raised on the constitutional legitimacy of the Campania legislation – observed that

> if the Italian legislature is certainly allowed to dictate rules, not manifestly unreasonable and not in conflict with international obligations, regulating the entry and stay of non-EU citizens in Italy, and if it is possible to subordinate, not unreasonably, the provision of certain benefits, not aimed at remedying serious emergency situations, to the circumstance that the foreigner's entitlement to stay in the territory of the State demonstrates that it is not episodic and not of short duration –
>
> Once, however, the right to stay under the above-mentioned conditions is not in question, 'it is not possible to discriminate against foreigners, establishing, in their regard, particular limitations for the enjoyment of fundamental personal rights, recognised instead to citizens' (judgments no. 187 of 2010 and no. 306 of 2008)'.

The Court, in Judgment No 248 of 2015, emphasised that

> the protection of the certainty of legal relationships, in so far as it is linked to the instruments for the protection of personal credit, does not allow the attachment of emoluments to be denied outright but to be attenuated for particular situations whose identification is reserved to the legislature's discretion.

Particularly significant is the sentence in which the Court held that the Friulian law on welfare benefits was constitutionally illegitimate insofar as it established that, for foreigners, they could only benefit from it if they had been resident in the region for at least five years (sentence no 222 of 2013). While admitting that the legislature may reserve certain welfare benefits only for citizens and persons treated as such residing in Italy, whose status is in itself capable of generating an adequate link between participation in the political, economic and social organisation of the Republic, and the granting of the benefit, the Court held that

> it is not necessarily the case that a link deserving of protection cannot emerge with regard to the position of a person who, although deprived of status, has nonetheless legitimately established a strong link with the community in which he resides and of which he has become a part, by having established there a stable prospect of working, family and emotional life, the protection of which is certainly not anomalous in the light of the legal system in force.[5]

In such cases, in view of the prejudice that may result from the indiscriminate exclusion of foreigners from social benefits, particular care must be taken in identifying the link that connects the benefit to the status of citizen, rather than to the contribution made by the individual to the society in which he is integrated.

The legislator, therefore, in order to remove any restrictions on access to social benefits from a judgement of inequality and manifest unreasonableness,

> is required to look not only, in the past, at the duration of residence in the national or local territory beyond a minimum time threshold, but also, in the future, at the presence or absence of suitable indices testifying to the tendentially stable link between the person and the community.

IV. EUROPEAN CULTURAL IDENTITY

National identity is now joined by European identity. The relationship is biunivocal, because each nationality has made a contribution to the construction of the idea of Europe and to European culture. On the other hand, belonging to Europe – either within the continent or as an island close to it – is a source of enrichment for each country that is part of it.

The construction of modern Europe developed over a long historical process. The very concept of Europe has changed over time. And it is worth remembering, in this arduous path of cultural construction, Paul Hazard, Academician of France and lecturer at the Collège de France, who in his best-known book, *La crise de la conscience européenne*, published in 1935, wondered what Europe was. It was a new order that came into being in the course of less than half a century, from 1680 to 1715, in which great psychological, philosophical and technical changes took place in the collective imagination. To the crisis of the ancient and medieval tradition, European thought reacted with immense reconstruction work that followed a laborious path: Locke's empiricism; the deism and natural religion professed by Boyle, Bayle, Collins and Toland; the natural

[5] Art 8 of the European Convention for the Protection of Human Rights and Fundamental Freedoms, signed in Rome on 4 November 1950, ratified and made enforceable by Act No 848 of 4 August 1955; Art 13(2) *bis*, of Legislative Decree No 286 of 1998).

law of Grotius, Pufendorf, Spinoza, Cumberland, Fénelon, Thomasius and Gravina; Mandeville's social morality; Fontenelle and Shaftsbury's search for happiness on earth; the science and progress of Descartes and Newton; the new humanity and Romanticism of Rousseau and Pope; the picturesque life, laughter and tears; and then the birth of the idea of nationhood in German culture; ending with the psychology of restlessness.

It is the Europe of ideas that is at the heart of the idea of Europe, not the Europe born in religious wars, struggles between powers, exploitation of the masses, the slave trade.

But how was Europe formed? Historians do not agree on this point, and the debate around it is passionate.

Ideological aspects also come into play: the 1930s saw the clash between Romanism and Germanism.

The Axis powers expressed, through their intellectuals and political exponents, the unitary agendas of (allegedly cultural) symbols that brought (some) European peoples closer together and made them 'superior' to others. This line of thought matured in the second half of the nineteenth century in the writings of historians and jurists. Two traditions that were initially opposed to each other, as taught by the medieval history of Europe and Italy in particular, then partly merged in the events of coexistence, the standardisation of law, and unitary political paths. From the contact of the two traditions, the modern history of Europe is to be born. A volume, published in Italy by Sansoni and in Germany by Luetke, reflects this conception. The volume collects the lectures given by a large number of intellectuals versed in the various disciplines, all of which retrace the passages of histories that were at first parallel, then intersecting, then unitary of the peoples governed by 'Roman civilisation' and the peoples governed by 'Germanic civilisation'.

It examines myths, lineages, law, national revivals, political doctrine, language, mystics, poetry, the arts, music, theatre, the Renaissance and Romanticism, the art of war, economics, philosophy, all in an attempt to portray the meeting of the two civilisations as the cement of the modern human journey.

But beyond the historical contingencies, beyond the indubitable facts of the encounter of these civilisations, the theses propounded here are completely outlandish. One does not realise, on a historical level, that 'Germanism' had pervaded not only Germany, but all regions of northern Europe, and had then spread to the south, reaching as far as Sicily. And it is not considered that the places of contact, exchange, transplantation and osmosis, revisited in those writings, introduced completely arbitrary boundaries, because each of the expressions of the sciences and arts referred to may have originated in one place, but they had then spread to all regions of Europe, and from there, with the grafts and alterations that are typical of all migrant thought, they had once again been relocated to their countries of origin. This process of mutual enrichment could not only be attributed to Germany and Italy, but involved all the countries of continental and even insular Europe.

The philosopher Giovanni Gentile, one of the few critical voices in that context, was aware of this inherent contradiction in the thesis that sees the rebirth of Europe in the binomial 'Romanity and Germanism'. He traces the welding of Romanity and Germanism in nineteenth-century thought that contrasts with the Enlightenment, in the thought that relies on the historical reality that arises from below, from the 'rudimentary forms of the spiritual life of the people'. From these foundations Gentile gives rise to the idea of the *nation*, which has a spiritual foundation but also a natural foundation (the land, the language, the customs of the people); and the belief – which he calls a 'half-truth' – that nations 'are made by God, not by men'. Half-truth because the nation 'is not a natural datum, but a reality affirmed (theoretically and practically) by conscience'. And, given the circulation of thought, 'questions about the pure national character of each philosophy and the possible influences it may be subjected to by other philosophies are evidently emptied of real interest'.

The juridical aspects are more complex, involving both the medieval and modern tradition, the phenomenon of the Reconciliation of Roman Law in Germany, and the Historical School movement, which spread throughout continental Europe from the second half of the nineteenth century until the first half of the twentieth century, with the dogmatic scaffolding of Pandectics.

Within the framework that was outlined – of the coexistence of Romanity and Germanism – a great jurist of the 1930s, Mariano d'Amelio, then first president of the Court of Cassation, traced the stages of this binary history. The synthesis of the two traditions is represented precisely by a Romanist, Theodore Mommsen.

According to Stobbe, the fundamental difference in the structural nature of the two traditions was that Germanic law, as indigenous law, was largely customary, and therefore *ius incertum*, lacking general principles and composed of particular rules of a concrete nature, totally unsuited to the needs of a developing trade. By contrast, Roman law, as written law, was known to all and adaptable to ever-changing needs.

But d'Amelio also emphasises the currents against slavish adherence to Roman law that were unleashed in late nineteenth-century Germany and later found nourishment in Nazi cultural and academic policy.

The diatribe on the usability of Roman law began in the mid-nineteenth century with the debate between Schmidt and Ihering on the configurability of this 'system' as a framework of absolute principles. It continues with Beseler, who attacks the Historical School, and in particular Savigny, for the lack of legitimacy of the doctrine that had chosen Roman law as the repository of rules not wanted by the people.

Authoritative scholars like Bernard Windscheid had raised their voices in defence of Roman law, whose paternity German law could not repudiate. He emphasised that

> Roman law is not absolute law: absolute law does not exist; in the legal field as in any other, truth is revealed only by the assiduous and continuous work of the spirit. But Roman law is the result of the legal work of that part of mankind to which, of all the peoples that have appeared so far in the history of the world, was granted the greatest aptitude for the culture of law. Roman law is not law, just as the art of Greece is not art; but the intellectual patrimony of mankind was not increased by the work of Greek art to any greater extent than it was increased by the work of Roman law.[6]

Homage to Roman law in Germany did not stop even with the codification of 1896–1900. The union dissolved with the Nazi authorities' assertion of the nationality of Germanic law.

Hence Koschaker's heartfelt defence of Roman law.

Koschaker's thesis is very suggestive, is still widespread in Western thought, and requires in-depth reflection that places its meaning in the context of the cultural and political climate in which it arose. A historian of Roman law and ancient Oriental law, Paul Koschaker (1979–1951), after teaching in his homeland, at the University of Graz, continued his teaching at leading German universities, in particular Leipzig, Berlin and finally Tübingen. During his Berlin years, he wrote an essay on the crisis of Roman law, *Die Krise des roemischen Rechts und die romanistische Rechtswissenschaft* (1938), later collected, with other essays, in a book that appeared in 1947, and translated into Italian with the title *L'Europa e il diritto romano*. It is an essay on the method of studying Roman law, understood as an *art*, born from the practice of solving concrete cases by Roman jurists, and then transformed into a dogmatic science in the medieval legal tradition. In order to maintain its teaching and formative function in the course of law studies, Koschaker emphasises its legal structure, rather than its historical analysis, which would draw this subject into the realm of historical studies and remove it from legal studies.

This crisis arose in Germany at the same time as the introduction of the German Civil Code: the *BGB* attracted all the attention of jurists, and Roman law remained in the background. Koschaker tries to show that 'Roman law constitutes a significant, though not the most important, part of European civilisation and is therefore inextricably linked to Europe'. Its crisis is combined with the decline of Europe following the First World War.

Koschaker shows that modern law has its roots in a combination of Roman law, Germanism and Christianity. He argues that

> Europe is first and foremost a cultural phenomenon, an unmistakable synthesis of Germanic cultural elements and classical, predominantly Roman cultural elements,

[6] B Windscheid, *Pandette* (1886) vol I, It trans (Turin, UTET, 1930) 3.

> from which Christianity cannot be separated, and which together determined the cultural situation of the higher social classes in the various European countries, also penetrating the masses through Christianity.

Europe 'is not a geographical and natural fact, but rather a product of history'. The *imperium Romanum* was a Mediterranean empire; with the shattering of the Byzantine empire and the Islamic invasion, the Christian West relied on the Franks, and the new concept of 'Europe' was born with the Carolingian empire and the investiture given by the Pope to Charlemagne. The entire history of Western law, based on the study of Roman law, steeped in Germanic and Christian values, winds its way, according to Koschaker, through the centuries up to the Reconstruction of Roman law in Germany.

Koschaker's thesis, illustrated in his stance against the arginalization of Roman law in law teaching advocated by Nazi university policy, made a huge impression in the legal culture of the time. And another great scholar of Roman law, Francesco De Martino, in his 1941 paper on 'Individualism and Private Roman Law', taking up Koschaker's position, came down in defence of Roman law as it was represented by National Socialism, ie as the 'law of capitalism'. De Martino emphasises that this way of interpreting the phenomenon was a mystification: the Nazis were fighting against the civil principles inherited from Roman law because they opposed the protection of free personality. Roman law – according to De Martino – must rather be understood as a body of rules based on freedom against absolutism, ie against unlimited state power. On the other hand, superimposing the capitalist conception of political and economic relations on Roman law could only be an anti-historical stretch.

At the outbreak of the Second World War and in the course of the wartime operations and the occupation by Nazi-fascist forces of many European countries, the idea of Europe takes on an even different meaning. It evokes the demands for peace and freedom from totalitarianism. And to make these demands concrete, many think of creating a European-level organisation – a federal state, or a confederation, or a superstate body with certain competences – that embodies these values. These are academics, politicians and even jurists, Each with his own angle, derived both from ideological positions and from different perspectives, but all oriented towards the search for values common to a society – a European society – with which to proceed with the reconstruction of the now devastated western civilisation.

Even at this juncture, history, or rather, the use of history, helps to cement the noble aspirations of democratic spirits.

It may seem remarkable that in precisely the same years two historians – the Italian Federico Chabod and the Frenchman Lucien Febvre – dedicated their university courses to analysing the *idea of Europe*. It is remarkable and moving at the same time, considering that by then the great conflict had deflagrated and was ongoing. The two historians are animated by intentions that are not explicitly expressed, but clearly decipherable in their pages.

In the academic year 1943–1944, Federico Chabod gave a course on European history at the Faculty of Letters at the University of Milan, the themes of which would be taken up again, once the war was over, in the lecture he gave in January 1947 at the University of Rome. Times then were stormy: in those months, Italy was divided in two, the South already liberated by the Allies, the North still under the fascist Government collaborating with the Nazi forces.

According to Chabod, the modern idea of Europe should not be confused with its geographical or physical idea. What is relevant is Europe understood in a political, cultural and moral sense, because this is the *idea* that penetrates the *forma mentis*, the way in which modern people feel the term 'Europe'. 'In history,' Chabod warns, 'only that which has self-consciousness has a place'. Therefore, the idea of Europe that historians trace back to Isocrates, who distinguished between Europe and Asia; to Herodotus, who delineated the geographical borders of Europe; to Augustus, who conceived it as the object of conquest of new territories to Roman domination; to Christianity, which defined the border between civilisation and barbarism; to Charlemagne himself, who together with the Pope conceived it as the Roman Empire of the West, a bulwark against Arab invasion, is a mutilated idea.

Likewise partial is the idea of the Humanists who conceive of Europe as the region in which cultural, moral and spiritual affinities and customs mature. What matters is the *political idea* of Europe, as a 'political body' in which states balance each other's powers. Chabod traces this idea in more recent times, particularly during the Enlightenment, in the pages of Frederick the Great, Voltaire and Montesquieu. The Enlightenment saw Europe as a land of *freedom*. But their opinions were not unequivocal: some attributed the origin of the new civilisation to Germanism, while Voltaire insisted on the opposition between Europe and Asia, and recognised Europe alone as the home of letters and sciences.

Chabod emphasises how the idea of Europe blurred with the birth of the *nation*, built through the contribution of Rousseau. But the idea did not die. Metternich and Castlereagh conceived of it as a whole, an overall political body with its parts in balance, to the point that Castlereagh himself thought of a 'Commonwealth of Europe'. And even in the Romantic era, with the consolidation of the idea of the nation, the need to place western nations in a unitary framework does not disappear: the revolutionary Mazzini or the conservative De Maistre believe that the rights of nations must be balanced with those of Europe.

In the academic year 1944–1945, Lucien Febvre, one of the founders of the French historical school of the *Annales*, also gave a course of lectures at the Collège de France on 'Europe. Genesis of a civilisation'.

Febvre also distances himself from the geographical idea of Europe, but wonders how this name, which is not given by nature, came about. This name seems to date back to 520 BC, to Hecataeus of Miletus, who, in describing the *orb terraqueo*, distinguished three regions: Europe, Asia and Libya. Europe soon became a category of the spirit. And its conceptual boundaries change over time according to economic and political influences. Europe becomes confused with the Mediterranean civilisation, then with the borders of the Roman Empire. The political failure of the Empire is succeeded by the victory of Roman, then European, culture. For Febvre – who echoes a statement by Marc Bloch – Europe in the modern sense was born when the Roman Empire collapsed: its germs can be traced in the Carolingian Empire and in the West's opposition to the Arab conquest. It is therefore an idea eminently based on *culture*: 'the collaboration in the same work of civilisation, the participation in the same ideal of culture, in the same ideal of life, the participation, the collaboration, of very different peoples'. But Europe also means the Christianity of the crusades, the feudalism of the political system, the economic revival, the search for gold, the republic of letters, the land of revolutions and new freedoms, the land of nations. That is why Europe – 'fetish word, remedy word, salvation word' – postulates a 'European republic'. In the conclusion of a fascinating and valuable reconstruction of this idea, Febvre reminded his students, in occupied France, that

> Europe is the necessary end of that long march towards unity and concentration, begun and pursued by all European countries for more than a millennium, from the time when the Carolingian Empire gave a sort of first prefiguration to Europe. This was said by the great spirits, the generous romantic spirits of the nineteenth century. How could we, along with them, not say it, we men of the twentieth century?

RW Mackay published *Federal Europe* in London in 1940. Altiero Spinelli, in confinement at Ventotene, writes in 1941, together with other prisoners, a *Manifesto* describing the aspiration of a free Italy in a free and united Europe. Thomas Mann, in his message delivered on the New York radio on 29 January 1943, professes his idea of European unity and proclaims the need to found a 'federation of free states with equal rights, capable of flourishing their spiritual independence and their traditional culture subject at the same time to the common law of reason and morality'.

And as early as 1940, when Belgium, Holland and Luxembourg were invaded by the Nazis, the *Commission pour l'étude des problèmes d'après guerre* (CEPAG) was set up, which, with the help of PH Spaak and H Pierlot, was concerned about the future of Europe. It is the economic and social, but above all the political issues that are examined with lucidity and far-sightedness, pushing the need to achieve a European union that would discourage the outbreak of further atrocious wars and promote democracy and the progress of the European peoples.

The outcome of these ideals and currents would be the establishment of the Communities and then the foundation of the European Union: a slow and difficult path marked by the Treaty of Rome, the Single Act, the Treaty of Maastricht, the Treaty of Amsterdam, the European Charter proclaimed in Nice.

At the end of the war, the idea of Europe rose from the ashes of the conflict. Historians promoted a further refinement of this idea. Oscar Halecki, a graduate of Krakow, a member of the Polish Academy and later a professor at Fordham University in New York, posed in 1950 the problem of the chronology of the history of Europe, with its geographical limits, natural divisions and temporal scans, claiming the inclusion of Eastern Europe in European history *tout court*.

The deepest and clearest roots of Europe as a whole in the twentieth century are *cultural* ones. According to contemporary historians, they lie in the early Middle Ages: the use of the Latin language, the civilisation of writing, centres of learning – and the birth of universities – are some of the factors that historians combine with legal factors: written law, schools of law, the universality of laws, the notion of citizenship and *res publica* constitute what Michel Baniard, a professor at the University of Toulouse, calls the 'cultural safeguards' of European civilisation.

Law does not always stand out among the hallmarks of European identity. But for many, one of the fundamental aspects of this identity is the construction of *human rights*, in the dual version of the values defended by Christianity and the values defended by the Enlightenment.

The search in the historical tradition for European roots and thus for the distinctive features of European identity can be a reflection of a bitter awareness, namely that since the nineteenth century, with the consolidation of *nations* and with the crediting of the *idea of nationhood* and nationalist ideologies, the 'ideal' Europe has shattered against reality and that today its unity must be recomposed also through the falsification of history.

What place does the legal factor occupy in the construction of European identity and consciousness? It has already been emphasised that in the analysis of historians, the legal factor is not of fundamental importance. Legal historians, for their part, have attempted to write the history of 'European law', but in most cases, one is in the presence of a history of medieval law overlaid with the European dimension.

The problem is more complex than one might think at first glance. In a dense and refined book[7] Antonio Padoa Schioppa warns us that for seven centuries, up to the end of the eighteenth century,

> continental Europe modelled and practised a single great system of supranational law, founded on a multi-layered normative structure, which gave rise to a sort of common 'republic of legal culture', so that for each national experience it is not possible to isolate the territorial boundaries of this phenomenon.

The legacy of the Justinian *Corpus iuris* was reconstructed and modelled by the Glossators, then taken up by canon law with Gratian's *Decretum*, then

[7] *Italy and Europe in the History of Law* (Bologna, Il Mulino, 2004) 3.

reformulated by the Commentators, by the Cultic School, until the fall of the *Anciѐn Régime*. The break with the past was consolidated with the first codifications of the nineteenth century, although the traces of Roman law reworked in those seven centuries did not disappear.

England also played a role in this epic of reworked Roman law. But for political, religious, and even national identity reasons, historians of *common law* for a long time attempted to isolate the English experience from continental experiences and maintained a reductive attitude towards both Roman law and canon law, consummating the attempt to create an absolute originality of common law that is now being reconsidered. According to Baker[8] the influence of Roman law – which was lacking during the Roman domination of Anglia – occurred in the early Middle Ages and then through canon law, but it left very few traces: a few terms or notions (such as *aequum et bonum*, *dominium*, *nudum pactum*, *res nullius)* but subsequently the construction of an autonomous body of rules ended up distancing English law from continental law. And Plucknett[9] also follows this line, even if he makes a few concessions: he points out that the Glanville treatise shows a certain familiarity with Roman law, that the *Domesday Book* was written with the typical intonation of Italian jurists, that Thomas Becket brought Vicario to England, and to Vicario we owe the official teaching of Roman law on the island. If one adds to these influences also the last flashes of Romanism introduced by the Stuarts, one realises that these are entirely marginal phenomena. However, in the nineteenth century, the study of Roman law flourished again: a fascinating survey shows us how John Austin took great advantage of this in the systematic construction of common law.[10]

The study of Roman law in England is still flourishing, but has led – according to Markesinis[11] – to a peculiar situation. That is to say, it seems that English scholars of comparative law have subsequently exchanged Roman law for continental law, and thus for many years have drained the interest and richness of continental models in favour of an imaginative representation of the law of non-insular Europe. This gave rise to two opposing reactions: the aversion of many contemporary English jurists studying European private law to any trace of Roman law, on the one hand, and the claim by other scholars to assign Roman law the role of the fundamental basis of European private law.[12]

None of them, however, whatever orientation they belong to, doubt that the legal component is an essential part of European culture and identity.

If one thinks that the components of identity should also include the subject and subjectivity, citizenship, fundamental rights, the model of democratic management of power, one must agree on the essentiality of the legal factor.

[8] *An Introduction to English Legal History* (London, Butterworths, 1975).

[9] *A Concise History of the Common Law* (London, Butterworths, 1956).

[10] MH Hoeflich, *Roman Law and Civil Law* (Athens, Georgia, 1997).

[11] *The Comparative Method* (It trans) (Milan, Giuffré, 2004).

[12] G Alpa, *Il diritto privato nel prisma della comparazione* (Turin, Giappichelli, 2004) 73ff.

Two questions then arise: whether the legal factor is essential in the construction of national identities; and whether the European identity should be conceived as a larger national identity.

If one associates the idea of identity with that of conscience, the legal aspect of national identities is not particularly important. The common man feels English, French, German, Spanish, Italian because of the language he speaks, because of the culture he is the bearer of, because of the 'mentality' of which he is the expression, certainly not because of the rules of behaviour to which he conforms.

For European identity – in the sense that contemporaries take it – however, it is different. The 'united' Europe came into being in the mid-1950s and was founded on three pillars: the economic pillar; the social pillar; and the legal pillar. The unitary economic and social space could not have taken shape without the contribution of law. The evolution of the Union thus rests eminently on its legal structure[13] and its judicial area.[14]

Hence the *acquis communautaire*, which in many areas of economic and social relations has already introduced uniform and harmonised law. Hence the search for a constitutional foundation – identified in the Charter of Rights and the Constitutional Treaty and now in the Constitutional Charter of the European Union, signed in Rome on 29 October 2004 – and the drives towards the creation of a European judicial area. Hence, finally, the plans to codify European private law.

At the European level, the legal factor plays a far more important role than it does in national experiences. From a static point of view, it is one of the pillars cementing the Union, an element ensuring solidity and continuity in the construction of a united Europe. In this sense, it is irrelevant whether the European Union will become a supranational body to which limited unitary functions will be assigned, a federation in which national identities will be retained, or a real state with a regional basis.

From a dynamic point of view, the legal factor plays an even more prominent role, because it becomes one of the driving forces behind the Europe of the future. Indeed, it is from the legal dimension that the building of the new Europe started.

In this perspective, how should the legal culture that is taking root in Europe today be viewed?

The situation in which we live is quite different from that described by Carl Schmitt in his insightful essay, 'The Construction of European Legal Science'.[15] Not that ideas expressed in Schmitt's essay are to be reproved; on the contrary, Schmitt in some respects seems a prophet of the condition that has arisen: the

[13] S Cassese, *Lo spazio giuridico globale* (Roma-Bari, Laterza, 2003).
[14] SM Carbone, *Lo spazio giuridico europeo* (Turin, Giappichelli, 2000).
[15] *La situazione della scienza giuridica europea*, (1944) (It trans) (Quodlibet, Macerata, 2020).

science of European law is certainly a historical fact, Roman law has played a leading role in the formation of law in Europe, the crisis of state legality has been confirmed. However, the *rule of law* has not abdicated its essential function in any democratic order (and the preamble to the European Constitution emphasises this fundamental political choice), nor can we say that Savigny's paradigm, which identified the origin of law in the *Volkgeist*, has been incorporated into the formation of current European law; nor can we admit that only the science of law is the last asylum of European consciousness. Roman law critically reconsidered, as we learn from the contributions of Riccardo Orestano and his student Massimo Brutti, together with canon law, can indeed be considered one of the roots of European private law.

Contemporary observers consider that the legal culture reflected by Community law is the originator of an impressive production of rules, in which the extension of the economic space is associated with the protection of the individual, understood as worker, consumer, tourist, victim of the deterioration of the environment.

Legal integration postulated the prevalence of EU law over national laws and thus contributed to the creation of what Gessner Volkmar, lecturer at the University of Bremen called a 'common legal structure'. However, the Sutherland Report revealed the distance between the body of EU law and the individual national systems. In addition, the differences between the systems of the Member States still appear considerable; eg in judicial style, intervention in the market with regulatory measures, or the techniques of the relationship between the individual and the Administration, which vary from the Swedish ('contact culture', based on consensus and reliance) to the English ('negotiation culture' based on conflict and reliance) to the German ('regulatory culture' based on conflict and low reliance), the latter being similar to the Italian culture. So do the levels of consumer protection and modes of dispute resolution (formal and informal).

Volkmar then wonders whether European legal integration is doomed to maintain its fictitious character and what the remedies to this fiction might be. The *acquis communautaire* is an essential instrument in this direction, but the differences that still exist in the legal cultures of the Member States can be a serious obstacle to legal integration. Exchanges of professors and students, joint programmes, and mutual recognition of qualifications are not sufficient, nor can they exhaust the problems, because 'a legal culture is rooted very deeply in society and cannot easily and quickly be changed by top-down measures'. Nor can it be forgotten that European legal culture is now being undermined by the globalisation of trade and commerce in general. Uniform contracts, standard contract forms, general terms of business, codes of conduct and even international courts are now the unifying factors of this global legal culture.

European legal thought can also be described from the opposite perspective to that of standardisation: it is the perspective of the coexistence of different cultures and the complex administration that arises from it. Claude Lévi-Strauss spoke of progress in the case of a 'coalition of cultures'. In his wake, André-Jean Arnaud resorts to evocative images to represent European legal thought as a meeting point, an intersection (*carrefour*), a cradle (*berçaeau*), a cornucopia (*foison*). The *carrefour* is given by the meeting of Roman law, feudal law and canon law, the *berceau* by the standardisation of law under the influence of modern axiomatic natural law, the *foison* by the coexistence of Anglo-Saxon and Scandinavian, Germanic, French-speaking and Latin traditions. National laws are not – according to Arnaud – an obstacle to the harmonisation and standardisation of European law insofar as legal science, as a cognitive activity, has no boundaries. It is therefore necessary to start from the premise that legal pluralism is the basis of European legal thought, but does not constitute a brake on it: the reality of the European Communities itself is a permanent challenge to traditional legal thought.

V. EUROPEAN CITIZENSHIP

State citizenship is not replaced by, but added to, European citizenship, ie the *status* deriving from a citizen's membership of an EU Member State.[16]

This citizenship is not acquired directly, but by a mediated route in that the person already has the *status* of Italian, or French, etc, citizenship.

If he loses this *status*, h also loses European citizenship (so-called dual citizenship).

European citizenship is also a summary of rights and duties. These were provided for in the Maastricht Treaty (Articles 8–8E), in force since 1 January 1993, where the rights and duties introduced by the Treaty of the European Economic Community are reconfirmed and supplemented, and are now enshrined in Article 20 of the Treaty on the Functioning of the European Union and in Chapter V of the Charter of Fundamental Rights of the European Union.

These rights include: the right to reside and move freely within the territory of the Member States, once recognised only for those who moved from their own State to another Member State of the Community for reasons of work and now recognised without limits; political rights, for active and passive voting in the European Parliament as well as for local elections in the place where one resides, even if it belongs to a State other than the one of which one is a national the right to petition the European Parliament; the right to complain to the European Ombudsman; the right to diplomatic protection in third countries where the state of which one is a national does not have diplomatic representation (in this case, protection is offered by any other EU Member State that has representation in the third state).

[16] E Meehan, *Citizenship and the European Community* (London, Sage, 1993).

Alongside these rights, there are, in EU law, the right of equality (Article 20 of the Charter of Fundamental Rights of the European Union), ie 'non-discrimination', and the specifications of the right of incumbency, ie freedom of movement and residence, freedom of establishment and the exercise of a profession, or employed and self-employed work, freedom of economic initiative, and freedom of transfer of goods and capital.

The Rome Convention, concluded between the states belonging to the Council of Europe on 6 November 1990, also guaranteed citizens of the Council's Member States the right to directly appeal to the Strasbourg Court of Human Rights.

State and European citizenship, however, still have many limitations.

The former is conformed to differently in individual states: there are states that attribute it by the mere fact of being born in their territory (*jure soli*) and others that attribute it by being descendants of citizens (*jure sanguinis*), others that combine the two connecting criteria; others that, due to their federal form, also distinguish citizens internally by their belonging to a nation, an ethnic group, or a linguistic group; there are restrictions concerning civil servants, members of the Armed Forces, prisoners, those in forced residence, and, of course, foreigners. However, the difference between citizen and foreigner diminishes with the strengthening of the European Union.

In every state, even within the European Union, measures have been introduced concerning immigrants from third countries. In this regard, we speak of non-EU 'citizens'.

The rights of European citizens were strengthened by the Treaty of Amsterdam.[17]

VI. IMMIGRANTS

The regulation of 'immigration' into Italy by citizens of other non-EU states and by 'stateless persons' (ie persons without citizenship) – both categories concerning 'foreigners' – has been the subject of numerous legislative interventions in recent times, often inspired by European sources. If in the first phase these interventions appear mostly aimed at safeguarding the dignity of the foreigner in relations with Italian citizens, in the second phase they take on an emergency character and focus – more frequently according to a repressive and securitarian logic[18] – on the operational problems related to border control and the administration of incoming migratory flows.

The basic law (Turco-Napolitano law, no 40) was promulgated on 6 March 1998. A few months after the basic law, the Consolidation Act on Immigration

[17] A Tizzano, *The Treaty of Amsterdam* (Padua, Cedam, 1998).

[18] This is already evident from the express reference to the issue of public safety in two of the most important measures mentioned in the text, namely the Bossi-Fini law and the recent Salvini decree.

and the Legal Status of Foreigners (Legislative Decree 25-7-1998, no 286) was approved, which gathered together the scattered provisions on the subject and was variously and repeatedly amended in the following years. Corrective provisions were introduced by legislative decree no 113 of 13-4-1999, while the regulation implementing the aforementioned Consolidated Act was approved by presidential decree no 394 of 31-8-1999. The legislator then intervened – to limit the references to some of the most relevant provisions – with l 30-7-2002, no 189 (Bossi-Fini law), which provides for amendments to the legislation on immigration and asylum; with lgs d 10-8-2007, no 154 implemented 2004/114 EC on the conditions of admission of third-country nationals for reasons of study, pupil exchange, unpaid training or voluntary service; with l 15-7-2009, no 94 (the so-called 'security package'), which modifies the rules on the marriage of a foreigner in Italy and the acquisition of nationality by his spouse,[19] as well as introducing the offence of illegal entry and residency in the territory of the State (Article 10 *bis* TU); by dl 17-2-2017, no 13 (the Minniti Decree), converted with amendments by l 13-4-2017, no 46, on urgent provisions for the acceleration of proceedings on international protection, as well as for the fight against illegal immigration; finally, lastly, by dl 4-10-2018, no 113 (the Salvini Decree), converted by l 1-12-2018, no 132, also containing urgent provisions on international protection and immigration, as well as public safety.

Article 2 of the Consolidated Act identifies the 'rights and duties' of the foreigner, who is guaranteed the 'fundamental rights of the human person' provided by Italian law, international conventions and generally recognised principles of international law.

The foreigner is granted equal treatment for the 'judicial protection of rights and legitimate interests', in relations with the public administration and in access to public services. The foreigner must comply with the 'obligations' laid down in the legislation in force (this paragraph is entirely pleonastic or tautological). Entry into Italian territory is permitted only to those who are in possession of a passport or a valid document (Article 4, § 1), for a period of no more than 90 days (Article 4, § 4), except for derogations provided for by law; according to Article 5, a 'residency permit' is provided for longer periods (from three months to two years) for study and work reasons; and for longer periods for subordinate or autonomous work and for family reunification (Article 5, § 3, letter d), without prejudice to the fact that the 'residence permit' is granted without prejudice, in the first case, to the need for the prior stipulation of a residency contract for subordinate work between an Italian employer or a foreigner legally residing in Italy and the foreigner. This contract of stay, signed at the competent immigration office, must necessarily contain, pursuant to Article 5 *bis*, the employer's

[19] See in this regard G Tucci, 'Il matrimonio dello straniero in Italia nella tradizione della nostra codificazione civile da Pasquale Stanislao Mancini al "Pacchetto Sicurezza"' in G Tucci, *La giustizia e i diritti degli esclusi* (Naples, Editoriale Scientifica, 2013) 91ff.

guarantee of the availability of accommodation for the worker and the commitment to pay the travel expenses for the worker's return to his country of origin.

Chapter II of Title II of the Consolidated Act deals with border control and regulates the two fundamental measures of the rejection of foreigners who do not meet the requirements for entry into the state (Article 10) and administrative expulsion, ordered by the Minister of the Interior for reasons of public order or state security, in the cases and with the procedures laid down in Article 13.[20] It should be noted that, pursuant to Article 19, expulsion or refoulement to a state 'in which the foreigner may be persecuted for reasons of race, sex, language, nationality, religion, political opinion, personal or social conditions, or may risk being returned to another State in which he is not protected from persecution' may in no circumstances be ordered; the same prohibition extends to refoulement, expulsion or extradition to a state if 'there are substantial grounds for believing that the person would be in danger of being subjected to torture there'.

Special rules are laid down in Titles III to V of the T.U. for work, study, health care and social security.

Chapter IV of Title V deals most directly with the integration of foreigners residing in Italy and the protection of their dignity as persons. Article 42 regulates the social integration measures that the state undertakes to put in place; Article 42 *bis* provides for a residence permit for 'acts of particular civic value', while Article 43, which follows in the wake of copious EU regulations, prohibits 'acts of discrimination' (Article 43) on racial, ethnic, national or religious grounds, by private individuals and by employees of public administrations. According to the Consolidated Act, discrimination is defined as

> any conduct which, directly or indirectly, results in a distinction, exclusion, restriction or preference based on race, colour, ancestry or national or ethnic origin, religious beliefs and practices, and which has the purpose or effect of destroying or impairing the recognition, enjoyment or exercise, on an equal footing, of human rights and fundamental freedoms in the political, economic, social and cultural fields and in any other area of public life.

Acts of discrimination, within the meaning of Article 43(2), include in any case the commission or omission of an act by a public official or person in charge of a public service that unfairly discriminates against a person 'solely because of his or her status as a foreigner or as a member of a particular race, religion, ethnic group or nationality'; the conduct of a person who imposes more unfavourable conditions or refuses to provide goods or services offered to the public to a foreigner solely because of his status as a foreigner or as a member of a particular race, religion, ethnic group or nationality or who unlawfully refuses

[20] For details see A Di Muro, *Il diritto dell'immigrazione. An updated guide to Law No. 132/2018 Decree 'Salvini'* (Turin, Giappichelli, 2019) 65ff.

or renders more disadvantageous access to employment, housing, education, training and social services; who impedes the exercise of an economic activity legitimately undertaken; or any act or conduct by the employer or its servants which produces a prejudicial effect by discriminating, even indirectly, against workers by reason of their membership of a particular race, ethnic or linguistic group, religious denomination or nationality. Lastly, it is worth noting the clarification contained in the third paragraph, which extends the application of the prohibition of the relevant remedies 'to xenophobic, racist or discriminatory acts committed against Italian citizens, stateless persons and citizens of other Member States of the European Union present in Italy'.

Discriminatory acts are subject to 'inhibition', and 'compensation for damages', both pecuniary and non-pecuniary, (Article 44), as well as criminal sanctions, where applicable.

Two other particularly relevant blocks of regulations concur with this first body of legislation: (a) the internal regulatory level discipline composed of numerous decrees of the Ministry of the Interior establishing and regulating the operation of reception centres for migrants, such as the Centri di soccorso e prima accoglienza (CPSA), the Centri di accoglienza (CDA), the Centri di accoglienza per richiedenti asilo e rifugiati (CARA) and the centri di identificazione e espulsione (CIE);[21] and (b) the dense European legislation aimed at implementing a common asylum policy and, therefore, at establishing minimum guarantees regarding the detention of migrants and uniform procedures for the recognition of international protection or refugee status (eg the Dublin III Regulation, no 604 of 2013, Directives 32 and 33 of 2013, on reception conditions and recognition of international protection status).[22]

The result is an immigration law articulated on several levels[23] and often inspired by logics that are not perfectly coherent with each other, which alternate, depending on the sources involved and the historical context from which the measures in question emanate, the values of solidarity and respect for human dignity with the securitarian paradigm of control and marginalisation of the 'different'.[24] The friction between the normative logics of reference dramatically reflects an involution of social relations and the widespread attitude of the population towards the migration problem.

The jurisprudence offers a truly emblematic cross-section of the growing feeling of intolerance and the re-emergence of impulses that one would not

[21] On the changes introduced by the so-called Salvini Decree, see M Giovannetti, *Disposizioni in materia di accoglienza dei richiedenti asilo, in Curi, a cura di, Il decreto Salvini. Immigration and Security* (Pisa, Pisa University Press, 2019) 147ff.

[22] G Mirate, 'Migration flow management and state responsibility: problematic reflections between domestic regulations, administrative practices and ECHR jurisprudence' (2017) *Responsabilità civile e previdenza* 431.

[23] For an overview see G Dell'Osta, *Immigrazione e cittadinanza: nuove regole, diritti, giurisdizione* (Milan, Giuffré, 2019).

[24] S Rodotà, *Solidarietà. Un'utopia necessaria* (Roma-Bari, Laterza, 2014) 110ff.

hesitate to define as racist, especially in the richest and most advanced parts of our country, in the indifference and sometimes even with the complicit support of part of the political class.[25] It will be sufficient to limit ourselves to describing two main lines of intervention: that of domestic jurisprudence on the prohibition of discrimination; and that of European jurisprudence on respect for human rights in the context of border rejection procedures, expulsion and detention of foreigners.

From the first point of view, the jurisprudence of merit and legitimacy has been called upon to deal with numerous cases of discriminatory acts carried out by both public administrations and private individuals in the exercise of their negotiating autonomy.[26] For example, the use of the term 'clandestine' to designate asylum-seekers in a political poster affixed by the Lega Nord in the municipality of Saronno;[27] the issuance of a municipal circular that made the enrolment of a non-EU child in a nursery school conditional upon the family obtaining a residence permit;[28] the use of the term 'clandestine' to designate asylum-seekers in a political poster affixed by the Lega Nord in the municipality of Saronno; the issuance of a municipal circular that made the enrolment of a non-EU child in a nursery school conditional upon the family obtaining a residence permit; the refusal of a birth allowance to a foreign national holding a residence permit for employment reasons, in application of the provision – considered contrary to European law – limiting the granting of this allowance to non-EU foreigners holding a long-term residence permit;[29] the conduct of a shopkeeper, who had refused to serve non-EU customers, in this case North Africans, solely because they were non-EU customers and belonged to a category of subjects prejudicially considered to be illegal and not working[30] the conduct of an insurance company that offered policies in which the premium was directly influenced by the insured person's state of birth.[31]

From the second point of view, there are many interventions of the case law of the Strasbourg Court and the Court of Justice in the field of immigration that are worthy of reflection.[32] For the purposes herein, it will suffice to mention two of the best-known pronouncements of the European Court of Human

[25] In place of many see G Tucci, 'Principle of equality and discrimination by nationality and citizenship: bonus bebè and "Padano" racism' in Tucci (n 19) 65ff.

[26] On the latter profile see the recent monographic survey by P Donadio, *Models and issues of anti-discriminatory contract law* (Turin, Giappichelli, 2017); see also D Maffeis, 'La discriminazione contrattuale e la dignità della persona' in F Caggia and G Resta (ed), *I diritti fondamentali in Europa e il diritto privato* (Rome, Roma Tre Press, 2019) 135ff.

[27] Tribunal Milan, 22 February 2017.

[28] Tribunal Milan, ord 11 February 2008.

[29] Tribunal Milan, 2 December 2016, in Foro it, 2017, I, 352.

[30] Cassazione penale 11 October 2006, in Giustizia penale, 2008, II, 43.

[31] See in this regard Tucci (n 19).

[32] G Panella, 'The evolution of the jurisprudence of the European Court of Human Rights on immigration and the position of the Court of Justice of the European Union' in G Panella, *European Integration Studies* (Milan, Giuffré, 2018) 599ff.

Rights, which exemplify the kind of problems with which modern migration law is called upon to deal on a daily basis: *Hirsi Jamaa v Italy*[33] and *Khlaifia and others v Italy*.[34]

The first relates to the issue of the refoulement at sea of Somali and Eritrean migrants from the Libyan coast, carried out in international waters by patrol boats of the Italian Guardia di Finanza and Italian Coast Guard. This refoulement, which was followed by the forced return within Libyan territorial seas, had been carried out within the framework of a series of bilateral agreements concluded between Italy and Libya in order to exercise control over migratory flows also through interposition actions. In the Court's opinion, the refoulement in international waters and the forced transfer to Libya constituted a violation of the European Convention on Human Rights, due to the principle – also reiterated in Article 19(2) of the EU Charter of Rights – of *non-refoulement*. According to this principle, a state may not refuse or return a person to territories where his life or fundamental freedoms would be threatened;[35] in the present case, the forced transfer to Libya by the Italian authorities, without any identification of the migrants, constitutes a violation of Article 3 of the Convention, in light of the risk of being subjected to inhuman or degrading treatment once returned to the Libyan coast and from there to their country of origin. In addition, the Court found a violation of the prohibition of collective expulsions in Article 4 of the Fourth Protocol to the Convention, as well as of Article 13 ECHR (right to an effective remedy), by reason of the failure to guarantee a redress procedure granted to victims to challenge the measures applied by the state.

The second case concerned, in addition to the issue of collective expulsion, the compatibility of the domestic regulation of administrative detention in immigration centres with the Convention.[36] It concerned, in particular, a group of Tunisian citizens who had fled their country following the unrest caused by the Arab Spring and were intercepted at sea by coastguard forces and there transferred first to the rescue and first reception centre of Lampedusa and then on board ships moored in the port of Palermo. The Court examined the admissibility of the detention regime in light of Article 5 of the Convention.[37] This provision guarantees, in its first paragraph, the fundamental right to liberty and security of every person, but is without prejudice to the power of states (Article 5(1)(f)) to restrict the freedom of foreigners irregularly present on their territory. Starting from the assumption that the restrictive measures must be proportional to the aim pursued (the return of the foreigner) and that the

[33] ECtHR, 23 February 2015, App no 27765/09.

[34] European Court of Human Rights, Grand Chamber, 15 December 2016, App no 16483/12.

[35] On the subject, Panella (n 32) 602–03.

[36] For more on the administrative detention regime, see V Berlingò, L'humanitas e la fondamentalità del diritto: il 'trattamento' degli immigrati irregolari (2017) 3 *Diritto amministrativo* 529.

[37] For the necessary insights see Mirate (n 22).

conditions of detention must be appropriate, since it was dealing with persons who have left their country of origin, but have not committed crimes, the Court came to the conclusion that the detention regime at the CPSA in Lampedusa lacks, both procedurally and substantively, the minimum guarantees that would allow it to pass the test of compatibility with the ECHR. Consequently, the conduct of the Italian State was found to be in violation of Article 5(1), (2) and (4) of the Convention.

15

Person, Dignity, Identity

I. FACTORS IN THE MODERN CONCEPTION OF THE PERSON

At the Festivalfilosofia 2019 dedicated to the *person*, and organised in Modena, a number of speeches dealt with the *dignity* of man, a topic on which a huge number of contributions from philosophers, historians, anthropologists, psychologists and particularly jurists have been collected. For jurists, human dignity is not a 'problem, nor is it a word with too many misunderstandings, which would make one doubt its usefulness', as Michael Rosen argues,[1] but rather 'a surplus value, since it is the heart of the personalist principle, which, together with the egalitarian principle, underpins the great edifice of contemporary constitutionalism' (Silvestri),[2] a value that implies freedom of self-determination to be balanced with (but not opposed to) fundamental rights (Ridola), the foundation of personalism and the legal meaning of 'person' (Rodotà). In his book *Dignity. History and Meaning*,[3] Rosen was more generous, or at least more cautious, commenting on the passages of Kant's various books that deal with the subject, discussing in particular Kant's statements that humanity in itself is dignity, that man must not be treated as a means but as an end, and that morality stops when dignity is violated.

Of course, the expression 'dignity' is polysense, as its history and the different meanings in which it can be used demonstrate. 'Dignity' can be an ambivalent and ambiguous word, if instrumentalised to achieve results that contrast with the essence of humanity expressed in the individual-person, but this does not mean that it should be considered a concept to be dispensed with, or even to be reproved. The regimes that have trampled on it, those that still do not recognise it, are branded – commendably – as totalitarian regimes (Arendt), as regimes that trample on rights. Its proclamation, in the Declarations of Rights, in the Constitutional Charters, in the European Charter of Fundamental Rights is not superfluous; indeed, after the horrors of Auschwitz and the Gulag, it has become a guarantee and a promise.

[1] In his intervention *La Repubblica* (8 September 2022) 39.

[2] I Kant, *Metaphysics of Morals* (trans MJ Gregor) (1785) (New York, CUP, 1996); O Sensen, *Kant on Human Dignity* (Berlin, De Gruyter, 2011).

[3] M Rosen, *Dignity. Its History and Meaning* (Harvard, Harvard University Press, 2012).

In other words, for jurists, the concept of dignity is fundamental and irrepressible. Quite different is the concept of *identity*, also discussed at Festivalfilosofia. Here, law has played a different role, indeed, we could say it has been 'perverse', because it is only since the end of the Second World War that identity has become a yardstick for the exaltation of the person, having for centuries, indeed for millennia, been used to diversify and thus demean the person. One need only think of the statuses of the slave, the serf, the *sans-culottes*, the non-proprietor, the illiterate, the poor, the heretic, the Jew, the woman, the foreigner, the immigrant, which were conceived to oppress people, and law was a tool to achieve this result. The problem today is how to restore dignity, including through identity, to those who are still deprived of it. Identity classification must therefore pass through criteria and paradigms that must be corrected in the light of the constitutional concept of dignity. This is the great gamble of the West, which counts on the support of jurists and, of course, the rulers of states, the European Union and people of goodwill: beyond identity, to reaffirm the concept of humanity inherent, as Kant taught us, in the very concept of the individual-person. Because fundamental rights, freedoms and the principle of equality, and therefore dignity, are non-negotiable, nor can they be legally or economically compressed.

Rosen, then, does not bother to consider the problems of the digitised society: it is no coincidence that the European Personal Data Regulation, in affirming the principle of economic freedom in the collection and use of data, proclaims the irrepressible rights of the individual against the managers of the databases, to whom it imposes an objective responsibility for their violation. Here too, the dignity of the person is connected with the identity – digital (ie virtual) – reconstructed on the basis of the data collected by the network and attributed to the person.

Dignity is also a religious concept, and a pillar of the Christian conception of the person. But, to remain within the confines of secularism, one can share with Rosen his conclusion today: we must not use this concept as a mask, and when we use it, we must make explicit the meaning we wish to attribute to it.

And yet identity does not escape the imperatives of law, for which identity is not a fact but a construction.

II. THE IRREPRESSIBLE IDENTITY

Can we therefore remove the notion of identity, given that over the centuries it has served to stifle the person rather than to enhance their qualities and value?

Divergent answers from different cultural backgrounds argue that we cannot.

On the moral level, Kwame Antony Appiah states that it is not necessary to take an attitude towards identity of favour or disfavour: what is important is to understand how it is constructed, so to speak, on the physiological level.

If shortcomings are found, it will be up to others to identify the cure. Following the teachings of John Stuart Mill, he points out that what matters is to leave each individual free to realise his own life programme, since it is not the status one acquires that is important, but the model of life one wishes to pursue.[4] The ethics of identity in this view becomes *the ethics of individuality*. Identity – and individuality – are thus closely connected with *freedom*: what matters is not to be different from others, but rather to enjoy the freedom to construct oneself. But, Appiah emphasises, we must take into account three factors: the inventive capacity of each of us, who wants to design our lives according to our own aspirations, our own ideals; the authenticity of this image, which corresponds to what we actually achieve; and the collective dimension of individual identity.

This collective dimension is particularly important for jurists, because the law, which is the result of the decisions of the collective, constructs for its part the path of the identity of each one of us, from the moment of birth to the end, and the identity constructed by the individual is a continuous duel between the identity one would like to have and the identity that society imposes on us.

In ethical terms, individuality, ie individual identity, implies that we have duties towards ourselves, and social identity implies that we have duties towards others. Solidarity is triggered towards those who are similar to us, so as to be an aggregating factor of many individualities. In order to guarantee this opportunity to all, it is necessary to achieve the totality of human rights, and to safeguard individualities and thus differences, because 'in a single society there is no wisdom'.[5]

It is clear, then, that it is not enough to claim more freedom for everyone; everyone must be enabled to make free choices in life. And here, of course, radical liberalism clashes with factual reality, today made even more difficult to govern due to the current economic crisis.

On an anthropological level, Francesco Remotti warns us against the notion of identity, which he describes as controversial, unstable, equivocal, whether it is assumed on an individual level or seen on a collective level. The plural nature of the self must guide us against attempts at simplification and standardisation, especially against attempts at classification that end up being oppressive of each individual's way of being.[6] Remotti realises that

> The anthropologist, the sociologist, the psychologist comes across subjects (individuals or groups) who speak of identity, who invoke identity, who affirm their own identity: perhaps, then, identity does not exist? Identity exists at least at the level of discourse, just as it exists at the level of identity-inspired practices.

[4] A Appiah, *The Ethics of Identity* (Princeton, Princeton University Press, 2005) 5.
[5] ibid 252.
[6] F Remotti, *Against Identity* (Roma-Bari, Laterza, 1996).

It is therefore necessary to 'come to terms with identity'. But his point is that identity becomes an obsession, and therefore, we need to understand the reason for it, because it chases us all our lives; but we also need to put it aside, because identity is elusive and constantly changing.[7] Drawing on Hume's studies on the intellect, Remotti argues that identity is elusive because it is based on two elements that are themselves unstable: memory, which is selective and therefore partial; and imagination, which constructs changing worlds, outside of reality. However, we cannot do without identity, which, in a social context, implies *recognition*. Recognition is linked to the idea of rights: 'A subject is recognised when he is granted rights, beginning with those of existence and survival. In a certain sense, this notion of rights encompasses all the contents listed above (existence, needs, characteristics)'.[8] In other words, Remotti argues,

> the idea of the individual is a sort of cultural conquest, which the societies usually dealt with: it is the theme of modern individualism, that is, of the unique and unrepeatable character of the individual. It should be pointed out that many societies in which we have encountered the individual conception of the person fully recognize his or her unrepeatable character. Precisely by thinking of the person as individual and plural, i.e. made up of many relationships, it is easy to admit that the combination of relationships is unrepeatable. Each of us is an 'individual', but at the same time represents a unique situation. I am unique and unrepeatable not as an isolated individual but as an individual admitted into social relations.

And he states:

> In this way, unrepeatability is not only not lost at all, but rather enhanced. As can be seen, one can very well speak of uniqueness and unrepeatability without appealing to the concept of personal identity. Not being an unrepeatability of substance, unrepeatability is also a highlighting of how today you are like this but tomorrow you will be made in another way, because situations have changed, because you have entered into another bundle of relationships: there is an unrepeatability of situations within the self.[9]

On a psychological level, what is relevant is the ego, the subconscious and the unconscious, the ego's relations with the outside world, the ego-other-me relationship. Also explored are the relationships with the body, the projections of the mind, and the ways of 'recognising' a subject within a group and of this within a larger, more inclusive community.[10]

The problem of identity thus merges with the analysis of human nature throughout the entire course of philosophical thought: each philosopher poses

[7] F Remotti, *The obsession with identity* (Roma-Bari, Laterza, 2010).

[8] F Remotti, 'L'ossessione identitaria' (2011) XXV *Rivista Italiana di Gruppoanalisi* 9.

[9] ibid 28.

[10] In the extensive literature see for early references G Jervis, *La conquista dell'identità. Essere se stessi, essere diversi* (Milan, Feltrinelli, 1997); M Marzano, *Il diritto di essere io* (Roma-Bari, Laterza, 2014).

the problem of who we are and endeavours to answer this question with the methodological choices aligned to his system of thought. The nature of the person becomes an interpretative key to the entire history of philosophy.[11]

The person is a central notion in the world of law, and so is his identity. But as mentioned, it is only recently that *individual* identity has been given value.

If for other sciences the question is whether we can dispose of identity, this question makes no sense for law. The answer in law is negative. As long as a society is built on roles – and it could not be otherwise – man is destined to be the *person* Gaius spoke of, and to be identified in the three forms that have been described: by what he feels he is, by what he wants to appear to be, and by what society imposes on him to be. The relationship between identity and a person is measured by the ways in which identity is constructed, by the extent of the space available to the person to construct an identity, by the greater or lesser coercive force with which identity is imposed on each subject.

Hence the need to defend fundamental rights.

In the imagination of jurists, identity spans the centuries in a continuum of rules, theories, concepts.

It is a laboratory for jurists, who use it from time to time, depending on the purposes pursued, either to discriminate or to protect the individual. Ultimately, identity is neither a photograph nor an end point: identity is a tool, which from time to time can fulfil a liberating or persecutory function. And the level of civilisation of a society is determined by the extent to which it is able to guarantee everyone the *right to be themselves*.

[11] See eg W Bourgeois, *Persons. What Philosophers Say About You* (Waterloo, Canada, 1995); Pojman, *Who are we? Theories of Human Nature* (Oxford, OUP, 2006).

16

Biological Identity and Digital Identity

I. BIOLAW

UP TO THIS point, it would appear that the principle (value, fundamental right, limitation) of personal dignity is universally recognised and that it has been afforded precise protection in national and EU legal systems. But the problem is open. The greatest friction is to be found in the area of biolaw, in which the rights of the individual (ie the right to self-determination) must be reconciled with the values shared by the community in the area of assisted procreation and protection of the embryo, surrogacy, reaction to therapeutic measures, trans-sexuality and relations between gender and physical sex; and in the area of the expression of religious beliefs through their symbolic representation, such as the veil for Islamic women and the cross for Catholics. In these matters, human dignity often plays a complex role, and the expression presents a semantic ambiguity that lends itself to providing an alibi for opposing solutions to the problems posed to the jurist.

It was precisely human dignity that Paul VI's declaration on religious freedom, *Dignitatis humanae* of 7 December 1965, appealed to. The Congregation for the Doctrine of the Faith also appealed to human dignity in its *Dignitas Personae* Instruction on Certain Questions of Bioethics of 8 September 2008, # all questions concerning the use of embryos being dealt with in this way and from a restrictive perspective, thus extending the principle of dignity from the living person to the person *in nuce*.

Yet, it is precisely human dignity that the Oviedo Convention of 4 April 1997 refers to in order to allow, within certain limits, the scientific research, transplantation, the use of stem cells and embryos:

> The Parties ... – it states – shall protect the human being in his dignity and identity and guarantee to every person, without discrimination, respect for his integrity and his other fundamental rights and freedoms with regard to the applications of biology and medicine.

The conflict between values – ethical, religious, and human dignity – has been resolved with different outcomes depending on the adjudicating courts and the historical phases in which they arose.

In Italy, the first emblematic pronouncements concerned transfusions given to Jehovah's Witnesses, a conscious person who due to suffering no longer wished to be fed and cared for (*Welby*[1]) and a girl who had been in a deep coma for many years, whose father believed that she should no longer be fed and cared for because the coma was irreversible and it was not decent to continue to ravage the girl's body (*Englaro*[2]).[3]

In this context, the principle of dignity was invoked both in favour of the prohibition of transfusions, the lawfulness of the cessation of therapeutic treatment, and the cessation of artificial life, and in favour of the obligatory nature of transfusion in the case of a believer in a state of natural incapacity, the conscious patient, and the unconscious patient.

In its judgment of 23 February 2007 No 4211 concerning the refusal of blood transfusions by a Jehovah's Witness, the Court held that:

> With regard to the refusal of certain therapies, as a right based on the combined provisions of Article 32 of the Constitution, Article 9 of the Law of 28 March 2001 n. 145 (ratifying and executing the Council of Europe Convention for the Protection of Human Rights and Dignity of the Human Being with Regard to the Application of Biology and Medicine), and 40 of the Code of Medical Ethics, even in the presence of an express pre-emptive rejection, it cannot be excluded that the doctor in the face of an unforeseen and unforeseeable worsening of the patient's condition and in the presence of circumstances that prevent the effective verification of the persistence of such dissent, may consider it certain or highly probable that such dissent is no longer valid and, consequently, perform the treatment already redefined, if the same is indispensable to save the patient's life.

The *Welby* case was easier to solve because the patient was finally conscious and capable of expressing his will and therefore determined to interrupt his own suffering. Invoking the principle of self-determination, on the basis of which it is possible to redefine futile therapy, artificial respiration and feeding, the Court of Rome declared that there was no need to proceed against the treating doctor who had acceded to the patient's will.

In the case of Eluana Englaro – which involved ordinary judges, administrative judges, the higher courts and even the Parliament in its tormented phases – the situation was more difficult because the patient was not conscious and her will was expressed by her father and the special curator. The Court of Cassation specified that the judge could only authorise the interruption of treatment if there are two competing circumstances: (a) the irreversibility of the patient's condition of vegetative state, scientifically grounded, so that there is, according to internationally recognised scientific standards, no possibility of recovery of consciousness and the ability to perceive; and (b) the unambiguous

[1] Criminal Tribunal Naples, 17 October 2007, No 2049.

[2] Italian Court of Cassation, 16 October 2007, No 21748.

[3] All these decisions are discussed by G Alpa, *Cos'è il diritto privato?* (Roma-Bari, Laterza, 2008); American edition: *What is Private Law?* (trans A Lordi) (Durham, Carolina Academica Press, 2010).

ascertainment of the patient's will, on the basis of elements drawn from her experience, personality and ethical, religious, cultural and philosophical convictions, about the refusal to continue the treatment.

The valuable and learned explanatory statement, in which reference is made to many cases decided by foreign courts and the jurisprudence of the European Court of Human Rights, states that:

> The preaching of the non-availability of the right to life, unlike what happens with other constitutional and fundamental rights, is linked to the fact that, on the map of modern constitutionalism, it constitutes a right that is different from all others: life is an indispensable prerequisite for the enjoyment of any human freedom and, precisely for this reason, it cannot be accepted that the person alienates the decision on his or her survival to others or that the right is extinguished by renunciation.
>
> Religious identity cannot therefore invest the sphere of the person's dignity and cannot demand that practices that harm the physical integrity can be permitted.

II. RELIGIOUS SYMBOLS

It is in this light that the Strasbourg Court's ruling on the exposure of the cross (the *Lautsi* case of 3 November 2009[4]) can be read, particularly where it states that:

> The compulsory display of a confessional symbol in the public sector in special situations that depend on government control, particularly in classrooms, violates the right of parents to educate their children according to their convictions and the right of schoolchildren to believe and not to believe.

The case was then reformed by the Grande Chambre on 18 March 2011, according to which:

> The State's choice to give greater visibility to the country's majority religion through the simple display of a religious symbol (such as the cross) in schools is legitimate, as long as this choice does not lead to actual indoctrination. The mere display of the cross in classrooms, unaccompanied by compulsory teaching of Christianity or forms of intolerance towards pupils of a different religion, does not violate the right of parents to guide their children in their own lives towards an education in conformity with their religious convictions (Article 2 of Protocol No. 1).[5]

But the problem is an open one, since it is a question of balancing the right to freedom of expression and freedom of religious belief.

In both areas, we are dealing with issues in which dignity is closely connected with the right to life and the expression of religious sentiments, and

[4] ECHR, Tribunal, 3 November 2009.

[5] ECHR, Grand Chamber,(which reversed the judgment), 18 March 2011; see A Leoni, L'"Affaire Lautsi c. Italie": la vicenda giudiziaria dell'esposizione del crocifisso nelle aule scolastiche' (April 2011) *Stato, Chiese e pluralismo confessionale*, available at www.statoechiese.it.

the investigation of this issue must therefore take place in the context of the commentary on the articles of the Charter of Fundamental Rights that are connected to and directly follow Article 1.

III. THE RIGHT TO GENETIC IDENTITY

A new personal right has been identified by American jurists and bioethicists: the *right to genetic identity*. This right has a complex structure; in fact, it starts from the protection of the genome understood as the direct biological link between generations; this genetic heritage is a means of identification of the person. This legal situation includes:

(a) the individual's right to know his genetic heritage (the so-called right to information);
(b) the individual's right to the preservation of his genetic heritage, and thus to the prevention of genetic manipulation.

Problems of privacy therefore arise, so that knowledge of the individual's genetic heritage does not fall into the hands of third parties. Issues also arise in relation to the protection of the child, since genetic manipulation alters the physiognomy and physical manifestation of the child.

However, a blanket protection would be excessive and in conflict with the individual's own interests: the assessment of the genetic heritage is in fact useful in the prenatal phase to help prevent genetic disease, and to diagnose and treat genetic diseases in children and adults.

However, the patenting of processes for human cloning or the genetic modification of embryos is excluded.[6]

IV. THE RIGHT TO SEXUAL IDENTITY

The right to determine one's sex corresponding to one's psychosomatic reality has been recognised in society and in the legal system that regulates it.

In addition to this right, which entails a later and more precise definition of sexual identity, there is another right, relating to sex change. For this, the orientation of jurisprudence is not clear-cut. A change of sex, in fact, runs counter to the public interest in the certainty of relationships and orderly coexistence; there are rulings that give precedence to this public interest over the individual's interest in undergoing medical treatment to acquire the sex that,

[6] Court of Justice of the European Union (CJEU) 9 October 2001, fn 377 in *Foro italiano* (2001) IV, 25.

from a psychological point of view, seems best suited to express his personality. However, there are also judgments in which the constitutional principles that ensure the protection of the individual's personality (Articles 2 and 3 of the Italian Constitution) make it possible to overcome the public requirement to prohibit any change in sex, and therefore legitimise the individual to undergo treatment to realise his aspirations and to have his new sexual identity recognised, even formally.

The principles of respect for the individual seem to be the inspiration behind Law 164 of 14 April 1982 (containing regulations on the rectification of sex attribution), which makes it possible to change the sex on a birth certificate from the one stated therein 'following intervening changes in the person's … sexual characteristics' (Article 1). The law had given rise to an interesting family and personal affair concerning a couple united in marriage and with children. The husband had changed sex and, on the basis of Article 2 of the aforementioned law, the marriage was dissolved, because civil unions between persons of the same sex were not (yet) recognised in the Italian legal system. The former spouses appealed against the decision of the civil registrar's office that had recorded the dissolution in the civil status register. The subsequent proceedings in the Court of Cassation, following the confirmation of legitimacy by the Court of Appeal, were suspended due to the referral of the law to the Constitutional Court.

The reasoning of the Constitutional Court, which in Judgment No.170 of 2014 upheld the appeal and declared the constitutional illegitimacy of Articles 2 and 4 of the aforementioned law, is very straightforward. First of all, the Court ruled that

> Articles 8 (on the right to respect for family life) and 12 (on the right to marry and form a family) of the ECHR, as interpreted by the European Court of Human Rights (H. v. Finland – decision of 13 November 2012; Schalk and Kopf v. Austria – decision of 22 November 2010), could be applied in the present case, pursuant to the alleged violation of Articles 10, first paragraph, and 117, first paragraph, of the Constitution

because

> in the absence of a consensus between the various national States on the subject of same-sex unions, the European Court of Human Rights, on the assumption of the margin of appreciation consequently granted to them, affirms that any forms of protection for same-sex couples are reserved to the discretion of the national legislator.

Instead, it considered pertinent the reference to Article 2 of the Constitution, as already affirmed in Judgment No 138 of 2010, in which it was stated that social groups

> also include same-sex unions, understood as stable cohabitation between two persons of the same sex, who have the fundamental right to freely live as a couple,

> obtaining – within the time, methods and limits established by law – legal recognition with the related rights and duties. In that same judgment, however, it was also stated that … the aspiration to such recognition – which necessarily presupposes a general discipline, aimed at regulating the rights and duties of the members of the couple – cannot be realised only by putting same-sex unions on an equal footing with marriage

This was confirmed, moreover, by the diversity of choices made by countries that have so far recognised such unions.

In other words, the Constitutional Court held that, in this particular situation, the couple was not just any union, but that, since the two former spouses continued to live together with their original affection and children, the law could not divide them, forcing them into estrangement.

Consequently, the Court of Cassation overturned the appealed decision because, quoting a passage from the Constitutional Court's decision,

> it is not seriously contestable that the principle of the immediate and uninterrupted necessity of a status substantially comparable, in terms of the rights and duties of reciprocal financial and moral assistance, to that deriving from the marriage bond for married couples in the appellants' situation is imperative.

So, the recognition of the rights and duties deriving from the marriage bond was reserved for the couple, pending the intervention of the legislature in the field of civil unions.

However, the law is also objectionable in another respect: when it allows sex changes only after surgery to alter sexual attributes.

In this regard, the Constitutional Court – first in Judgment No 221 of 2015, then in Judgments Nos 180 and 185 of 2017 – specified that a constitutionally oriented interpretation of Law No 164 of 1982 makes it possible to exclude the need for the medical intervention for the purpose of rectifying the sex attainment registry:

> In Law No. 164 of 1982, the realisation of the individual's right to the recognition of his or her right to personal identity, of which gender identity is a part, finds its realisation through a judicial procedure that guarantees, at the same time, both the individual's right and those public needs for the certainty of legal relations, on which the importance of civil registers is based.[7]

The most recent jurisprudence of legitimacy and merit have also adhered to this approach: to obtain the rectification of civil status documents in accordance with the true sexual identity of the person concerned. It is no longer necessary for a priority medical-surgical and/or psychological intervention to be carried out in order to change one's legal primary sexual characteristics, and the lack of surgery cannot is not in itself sufficient reason to exclude the change of sex from the registry documents. Rather, it is sufficient to demonstrate, through the

[7] Italian Constitutional Court, 13 July 2017, fn 185.

medical-surgical and/or psychological treatment the individual has undergone, the necessity of that choice.[8]

On this point, the European Court of Human Rights has noted a violation of Article 8 ECHR on the

> right to respect for private and family life by a Contracting State which does not provide for the possibility of obtaining a change of name of an individual entered in the civil status register as a male person, but whose sexual identity is now peacefully female, although still awaiting a sexual transition surgery.

V. HUMAN RIGHTS AND GENDER

The most complicated cases concern the *gender* of an individual. Identity plays an essential role here, right from birth; it affects the individual throughout life.

The judges of the European Court of Human Rights are aware of this, both when they deny the individual to change his identity and when they accept it.

Two examples apply in this context.

The 1986 case of *Rees v UK*[9] concerned a woman who had undergone sex reassignment surgery and had asked for her documents to be amended on the basis of her sex at birth. The European Court of Human Rights balanced the interests at stake and, noting that in the United Kingdom and most European countries, the rectification of civil status documents was not permitted even if the person concerned had biologically and physically changed, grounded its decisions on Article 8 of the ECHR (which protects the right to privacy) and Article 14 (which protects the right to start a family) by stating that 'it cannot be said, for the time being, that there is a unity of views in this matter, and that on the whole, it seems going through a transitional phase, in which states have a large margin of appreciation'.

On the contrary, in the following years, as the orientations of legislators and judges in most states have changed, the Court has found for the violation of these rights. This is the case for the rectification of the first name (*SV v Italy* 55216/08, 11 October 2018); while for the rectification of civil status documents in the case of sex change (*P v Ukraine*, No 40296/16), the appeal was deemed inadmissible because the three levels of proceedings required for access to the Court had not been completed. However, in the case of *AP, Garçon and Nicot v France* the Court completely changed its position, noting that sexual identity is a relevant aspect of a person's identity and therefore if obstacles are placed in the way of its exact registration, Articles 8 and 14 ECHR are violated.[10]

[8] Italian Cassazione civile., 20 July 2015, No 15138; similarly, Trib. Milan, 1 March 2018, No 2491 and Trib. Trani 6- December 2018, No 2461 (see www.iusexplorer.it).

[9] Case No 9532/81, decision of 10 October 1986.

[10] Case Nos 79885/12, 52471/13 and 52596/13, 6 April 2017.

In the Constitutional Court's creative process of rights, many personal rights have been recognised, including, most recently, the right to *gender*, ie the right to have one's sexual gender recognised without the expectation that it conforms to the person's physical nature. This implies the person's freedom to express a sex other than the one that his physical manifestation might be expected to give him; a freedom that is expressed in not being forced to undergo a surgical intervention to ensure the identity between sexual awareness and sexual appearance.

In two subsequent rulings, the Italian Constitutional Court affirmed this right. In Case No 180/2017 (no name was revealed for privacy reasons) the judge rapporteur, Giuliano Amato, explained that:

> A rigorous judicial ascertainment of the manner in which the change has taken place and of its definitive character is unavoidable. With respect to this, surgical treatment constitutes an eventual instrument that helps to guarantee, by means of a tendency for somatic features to correspond to those of the sex to which one belongs, the achievement of the person's full psychological and physical well-being.

This perspective should be taken when reading the reference, contained in Article 31 of Legislative Decree no 150 of 2011, to the possibility ('When it is necessary') of medical-surgical treatment for the adjustment of sexual characteristics. That provision reiterates, almost 30 years after the introduction of Law No 164 of 1982, that the necessity of surgery in relation to the specificities of the case should be left to the judge's discretion.

Recourse to the surgical modification of sexual characteristics is therefore authorised as a guarantee of the right to health, ie where it is intended to allow the person to achieve a stable psycho-physical balance, particularly where the divergence between anatomical sex and psychosexuality creates turmoil for the individual.

The increasing protection of the health of the individual over the correspondence between anatomical sex and registry sex leads to the conclusion that surgical treatment is not a prerequisite for access to the rectification procedure – as suggested by the referring party – but a possible means of achieving full psycho-physical well-being.

The hermeneutic path highlighted above recognises, therefore, the role of the provision in question as a guarantee of the right to gender identity and an expression of the right to personal identity (Article 2 of the Constitution and Article 8 of the ECHR) as well as an instrument for the full realisation of the right, which also has constitutional coverage, to health (Constitutional Court no 221 of 2015).

The right to *gender* goes beyond the right to personal identity (ie the ideal identity) because it demystifies the idea of nature that jurists have codified for millennia. It considers the person to be a unique being (physically and mentally), with a right to self-determination following his natural inclinations, and who can choose to change the body sex into the other, more psychologically appropriate, sex.

VI. DIGITAL IDENTITY

Technological innovations have led to the creation of a new type of identity, which emerges from the collection of data about a person. Purchases, travel, bookings of houses and hotels, economic transactions, and countless acts of daily, family and work life are recorded using digital technologies. This data, carefully collected and manipulated (or 'processed') leads to the shaping of a person's way of being. This digital identity, however, does not reflect the individual's real or public identity, but an incomplete identity that emerges from the manipulation of data collected in individual acts. In order to enable the individual to control the collection, processing and dissemination of data concerning him, the European Charter of Fundamental Rights has provided for an ad hoc provision related to the right to privacy:

> Article 7 Respect for private and family life
>
> Everyone has the right to respect for his or her private and family life, home and communications.
>
> Article 8 Protection of personal data
>
> 1. Everyonc has the right to the protection of personal data concerning him or her.
> 2. Such data must be processed fairly, for specified purposes and with the consent of the person concerned or on another legitimate basis laid down by law. Everyone shall have the right of access to the data collected concerning him or her and the right to have them rectified.
> 3. Compliance with these rules shall be subject to control by an independent authority.

Commenting on these provisions, Stefano Rodotà, in his capacity of Privacy Guarantor said:

> Without strong protection of information about them, people are increasingly at risk of being discriminated against because of their opinions, religious beliefs, health conditions: privacy thus presents itself as a fundamental element of the society of equality. Without strong protection of data on political beliefs or membership of parties, trade unions and associations, citizens are at risk of being excluded from democracy: Thus privacy becomes an essential condition to be included in the society of participation. Without a strong protection of the 'electronic body', of all the information collected on our account, personal freedom itself is in danger, it becomes so clear that: privacy is a necessary tool to defend the society of freedom, and to oppose the pushes towards the construction of a society of surveillance, of classifying, of social selection.

Information technology has transformed the individual, adding a virtual dimension to his corporeal reality. The free circulation of data and the possibility of commercialising them by the person concerned (without limits, unless a legal barrier is erected, dictated by respect for the dignity of the individual), balanced by the the right to be forgotten and the strengthening of control with the multiplication of the responsible parties, appears to be more of a regression with a mercantilist flavour than progress in the guarantees of individual rights.

This matter was governed by the European Union's General Data Protection Regulation (Regulation No 2016/679, GDPR), which brought in rules concerning the construction of the market of personal data, an essential component of the digital market. The Regulation concerns their circulation and thus the authorisation, or consent by the person concerned, to their acquisition, processing and use, and also the ownership of databases created by economic operators.[11] Another Regulation relates to contracts with digital content, among which data of a personal nature may be found.[12] There are of course, other developments, intertwined with the worlds of information technology, cybernetics and artificial intelligence, but for the time being, literature, case law, acts of independent authorities, resolutions of European and international socio-economic bodies, and codes of conduct focus mainly on personal data and their relationship with the market.[13]

VII. THE US MODEL

At least three tendencies can be isolated in the North American experience: the liberalist one, which considers data as goods in and of themselves, as if they were *new properties* (*commodities*) that are freely negotiable on the market; the one that transforms data into rights assimilable to copyright, and therefore makes them the object of exchange; and the one, so to speak, which comes close to the Italian model and classifies them among the rights of the person, with the limitations and guarantees provided for by the ordinance, while still

[11] 'Strategia per il mercato unico digitale in Europa' COM2015/192); G Simeone, 'Mercato unico digitale; in *Encyclopedia Diritto on line* (2016), available at www.treccani.it/enciclopedia/mercato-unico-digitale_%28Diritto-on-line%29; C Prins (ed), *Digital Democracy in a Globalized World* (London, Elgar, 2017); OECD, *Key Issues for Digital Transformation in the G20* (Berlin, 12 January 2017); European Commission, Foley et al (eds), 'International Digital Economy and Society Index 2018, Smart 2017/0052', Final Report (Bruxelles, 2018).

[12] See European Parliament, *Contracts for the supply of digital content and personal data protection*, PE 603.929, Brussels,2017; European Council, Paper on the Digital Market, Bruxelles, 11 April 2017, 8229/17; A De Franceschi, *European Contract Law and the Digital Single Market. The Implication of the Digital Revolution* (Cambridge, CUP, 2017).

[13] A Montelero, *Il costo della privacy tra valore della persona e ragioni dell'impresa* (Milano, Giuffré, 2007); S Rodotà, *Il mondo nella rete. Quali diritti, quali vincoli* (Roma-Bari, Laterza, 2014); N Zorzi Galgano, *Persona e mercato dei dati.Riflessioni sul GDPR* (Padova, Cedam, 2019); M Wiggers, *Digital Competition Law in Europe* (Alphen and der Rijn, Wolters Kluwer, 2023).

being more liberal than European models because, data can be freely traded on the market.

The liberalist tendency is typical of the legal analysts of the Chicago School, whose coryphaeus is the 'first' Posner, who represented the most determined wing of the conception of rights and law grounded on the reasons of the market.[14] The discourse at the end of the 1970s was more about privacy than *personal data*. But the arguments can be homologous for the two sectors. Posner is not concerned with early privacy, created by Warren and Brandeis, understood in the forms of the public's curiosity about the lives of others and the conflict between individuals and the media, but with *informational privacy*, ie privacy linked to the information economy, following Stigler's insights.[15] Hence the conception of *property rights* that insist on private information, such as trade secrets. And the favour for transparency, when the information does not concern the market but private facts; unless we are talking about subjects who have notoriety, and then their images or information concerning them have an economic value that cannot be disregarded (*right to publication*). There are other cases in which Posner admits the protection of privacy, such as the case of erroneous information, information that distorts the right to personal identity, and trespassing. In all these cases, the rules of tort, rather than the rules of contract, apply.

Proponents of the 'purchase' of data by the data subject and its commercialisation, such as Paul Schwartz, make no secret of the arguments militating against this thesis, which range from market failure to the inability of the data owner to negotiate data to the free transparency of information (which implies the connotation of personal data as 'common goods'), but surpass them all by proposing a case-by-case and data-to-data distinction. And they also consider the positive aspects: the commercialisation of data reduces transactional costs, supports technological development, and enables individuals to obtain more services.

The firm belief of the liberalists is that the commercialisation of personal information benefits not only businesses but also consumers: businesses, because they can, through profitability, better satisfy consumer preferences and develop technology and innovation to offer better products; and consumers, because the subsequently more varied choice of products and services is better suited to their needs.

The problem, if anything, lies in the way in which the information is accessed: hence the need to impose control rules that can pre-empt the company's wrongdoing, given that the instrument of compensation for damages

[14] R Posner, 'The Right to Privacy" (1981) 12 *Georgia Law Review* 393; R Posner, *The Economics of Justice* (Cambridge, Harvard University Press, 1981); in response to Posner see G Calabresi, The Future of Law and Economics: Essay in Reform and Recollection (Yale, Yale University Press, 2016).

[15] GJ Stigler, 'An Introduction to Privacy in Economics and Politics' (1980) 9 *The Journal of Legal Studies* 623.

appears ineffective because it is late, intervening when the damage has already occurred.

At the same time, an apparent contradiction is highlighted: the person has a digital identity with which he identifies himself or is identified, but precisely for this reason he should not 'own' it; on the other hand, third parties can appropriate it, and can exercise a proprietary right over it: and indeed the (also European) regulation of databases protects the property of those who have collected others' data.[16]

This apparent contradiction, however, is not blunt: there are thousands of data that can be transferred to a person, and selecting them in order to collect, assimilate and count them requires a sophisticated activity that has a cost, and therefore it is only right that those who have carried out this work should be remunerated. On the other hand, it is a different matter to the person 'who appropriates himself': this is a topic that our literature has debated since the time of the creation of the general right of personality, but the European choice had been not to consider the subject as an object of self-property.

The analogy with copyright (of English ancestry, recalls Diane Zimmerman)[17] protects the interested party, the owner of the data, against their illegal use: the argument is suggestive, but, as can be understood, we are in the presence of rights that in *common law* (this time in England) have not had their own codicil configuration, as has happened in Italy with the right to the image, and therefore the analogy is completely useless.

In order to overcome the impasse, it is argued that the copyright under discussion is a special kind of copyright: recognising a property right to the interested parties is in line with the formation of a *cyberspace* economy, because it favours the circulation of information by the database owners and avoids negotiation with each owner.

But therein lies the contrast between the North American model and the European model: copyright in Europe also has a moral value; personal data in Europe are fundamental rights. For this reason, Pamela Samuelson, an exception among American authors, who are predominantly oriented towards the conception of data grounded in economic categories, suggests taking the European model into account and placing restrictions on the circulation of data in consideration of the values of the individual and the moral interest of data in itself.[18]

There is no shortage of authors in the United States who invoke the protection of dignity to advise against the commercialisation of data – or of

[16] S Spiekermann, 'Personal Data Markets' (2015) 25 *Electronic Markets* 91.

[17] D Zimmerman, 'Living Without Copyright in a Digital World' (2007) 70 *Albany Law Review* 1375.

[18] P Samuelson, 'Privacy As Intellectual Property?', available at people.ischool.berkeley.edu/~pam/papers/privasip_draft.pdf.

privacy – for the sake of personal protection, such as Jennifer Rothman.[19] And authors who, while adopting the copyright model, emphasise its moral aspects.[20]

One can understand the doubts and uncertainties plaguing Italian doctrine: the digital market has its own requirements, we cannot be too intransigent; the right balance must be found; *homo dignus* is also *homo economicus*, and globalisation has its own rights. The markets no longer have any configuration, Big Data their hardly controllable force. And the European (continental) model must not be abandoned. We can think of a set of coordinated initiatives, taking advantage of the proposals and rules already in force from the Union – the broad interpretation of Article 8 of the Charter of Fundamental Rights; the broad definition of the right to privacy; the valorisation of consent and withdrawal; the strengthening of controls on the digital market – without arriving at the definition of the data-person relationship in terms of property.

The French doctrine is predominantly oriented in this sense: property is defined as a 'false good idea', a 'dangerous illusion', sensational cases such as Cambridge Analytica alarm public opinion, and the Regulation seems to contain a contradiction, on the one hand strengthening the rights of the individual, on the other hand favouring the circulation of data; a new social compromise is also called for, and economists themselves express doubts about the exchange of data and goods or services.[21]

[19] J Rothman, *The Inalienable Right of Publicity* (2012) 101 *Georgetown Law Journal* 185.

[20] J Ritter and A Mayer, 'Regulating Data As Property: A New Construct For Moving Forward' (2018) 16 *Duke Law & Technology Review* 221.

[21] The Internet is flooded with speeches against the ownership of personal data, as shown in the 2018 *Le Monde* forum.

By Way of Conclusion

CAN WE THEREFORE do away with identity, since over the centuries it has served to suffocate the person rather than to enhance his qualities and value?

Sources from a variety of cultural backgrounds indicate that we cannot.

At the moral level, Kwame Anthony Appiah states that it is not necessary to adopt a position in relation to identity: what is important is to understand how it is constructed, so to speak, on the fixed level. If there are shortcomings, it will be up to others to identify the remedy. Following the teaching of John Stuart Mill, he points out that each individual should be free to realise his own life plan, since it is not the status one acquires that is important, but the life model one wishes to pursue.[1] The ethics of identity in this view becomes the *ethics of individuality*. Identity – and individuality – are thus closely connected with *freedom*: what matters is not to be different from others, but to enjoy the freedom to construct oneself. But, Appiah emphasises, we have to take into account three factors: the inventive capacity of each of us, design our lives according to our own aspirations, our own ideals; the authenticity of this image, which corresponds to what we actually achieve; and the collective dimension of individual identity.

The collective dimension is particularly important for jurists, because the law, which is the result of the decisions of the community, constructs for its part the identity of each of us, from the moment of birth to its end, and the identity constructed by the individual is a continuous duel between the identity one would like to have and the identity that society imposes on us.

In ethical terms, 'individuality', ie individual identity, implies that we have duties towards ourselves, and 'social identity' implies that we have duties towards others. Solidarity is triggered towards those who are similar to us, so it is a unifying factor for many individualities. In order to guarantee this opportunity for all, it is necessary to achieve global human rights and safeguard individualities and thus differences, because 'in a single society there is no wisdom'.[2]

It is clear, then, that it is not enough to demand more freedom for everyone: everyone must be put in a position to make free life choices. And here, of course, radical liberalism clashes with factual reality, which today is even more difficult to govern due to the current economic crisis.

On an anthropological level, Francesco Remotti warns us against the notion of identity, which he describes as controversial, unstable and equivocal, whether

[1] *The Ethics of Identity* (Princeton, Princeton University Press, 2005) 5.
[2] ibid 252.

it is assumed on an individual level or seen on a collective level. The plural nature of the ego must guide us against attempts at simplification and standardisation, especially attempts at classification that end up oppressing each individual's way of being.[3] Remotti realises that:

> The anthropologist, the sociologist, the psychologist comes across subjects (individuals or groups) who speak of identity, who invoke identity, who affirm their own identity: is it therefore the case that identity does not exist? Identity exists at least at the level of discourse, just as it exists at the level of identity-inspired practices.

It is therefore necessary to 'come to terms with identity'. But his point is that identity becomes an obsession that chases us all our lives, and we need to understand why this is and put it aside, because identity is elusive and constantly changing.[4] Drawing on Hume's studies of the intellect, Remotti argues that identity is elusive because it is based on two elements that are themselves unstable: memory, which is selective and therefore partial; and imagination, which creates changing worlds outside of reality. However, we cannot do without identity, which, in a social context, implies *recognition*. Recognition is linked to the idea of rights: 'A subject is recognised when he or she is granted rights, starting with those of existence and survival. In a certain sense, this notion of rights encompasses all the contents listed above (existence, needs, characteristics)'.[5] In other words, the idea of the individual is a kind of cultural achievement, at which the societies that anthropologists usually deal with do not have yet to arrive: it is the theme of modern individualism, ie the unique and unrepeatable character of the individual. It should be pointed out that many societies in which we have encountered the individual conception of the person recognise his unrepeatable character. It is precisely by thinking of the person as individual and plural, ie built from many relationships, that the combination of relationships is understood to be unrepeatable. Each of us is an 'individual', but at the same time represents a unique situation. I am unique and unrepeatable not as an isolated individual but as an individual couched in social relations.

> In this way, unrepeatability is not only not lost at all, but rather enhanced. As can be seen, one can very well speak of uniqueness and unrepeatability, without thereby appealing to the concept of personal identity. Since it is not an unrepeatability of substance, unrepeatability is also a highlighting of how today you are this way but tomorrow you will be made another way, because situations have changed, because you have entered into another bundle of relationships: there is 'an unrepeatability of situations within the self.[6]

On a psychological level, what is relevant is the ego, the subconscious and the unconscious, the ego's relations with the outside world, the ego-other-me

[3] F Remotti, *Contro l'identità* (Roma-Bari, Laterza, 1996).
[4] F Remotti, *L'ossessione dell'identità* (Roma-Bari, Laterza, 2010).
[5] F Remotti, 'L'ossessione identitaria' (2011) XXV *Rivista Italiana di Gruppoanalisi* 9.
[6] ibid 28.

relationship. And also explored are relations with the body, projections of the mind, and the ways of 'recognising' a subject within a group and of this within a larger, more inclusive community.[7]

The problem of identity thus merges with the analysis of human nature throughout the history of philosophical thought: every philosopher poses the problem of who we are and strives to answer this question with the methodological choices appropriate to his system of thought. The nature of the person becomes an interpretative key to the entire history of philosophy.[8]

The person is a central notion in the world of law, and so is his identity. But as mentioned above, it is only recently that *individual* identity has been valued.

While other sciences ask whether we can do away with identity, this question makes no sense for law. The answer on a legal level is negative. As long as a society is built on roles – and it could not be any other way – man is destined to be the *person* Gaius spoke of, and to be identified in the three forms that have been described: by what he feels he is; by what he wants to appear to be; and by what society requires him to be. The relationship between identity and the person is measured by the ways in which identity is constructed, by the size of the spaces in which a person can construct an identity, by the degree of coercion with which identity is imposed upon each subject.

Hence the need to defend fundamental rights. In the imagination of jurists, identity crosses the centuries in a continuum of rules, theories, concepts.

It is a laboratory for jurists, who use it from time to time, depending on the conclusion pursued, either to discriminate or to protect the individual. Ultimately, identity is neither a photograph nor a point of arrival: identity is an instrument, which from time to time can fulfil a liberating or persecutory function. And the level of civilisation of a society is determined by the extent to which it is able to guarantee everyone the *right to be themselves*.

[7] G Jervis, *La conquista dell'identità. Essere se stessi, essere diversi* (Milan, Feltrinelli, 1997); M Marzano, *Il diritto di essere io* (Roma-Bari, Laterza, 2014).

[8] W Bourgeois, *Persons. What Philosophers Say About You* (Waterloo Canada, Wilfrid Laurier University Press, 1995); P Pojman, *Who are we? Theories of Human Nature* (Oxford, OUP, 2006).

Index

www.ingramcontent.com/pod-product-compliance
Ingram Content Group UK Ltd.
Pitfield, Milton Keynes, MK11 3LW, UK
UKHW021543041026
15470UKWH00019B/734